Cochran's
German
Review
Grammar

Versteigerung

Cochran's German Review Grammar

THIRD EDITION

Revised and edited by

JONATHAN B. CONANT

Brown University

PRENTICE-HALL, INC., *Englewood Cliffs, New Jersey*

Library of Congress Cataloging in Publication Data

COCHRAN, EMORY ELLSWORTH.
   Cochran's German review grammar.

   SUMMARY: A reference and review grammar of German
for second year students.
   Published in 1934 and 1963 under title: A practical
German review grammar.
   1. German language—Grammar—1950–   [1. German
language—Grammar] I. Conant, Jonathan B., date
II. Title.
PF3111.C57 1974   438'.2'421   73–21535
ISBN 0-13-139501-7

PRENTICE-HALL INTERNATIONAL, INC., *London*
PRENTICE-HALL OF AUSTRALIA, PTY. LTD., *Sydney*
PRENTICE-HALL OF CANADA, LTD., *Toronto*
PRENTICE-HALL OF INDIA PRIVATE LIMITED, *New Delhi*
PRENTICE-HALL OF JAPAN, INC., *Tokyo*

Preface

This new edition of Cochran's grammar is intended principally for students of German who have advanced beyond their first year of study but are not expert enough, or whose needs are not sophisticated enough, for them to use the Duden *Grammatik* and similar tools.

Language is always changing, and any grammar is necessarily an imperfect snapshot, recording as much of what it sees as it can. The grammar can never be more than a guide, for the language it seeks to describe has already changed by the time the book is published. So the first practice the user should adopt is: allow the language itself to update the grammar. Always seek the advice of native speakers of German, read magazines and newspapers, watch motion pictures, listen to the radio. While the basic statements of the grammar will change very little, matters of idiom and syntax can be only sketchily represented in these pages, and are subject to wide variation in the living language.

The author of a book like this tries to answer the needs of his audience. When Emory Cochran first wrote the book from which this third edition derives, English-speaking students of German needed both a reference and a review grammar. Now the need for a review grammar of German is less acute, for there are many available; but good reference grammars for the non-specialist do not exist. Accordingly, while the present edition is as useful as ever as a review grammar, it emphasizes by its organization its function as a reference work. Professor Cochran relied heavily on cross-references and footnotes; I have largely removed these and instead expanded the index. The second practice the user should adopt is: use the index. It may be at the end of the book, but it is the real door to what lies within.

Those who have used the earlier editions of this book will find that the exercises, somewhat reduced in number, have been moved from the body of the text to a separate section at the back where they will not interfere with the grammar presentation. I hope their new position will prove advantageous to the student. As for the organizational revision of the grammar itself, I have integrated the illustrative examples and the explanatory notes, striving wherever possible to begin each section with fundamental statements and to follow the examples with more detailed comment, as required. Most of the words are Cochran's, most of the organization mine.

A word on terminology. Most users will come to this book from an elementary text. It is impossible to eliminate the trauma which new and unfamiliar terms for old grammatical acquaintances can cause, but attempts have been made to minimize it. Although the terms "strong" and "weak" cannot be defended scientifically, they are retained because they are still in general use and are mnemonically useful for the student, if not for the professional linguist. Wherever possible, alternatives to this terminology have been provided in the explanations. Because of their convenience, the terms Subjunctive I and Subjunctive II, which are now used by the more detailed grammars, have been adopted here. Similarly, it is expedient to call *sich amüsieren* a "reflexive verb" and *fahren* an "intransitive verb." Ultimately, however, the systematic differentiation that we make between parts of speech will give way to a deeper understanding of how grammar elements function in the living language.

I wish to thank my colleagues at Brown University, who have never objected to late-night queries on points of grammar and usage. But, for better or worse, what appears here is my responsibility.

J. B. C.

Contents

Cochran's
German
Review
Grammar

CHAPTER 1

Principles
of Case

§1. CASE IN ENGLISH

Case shows the relation which a noun or pronoun bears to other words in a sentence. This relation is indicated in English by three cases: *nominative, possessive,* and *objective.*

    A. The nominative case. This case has three common uses:

    (1) As subject of a verb: ***My friend*** *is at home.*

    (2) As predicate noun: *He is **my friend**.*

    (3) As noun of address: *Please visit me,* **Mr. Smith.**

    B. The possessive case. As its name implies, this case denotes ownership. In English, but not in German, an apostrophe indicates the possessive case: *The **boy's** books are on the table.* Or with a plural possessive: *The **boys'** books are on the table.*

    C. The objective case. The chief uses of this case are:

    (1) As direct object of a verb: *He loves* ***his son.***

A transitive verb in the active voice requires a complement, which is called a "direct object." Only transitive verbs take direct objects. The complement which must follow such a verb indicates the recipient of the action. (In the preceding example the *son* receives his father's love.) Stated differently, a direct object denotes person or thing acted upon: *He threw* ***the ball.*** Here the ball was the thing acted upon. A direct object answers the question *what?* or *whom?* after the verb. Referring to the two examples given above: *Loves whom?* ***The son.*** *Threw what?* ***The ball.*** *Son* and *ball* are, therefore, direct objects.

    (2) As indirect object of a verb.

A noun or pronoun denoting the person to or for whom (or the thing to or for which) something is done is called the "indirect object." English usually supplies *to*:

> *She gave **the children** the apples.*
> or: *She gave the apples **to the children**.*

In the first sentence *children* is the indirect object; *apples*, the direct object.

> *She showed **me** the pictures.*
> or: *She showed the pictures **to me**.*

In the first sentence *me* is the indirect object; *pictures*, the direct object.

(3)   As object of a preposition: *They ran after **him**.*

§2. CASE IN GERMAN

There are four cases in German: *nominative, genitive, dative,* and *accusative.* One must distinguish carefully between transitive and intransitive verbs. Most verbs that are transitive in English are also transitive in German. An intransitive verb —e.g., **sein,** *to be,* and **gehen,** *to go*—is one that cannot take a direct object:

> Er ist **mein Bruder.**
> *He is my brother.*

A. Nominative case. The use of the German nominative corresponds to that of the English:

(1)   As subject of a verb:

> **Mein Freund** ist nicht zu Hause.   **Das Kind** wird müde.
> *My friend is not at home.*   *The child is getting tired.*

(2)   As predicate noun:

> **Er** ist **mein Freund.**   **Er** wurde **mein Freund.**
> *He is my friend.*   *He became my friend.*

(3)   As noun of address:

> Bitte, besuchen Sie mich, **Herr Müller!**
> *Please visit me, Mr. Mueller.*

B. Genitive case. The genitive corresponds to the English possessive case or to the objective case preceded by *of* to denote possession:

> Die Eltern **jener Kinder** sind sehr arm.
> *The parents of those children are very poor.*
> Die Federn **des Jungen** liegen auf dem Tisch.
> *The boy's pens are (lying) on the table.*
> Die Federn **der Jungen** liegen auf dem Tisch.
> *The boys' pens are (lying) on the table.*
> Die Kinder **der Frau** spielen Ball.
> *The woman's children are playing ball.*

Der Bruder **des Mädchens** ist in der Schule.
The girl's brother is in school.

(1)   With proper nouns (i.e., names) German denotes the genitive by adding an apostrophe if the noun ends in an *s* sound; other names simply add *s* without apostrophe:

Voß' Werke, *the works of Voss*
Goethes Werke, *Goethe's works*

(2)   In German the genitive usually follows the noun to which it refers; the genitive of proper nouns, however, ordinarily precedes the noun, as shown in the examples above.

(3)   Possessive adjectives and pronouns must not be confused with the possessive (i.e., German genitive) case:

Seine Feder liegt auf dem Tisch.
His pen is on the table.

Seine is *nominative* singular to agree with the word **Feder**, which it modifies; it is feminine for the same reason.

C.   Dative case.   The dative is regularly used as the case of the indirect object:

(1)   Er hat **den Kindern** die Äpfel gegeben.
      *He gave **the children** the apples.*
or: *He gave the apples **to the children.***

(2)   Sie zeigte **dem Manne** das Bild.
      *She showed **the man** the picture.*

(3)   Ich werde **der Dame** das Buch geben.
      *I shall give **the lady** the book.*

(4)   Ich werde es **ihr** geben.
      *I shall give it **to her.***

As shown in examples (3) and (4), if the direct object is a noun, the dative precedes the accusative; if the direct object is a personal pronoun, the accusative precedes the dative.

D.   Accusative case.   The accusative is the case of the direct object. Remember that only transitive verbs take direct objects:

Er liebt **seinen Sohn.**   Ich habe **Sie** nicht gehört.
*He loves **his son.***   *I did not hear **you.***

Er wird **das Gedicht** lesen.   Wir lieben **unsere Freunde.**
*He will read **the poem.***   *We love **our friends.***

E.   Other uses of the genitive, dative, and accusative cases—e.g., with prepositions, adjectives, special verbs, etc.—will be discussed in subsequent chapters. The preceding examples have shown that the functions of the English "objective" case are divided among the genitive, dative, and accusative cases in German.

F.   In contrast to English, where the case of an appositive is not distinct, appositives in German must always agree in case with the nouns or pronouns to which they refer:

Sein Bruder, **der Ritter**, war sehr berühmt.
His brother, the knight, was very famous.

Ich werde meinem Freunde, **dem Advokaten,** die Bücher geben.
I shall give the books to my friend, the lawyer.

CHAPTER 2

Principles
of Tense

§3. TENSE IN ENGLISH

A verb—e.g., *write, wrote, written*—has six tenses. The following sentences illustrate the use of these tenses.

A. **Present:** *I write the letter. I am writing the letter. I do write the letter.*

B. **Past:** *I wrote the letter. I was writing the letter. I did write the letter.*

C. **Present Perfect:** *I have written the letter.*

D. **Past Perfect:** *I had written the letter.*

E. **Future:** *I shall write the letter.*

F. **Future Perfect:** *I shall have written the letter.*

§4. TENSE IN GERMAN

The German verb also has six tenses. These are, however, less rich in forms than the English tenses and are somewhat differently named. As in English, each verb has three principal parts—e.g., **schreiben, schrieb, hat geschrieben,** *to write.*

A. **Present:**

Ich schreibe den Brief.
I write the letter.
I am writing the letter.
I do write the letter.

5

B.   Past (or **Simple Past**):   **C.   Perfect** (or **Compound Past**):

Ich **schrieb** den Brief.   Ich **habe** den Brief **geschrieben**.
*I **wrote** the letter.*   *I **have written** the letter.*
*I **was writing** the letter.*   *I **wrote** the letter.*
*I **did write** the letter.*   *I **did write** the letter.*

In German there are no progressive forms (i.e., *am, are, is, was, were* followed by the present participle ending in *-ing*), nor does German have any emphatic forms with *do does,* and *did.* The English present tense can be translated in one way only: *he is playing, he does play,* and *he plays* are all **er spielt**. Similarly, *was* or *were* followed by the present participle ending in *-ing* must become the past tense: *he was writing* = **er schrieb**; *they were playing* = **sie spielten**.

D.   Past Perfect:

Ich **hatte** den Brief **geschrieben**.
*I **had written** the letter.*

E.   Future:

Ich **werde** den Brief **schreiben**.
*I **shall write** the letter.*

F.   Future Perfect:

Ich **werde** den Brief **geschrieben haben**.
*I **shall have written** the letter.*

§5.   COMPARISON OF ENGLISH AND GERMAN TENSES

The following table shows the extent of correspondence between English and German tenses in their fundamental use. Special and idiomatic uses are explained in later chapters.

ENGLISH	GERMAN	TENSE
I write *I am writing* *I do write*	ich schreibe	PRESENT
I wrote *I was writing* *I did write* *I have written*	ich schrieb (SIMPLE) ich habe geschrieben (COMPOUND)	PAST
I had written	ich hatte geschrieben	PAST PERFECT
I shall write	ich werde schreiben	FUTURE
I shall have written	ich werde geschrieben haben	FUTURE PERFECT

A. The German simple past and compound past (or perfect) tenses refer to the same time in the past and are to some extent interchangeable. English *he wrote* may be rendered either **er schrieb** or **er hat geschrieben.**

(1) The compound past predominates in spoken German while the more abrupt simple past may be favored in the written language. The former may be used in written German to signify instantaneous (as opposed to continuous) past action.

(2) In conversation the compound past is ordinarily used when referring to *a single event* that has taken place.

> *We saw the children yesterday.*
> Gestern **haben wir** die Kinder **gesehen.**
> *When did you see them?*
> Wann **haben Sie** sie **gesehen?**

(3) The past is regularly used to express two or more acts that occurred at the same time in the past:

> Er **spielte** Ball, während der Bruder einen Spaziergang **machte.**
> *He played ball, while his brother took a walk.*

(4) In both the spoken and written language, the past is regularly used for narrating and describing past events, especially when such events are related as *a chain of facts*:

> Er kam, er sah, er siegte.
> *He came, he saw, he conquered.*
> Die Mutter ging in die Stadt, kaufte sich einen neuen Hut und kam um vier Uhr nach Hause.
> *Mother went to the city, bought herself a new hat, and came home at four o'clock.*

B. The German past perfect corresponds in use and meaning to the English past perfect:

> **Wir hatten** ihn schon **besucht.**
> *We had already visited him.*

C. The future tense is used chiefly as in English:

> Morgen **wird** mein Freund **ankommen.**
> *My friend will arrive tomorrow.*

D. The future perfect tense in its literal sense is as rare in German as it is in English:

> **Er wird** das Buch **gelesen haben.**
> *He will have read the book.*

CHAPTER 3

Definite
and Indefinite Articles
Negation

§6. USES OF THE DEFINITE ARTICLE (*DER*)
AND THE INDEFINITE ARTICLE (*EIN*)

The examples that follow illustrate the resemblances and the differences between German and English in the use of articles.

A. Geographical names. As in English, the names of countries, states, and cities are generally used without a definite article. This applies almost invariably if the name of the country is neuter (as most are, e.g. Deutschland, Frankreich, Spanien, England, Kanada).

Waren Sie je in Deutschland oder Frankreich?
Were you ever in Germany or France?

Er wurde in Bayern geboren. Ja, in München.
He was born in Bavaria. Yes, in Munich.

Here are the most common exceptions:

(1) The definite article (here, in the dative case) is required if the name of the country is feminine or plural:

Sie war Verkäuferin in **der** Schweiz.
She was a salesgirl in Switzerland.

Er knipste viele Mädchen in **den** Niederlanden.
He took snapshots of many girls in the Netherlands.

Other examples: die Türkei, die Tschechoslowakei, die Normandie, die Pfalz, die Vereinigten Staaten.

(2) The definite article is always required if the name of the country is preceded by an adjective:

Waren Sie je in **dem schönen** Deutschland?

(3) Certain masculine and some neuter names of countries require or may use the definite article: der Balken, der Sudan, das Elsaß, der Irak, der Iran.

B. Parts of body; clothing. The definite article is ordinarily used with parts of the body or articles of clothing, provided there is no doubt as to the possessor. English uses the possessive instead of the article.

Er setzt (sich) **den** Hut auf.   Was hat sie in **der** Hand?
*He puts **his** hat on.*   *What has she in **her** hand?*

Was haben Sie in **der** Tasche?
*What have you in **your** pocket?*

C. Temporal references. The definite article is used in German when referring to the seasons, months of the year, and days of the week. In English the article is regularly omitted in such cases.

Der Frühling ist gekommen.   **Am** Samstag haben wir keine Schule.
Spring is here.   *We have no school on Saturday(s).*

Im Juli und **im** August haben die Schüler Ferien.
In July and August the pupils have vacation.

D. German requires the article, but English omits it in such phrases as: *to go to school, to church, etc., to be in school, in church, etc.,* and *after school.*

Er ist in **der** Schule.   Sie ist in **der** Kirche.
He is in school.   *She is in church.*

Er geht in **die** Schule.   Sie geht in **die** Kirche.
He goes to school.   *She goes to church.*

Nach **der** Schule spielt er Ball.
After school he plays ball.

E. Price, frequency, rate. Where English uses the indefinite article *a* in the sense of *per*, the German idiom requires the definite article.

Ich besuche ihn zweimal **die** Woche (*or* **in der** Woche *or* **wöchentlich**).
I visit him twice a week.

Es kostet zwei Mark **das** Pfund.
It costs two marks a pound.

F. Names of streets. Contrary to English usage, German often includes the definite article with names of streets. In addresses, however, the article is omitted.

Er wohnt in **der** Friedrichstraße.
He lives in Frederick Street.

Herrn Leopold Kaminfeger, 3407 Bad Tölz,
Haufenstraße 46, BRD.

G. General statements. The definite article is frequently used before nouns in general statements. In sentences of a proverbial nature, however, it is often omitted.

Das Leben ist kurz.   **Der** Mensch ist sterblich.
Life is short.   *Man is mortal.*

Not bricht Eisen.
Necessity knows no law. (lit. *Necessity breaks iron.*)

H.   Infinitives used as nouns are neuter and require the definite article.

Das Schreiben ist schwer.
Writing is difficult.

I.   Nouns in series.   German usage requires the repetition of the definite article in a series of nouns of different gender. This same rule applies to the indefinite article, to adjectives, and to possessives.

Der Hund und **die** Katze sind Haustiere.
The dog and cat are domestic animals.

Der Vater und **die** Mutter sind nicht zu Hause.
Father and mother are not at home.

ein Mann und **eine** Frau, *a man and woman*
guter Wein und **gutes** Bier, *good wine and beer*
sein Säbel und **seine** Rüstung, *his sword and armor*

The article should be repeated with nouns of the same gender if the nouns are contrasted:

der Vater und **der** Sohn, *father and son*

J.   Vocation.   The indefinite article is omitted before an *unmodified* predicate noun denoting vocation, rank, or station in life. But if such a noun is modified by an adjective, the indefinite article must be used.

Sein Vetter ist Arzt.   Er ist **ein guter** Arzt.
*His cousin is **a** physician.*   *He is a **good** physician.*

K.   Meals.   The German idiom requires the definite article before names of meals.

Wir haben Kaffee und Brötchen **zum** Frühstück.
We have coffee and rolls for breakfast.
Das Mittagessen ist fertig.
Dinner is ready.
Nach **dem** Abendessen haben wir die Zeitung gelesen.
After supper we read the newspaper.

L.   The superlative **meist-** must be preceded by the definite article.

Die meisten Schüler lesen Geschichten gern.
Most pupils like to read stories.

M. A few common expressions that use the indefinite article in English require the definite article in German. These must be memorized.

In der Regel bleibt er vormittags zu Hause.
As a rule he stays at home in the forenoon.

Zur Abwechs(e)lung gehen wir an den Strand, anstatt in die Berge.
For a change we are going to the beach instead of to the mountains.

Er wurde krank und verlor **zur Folge** seine Stellung.
He became ill and as a result lost his position.

N. *What a, what kind of a, such a.* In these expressions the indefinite article is used both in German and in English, and there are a number of variations possible.

  (1)   **Welch ein** Erfolg!   **Welch eine** Stadt!
         What a success!   *What a city!*

Welch (the uninflected form of **welcher**) followed by **ein** commonly occurs in exclamations; **ein** agrees with its noun.

  (2)   Mit **was für einer** Feder schreiben Sie?
         *With **what kind of** (a) pen are you writing?*

In the interrogative phrase **was für ein, für** lacks the force of a preposition and hence does not determine the case of the following noun.

  (3)   ⎰**Eine solche** Hitze habe ich nie erlebt.
       ⎨**Solch eine** Hitze habe ich nie erlebt.
       ⎱**So eine** Hitze habe ich nie erlebt.
       *I have never experienced **such** (a) heat.*

Such a may be translated in three ways: by **solch-** following the indefinite article and declined like a adjective; by **solch** preceding the indefinite article and undeclined; by **so** followed by the indefinite article. In each case the article is declined regularly.

One may also say: **Solche** Hitze habe ich nie erlebt. Here the indefinite article disappears from both the English and the German. **Solch-** is inflected like **dieser,** and has the plural **solche:**

Solche Menschen gibt es.
*There are **such** people.*

O. Unlike English, German uses no article in the following instances:

  (1)   Ich habe **hundert** Bücher gekauft.
         I bought a hundred books.

         Es sind **tausend** Jahre her.
         A thousand years have passed.

The German equivalent of *a hundred* modifying a noun is simply **hundert.** Similarly *a thousand* is **tausend.**

(2) Er hat **Kopfweh.**   Sie hat **Halsweh.**
     He has a headache.   *She has a sore throat.*

To express **an** ache or pain, **-weh** is attached and the noun is used without any article. Other examples: **Magenweh,** *a stomach ache;* **Zahnweh,** *a toothache.*

P. The idiom **machen zu** requires the definite article in German where none is present in English.

Man machte ihn **zum** Führer.
He was made leader.   (or: *They made him leader.*)

Listed below are some common phrases that use the definite article in German but not in English.

zum Beispiel (abbr. z.B.), *for example* (abbr. *e.g.*)
zum Nachtisch, *for dessert*
zum Schluß, *in conclusion, finally*
zum Teil, *partly, to some extent*
mit der Post (Luftpost) schicken, *to send by mail (airmail)*
mit der Eisenbahn (Straßenbahn, Untergrundbahn, Hochbahn), *by rail*
    (streetcar, subway, elevated railway)
mit dem Dampfer, *by steamer*
in der Nacht, *at night*
in der Tat, *in fact, in reality, indeed*
im Bett, *in bed*
beim Namen nennen, *to call by name*

Q. Personal names are not normally preceded by the definite article. Demands of style may cause exceptions (colloquial writing: „Da kommt der Leo!"). Here are some more common exceptions and the difficulties they pose:

(1) Personal names modified, either attributively or by apposition, frequently have the definite article.

Die kleine Marie spielte mit ihrer Puppe.
Little Mary was playing with her doll.

Karl **der** Große hat viele Klöster und Schulen bauen lassen.
Charlemagne built many monasteries and schools.

(2) Where the name is followed by both the article and an adjective, all elements of the phrase are normally inflected. Where the name is preceded by a title without article, the name only is inflected. Where the name is preceded by title with article, only the title (and article) is inflected.

Voltaire lebte am Hofe Friedrichs **des** Großen.
Voltaire lived at the court of Frederick **the** *Great.*

König Friedrichs Schloß war in Potsdam.

or: Das Schloß **des** Königs Friedrich war in Potsdam.
           King Frederick's castle was in Potsdam.

(3)   **Herr** as a title is regularly inflected, even without the article, when it precedes a name:

Herrn Wagners Hut, *Mr. Wagner's hat*
ein Brief an Herrn Wagner, *a letter to Mr. Wagner*

R.   Kein, which follows the same inflection as **ein,** is used to convey *not a, not any*.

Das ist **kein** übler Einfall.
*That is **not a** bad idea.*

Ich habe leider **keinen** Fernsehapparat.
*Unfortunately I have **no** (**haven't any**) television set.*

§7.   NEGATION WITH *NICHT, NIE, NIEMALS*

Nicht stands at the end of clauses which it entirely negates, but it *precedes* in other instances, as shown below. **Nie** and **niemals** follow the same rules as **nicht.**

A.   At end of clause.

Er hat das Buch **nicht.**   Er hatte den Bleistift **niemals.**
He does not have the book.   *He never had the pencil.*

B.   Before separable prefix.

Sie sieht ihn **nicht** an.   Sie sah ihn **nicht** an.
She does not look at him.   *She did not look at him.*

Sehen Sie ihn **nicht** an!
Do not look at him.

C.   Before infinitive.

Wir werden es ihm **nicht** geben.   Wir werden es **nie** ansehen.
We shall not give it to him.   *We shall never look at it.*

D.   Before participle.

Ich habe es ihm **nicht** gegeben.   Ich habe es **niemals** angesehen.
I have not given it to him.   *I have never looked at it.*

E.   Before predicate adjective.

Er ist **nicht** schläfrig.   Sie war **nie** schläfrig.
He is not sleepy.   *She was never sleepy.*

F. Before prepositional phrase.

Sie ist **nicht** zu Hause.   Das Kind spielt **nicht** auf der Straße.
She is not at home.   *The child is not playing on the street.*

Er ist **nie** nach Europa geflogen.
He has never flown to Europe.

G. Before adverbs.

Er ist **nicht** hier.
He is not here.

H. Before predicate nouns.

Er ist **nicht** Arzt.   Er war **nie** Arzt.
He is not a physician.   *He was never a physician.*

I.   In contrastives.

Sie hat **nicht** die Feder **sondern** den Bleistift.
She does not have the pen but the pencil.

J.   Er versteht es **gar nicht.**   Er hat **gar nichts.**
         He does not understand it at all.   *He has nothing at all.*

Ich verstehe **gar nicht,** warum du weinst.
I don't understand at all why you are crying.

CHAPTER 4

Adjective Declension

§8. THE WEAK ADJECTIVE DECLENSION

As applied to German adjective declension, the terms "weak" and "strong" identify inflectional endings as, respectively, non-distinctive or distinctive. A distinctive ending or form is one which shows the gender, case, and number of the noun following; this statement yields the following rules:

1. Adjectives preceded by **der**-words and inflected **ein**-words (i.e., distinctive forms) have *weak* (i.e., non-distinctive) endings.
2. Adjectives either unpreceded or preceded by uninflected **ein**-words have *strong* endings.

It is convenient to establish a paradigm of weak endings for adjectives following **der**-words, one of strong endings for adjectives unpreceded by either **der**- or **ein**-words, and a mixed declension for adjectives preceded by **ein**-words.

The **der**-words are: **der** (the definite article), **dieser** (*this*), **jener** (*that*), **jeder** (*each* or *every*), **mancher** (*many a*), **solcher** (*such* or *such a*), and **welcher** (*which* or *what*). Below are some examples of their use with the weak adjective declension.

A. Singular number.

(1) The nominative case:

Der deutsche Rhein entspringt in der Schweiz.
The German Rhine has its source in Switzerland.

Die alte Stadt Heidelberg liegt am Neckar.
The old city of Heidelberg is situated on the Neckar.

Dieses deutsche Buch gefällt mir.
I like this German book.

(2) The genitive case:

Der Vater **des** kleinen Jungen ist zu Hause.
The little boy's father is at home.

15

Die Straßen **der** alten Stadt sind sehr eng.
The streets of the old city are very narrow.

Die Eltern **des** kleinen Kindes sind auf dem Lande.
The little child's parents are in the country.

(3)   The dative case:

Er gab **dem** alten Mann ein Buch.
He gave the old man a book.

Ich zeigte **der** guten Frau das Bild.
I showed the good woman the picture.

Er wohnt in **jenem** neuen Haus.
He lives in that new house.

(4)   The accusative case:

Welchen alten Mann haben Sie gesehen?
What old man did you see?

Er besuchte **die** alte Dame.   Wir kauften **das** große Haus.
He visited the old lady.   *We bought the large house.*

B.   Plural number.

(1)   The nominative case:

Die kleinen Bleistifte (Federn, Bücher) liegen auf dem Tisch.
The small pencils (pens, books) are (lying) on the table.

(2)   The genitive case:

Die Eltern **der** fleißigen Schüler (Schülerinnen, Kinder) sind zufrieden.
The parents of the diligent boy pupils (girl pupils, children) are satisfied.

(3)   The dative case:

Er wird **den** armen Männern (Frauen, Kindern) helfen.
He will help the poor men (women, children).

(4)   The accusative case:

Ich habe **die** alten Bäume (Burgen, Dörfer) gesehen.
I have seen the old trees (castles, villages).

C.   Summary of the weak adjective declension.   In the paradigm below, **dieser** stands for any **der**-word, and the ending after the dash is that of any following adjective.

| | SINGULAR | | | PLURAL |
	MASCULINE	FEMININE	NEUTER	ALL GENDERS
Nom.	dieser –e	diese –e	dieses –e	diese –en
Gen.	dieses –en	dieser –en	dieses –en	dieser –en
Dat.	diesem –en	dieser –en	diesem –en	diesen –en
Acc.	diesen –en	diese –e	dieses –e	diese –en

§9. THE STRONG ADJECTIVE DECLENSION

The sentences below illustrate the "strong" endings employed when the adjective is unpreceded. Note that they are identical with the endings of **dieser** and other **der**-words, with one exception: the genitive singular of the masculine and neuter have **-en** instead of the expected **-es**.

A. Singular number.

(1) The nominative case:

Arm**er** Mann, was fehlt Ihnen?
Poor man, what is the matter with you?

Lieb**e** Frau, wo sind Ihre Kinder?
Dear woman, where are your children?

Lieb**es** Kind, wo ist deine Mutter?
Dear child, where is your mother?

(2) The genitive case:

Er bestellte ein Glas rot**en** Weines (or rot**en** Wein).
He ordered a glass of red wine.

Er trank ein Glas erfrischend**er** (or erfrischend**e**) Limonade.
He drank a glass of refreshing lemonade.

Er gab mir ein Glas kalt**en** Wassers (or kalt**es** Wasser).
He gave me a glass of cold water.

Er hatte nur ein Stück trock(e)n**en** Brotes (or trocken**es** Brot).
He had only a piece of dry bread.

Ordinary conversation employs the optional forms in parentheses, which are not genitives but accusatives in apposition with preceding nouns.

(3) The dative case:

Er ist ein alter Mann mit lang**em** Bart.
He is an old man with a long beard.

Er schreibt mit rot**er** Tinte.
He writes with red ink.

Sie ist eine alte Frau mit weiß**em** Haar.
She is an old woman with white hair.

(4) The accusative case:

Gut**en** Morgen![1]   Gut**e** Nacht![1]
Good morning.   *Good night.*

Kaufen Sie frisch**es** Brot!
Buy fresh bread.

---

[1]Accusative because a verb of wishing is implied: *I wish you a good morning (good night).*

B. Plural number.

(1) The nominative case:

Alte Freunde sind gute Freunde.
Old friends are good friends.

(2) The genitive case:

Sie kaufte sich vier Paar feinster Handschuhe.
She bought (herself) four pairs of the finest gloves.

(3) The dative case:

Die schweren Wagen wurden von kräftigen Pferden gezogen.
The heavy wagons were drawn by strong horses.

(4) The accusative case:

Kurze Geschichten liest er am liebsten.
He likes best to read short stories.

Sie hat drei kluge Kinder.
She has three bright children.

Cardinal numbers other than **ein** require the following adjective to have strong endings.

§10. THE MIXED ADJECTIVE DECLENSION

The sentences below illustrate the endings employed when the adjective is preceded by an **ein**-word. The **ein**-words are: **ein** (the indefinite article), **kein** (the negated indefinite article), and the possessives **mein** (*my*), **dein** (*your*), **sein** (*his* or *its*), **ihr** (*her* or *their*), **unser** (*our*), **euer** (*your*), and **Ihr** (*your*).

A. Singular number.

(1) The nominative case:

Ein fleißiger Schüler fällt selten durch.
A diligent pupil rarely fails.

München ist **eine** schöne Stadt.
Munich is a beautiful city.

Ein deutsches Buch liegt auf dem Tisch.
A German book is (lying) on the table.

(2) The genitive case:

Das ist der Rat **eines** guten Arztes.
That is the advice of a good physician.

Er ist der Sohn **einer** berühmten Sängerin.
He is the son of a famous singer (fem.).

Sie ist die Mutter **eines** klugen Kindes.
She is the mother of a bright child.

(3)   The dative case:

Er machte einen Spaziergang mit **einem** alten Freund.
He took a walk with an old friend.

Er gab **einer** alten Frau etwas Geld.
He gave an old woman some money.

Er hatte **einem** armen Kind geholfen.
He had helped a poor child.

(4)   The accusative case:

Ich werde **einen** kleinen Hund kaufen.
I shall buy a little dog.

Sie hat **eine** interessante Geschichte erzählt.
She told an interesting story.

Haben Sie je **ein** deutsches Buch gelesen?
Did you ever read a German book?

B. Plural number.

(1)   The nominative case:

Meine kleinen Bleistifte (Federn, Bücher) liegen auf dem Tisch.
My small pencils (pens; books) are (lying) on the table.

(2)   The genitive case:

Die Bücher **meiner** fleißigen Schüler (Schülerinnen, Kinder) sind interessant.
The books of my diligent boy pupils (girl pupils, children) are interesting.

(3)   The dative case:

Er wird **meinen** armen Freunden (Freundinnen, Kindern) helfen.
He will help my poor friends (masc.) [*friends* (fem.), *children*].

(4)   The accusative case:

Haben Sie **meine** schönen Vögel (Blumen, Bilder) gesehen?
Have you seen my beautiful birds (flowers, pictures)?

Do not confuse **unser** and **euer** with **der**-words because they happen to end in **-er**. The endings of the "mixed" declension, outlined below, are added to **unser** and **euer**; if an ending is added, **unser** often and **euer** regularly lose an e:

Nom.   **unser lieber Freund,** *our dear friend*
Acc.   **unseren** (or: **unsren**) **lieben Freund**
Nom.   **euer alter Vater,** *your* (pl.) *old father*
Acc.   **euren alten Vater**

C. **Summary of the mixed adjective declension.** In the paradigm below, the endings that differ from the weak declension are shown in boldface.

	MASCULINE		FEMININE		NEUTER		ALL GENDERS	
	SINGULAR						PLURAL	
Nom.	mein	**–er**	meine	–e	mein	**–es**	meine	–en
Gen.	meines	–en	meiner	–en	meines	–en	meiner	–en
Dat.	meinem	–en	meiner	–en	meinem	–en	meinen	–en
Acc.	meinen	–en	meine	–e	mein	**–es**	meine	–en

§11. ADJECTIVES IN A SERIES; DERIVED FROM NAMES OF TOWNS; USED AS NOUNS

A. **Adjectives in a series.** Two or more descriptive adjectives modifying the same noun have the same endings:

ein guter alter Mann = *a good old man*
der gute alte Mann = *the good old man*

B. **Adjectives derived from names of towns.** Adjectives are formed from names of towns by adding –er. Such adjectives are capitalized and are indeclinable:

eine Hamburger Zeitung = *a Hamburg newspaper*
das Heidelberger Schloß = *Heidelberg Castle*

C. **Adjectives used as nouns.** Adjectives used as nouns are capitalized but keep their adjective endings:

die Reichen und die Armen = *the rich and the poor*
der Reiche = *the rich man*
ein Armer = *a poor man*
die Arme = *the poor woman*
Er besuchte Reiche und Arme. = *He visited rich and poor.*

§12. ADJECTIVES AFTER *ALLE*; *VIELE, WENIGE, ANDERE, EINIGE, MEHRER*, ETC.

A. **Alle**, when followed by a *descriptive* adjective, functions as a **der**-word:

Alle guten Menschen liebten ihn.
All good people loved him.
Aller guten Dinge sind drei.
All good things come in threes.
lit.   *There are three **of all** (gen. pl.) good things.*

In **allen** deutschen Städten hatte er Bekannte.
He had acquaintances in all German cities.
Er liest **alle** deutschen Zeitschriften gern.
He likes to read all (the) German magazines.

Limiting words such as **diese** and **seine** are not descriptive adjectives:

alle die**se** Bücher, *all these books*

B.   Viele, wenige, andere, einige, and **mehrere,** when not preceded, take strong endings; any adjectives following them will have the same endings.

Er hat **viele** liebe Freunde.
*He has **many** dear friends.*

Wenige ehrliche Männer würden das billigen.
***Few** honest men would approve of that.*

Andere gute Gründe hat er mir gegeben.
*He gave me **other** good reasons.*

Wir haben **einige** alte Damen getroffen.
*We met **some** old ladies.*

Mehrere wichtige Dinge haben Sie vergessen.
*You forgot **several** important things.*

C.   Manch– is used chiefly in the singular; one may say either:

mancher liebe Freund
or: **manch** lieber Freund ⎬ ***many** a dear friend*

Similarly:

welch**es** schöne Haus
or: **welch** schön**es** Haus ⎬ ***what** a beautiful house*

solch**es** gute Wetter
or: **solch** gut**es** Wetter ⎬ ***such** good weather*

CHAPTER 5

Nouns

§13. STRONG, WEAK, MIXED, AND IRREGULAR NOUNS

The terms "weak" and "strong" as applied to German nouns identify plural formation as, respectively, uniform (endings in **-n** or **-en** for all weak nouns) or differentiated (various combinations of umlaut and endings in **-**, **-e**, **-er**). Mixed nouns have strong singular and weak plural inflections. All nouns in German have **-n** in the dative plural; the other three plural cases are always identical.

    A. **Strong nouns** fall into three classes according to their plural formation: (1) no ending, with frequent umlaut; (2) **-e**, with frequent umlaut; and (3) **-er**, with umlaut wherever possible. Strong masculines and neuters form their genitive singular by adding **-s** or **-es**. (For paradigms of the strong declension, see §98A.)

    (1)   Mein Onkel besucht mich.
            My uncle is visiting me.
            Das Haus meines Onkels liegt an einem schönen Fluß.
            My uncle's house is situated on a beautiful river.
            Meine Onkel wohnen auf dem Lande.
            My uncles live in the country.

    (2)   Mein Freund ist nicht zu Hause.
            My friend is not at home.
            Die Mutter meines Freundes ist in Deutschland.
            My friend's mother is in Germany.
            Meine Freunde werden ihm helfen.
            My friends will help him.

    (3)   Das Kind spielt mit dem Hund(e).
            The child is playing with the dog.

Die Eltern des Kind**es** sind arm.
The child's parents are poor.

Die Kind**er** gehen jetzt nach Hause.
The children are going home now.

B.   Weak nouns. The masculines have **-n** or **-en** in all singular cases except the nominative; no feminine nouns in German except proper names have endings in the singular; there are no weak neuter nouns. (For weak declension paradigms, see §98 **B**.)

(1)   Der Jung**e** heißt Fritz.
The boy's name is Fred.

Der Vater des Jung**en** ist Advokat.
The boy's father is a lawyer.

Er hat dem Jung**en** ein deutsches Buch gegeben.
He gave the boy a German book.

Ich habe den Jung**en** auf der Straße getroffen.
I met the boy on the street.

Die Jung**en** gehen in die Schule.
The boys go to school.

Die Bücher der Jung**en** liegen auf dem Tisch.
The boys' books are (lying) on the table.

Er hat den Jung**en** die deutschen Bücher gegeben.
He gave the boys the German books.

Ich habe die Jung**en** auf der Straße getroffen.
I met the boys on the street.

(2)   Die Frau ist meine Freundin.
The woman is my friend.

Der Vater der Frau ist in Europa.
The woman's father is in Europe.

Die Frau**en** machen einen Spaziergang.
The women are taking a walk.

Die Kleider der Frau**en** sind schön.
The women's dresses are beautiful.

C.   Mixed nouns. These are characterized by strong declension in the singular, weak in the plural (see paradigms in §98 **C**).

Mein Vetter ist Lehrer.
My cousin (masc.) *is a teacher.*

Der Freund meines Vetter**s** ist Arzt.
My cousin's friend is a physician.

Meine beiden Vettern besuchen mich.
My two cousins are visiting me.

D.   Irregular nouns.   There are a few irregular nouns which do not fit into any of the preceding classifications, e.g.,

Er hat ein gutes Herz.
He has a good heart.

Er sprach aus dem Grunde des Herzens.
He spoke from the depths of his heart.

Ich tue es von Herzen (sing.) gern.
I do it with all my heart.

Sie sind zwei Herzen und ein Schlag.
They are bosom friends (lit. *two hearts and one beat*).

E.   Weak feminine nouns in **-in** have **-innen** throughout the plural:

Sie war meine Lehrerin.
She was my teacher.

Kennen Sie diese Lehrerinnen?
Do you know these teachers (fem.)?

F.   Nouns ending in -nis double the **s** when it is followed by an ending:

Das war ein interessantes Erlebnis.
That was an interesting experience.

Er schrieb über seine Erlebnisse in Deutschland.
He wrote about his experiences in Germany.

G.   Plural noun forms:

Die Männer (Frauen, Kinder) arbeiten schwer.
The men (women, children) are working hard.

Die Kleider der Männer (der Frauen, der Kinder) sind zerrissen.
The men's (women's, children's) clothes are torn.

Er hat den Männern (den Frauen, den Kindern) geholfen.
He helped the men (the women, the children).

Er besuchte die Männer (die Frauen, die Kinder).
He visited the men (the women, the children).

H.   Masculine and neuter monosyllabics may take the optional ending **-e** in the dative singular:

Er half dem Manne (*or* dem Mann).
He helped the man.

Sie folgte dem Kinde (*or* dem Kind).
She followed the child.

Note:

The examples given in this chapter and the information and paradigms in the Appendices help to predict the oblique forms of many nouns, and therefore repay careful study. In general it is advisable to memorize with each noun its gender, genitive singular, and nominative plural.

CHAPTER 6

Verbs
Auxiliaries

§14. WEAK VERBS

The terms "weak" and "strong" as applied to German verbs identify tense formation as, respectively, regular (by suffix) or irregular (by internal vowel alternation). Thus, German weak verbs correspond to English "regular" verbs:

PRESENT INFINITIVE	PAST	PAST PARTICIPLE
hören	**hörte**	**gehört**
to hear	*heard*	*heard*

The following sentences illustrate the German weak verb in all six active tenses. Before proceeding to study them be sure to know the conjugation of the auxiliary verbs **haben, sein,** and **werden** (Appendix §102) and of the weak verb **lernen** (Appendix §103).

A. Sie liebt ihn.   Sie hatte ihn geliebt.
She loves him.   *She had loved him.*

Sie lieb**te** ihn.   Sie wird ihn lieben.
She loved him.   *She will love him.*

Sie hat ihn geliebt.   Sie wird ihn gelieb**t** haben.
She (has) loved him.   *She will have loved him.*

The stem of a verb is found by dropping final –**en** from the present infinitive: for **lieben** the stem is **lieb–**. To this stem are added (subject to some variation):

1. For the present tense, the present tense endings –**e**, –**st**, –**t**, –**en**, –**t**, –**en**.

2. For the simple past tense, the past suffix –**t**– and the past tense endings –**e**, –**est**, –**e**, –**en**, –**et**, –**en**.

3. For the past participle (used in forming the compound past, past perfect, and future perfect tenses), the participial prefix **ge**– and the suffix –**t**.

B. Er wartet auf mich.   Er hatte auf mich gewartet.
He is waiting for me.   *He had waited for me.*

Er wartete auf mich.   Er wird auf mich warten.
He was waiting for me.   *He will wait for me.*

Er hat auf mich gewartet.   Er wird auf mich gewartet haben.
He (has) waited for me.   *He will have waited for me.*

The past tense suffix is –et– instead of –t– if the stem of a verb ends in **t** or **d** (e.g., **reden, redete,** *to speak*) or if the stem ends in **m** or **n** preceded by a consonant other than **l** or **r** (e.g., **atmen, atmete,** *to breathe*; but **warnen, warnte,** *to warn*). In the same cases the past participle ending is –et instead of –t.

C. Ich studiere die Aufgabe.   Ich hatte die Aufgabe studiert.
I am studying the lesson.   *I had studied the lesson.*

Ich studierte die Aufgabe.   Ich werde die Aufgabe studieren.
I was studying the lesson.   *I shall study the lesson.*

Ich habe die Aufgabe studiert.   Ich werde die Aufgabe studiert
I (have) studied the lesson.   haben.
                                                  I shall have studied the lesson.

Verbs ending in –**ieren** are weak and do not take the participial prefix **ge**–. A few of the more common verbs in –**ieren** (usually of foreign origin) are: **regieren** (*to govern*), **probieren** (*to try*), **buchstabieren** (*to spell*), **telefonieren** (or **telephonieren**) (*to telephone*), **telegrafieren** (or **telegraphieren**) (*to telegraph*), **operieren** (*to operate*), **sich amüsieren** (*to have a good time*), **spazieren** (*to walk*), **studieren** (*to study*), and **sich interessieren für** (*to be interested in*).

D. Er beantwortet die Frage.   Er hatte die Frage beantwortet.
He answers the question.   *He had answered the question.*

Er beantwortete die Frage.   Er wird die Frage beantworten.
He answered the question.   *He will answer the question.*

Er hat die Frage beantwortet.   Er wird die Frage beantwortet
He (has) answered the question.   haben.
                                                  He will have answered the question.

Verbs (both weak and strong) with the inseparable prefixes **be–, emp–, ent–, er–, ge–, ver–, zer,** and sometimes **miß–** take no prefix in the past participle.

E. Ich mache die Tür zu.   Ich hatte die Tür zugemacht.
I am closing (or *close*) *the door.*   *I had closed the door.*

Ich machte die Tür zu.   Ich werde die Tür zumachen.
I was closing (or *closed*) *the door.*   *I shall close the door.*

Ich habe die Tür zugemacht.   Ich werde die Tür zugemacht
I (have) closed the door.   haben.
                                     I shall have closed the door.

Verbs (both weak and strong) with separable prefixes have the participial prefix **ge–** between prefix and verb.

§15. STRONG VERBS

German strong verbs correspond to English "irregular" verbs:

PRESENT INFINITIVE	PAST	PAST PARTICIPLE
singen	**sang**	**gesungen**
to sing	*sang*	*sung*

The sentences below indicate that the characteristics of strong verbs are: a change in the stem vowel of the present infinitive in the past and usually in the past participle, and the past participle ending in **–en.**

The best way to learn a verb is to memorize its principal parts and form sentences in the various tenses. Since many strong verbs change their stem vowels in the second and third persons singular of the present indicative, as well as in the past and often in the past participle, the present indicative should be learned together with the principal parts of a verb, e.g.,

sprechen, sprach, hat gesprochen, er spricht

For the complete conjugation of strong verbs, see Appendix II, §104. The principle parts of strong and irregular verbs are listed in §111.

A. Classes. Grammarians have divided strong verbs into seven classes (the ablaut series) according to the vowel changes which characterize each group. The details of this division are given below; they will not replace memorization, but may aid it.

(I)   Wir bleiben zu Hause.   Wir waren zu Hause geblieben.
       We stay at home.   *We had stayed at home.*

       Wir blieben zu Hause.   Wir werden zu Hause bleiben.
       We stayed at home.   *We shall stay at home.*

       Wir sind zu Hause geblieben.   Wir werden zu Hause geblieben
       We (have) stayed at home.   sein.
                                        We shall have stayed at home.

Class I: **ei—ie—ie** or **ei—i—i**: bleiben, blieb, geblieben; schneiden, schnitt, geschnitten.

(II)   Er gießt das Wasser ins Glas.
       He pours the water into the glass.

Er goß das Wasser ins Glas.
He poured the water into the glass.

Er hat das Wasser ins Glas gegossen.
He (has) poured the water into the glass.

Class II: **ie—o—o.** The **o** may be short or long: gießen, goß, gegossen; ziehen, zog, gezogen.

(III)	Sie singt das Lied.	(IV)	Er spricht zu schnell.
	She sings the song.		*He speaks too rapidly.*
	Sie sang das Lied.		Er sprach zu schnell.
	She sang the song.		*He spoke too rapidly.*
	Sie hat das Lied gesungen.		Er hat zu schnell gesprochen.
	She has sung the song.		*He has spoken too rapidly.*

Class III: **i—a—u.** These vowels are short: singen, sang, gesungen.

Class IV: **e—a—o.** The **e** and **o** of this class are sometimes long and sometimes short; short **e** becomes **i** and long **e**, **ie** in the second and third persons singular of the present indicative and in the singular familiar imperative:

sprechen, sprach, hat gesprochen, er spricht, sprich!
stehlen, stahl, hat gestohlen, er stiehlt, stiehl!

(V)	Sie liest das Buch.	(VI)	Er schlägt den Hund.
	She is reading the book.		*He strikes the dog.*
	Sie las das Buch.		Er schlug den Hund.
	She was reading the book.		*He struck the dog.*
	Sie hat das Buch gelesen.		Er hat den Hund geschlagen.
	She (has) read the book.		*He (has) struck the dog.*

Class V: **e—a—e.** The **a** is regularly long but the **e** varies both in the infinitive and in the participle; vowel changes in the present indicative and singular familiar imperative are the same as for Class IV:

lesen, las, hat gelesen, er liest, lies!
essen, aß, hat gegessen, er ißt, iß!

Class VI: **a—u—a.** The **u** is regularly long but the **a** varies in both cases; in the second and third persons singular of the present indicative the latter becomes **ä**, but not in the singular imperative:

schlagen, schlug, hat geschlagen, er schlägt, schlag(e)!
wachsen, wuchs, ist gewachsen, er wächst, wachs (wachse)!

(VII)	Er läuft nach Hause.	Er lief nach Hause.
	He runs home.	*He ran home.*

Er ist nach Hause gelaufen.
He has run home.

Class VII: All verbs of this class have **ie** or **i** in the past; the vowel of the past participle is always the same as that of the present infinitive; **a** changes to **ä** in the present indicative, but not in the singular familiar imperative (just as in Class VI):

> **laufen,** lief, ist gelaufen, **er läuft, lauf(e)!**
> **fangen,** fing, hat gefangen, **er fängt, fang(e)!**

Rufen (*to call*) is the only verb in this class with **u** as the stem vowel. The vowel is not modified.

> rufen, rief, hat gerufen, **er ruft, ruf(e)!**

Heißen [(tr.), *to bid, call;* (*intr.*) *to be called*] is the only verb with **ei** in the present infinitive which does not belong to Class I:

> heißen, hieß, hat geheißen, er heißt, heiß(e)!

B.   Imperatives.   The singular familiar imperative of strong verbs has no vowel ending if **e** is the stem vowel of the infinitive:

> sprechen,   **sprich!**
> lesen,   **lies!**
> Karl, sprich nicht zu schnell!   Lies das Buch!
> *Carl, don't talk too fast.*   *Read the book.*

A few verbs, however, such as **gehen, stehen,** and **heben,** which do not change the stem vowel in the present indicative, may have singular familiar imperative forms in –e: **geh(e)! steh(e)! heb(e)!**

All other strong verbs, including those with the stem vowel **a** (which becomes **ä** in the present indicative but not in the singular familiar imperative: **schlagen,** er schlägt, schlag(e)!) may or may not have a final **e** in the imperative. In conversation this **e** is usually omitted:

> Schlag(e) den Hund nicht.   Komm schnell nach Hause!
> *Don't hit the dog.*   *Come home quick.*

The present infinitive is often used as an imperative, particularly in giving commands to children and directions to the general public:

> Mund **halten!**   *Hold your tongue.*
> **Schweigen!**   *Be quiet.*
> **Umsteigen!**   *Change cars.*

The past participle is used with the force of an imperative in giving sharp commands and warnings:

> **Vorgesehen!**   *Look out.*
> **Aufgestanden!**   *Get up.*
> **Aufgepaßt!**   *Pay attention.*

§16. IRREGULAR WEAK VERBS

A. Certain weak verbs have stem vowel change:

Kennen Sie ihn?	Das Feuer brennt.
Do you know him?	*The fire is burning.*
Ich kannte ihn.	Es brannte.
I knew him.	*It was burning.*
Ich habe ihn gekannt.	Es hat gebrannt.
I knew him.	*It (has) burned.*

Sie denkt an mich.
She is thinking of me.

Sie dachte an mich.
She was thinking of me.

Sie hat an mich gedacht.
She (has) thought of me.

This change was occasioned by mutation of the present infinitive stem vowel and not by vowel gradation (ablaut); these irregular weak verbs are in no way related to strong verbs.

In the table below, note particularly that the present Subjunctive II of the first six verbs keeps the stem vowel of the present infinitive.

PRESENT INFINITIVE	PAST	PERFECT	PRESENT SUBJUNCTIVE II	
brennen	brannte	hat gebrannt	brennte	*to burn*
kennen	kannte	hat gekannt	kennte	*to know*
nennen	nannte	hat genannt	nennte	*to name*
rennen	rannte	ist gerannt	rennte	*to run*
senden	sandte (sendete)	hat gesandt (gesendet)	sendete	*to send*
wenden	wandte (wendete)	hat gewandt (gewendet)	wendete	*to turn*
bringen	brachte	hat gebracht	brächte	*to bring*
denken	dachte	hat gedacht	dächte	*to think*

The verb **wissen**, *to know,* and the modal auxiliaries (treated in Chapter 24) show similar stem vowel changes, but have a different historical origin and are therefore not listed here.

B. There are three German verbs meaning *to know*: **kennen, wissen,** and **können**, but they are used in different contexts:

(1) **Kennen** means *to know* in the sense of *to be acquainted with,* and may refer either to persons or to things.

Kennen Sie den Mann?   Er **kennt** Goethes Werke.
Do you know the man?   *He knows Goethe's works.*

(2) **Wissen** means *to know a fact.*

Ich **weiß**, daß er recht hat.   Ich **weiß** es.
I know that he is right.   *I know it.*

(3) **Können** (which usually means *to be able, can,* etc.) may mean *to know* in the sense of *having acquired knowledge by study.*

Er **kann** Deutsch.   Sie **kann** ihre Aufgabe nicht.
He knows German.   *She does not know her lesson.*

Wir **können** das Gedicht.
We know the poem.

§17. THE AUXILIARIES *HABEN* AND *SEIN*

A. Er **hat** den Brief geschrieben.   Sie **hatte** das Lied gesungen.
He has written (or wrote) the letter   *She had sung the song.*

Er **hatte** den Brief geschrieben.   Er **hat** die Tür zugemacht.
He had written the letter.   *He (has) closed the door.*

Sie **hat** das Lied gesungen.   Ich **hatte** eine Geschichte erzählt.
She has sung (or sang) the song.   *I had told a story.*

The sentences above indicate that all transitive verbs require the auxiliary **haben** to form their perfect tenses. The same holds true for the rare future perfect:

Er wird den Brief geschrieben **haben**.
He will have written the letter.

B. Er **ist** aufgestanden.   Sie **war** nach Hause gegangen.
He got up.   *She had gone home.*

Sie **waren** gekommen.   Er **ist** gekommen.
They had come.   *He has come (or came).*

Er **ist** nach Hause gegangen.   Er **war** aufgestanden.
He has gone home.   *He had gotten up.*

These sentences indicate that intransitive verbs require the auxiliary **sein** to form their perfect tenses, provided they denote a change of place. The same holds true for the rare future perfect:

Er wird gekommen **sein**.
He will have come.

Haben is used as an auxiliary when the action itself is emphasized rather than the goal toward which the action is directed:

Haben Sie lange geschwommen?
Did you swim long?

Here the *action* of swimming is important.

Ich **bin** über den Fluß geschwommen.
I swam across the river.

In this sentence the *goal*—the other side of the river—is implied.

C. Sie **ist** eingeschlafen.   Es **ist** kalt geworden.
She has fallen (or fell) asleep.   *It has become (or became) cold.*

Sie **war** eingeschlafen.   Es **war** kalt geworden.
She had fallen asleep.   *It had become cold.*

These sentences indicate that intransitive verbs require the auxiliary **sein,** provided they denote a change of condition.

D. Hier **hat** er gestanden.   Er **hat** nicht geschlafen.
Here he (has) stood.   *He has not slept (or did not sleep).*

Er **hatte** gestanden.   Er **hatte** nicht geschlafen.
He had stood.   *He had not slept.*

These sentences indicate that intransitive verbs are conjugated with **haben,** provided they do not denote a change of place or condition.

E. The following verbs are also conjugated with **sein:**

bleiben	blieb	ist geblieben	*to remain*
geschehen	geschah	ist geschehen	*to happen*
sein	war	ist gewesen	*to be*
gelingen	gelang	ist gelungen	*to succeed*
glücken	glückte	ist geglückt	*to succeed*

Geschehen, gelingen, and **glücken** are impersonal verbs:

Es ist ihm noch nicht gelungen, den Bleistift zu finden.
He has not yet succeeded in finding his pencil.

CHAPTER 7

Numerals

§18. CARDINAL NUMERALS

A. Zählen Sie von **eins** bis **ein**undzwanzig!
Count from 1 to 21.

The form **eins** is used in counting, except where **und** follows.

B. (1) **Ein** Bleistift liegt auf dem Tisch.
There is a (one) pencil on the table.

(2) Wie viele Bleistifte liegen darauf?   (*a*) **Einer.**
How many pencils are there on it?   *One.*

(3) **Ein** Buch gehört mir.   (*a*) **Ein(e)s** gehört mir nicht.
One book belongs to me.   *One does not belong to me.*

(4) Haben Sie **ein** Buch?   (*a*) Ja, ich habe **ein(e)s.**
Have you a book?   *Yes, I have one.*

When followed by a noun the numeral **ein** is declined like the indefinite article (examples (1), (3), and (4) above). If **ein** stands alone (i.e., as a pronoun) it has the endings of a **der**-word (examples (2*a*), (3*a*), and (4*a*) above).

C. **Der eine** Sohn war in der Stadt, der andere war auf dem Lande.
(The) one son was in the city, the other was in the country.

After a **der**-word **ein** has the weak endings, functioning as an adjective.

D. **Sein einer** Sohn war in der Schule.
His one son was in school.

After an **ein**-word, **ein** takes the customary endings of a descriptive adjective.

34

E.   Die Stadt Berlin hat über vier **Millionen** Einwohner.
The city of Berlin has more than four million inhabitants.

Million and **Milliarde** are weak feminine nouns and are always inflected.

F.   (1)   Es waren **hundert** Menschen da.
          There were a hundred people there.
          Ich habe viele **H**underte gesehen.
          *I saw many hundred*s.

      (2)   Es waren **tausend** Menschen da.
          There were a thousand people there.
          Ich habe viele **T**ausende gesehen.
          *I saw many thousand*s.

A hundred and *a thousand* are rendered by **hundert** and **tausend,** which are capitalized when used as nouns: **H**undert, **T**ausend. Observe the plurals **H**underte and **T**ausende.

G.   Das ist **eine Fünf.**   Er ist **eine Null.**
     That is a (figure) five.   *He is a nobody* (lit. *a zero*).

Cardinal members are feminine when used as nouns.

H.   Es ist **ein** Uhr (*or* **eins**).   Es ist eine **Uhr.**
     It is one o'clock.   *It is a watch.*

Ein takes no ending in the time phrase **ein Uhr,** *one o'clock.*

I.   Cardinal numbers rarely take endings in modern German, except, occasionally, the numbers two to twelve:

      durch **zweier** (*gen. pl.*) Zeugen Mund, *by the mouth of two witnesses*
      auf allen **vieren,** *on all fours*

J.   (1)   Ihre **beiden** Brüder spielen Schach.
          *Her **two** (or both her) brothers are playing chess.*

      (2)   Keiner von den **beiden** interessiert sich für die Musik.
          *Neither of the **two** is interested in music.*

      (3)   Welches von den **beiden** Häusern haben Sie verkauft?
          *Which of the **two** houses did you sell?*

      (4)   Meine **beiden** Schwestern sind musikalisch.

When referring to but two of a kind, English *two* (or *both*) is usually translated by German **beide** (with adjective inflection). Instead of **die beiden Männer** one may also say **beide Männer** without change of meaning.

K.   The cardinals.

0 = Null	11 = elf	30 = dreißig
1 = ein(s)	12 = zwölf	31 = einunddreißig
2 = zwei	13 = dreizehn	40 = vierzig
3 = drei	14 = vierzehn	50 = fünfzig
4 = vier	15 = fünfzehn	60 = sechzig
5 = fünf	16 = sechzehn	70 = siebzig
6 = sechs	17 = siebzehn	80 = achtzig
7 = sieben	18 = achtzehn	90 = neunzig
8 = acht	19 = neunzehn	100 = hundert
9 = neun	20 = zwanzig	101 = hundert(und)eins
10 = zehn	21 = einundzwanzig	200 = zweihundert

1000 = tausend   1,000,000 = eine Million
100,000 = hunderttausend   1,000,000,000 = eine Milliarde
1974 = neunzehnhundertvierundsiebzig

Note: All multiples of ten except *dreißig*, end in –**zig**.

§19. ORDINAL NUMERALS

Ordinal numerals are declined like adjectives.

A.   Das ist der **zweite** Fehler.
That is the second mistake.

Heute fehlt der **fünfte** Schüler in der **vierten** Reihe.
The fifth pupil in the fourth row is absent today.

Mein Geburtstag ist am **sechsten** Oktober.
also: Der **sechste** Oktober ist mein Geburtstag.
October 6th is my birthday.

Mein Freund wird am **achtzehnten** (18ten or 18.) oder am **neunzehn-ten** (19ten or 19.) dieses Monats abreisen.
My friend will leave on the 18th or 19th of this month.

Ordinals up to *nineteenth* (except *first, third, eighth,* and sometimes *seventh*) are formed by adding the suffix –**t** to the corresponding cardinals.

B.   Heute ist der **erste** Schnee gefallen.
The first snow fell today.

Das ist das **dritte** Buch, das er verloren hat.
That is the third book (that) he has lost.

Haben Sie das **achte** Kapitel gelesen?
Did you read the eighth chapter?

The ordinals *first, third,* and *eighth* are irregular.

C.   Heute ist der **zwanzigste** Juni.

or: Heute haben wir den **zwanzigsten** Juni.
         Today is June 20.

Goethe wurde am **achtundzwanzigsten** August siebzehnhundert-
neunundvierzig geboren.
Goethe was born August 28, 1749.

Was ist der Inhalt des **dreiunddreißigsten** Kapitels?
What are the contents of the thirty-third chapter?

Ordinals from *twentieth* upward are formed by adding –**st** to the corresponding cardinals.

D.   When used in dates, titles, etc., ordinals are usually abbreviated to
number and a period:

Heute ist der 20. Juni. *Today is June 20.*
die zweite Hälfte des 18. Jahrhunderts, *the second half of the 18th century*
die 3. Ausgabe, *the third edition*
Wilhelm I. (*read*: der Erste), *William I (the First)*

E. The Ordinals.   Some ordinals are listed below; irregular forms are
in boldface:

         1. = (der, die, das) **erste,** *first*
         2. = (der, die, das) zweite, *second*
         3. = (der, die, das) **dritte,** *third*
         4. = (der, die, das) vierte, *fourth*
         7. = (der, die, das) siebente or **siebte,** *seventh*
         8. = (der, die, das) **achte,** *eighth*
        19. = (der, die, das) neunzehnte, *nineteenth*
        20. = (der, die, das) zwanzigste, *twentieth*
        21. = (der, die, das) einundzwanzigste, *twenty-first*
        30. = (der, die, das) dreißigste, *thirtieth*
       100. = (der, die, das) hundertste, *hundredth*
      1000. = (der, (die, das) tausendste, *thousandth*

§20. DERIVATIVES FROM NUMERALS

A. Forms in –*mal*.   The indeclinable forms **einmal** (*once*), **zweimal**
(*twice*), **dreimal** (*three times*), etc. are formed regularly by adding –**mal** to the
corresponding cardinals:

Wir haben Deutsch **fünfmal** die Woche.
We have German five times a week.

B. Forms in –*erlei*. The indeclinable forms **einerlei** (*one kind of*), **zweierlei** (*two kinds of*), **dreierlei** (*three kinds of*), **wievielerlei** (*how many kinds of*), etc. are formed regularly by adding –**erlei** to the corresponding cardinals:

> **Wievielerlei** Fragen stellt die Prüfung? **Dreierlei.**
> *How many types of questions does the test ask? Three types.*

C. Forms in –*ens*. The adverbial forms **erstens** (*first, in the first place*), **zweitens** (*secondly*), **drittens** (*thirdly*), etc. are formed by adding –**ens** to the stem of the corresponding ordinals:

> Sie konnte mich nicht besuchen: **erstens** war sie beschäftigt, **zweitens** hatte sie kein Reisegeld.
> *She could not visit me: in the first place, she was busy; secondly she had no money for traveling.*

D. Forms in –*fach*. The declinable adjectives **dreifach** (*triple, threefold*), **vierfach** (*fourfold*), etc. are formed by adding –**fach** to the corresponding cardinals:

> Er trägt eine **dreifache** Krone.
> *He wears a triple crown.*

Similarly with forms in –**stufig**, e.g., **dreistufig** (*with three steps*). For *double* or *twofold* one may say **doppelt**, **zweifach**, or **zwiefach**.

E. Fractions. The fractions **ein Drittel** (*a third*), **ein Viertel** (*a fourth*), **ein Zwanzigstel** (*a twentieth*) etc. are neuter nouns formed by adding –**el** to the stem of the corresponding ordinals:

> **Zwei Drittel** von einundzwanzig ist vierzehn.
> *Two thirds of twenty-one is fourteen.*

The preceding explanation is a simple and practical one for the formation of fractions. What actually happens, however, is that the suffix –**tel** (from **Teil**, *part*) is added to the stem of an ordinal, which drops the final **t**; thus **dritt**– plus –**tel** (literally *third part*) becomes **Drittel.**

F. *Halb* and combinations with *halb*.

(1) **Halb** is the adjective for *half*:

> Er hat einen **halben** Apfel gegessen.
> *He ate half an apple*

(2) Die **Hälfte** is the noun for *half*:

> Die andere **Hälfte** hat er der Schwester gegeben.
> *He gave his sister the other half.*

The form **anderthalb**, *one and a half*, takes no ending and is followed by a plural noun:

Ich wartete **anderthalb** Stunden.
I waited an hour and a half.

The same applies to the forms **zwei(und)einhalb,** *two and a half,* **sechs-(und)einhalb,** *six and a half,* etc.

In **acht(und)einhalb** Jahren kehrt er zurück.
In eight and a half years he will return.

CHAPTER 8

Comparison
of Adjectives
and Adverbs

§21. USES OF THE COMPARATIVE AND SUPERLATIVE

In German as in English, adjectives have three degrees of comparison: positive, comparative, and superlative:[1]

> spät, spät**er,** spät**este** (am spat**esten**)
> *late, later, latest*

As illustrated below, the comparative is formed by adding –**er** to the stem (i.e., the uninflected form) of an adjective; the superlative, by adding –**(e)st.** This closely parallels the procedure in English: *faster, fastest.* But note that German does not use *more* and *most* in comparisons: *more interesting* = **interessanter;** *most interesting* = **am interessantesten.**

A. Das Eisen ist schwer.   Karl ist stark.
   Iron is heavy.   *Carl is strong.*

   Das Blei ist schwer**er.**   Fritz ist stärk**er.**
   Lead is heavier.   *Fred is stronger.*

   Welches Metall ist am schwer**sten?** Johann ist am stärk**sten.**
   Which metal is heaviest?   *John is strongest.*

                    Der Mond ist groß.
                    The moon is large.

                    Die Erde ist größ**er.**
                    The earth is larger.

                    Die Sonne ist am größ**ten.**
                    The sun is largest.

   (1) Adjectives of one syllable with the vowels **a, o,** or **u** usually take umlaut in the comparative and superlative degrees: **alt, älter,** der **älteste** (am **ältesten**).

---

[1]Certain adjectives have no comparatives because of their meaning: **halb** (*half*), **mündlich** (*oral*), **neunfach** (*ninefold*), etc.

The following are the most common adjectives that take umlaut in forming the comparative and superlative degrees: **alt, arm, dumm, fromm, grob, groß, hart, hoch, jung, kalt, klug, krank, kurz, lang, nah(e), scharf, schwach, schwarz, stark, warm.** The comparative of **rot** may be either **röter** or **roter.**

(2) The superlative form with **am,** known as the "adverbial superlative," is used either as a predicate adjective or as an adverb: Er singt **am lautesten** = He sings **loudest.**

The English equivalent of the adverbial superlative does not have the definite article (**am** = **an dem**), wherein it differs from the "relative superlative" (explained in **B**).

B. (1) Karl ist ein starker Junge.   Johann ist der stärk**ste** Junge.
Carl is a strong boy.   *John is the strongest boy.*

Fritz ist ein stärk**erer** Junge.   Er ist der stärk**ste.**
Fred is a stronger boy.   *He is the strongest.*

(2) Marie ist eine gute Köchin.   Luise ist die be**ste** Köchin.
Mary is a good cook.   *Louise is the best cook.*

Klara ist eine bess**ere** Köchin.   Sie ist die be**ste.**
Clara is a better cook.   *She is the best.*

(3) Er schreibt einen kurzen Satz.
He writes a short sentence.

Er schreibt einen kürz**eren** Satz.
He writes a shorter sentence.

Er schreibt den kürz**esten** Satz.
He writes the shortest sentence.

The superlative with the definite article, known as the "relative superlative," is used both when a noun is expressed and when it is understood.

C. Es war eine dunkle Nacht.   Es war eine dunkl**ere** Nacht.
It was a dark night.   *It was a darker night.*

Es war die dunkel**ste** Nacht.
It was the darkest night.

Adjectives and adverbs of more than one syllable do not take umlaut.

D. Es wird immer heißer.   Es wurde immer schlimmer.
It is getting hotter and hotter.   *It was getting worse and worse.*

Immer followed by the comparative is used to express continuous increase in the quality denoted by the adjective. Two comparatives, as in English, may also be used: Es wurde **schlimmer** und **schlimmer.**

E. Er ist **stolz.**   Er geht **stolz.**
He is proud.   *He walks proudly.*

Many German adjectives may, without change of form, be used as adverbs.

The comparative of adverbs must always end in –**er** and the superlative (unless used absolutely) must use the invariable **am**-form:

Er geht langsam.   Er geht langsam**er**.
He walks slowly.   *He walks more slowly.*

Er geht am langsam**sten**.
He walks most slowly.

F. (1) Sie sang aufs schön**ste**.
            She sang most beautifully.

            Das Rauchen ist aufs streng**ste** (*or* streng**stens**) verboten.
            Smoking is very strictly forbidden.

       (2) Das ist höch**st** interessant.
            That is extremely interesting.

            Die Reise war äußer**st** gefährlich.
            The trip was exceedingly dangerous.

The superlative adverb in **aufs,** known as the "absolute superlative," denotes merely a very high degree without any actual comparison.

Another form of the absolute superlative is **höchst** or **äußerst**—or some similar word in the sense of *very*—followed by the positive degree.

Note that, while both the adverbial and relative superlatives express real comparison, the absolute superlative does not.

G. Sie ist die allerschön**ste** auf der Welt.   Sie tanzt am allerbes**ten**.
        She is the most beautiful in the world.   *She dances best of all.*

        Sie ist die schön**ste** von allen.   Sie schreibt am allerschön**sten**.
        She is the most beautiful of all.   *She writes most beautifully of all.*

        Das ist das allerbes**te**.
        That is the best of all.

Aller (gen. pl. of **all**) may be used to strengthen the superlative adjective or the superlative adverb. It is then invariable and serves for all cases and genders.

H. Die Reise war **mehr** anstrengend als interessant.
        The trip was more strenuous than interesting.

Mehr followed by the positive degree is used when two qualities of the same individual or thing are compared; *than* = **als**.

I. Wir besuchen eine **ältere** Dame.
        We visit an elderly lady.

        Sie wohnt hier seit **längerer** Zeit.
        She has lived here for some time.

The comparative degree may be used absolutely, without any idea of comparison.

Note that endings are added to the stem of the comparative and superlative, just as they are to the uninflected form of an adjective in the positive degree: ein armer Mann, ein ärmerer Mann, der ärmste Mann.

J.   **The use of *als* and *wie* in comparisons.**

(1) **Als** is used **after the comparative degree:**
Sie ist **fleißiger als** ihr Bruder.
She is more industrious than her brother.

(2) **Wie** is used after the positive degree (affirmative or negative):
Sie ist ebenso **fleißig wie** ihr Bruder.
She is just as industrious as her brother.
Sie ist nicht so **fleißig wie** ihr Bruder.
She is not as industrious as her brother.

§22. IRREGULAR FORMATIONS OF THE COMPARATIVE AND SUPERLATIVE

A.   Adjectives ending in –d, –t, or an *s* sound (written s, z, ß, or sch) add –est to form the superlative: kurz, kürzer, der kürzeste, am kürzesten.

Present participles used as adjectives do not insert e before the superlative ending: **reizend** (*charming*), der reizend**ste** (*the most charming*).

B.   Adjectives ending in –e drop it before a comparative ending: **weise** (*wise*), **weiser** (*wiser*).

C.   Adjectives ending in –el, –en, and –er usually drop the e before a comparative ending: **dunkel, dunkler, der dunkelste, am dunkelsten** (*dark*). The e is also frequently dropped before an ending in the positive degree:

eine **dunkle** Nacht, *a dark night*

D.   Adjectives that never or sometimes take umlaut.   Although the general rule is that adjectives of one syllable take umlaut in the comparative and superlative degrees, there are exceptions.

(1) Adjectives that never take umlaut: **klar, rasch, voll, froh, lahm, rund, starr, schlank,** and all au-stems: **laut, blau, schlau,** etc.

(2) Adjectives that sometimes take umlaut, although occurring also without it: **blaß, glatt, karg, naß, rot, schmal.**

E. Irregular comparison of adjectives and adverbs.

(1) The following adjectives have irregular comparatives:

groß (*large*)	größer	der größte	am größten
gut (*good*)	besser	der beste	am besten
hoch (*high*)	höher	der höchste	am höchsten
nah (*near*)	näher	der nächste	am nächsten
viel (*much*)	mehr	der meiste	am meisten

When **hoch** in the positive takes an ending, the –c– is dropped:

ein **hoher** Berg, *a high mountain*

(2) The following adverbs are irregular in their comparison:

| bald (*soon*) | eher | am ehesten |
| gern (*gladly*) | lieber | am liebsten |

Früher (*sooner*) is quite frequently used instead of **eher**; it is also very often used in the sense of *formerly*.

Gern is used idiomatically with **haben** to translate the English verb *to like*, provided what is liked is the direct object of the verb:

Ich **habe** Tee **gern.**   Ich **habe** Limonade **lieber.**
I like tea.   *I prefer soda.*

Ich **habe** *Bier* **am liebsten.**
I like beer best.

If the action of the subject of a sentence is the point of comparison, merely add **gern**:

Er spricht **gern.**   Er spricht **lieber.**
He likes to talk.   *He prefers to talk.*

Er spricht **am liebsten.**
He likes best to talk.

Here the act of talking is the point of comparison.

CHAPTER 9

Expression
of Time and Date

§23. THE DAYS, MONTHS, AND SEASONS

The days of the week, the months, and the seasons are all masculine. The seasons regularly have the definite article; the days of the week and the months have the definite article when they are used with a preposition. Contraction of preposition and definite article is usual: **in dem** becomes **im, an dem** becomes **am.**

A. The days of the week.

    (1)   Es war **am** Dienstag, dem 21. Juni.
        It was on Tuesday, June 21.

In phrases such as *on Monday(s), on Tuesday(s), etc.,* English omits, but German requires, the definite article after the preposition. In German **an + dem** becomes **am.** The preposition, however, may be omitted both in English and German:

        Montag (acc.) war ich beschäftigt.
        I was busy (on) Monday.

    (2)   **Letzten** Donnerstag war ich bei meinem Freund.
        Last Thursday I was at my friend's house.

        Nächsten Sonntag wird er mich besuchen.
        He will visit me next Sunday.

        Jeden Freitag gehe ich ins Theater.
        Every Friday I go to the theater.

As illustrated by **letzten, nächsten,** and **jeden** in the sentences above, the *accusative* denotes *definite* time.

Instead of **jeden Freitag** (Montag, Dienstag, etc.) one may also say **Freitags, des Freitags,** or **alle Freitage.**

    (3)   **Eines** Sonntags war ich auf dem Lande.
        One Sunday I was in the country.

The *genitive* case is used to denote *indefinite* time.

B.   The months.

  (1)   Es war **im** März (Dezember).
It was in March (December).

      Sein Geburtstag ist **am** 17. Oktober.
His birthday is on October 17.

  (2)   As the heading of a letter:
den 22. Mai, *May 22nd.*

The date in the heading of a letter is in the accusative case.

C.   The seasons.

  (1)   **Im Frühling** singen die Vögel.
The birds sing in spring.

  (2)   **Jeden Sommer** macht er eine Reise.
He takes a trip every summer.

      Letzten Herbst war sie in der Schweiz.
She was in Switzerland last fall.

      Nächsten Winter werden wir zu Hause bleiben.
We shall stay at home next winter.

§24.   HOURS, MINUTES, AND IDIOMATIC TIME EXPRESSIONS

A.   Hours.

Wieviel Uhr ist es?
or: Wie spät ist es?
What time is it?

Es ist ein Uhr.
or: Es ist eins.
It is one o'clock.

Es ist halb vier.
It is half past three.

Es ist Viertel nach zwölf.
or: Es ist Viertel eins.
It is a quarter after twelve.

Es ist Viertel vor elf.
or: Es ist drei Viertel elf.
It is a quarter to eleven.

B. Minutes.

Es ist zehn Minuten nach acht.
It is ten minutes after eight.

Es ist sieben Minuten vor zwei.
It is seven minutes to two.

C. Idiomatic time expressions.

Er wird **um** sieben Uhr kommen.
*He will come **at** seven o'clock.*

Er wird **ungefähr um** sieben Uhr kommen.
*He will come (at) **about** seven o'clock.*

Der wievielte **ist** heute?

or: **Den** wievielten **haben** wir heute?
What is today's date?

Heute ist der 25. Januar.

or: Heute haben wir den 25. Januar.
Today is the 25th of January.

Der wievielte ist morgen?
What is tomorrow's date?

Morgen ist der 26. Januar.
Tomorrow is January 26.

Vor zwei Stunden		*two hours ago.*
Vor acht Tagen	erhielt ich den Brief.	*a week ago.*
Vor einem Monat	*I received the letter*	*a month ago.*
Vor drei Jahren		*three years ago.*

Heute **über acht Tage** wird er abreisen.
*He will leave **a week from** today.*

Sie geht **auf** einen Monat aufs Land.
*She is going to the country **for** a month.*

§25. PERIODS OF THE DAY IN TIME EXPRESSIONS

A. Adverbial phrases denoting time.

(1) am Morgen (morgens *or* des Morgens), *in the morning*
am Vormittag (vormittags *or* des Vormittags), *in the forenoon*
am Mittag (mittags *or* des Mittags), *at noon*
Wir essen zu Mittag. *We eat dinner.*
am Nachmittag (nachmittags *or* des Nachmittags), *in the afternoon*
am Abend (abends *or* des Abends), *in the evening*
Wir essen zu Abend. *We eat supper.*
am Tage, *in the daytime*

The forms in parentheses are particularly common when denoting some customary or habitual action:

> **Vormittags** bin ich immer zu Hause.
> *I am always at home in the forenoon.*
> **Nachmittags** macht der Großvater ein Schläfchen.
> *In the afternoon grandfather takes a nap.*

(2)   in der Nacht, *at night*

(3)   gegen Abend, *toward evening*
       gegen Morgen, *toward morning*

B.   The accusative denotes definite time and duration of time.

> **Jeden** Abend (Morgen, Freitag, etc.) mache ich einen Spaziergang.
> *I take a walk every evening (morning, Friday, etc.).*
> Er arbeitete **den ganzen** Morgen (**die ganze** Nacht).
> *He worked all morning (all night).*

C.   Combinations with *heute, morgen, gestern*.   In combinations with these words, such time expressions as **morgen, vormittag, mittag,** etc. are not capitalized, since they function as adverbs:

> heute morgen, *this morning*
> heute vormittag, *this forenoon*
> heute mittag, *this noon*
> heute nachmittag, *this afternoon*
> heute abend, *this evening, tonight*
> heute nacht, *tonight*
> gestern morgen, *yesterday morning*
> gestern vormittag, *yesterday forenoon*
> gestern mittag, *yesterday noon*
> gestern nachmittag, *yesterday afternoon*
> gestern abend, *yesterday evening, last night*
> gestern nacht, *last night*
> vorige Nacht, *last night*
> vorgestern, *day before yesterday*
> morgen früh, *tomorrow morning*
> frühmorgens, *early in the morning*
> morgen vormittag, *tomorrow forenoon*
> morgen mittag, *tomorrow noon*
> morgen nachmittag, *tomorrow afternoon*
> morgen abend, *tomorrow evening* (or *night*)
> morgen nacht, *tomorrow night*
> übermorgen, *day after tomorrow*

CHAPTER 10

Prepositions

§26. PREPOSITIONS WITH THE ACCUSATIVE

The following seven prepositions, as illustrated below, govern the accusative case: **bis** (*to, until, as far as*), **durch** (*through, by means of*), **für** (*for*), **gegen** (*against*), **ohne** (*without*), **um** (*around*), and **wider** (*against*).

A. Bis:

Er hat **bis** zehn Uhr gewartet.
*He waited **until** ten o'clock.*

Er hat mich **bis** München begleitet.
*He accompanied me **to** (= **as far as**) Munich.*

Er ging **bis an** die Tür.
*He went **up to** (= **as far as**) the door.*

Er hat mich **bis auf** den Tod gequält.
He worried (lit. *tortured*) *me **almost to** death.*

Er war **bis vor wenigen** Jahren gesund.
***Until a few** years **ago,** he was well.*

Bis is usually followed by another preposition which determines the case of the following noun. If the noun is preceded by an article, a second preposition *must* be used with **bis.**

B. Durch:

Er ging **durch das** Zimmer.
*He went **through** the room.*

Der Löwe wurde **durch einen** Schuß getötet.
*The lion was killed **by** a shot.*

By usually becomes **von** with a passive verb to denote the *personal agent.* **Durch,** however, is often used to denote the means or instrument.

C. Für:

Die Mutter kaufte ein Geschenk **für die** Tochter.
The mother bought a gift for her daughter.

Wir lernen nicht **für die** Schule, sondern **fürs** Leben.
We do not learn for school but for life.

D. Gegen:

Was haben Sie **gegen ihn**?
What have you against him?

Es war **gegen den** Wunsch seines Vaters.
It was contrary to his father's wish(es).

Gegen Morgen sind sie weggefahren.
They left toward morning.

E. Ohne:

Ohne dich kann ich nicht leben.
I cannot live without you.

Ohne Freunde ist das Leben traurig.
Life is dreary without friends.

F. Um:

Der Gärtner baute einen Zaun **um den** Garten.
The gardener built a fence around the garden.

Kümmern Sie sich nicht **um mich**!
Don't worry about me.

G. Wider:

Er tat es **wider seinen** Willen.
He did it against his will.

Do not confuse the adverb **wieder** (*again*) with the preposition **wider** (*against*).

§27. USES OF *OHNE, UM,* AND *ANSTATT* WITH INFINITIVES

When followed by nouns or pronouns, **ohne** and **um** govern the accusative case, **anstatt** (or simply **statt**) the genitive. But when followed by an infinitive with **zu** they have these meanings:

A. Ohne:

Er sprach **ohne aufzustehen**.
He spoke without getting up.

B. Um:

Um zu verstehen, muß man aufpassen.
In order to understand, one must pay attention.

C. Anstatt:

(An)statt zu kommen, spielte er Ball.
Instead of coming, he played ball.

§28. PREPOSITIONS WITH THE DATIVE

The following nine prepositions, as illustrated below, govern the dative case: **aus** (*out of, of, from*), **außer** (*except, besides*), **bei** (*near, with, at, at the house of*), **mit** (*with*), **nach** (*to, toward, after, according to*), **seit** (*since*), **von** (*of, from, by*), **zu** (*to*), and **gegenüber** (*opposite*).

A. Aus:

Er kommt **aus dem** Hause.
He comes out of the house.
Was ist **aus ihm** geworden?
What has become of him?
Der Tisch ist **aus** Holz.
The table is (made) of wood.

B. Außer:

Außer meinem Bruder war niemand da.
Nobody was there but (or except) my brother.
Ich war **außer mir** vor Freude.
I was beside myself with joy.

C. Bei:

Das Haus steht **bei der** Kirche.
The house is near the church.
Bei wem wohnt er?
With whom (or At whose house) does he live?
Ich habe kein Geld **bei mir.**
I have no money with me.

D. Mit:

Sie reiste **mit der** Mutter.   Man ißt Suppe **mit einem** Löffel.
She traveled with her mother.   *One eats soup with a spoon.*

E. Nach:

Nach dem Frühstück geht er in die Schule.
After breakfast he goes to school.

Morgen fährt er **nach** Berlin.
Tomorrow he will go to Berlin.

In der Klasse sitzen die Schüler **nach dem Alphabet.**
*In class the pupils are seated alphabetically (**according to the alphabet**).*

Nach der Schule gehen sie **nach Hause.**
*After school they go **home.***

Der Sage nach ist Rübezahl Herrscher über das Riesengebirge.
According to the legend, Ruebezahl rules over the Riesengebirge (Giants' Mountains).

In the sense of *according to,* **nach** frequently follows its noun.

F. Seit:

(1) **Seit dem Krieg** habe ich ihn nicht gesehen.
*I have not seen him **since the war.***

(2) **Seit vier Monaten** wohne ich in diesem Haus.
*I have been living in this house **for four months.***

(3) **Seit wann** sind Sie hier?
How long have you been here?

Examples (2) and (3) illustrate the use of **seit** with the *present tense* for an action begun in the past and continuing in the present.

G. Von:

Der Zug kommt **von** Hamburg.
The train comes from Hamburg.

Das ist ein Gedicht **von** Goethe.
That is a poem by Goethe.

Was will er **von mir?**
What does he want from me?

Der Löwe wurde **von dem** Jäger getötet.
The lion was killed by the hunter.

H. Zu:

(1) Ich gehe **zu meinem** Bruder.
I am going to my brother's (house).

Following verbs of going, **zu** renders English *to,* when the action is

directed toward a person, and in such phrases as **zur Kirche** and **zur Schule**.[1]
Before the names of cities or countries, *to* is rendered by **nach**:

> Er reist **nach** Deutschland.   Er ging **nach** Berlin.
> *He is traveling to Germany*   *He went to Berlin.*

> (2) Er sagte **zu mir**: „Ich werde Sie **zu Weihnachten** besuchen."
> *He said to me: "I shall visit you at Christmas."*

The preposition **zu** is required, following **sagen**, to introduce a direct
quotation. In an indirect quotation the preposition is omitted:

> Er sagte mir, er würde mich zu Weihnachten besuchen.
> *He told me that he would visit me at Christmas.*

> (3) Er war nicht **zu Hause**.
> *He was not at home.*

I. **Gegenüber**:

> Er saß **mir gegenüber**.   Unser Haus liegt **dem Park gegenüber**.
> *He sat opposite me.*   *Our house is opposite the park.*

Gegenüber often follows the word it governs.

§29. PREPOSITIONS WITH THE DATIVE OR ACCUSATIVE

The following prepositions, as illustrated below, may govern either the
dative or accusative: **an** (*at, on, to*), **auf** (*on, upon*), **hinter** (*behind*), **in** (*in, into*),
neben (*beside, next to*), **über** (*over, about, across*), **unter** (*under, beneath, below,
among*), **vor** (*before, in front of, ago*), and **zwischen** (*between*).
The dative case is used in answer to the question *where?* or *when?*—i.e., when
the verb is one of *rest*. The accusative answers the question *whither?*—i.e., when
the verb denotes *motion toward some goal*.

A. **An**:

> Er steht **an der** Tafel.   Er geht **an die** Tafel.
> *He is standing at the board.*   *He is going to the board.*

> **Am** Sonntag brauchen wir nicht in die Schule zu gehen.
> *On Sundays we do not have* (lit. *need*) *to go to school.*

---

[1] **zur Schule gehen** means *to attend school*; **zur Kirche gehen** implies regular attendance
at church. *To enter the school (church)* is **in die Schule (Kirche) gehen**. One also hears **zum
Bahnhof** (*to the train station*), **zum Fest** (*to the festival*), etc., where **zu** functions as neutrally
as English *to*.

B. Auf:

Das Buch liegt **auf dem** Tisch.
The book lies on the table:

Sie ist **auf dem** Lande.
She is in the country.

Er legt das Buch **auf den** Tisch.
He puts the book on the table.

Sie geht **aufs** (= **auf das**) Land.
She is going to the country.

C. Hinter:

Der Hund liegt **hinter der** Tür.
The dog is lying behind the door.

Der Hund läuft **hinter die** Tür.
The dog runs behind the door.

D. In:

Sie ist **im** (= **in dem**) Zimmer.
She is in the room.

Sie kommt **ins** (= **in das**) Zimmer.
She comes into the room.

Im Winter sind die Nächte lang.
In winter the nights are long.

Er geht **im** Zimmer auf und ab.
He is walking up and down in the room.

E. Neben:

Ich saß **neben ihm.**
I sat beside him.

Ich setzte mich **neben ihn.**
I sat down beside him.

F. Über:

Eine Lampe hängt **über dem** Tisch.
A lamp hangs over the table.

Hängen Sie die Lampe **über den** Tisch!
Hang the lamp over the table.

Er sprach **über den** Krieg.
He spoke about the war.

Er wundert sich **über die** Schnelligkeit des Flugzeugs.
He marvels at the speed of the airplane.

G. Unter:

Er schlief **unter dem** Baum.
He was sleeping under the tree.

Er lief **unter den** Baum.
He ran under the tree.

Unter meinen Papieren habe ich diesen Brief gefunden.
I found this letter among my papers.

Er hält es **unter seiner** Würde.
He considers it beneath his dignity.

Das bleibt **unter uns.**
*That is **between** us.*

H. Vor:

Er steht **vor der** Klasse.   Er tritt **vor die** Klasse.
*He stands **before** the class.*   *He steps **before** the class.*

Vor kurzer Zeit überquerten die ersten Flieger den Ozean.
*A **short time ago** the first flyers crossed the ocean.*

I. Zwischen:

Er saß **zwischen mir** und **meinem** Bruder.
*He was sitting **between** me and my brother.*

Er setzte sich **zwischen mich** und **meinen** Bruder.
*He sat down **between** me and my brother.*

Note: Certain of the prepositions listed above may be used in set phrases, and in such situations the case is dictated and invariable. For example:

(1) **über** meaning *about* or *concerning* requires the accusative.
(2) **sich wundern über** always takes accusative.
(3) **vor** meaning *ago* requires the dative and must precede the noun it governs.

§30. *WO-* AND *DA-*FORMS

When a thing is referred to, interrogative and relative pronouns may be replaced by the prefix **wo–**, personal pronouns by **da–**, as objects of prepositions governing the dative or accusative cases. Pronouns referring to people cannot be so replaced. If the preposition begins with a vowel, the prefixes are **wor–** and **dar–**.

A. Womit, wodurch, woraus, wovon, woran, etc.

(1) **Womit** schreibt er?   **Wovon** spricht sie?
***With what** is he writing?*   ***Of what** is she speaking?*

Worüber wird die Geschichte erzählen?
*What will the story tell **about**?*

(2) Die Feder, **womit** [= mit der (*or* welcher)] ich schreibe, gehört meiner Schwester.
*The pen **with which** I am writing belongs to my sister.*

Die Bücher, **wovon** [= von denen (*or* welchen)] er sprach, gefallen mir.
*I like the books **of which** he was speaking.*

B.   Damit, dadurch, daraus, davon, daran, etc.

Er schreibt **damit.**   Sie spricht **davon** (or **darüber**).
*He is writing **with it.***   *She is talking **about it.***

Das Kind hat viele Spielsachen.   Es spielt **damit.**
The child has many playthings.   *It is playing **with them.***

§31.   CONTRACTIONS

A.   Common contractions.   The following are the most common contractions of prepositions with the definite article:

am	(= an dem)	**im**	(= in dem)
ans	(= an das)	**ins**	(= in das)
aufs	(= auf das)	**vom**	(= von dem)
beim	(= bei dem)	**zum**	(= zu dem)
fürs	(= für das)	**zur**	(= zu der)

B.   Other contractions.   Contractions other than those listed above are readily intelligible, provided one remembers that final –**m** stands for **dem** and final –**s** for **das**: **durchs** (= durch das), **ums** (=um das), **hinterm** (= hinter dem), etc.

§32.   PREPOSITIONS WITH THE GENITIVE

The following prepositions, as illustrated below, govern the genitive case: **während** (*during*), **wegen** (*on account of*), **trotz** (*in spite of*), **(an)statt** (*instead of*), **diesseits** (*on this side of*), **jenseits** (*on that side of*), **oberhalb** (*above*), **unterhalb** (*below*), **außerhalb** (*outside of*), **innerhalb** (*inside of* or *within*), and **um . . . willen** (*for the sake of*).

A.   Während:

Während der Nacht regnete es.   **Während des Tages** arbeiten wir.
During the night it rained.   *During the day we work.*

B.   Wegen:

Wegen des schlechten Wetters blieb er zu Hause.
or: **Des schlechten Wetters wegen** blieb er zu Hause.
*He stayed at home **on account of the bad weather.***

(1)   **Wegen** may precede or follow the noun it governs.

(2)   **Wegen** must follow when used with personal pronouns, which assume a form in –**t**: meinetwegen (*on my account*), deinetwegen [*on your* (sing. fam.) *account*], seinetwegen (*on his account*), ihretwegen [*on her* (*their*) *account*],

unsertwegen (*on our account*), euretwegen [*on your* (pl. fam.) *account*], Ihretwegen (*on your account*).

> Tun Sie es nicht **meinetwegen**!
> *Do not do it on my account.*

(3) **Meinetwegen** may also mean *for all I care.*

> **Meinetwegen** darf er das tun.
> *He may do that for all I care.*

C. Trotz:

> **Trotz des kalten Wetters** machte er einen Spaziergang.
> *He took a walk in spite of the cold weather.*

D. (An)statt:

> **(An)statt des Vaters** kam die Mutter.
> *Mother came instead of father.*
>
> **(An)statt des baren Geldes** gab ich ihm einen Scheck.
> *I gave him a check instead of cash.*

E. Diesseits:

> Der Dom ist **diesseits des Flusses**.
> *The cathedral is on this side of the river.*

F. Jenseits:

> Das Rathaus ist **jenseits des Flusses**.
> *The town hall is on that side of the river.*

G. Oberhalb:

> **Oberhalb des Dorfes** ist eine kleine Kirche.
> *Above the village there is a small church.*

H. Unterhalb:

> **Unterhalb der Kirche** ist eine schöne Wiese.
> *There is a beautiful meadow below the church.*

I. Außerhalb:

> Er wohnt **außerhalb der Stadt**.
> *He lives outside of the city.*

J. Innerhalb:

> **Innerhalb einer Stunde** muß ich fertig sein.
> *I must be ready within an hour.*

K.   Um ... willen:

Um Gottes (or **Himmels**) **willen!**
For heaven's sake!
Tun Sie es **um meinetwillen!**
Do it for my sake.

Note:

Other uses and meanings of common prepositions. Only the most common prepositions have been included in this chapter. There are many others—chiefly with the genitive and dative—which occur, for the most part, in the written language. The common prepositions have many other uses and meanings than those given above, particularly in idiomatic expressions and with certain reflexive verbs. The simplest conversation is apt to involve idioms with prepositions—e.g., the common phrase *in other words* = **mit** anderen Worten. The following sentences, which might be multiplied indefinitely, show that the same English preposition may have numerous German equivalents:

I thank you for the book.	*I ask you for the book.*
Ich danke Ihnen **für** das Buch.	Ich bitte Sie **um** das Buch.
He hopes for good weather.	*She longs for her friends.*
Er hofft **auf** gutes Wetter.	Sie sehnt sich **nach** ihren Freundinnen.
For what reason did he do that?	*For what price?*
Aus welchem Grunde hat er das getan?	**Zu** welchem Preise?

She has been here for two months.
Sie ist **seit** zwei Monaten hier.

Cologne is famous for its cathedral.
Köln ist **durch** den Dom (or **wegen** des Domes) berühmt.

He is looking for me.
Er sucht mich.

CHAPTER 11

Genitive, Dative, and Accusative Cases

§33. USES OF THE GENITIVE CASE

A. The genitive to denote indefinite time. The genitive case is frequently used to denote indefinite time:

Eines Tages (eines Morgens, eines Abends) besuchte er mich.
One day (one morning, one evening) he visited me.

Similarly with the adverbial forms **morgens** (*in the morning*), **abends** (*in the evening*), etc.

B. The genitive with certain verbs.

(1) A few verbs may take a genitive as sole object. These verbs should be noted in order to develop reading facility. In modern German, however, many such verbs are felt to be poetic, choice, pedantic or archaic. It is generally advisable to use other constructions in writing and conversation. Such alternative constructions are given in the examples that follow.

> (*a*) **Bedürfen:**
> Ich bedarf **Ihrer Hilfe.**
> Ich brauche Ihre Hilfe.
> *I need your help.*

> (*b*) **Denken:**
> Ich denke **seiner.**
> Ich denke an ihn.
> *I think (or am thinking) of him.*

> (*c*) **Gedenken:**
> Gedenke **deines Eides!**
> Erinnere dich an deinen Eid!
> *Remember your oath.*

(2)   A number of reflexive verbs may govern the genitive case, although other constructions are often possible:

(a)   **Sich erbarmen:**

Erbarmen Sie sich **meiner!**
Erbarmen Sie sich über mich!
Haben Sie Mitleid mit **mir!**
(*Have*) *pity* (*on*) *me.*

(b)   **Sich bedienen:**

Ich bediente mich **seiner Güte.**
Ich machte von seiner Güte Gebrauch.
I availed myself (or *made use*) *of his kindness.*

(c)   **Sich bemächtigen:**

Er hat sich **unseres Eigentums** bemächtigt.
Er hat unser Eigentum in Besitz genommen.
He took possession of our property.

(d)   **Sich erinnern:**

Er erinnert sich **des Vorfalls.**
Er erinnert sich an den Vorfall.
He remembers the incident.

(e)   **Sich rühmen:**

Er rühmt sich **seines Erfolgs.**
Er prahlt mit seinem Erfolg.
He boasts of his success.

(f)   **Sich schämen:**

Schämt er sich **seiner Armut?**
Schämt er sich über seine Armut?
Is he ashamed of his poverty?

(3)   Verbs of "judicial action" (e.g., **anklagen** and **beschuldigen,** *to accuse*) and certain verbs of separation or deprivation (e.g., **berauben,** *to rob*) take the genitive of the *thing* (that of which one is accused or from which one is separated) but the accusative of the *person*:

(a)   **Anklagen:**

Man hat **ihn des Diebstahls** angeklagt.
Er wurde **des Diebstahls** angeklagt.
He was accused of theft.

(b)   **Beschuldigen:**

Hast du **ihn der Unehrlichkeit** beschuldigt?
Did you accuse him of dishonesty?

(c) **Berauben:**

Er hat **mich meines ganzen Geldes** beraubt.
He robbed me of all my money.

Rauben, however, takes the dative of the person and the accusative of the thing:

Man hat **ihm alles** geraubt.
They robbed him of everything.

C. The genitive with certain adjectives. Certain adjectives govern the genitive ease, usually following the nouns they modify. Some of the common ones are:

(1) **Bedürftig** (*in need of*):

Sie ist **meines Trostes** bedürftig.
She is in need of my consolation.

(2) **Bewußt** (*conscious*):

Ich bin mir **keines Unrechts** bewußt.
I am not conscious of any injustice.

(3) **Fähig** (*capable*):

Er ist **einer solchen Tat** fähig.
He is capable of such a deed.

(4) **Froh** (*happy*):

Sie wird **ihrer hohen Stellung** nicht froh.
She is not happy in her high position.

Er ist froh über **den langen** Urlaub.
He is happy about the long vacation.

The adjective **froh** with the genitive and **werden** usually means *happy in.* To be *happy about* is **froh sein über,** which, like the verbal idiom **sich freuen über,** is followed by the accusative. The adjective may either precede or follow the prepositional phrase.

(5) **Gewahr werden** (*become aware of, perceive*):

Er wurde **seines Irrtums** gewahr.
He perceived (or became aware of) his mistake.

Gewahr is used only with **werden**; it sometimes takes the accusative.

(6) **Gewiß** (*certain*):

Er ist **seiner Sache** gewiß.
He knows what he is about.
He is sure of his case.

(7) **Mächtig** (*master* or *in control of*):

Er war **seiner Sinne** nicht mächtig.
He was not in (control of) his senses.

(8) **Müde** (*tired*):

Ich bin **dieses Treibens** müde.
I am tired of this activity.

Müde (*tired*) and **los** (*free, rid of*) very often govern the accusative in modern German:

Ich bin **es** müde.   Ich bin **es** los.
I am tired of it.   *I am rid of it.*

This is due to the fact that this **es** was genitive in the older language but came to be felt as accusative—a use of the accusative which spread to forms other than **es**:

Ich bin **ihn** los.
I am rid of him.

(9) **Sicher** (*sure*):

Sie sind **meines Bestands** sicher.
You are sure of my assistance.

(10) **Wert** (*worth*): In modern German this adjective usually governs the accusative but in a few idiomatic expressions it governs the genitive:

Es ist nicht **der Mühe** wert.   Es ist nicht **der Rede** wert.
It is not worthwhile.   *It is not worth talking about.*
It is not worth the trouble.

(11) **Würdig** (*worthy*):

Die Angelegenheit ist **Ihrer Unterstützung** würdig.
The affair deserves your support.
The affair is worthy of your support.

D. The genitive in idiomatic expressions:

Ich fahre **zweiter Klasse.**   Er ist **derselben Meinung.**
I travel second class.   *He is of the same opinion.*

Leichten (schweren) Herzens ging er an die Arbeit.
With a light (heavy) heart he went to work.

Sie ist **guter Laune** [or **guten Mut(e)s**].
She is in (a) good humor.

Meines Wissens verhalten sich die Tatsachen anders.
As far as I know, the facts are different.

Laß ihn **seines Weges** ziehen!
Let him go his way.

Many adverbs preserve traces of the genitive:

meinerseits, *on my part;* **glücklicherweise,** *fortunately;* **jedenfalls,** *in any event* (or *case*); **keineswegs,** *by no means;* **gewissermaßen,** *in a certain sense;* **links** (**rechts**)*, on* (*at* or *to*) *the left* (*right*); etc.

E.   When the genitive is not used.

(1)   Proper names used in apposition after, and names of months preceded by *of* are *not* in the genitive but in the same case as nouns preceding them:

> die Stadt **München,** *the city of Munich*
> im Monat **Mai,** *in the month of May*
> den 25. **Juni,** *the 25th of June* (as the heading of a letter)

(2)   Nouns of number, weight, measure, and kind are *not* followed by the genitive:

> drei Pfund **Butter,** *three pounds of butter*
> zwei Glas **Bier,** *two glasses of beer*
> eine neue Art **Teppich,** *a new kind of carpet*

Masculine and neuter nouns denoting measurement are usually in the singular, provided they follow a numeral: **drei** Pfund, **zwei** Glas, *etc.* Feminine nouns ending in –**e,** however, require the plural form:

> drei Tassen Tee, *three cups of tea*

Die Mark always has the singular form:

> zwanzig **Mark,** *twenty marks*

If the thing weighed or measured is modified by an adjective, the genitive *may* be used:

> ein Glas kalt**en** Wassers, *a glass of cold water*
> drei Pfund frisch**en** Fleisches, *three pounds of fresh meat*

In ordinary speech, however, the thing measured is in the same case as the preceding noun: ein Glas kalt**es** Wasser, drei Pfund frisch**es** Fleisch, etc.

§34.   USES OF THE DATIVE CASE

A.   The dative with certain verbs.   The following are a few of the more common verbs that govern the dative case:

(1)   **Antworten** (*to answer*):

> Antworten Sie **mir**!
> *Answer me.*

(*a*) **Antworten** takes the dative of the person. Observe, however, its idiomatic use with **auf** and the accusative:

Antworten Sie **auf die Frage!**
*Answer **the question.***

(*b*) **Beantworten,** on the other hand, takes a direct object:

Beantworten Sie die Frage!
Answer the question.

(2) **Befehlen** (*to command, order*):

Der Herr befahl **dem Diener**, bald zurückzukommen.
*The master ordered **the servant** to return soon.*

(3) **Begegnen** (*to meet*):

Er ist **mir** auf der Straße begegnet.
*He met **me** on the street.*

(4) **Danken** (*to thank*):

Er wird **ihnen** danken.
*He will thank **them.***

(5) **Dienen** (*to serve*):

Er hat **seinem König** treu gedient.
***He** has served **his king** faithfully.*

(6) **Drohen** (*to threaten*):

Er drohte **ihm** mit Schlägen.
*He threatened **him** with blows.*

(7) **Einfallen** (*to occur to, come to mind*):

Das war **mir** nie eingefallen.
*That had never occurred **to me.***
Was fällt **Ihnen** ein?
*What do you **mean**?*

(8) **Fehlen** (*to be the matter with, lack*):

Was fehlt **Ihnen?**   **Mir** fehlen zwei Bücher.
*What is the matter **with you?***   *I am short two books.*

(9) **Folgen** (*to follow*):

Er wird **den Männern** folgen.
*He will follow **the men.***

(*a*) In the sense of *follow*, **folgen** must be conjugated with **sein**:

Er war **mir** gefolgt.
*He had followed **me.***

(*b*) In the sense of *obey*, **folgen** is conjugated with **haben**:

Er hat **mir** gefolgt.
*He obeyed **me**.*

(10) **Gefallen** (*to please*):

Wie gefällt **Ihnen** das neue Buch?
*How do **you** like the new book?*

What one likes is the subject of the verb.

(11) **Gehorchen** (*to obey*):

Das Kind gehorcht **der Mutter**.
*The child obeys **its mother**.*

(12) **Gehören** (*to belong*):

Es gehört **mir**.
*It belongs **to me**.*

The preposition **zu** is not used with gehören if the verb denotes ownership; it is required if the verb is used in the sense of *to be a part of*:

Das Hause gehört **zum** (= **zu dem**) Gut.
The house belongs to (i.e., is a part of) the estate.

(13) **Gelingen** and **glücken** (*to succeed*):

Es ist **ihm** nicht gelungen (*or* geglückt), das zu tun.
He has not succeeded in doing that.

Both of these verbs are conjugated with **sein**, and both are impersonal. A thing may be the subject:

Dieser Plan ist mir nicht gelungen.
This plan did not turn out well for me.

(14) **Genügen** (*to suffice, satisfy*):

Es genügt **ihm** nicht ganz.
He is not quite satisfied with it.
It isn't enough for him.

(15) **Geschehen** (*to happen;* used only impersonally, see §62):

Es geschieht **ihm** recht.
*It serves **him** right.*

(16) **Gleichen** (*to resemble*):

Er gleicht **der Mutter**.
*He resembles **his mother**.*

(17) **Glauben** (*to believe*):

Ich glaube **Ihnen**.   Ich glaube **es** nicht.
*I believe **you**.*   *I don't believe **it**.*

Glauben takes the dative of the *person* but the accusative of the *thing*.

(18)   **Gratulieren** (*to congratulate*):

Ich gratuliere **Ihnen** zu Ihrem Erfolg.
*I congratulate **you** on your success.*

(19)   **Helfen** (*to help*):

Helfen Sie **dem armen Manne!**
*Help **the poor man.***

(20)   **Sich nähern** or **nahen** (*to approach*):

Ich näherte mich **der Stadt.**
*I approached **the city.***

(21)   **Nützen** (*to be of use, benefit*):

Was nützt **ihm** das?
*Of what use is that **to him?***

(22)   **Passen** (*to fit, be convenient, suit*):

Der Rock paßt **mir** nicht.
*The coat does not fit **me.***

Es paßte **mir** nicht, heute aufs Land zu gehen.
*It was not convenient **for me** to go to the country today.*

(23)   **Raten** (*to advise*):

Wozu raten Sie **mir**?
*What do you advise **me** to do?*

Raten, *to guess* (*at*) and **erraten,** *to guess* (*correctly*) both take the accusative:

Er kann raten, aber er wird es niemals erraten.
He can guess at it, but he will never succeed in guessing it.

(24)   **Schaden** (*to harm, hurt*):

Das wird **Ihrer Gesundheit** schaden.
*That will harm **your health.***

(25)   **Schmeicheln** (*to flatter*):

Der Maler hat **dem Mädchen** in diesem Bild geschmeichelt.
*The artist flattered **the girl** in this picture.*

Schmeicheln is often used with the dative reflexive:

Schmeich(e)le **dir** nicht!
*Don't flatter **yourself.***

(26)   **Trauen** (*to trust, believe in*):

Ich traue **ihm** nicht.
*I don't trust **him.***

(27) **Vergeben** (*to forgive*):

Vergeben Sie **ihnen!**
*Forgive **them.***

(28) **Widersprechen** (*to contradict*):

Widersprechen Sie **mir** nicht!
*Don't contradict **me.***

B. Verbs governing both dative and accusative. Many verbs such as **geben** (*to give*), **zeigen** (*to show*), and **sagen** (*to tell*) take an accusative of the *direct object* and a dative of the *indirect object*:

Ich werde es ihm geben.   Er wird mir das Bild zeigen.
I shall give it to him.   *He will show me the picture.*

Sagen Sie mir die ganze Wahrheit!
Tell me the whole truth.

C. Verbs of taking and stealing. Most verbs of taking and stealing have the thing stolen in the accusative but the person from whom it was taken in the dative:

Der Dieb hat **mir** die Uhr gestohlen.
The thief stole my watch.
lit.:   *The thief has stolen the watch **from me.***

D. The dative with certain adjectives. The adjectives listed below usually follow the nouns they modify.

(1) **Ähnlich** (*similar, resembling*):

Der Sohn ist **der Mutter** ähnlich.
*The son resembles **his mother.***

(2) **Angenehm** (*pleasant, agreeable*):

Das warme Wetter ist **mir** sehr angenehm.
I find the warm weather very agreeable.

(3) **Bekannt** (*known*):

Das Gedicht war **ihm** nicht bekannt.
Er kannte das Gedicht nicht.
He did not know the poem.

(4) **Bequem** (*comfortable*):
Mache es **dir** bequem!
Make yourself at home.

(5) **Böse** (*angry*):

Seien Sie **mir** nicht böse!
or: Seien Sie nicht böse auf mich!
*Don't be angry **with me.***

(6) **Dankbar** (*grateful*):

Er war **seinen Eltern** stets dankbar.
*He was always grateful **to his parents**.*

(7) **Feindlich** (**gesinnt**) (*hostile*):

Ich bin **Ihnen** nicht feindlich gesinnt.
*I am not hostile **to you**.*

(8) **Fremd** (*strange,* unknown):

Er ist **mir** fremd.
*He is a stranger **to me**.*

(9) **Freundlich** (*friendly*):

Seien Sie **ihm** freundlich!
or: Seien Sie freundlich gegen ihn!
Be friendly to (or *toward*) *him.*

(10) **Gelegen** (*opportune*):

Das kommt **mir** recht gelegen.
*That comes quite opportunely **for me**.*

(11) **Gleich** (*like, the same*):

Die Gestalten gingen **Gespenstern** gleich an uns vorüber.
***Like ghosts** the figures passed us.*

Es ist **mir** ganz gleich.
*It is all the same **to me**.*

(12) **Leicht** (*easy*):

Es war **dem Schüler** leicht, die Prüfung zu bestehen.
*It was easy **for the pupil** to pass the examination.*

(13) **Lieb** (*dear, charming*):

Es ist **ihm** sehr lieb.
He likes it very much.
lit: *It is very dear **to him**.*

Lieb is frequently used in the impersonal construction to express liking for;
it may be followed by a **daß**-clause:

Es ist **mir** lieb, daß Sie das sagen.
I am pleased to hear you say that.

(14) **Nah(e)** (*near*):

Das Dorf liegt **unserer Stadt** nahe.
*The village is near **our city**.*

Near is more frequently rendered by **in der Nähe:**

Er wohnt **in meiner Nähe.**
He lives near me.

(15) **Nützlich** (*useful*):

Der Beamte ist **dem Lande** nützlich.
*The official is useful **to the country**.*

(16) **Schwer** (*difficult*):

Diese Arbeit ist **den kleinen Kindern** schwer.
*This work is hard **for the little children**.*

(17) **Treu** (*true, faithful*):

Werden Sie **mir** treu bleiben?
Will you be (or *remain*) *true **to me**?*

(18) **Willkommen** (*welcome*):

Seien Sie **mir** herzlich willkommen!
You are heartily welcome.
I wish you a hearty welcome.

E.   The dative of possession.   English denotes possession with reference to parts of the body or to articles of clothing by the possessive adjective; the German idiom, however—usually with the dative—ordinarily uses the *definite article,* provided there is no doubt as to the possessor.

Ich wasche **mir die** Hände.	Ich wasche **dem Kinde die** Hände.
*I wash **my** hands.*	*I wash **the child's** hands.*
Er setzt (**sich**) **den** *Hut auf.*	Er setzt **dem Jungen den** Hut auf.
*He puts on **his** hat.*	*He puts **the hat on the boy's** head.*

F.   The dative of reference.   The dative is often used to denote the person concerned in a statement, or the person with reference to whom the statement holds good:

Schreiben Sie **mir** diese Aufgabe ab!	Es war **ihm** ein Rätsel.
*Copy this exercise **for me**.*	*It was a riddle **to him**.*

Notice that English does not always express such a dative:

Zu Hause nahm ich **mir** nur Zeit, mich anzuziehen und zu frühstücken.
At home I merely took time to dress and to have breakfast.

§35.   USES OF THE ACCUSATIVE CASE

A.   The accusative to denote definite time.

Letzten Monat war ich bei ihm.
***Last month** I was at his house.*

Nächsten Sommer wird er mich besuchen.
*He will visit me **next summer**.*

B. The accusative to denote duration of time.

Wir arbeiteten **den ganzen Tag.**
We worked all day.

Den ganzen Morgen spielte er Ball.
He played ball all morning.

C. The accusative to denote extent. The accusative case is used to denote extent, especially with such adjectives as **breit, dick, hoch, lang,** and **tief:**

einen Zoll **breit,** *an inch wide*   eine Meile **lang,** *a mile long*
einen Fuß **hoch,** *a foot high*   einen Ton **tiefer,** *a tone lower*
einen Fuß **dick,** *a foot thick.*   einen Kopf **größer,** *a head taller*

D. The double accusative. Certain verbs such as **lehren** (*to teach*), **nennen** and **heißen** (*to call*), and **schelten** and **schimpfen** (*to call names*) take two accusative objects:

Sie lehrte **ihn das Lied.**   Er nannte (*or* hieß) **mich seinen Freund.**
She taught him the song.   *He called me his friend.*

Er hat **ihn einen Narren** geschimpft (*or* gescholten).
He called him a fool.

The verb **kosten** (*to cost*) may take either the accusative or dative of the person, but always the accusative of the thing:

Es kostete **ihn** (*or* ihm) **einen Dollar.**
It cost him a dollar.

Das Buch kostete **mich** (*or* mir) zehn Mark.
The book cost me ten marks.

E. The cognate accusative. The cognate accusative repeats the idea contained in a verb:

Gar schöne **Spiele** spiel' ich mit dir. (Goethe)
I shall play very beautiful games with you.

Er starb **einen sanften Tod** (*or* eines sanften Todes).
He died an easy death.

The optional form indicates that **sterben** is sometimes followed by the genitive.

F. The absolute accusative. The accusative case is often used absolutely with some such word as *having* understood:

Den Stock unter dem Arm, ging er in den Wald.
***With** (i.e., **having**) **his cane** under his arm, he went into the forest.*

G.   The accusative in salutations.   Such expressions as **guten Morgen!
guten Abend! guten Tag!** etc., are in the accusative case because they imply
a verb of wishing: *I wish you a good morning (evening, day, etc.).*

H.   The accusative with *gewohnt, wert* and *entlang*.   The accusative is
used with **gewohnt** (*accustomed*), **wert** (*worth*), and **entlang** (*along*):

Er ist schwere Arbeit gewohnt.

or: Er ist **an** schwere Arbeit gewöhnt.

He is used to hard work.

Es ist ein**en** Dollar wert.   Er ging **das Ufer** entlang.
It is worth a dollar.   *He walked along the shore.*

(1)   The construction with **an** plus accusative and the past participle
gewöhnt is more common.

(2)   **Entlang** governs the dative occasionally and the genitive still less
frequently. It sometimes precedes the noun it governs.

I.   Compounds from intransitive verbs. Many intransitive verbs become
transitive when compounded:

(1)

Er folgte mir.   but: ⎧Er **be**folgte mein**en** Rat.
He followed me.   *He followed my advice.*
                             ⎨Er **ver**folgte **mich.**
                             ⎩*He pursued me.*

Er steigt auf den Berg.   Ich wohne in diesem Haus.
but: Er **be**steigt **den** Berg.   but: Ich **be**wohne dies**es** Haus.
He climbs the mountain.   *I live in this house.*

(2)   Similarly:

Er redete **mich an.**   Sie haben **den** alten Mann fast **über**fahren.
He addressed me.   *You almost ran over the old man.*

J.   Causatives.   Causative verbs, which require a direct object, must not
be confused with intransitive verbs of similar spelling. Causative verbs are
regularly weak.

(1)   Die Bäume **fallen** im Sturm. (intr.)
The trees fall in the storm.

Die Holzhacker **fällen** die Bäume.
The woodcutters fell the trees. (i.e., cause to fall, cut down)

(2)   Die Männer **ertrinken.** (intr.)
The men are drowning.

Sie **ertränken** ihren Kummer im Wein.
They drown their sorrow in wine.

INTRANSITIVE	CAUSATIVE
fallen, *to fall*	fällen, *to cause to fall*
ertrinken, *to drown*	ertränken, *to drown*
liegen, *to lie*	legen, *to lay*
sitzen, *to sit*	setzen, *to set*
versinken, *to sink*	versenken, *to sink*
erschrecken, *to be frightened*	erschrecken, *to frighten*
verschwinden, *to disappear*	verschwenden, *to squander*

CHAPTER 12

Special Uses
of Tense

§36. IDIOMATIC USE OF THE PRESENT
FOR THE ENGLISH PRESENT PERFECT

German uses the present tense to denote an action begun in the past and still continuing in the present. This construction, used where English uses a present perfect, must contain an adverbial expression of time (**schon, seit** plus the dative, **erst, zwei Monate, wie lange,** etc.).

Er **ist** schon zwei Monate hier.
*He **has been** here for two months.*
(i.e., he came here two months ago and is still here.)

Wie lange **lernen Sie** schon Deutsch?
*How long **have you been studying** German?*
(i.e., the person addressed began the study of German some time ago and is still studying it.)

Wir **arbeiten** schon einen Monat.
*We **have been** working for a month.*
(i.e., we began to work a month ago and are still working.)

Sie ist (schon) **seit drei Jahren** in dieser Stadt.
or: Sie ist **schon drei Jahre** in dieser Stadt.
*She has been in this city **for three years**.*
(i.e., she came three years ago and is still in the city.)

Seit wann wohnen Sie in dieser Stadt?
Since when have you been living in this city?
(i.e., the person addressed is still living in the city.)

Ich wohne **erst seit** zwei Monaten hier.
I have been living here for only two months.
(i.e., I began living here two months ago and am still living here.)

§37. USE OF THE PRESENT FOR THE FUTURE

The present tense is often used instead of the future, particularly when accompanying adverbs of time—such as **bald** and **morgen**—clearly show futurity. If the future indicative occurs in the main clause of a conditional sentence, the present indicative is ordinarily employed in the **wenn**-clause (just as in English). The present tense is also used for the future in other types of sentences, where there can be no chronological ambiguity.

Bald sind wir da.   Morgen reist mein Freund ab.
We shall soon be there.   *My friend will leave (is leaving) tomorrow.*

Wenn Sie sich beeilen, so werden Sie ihn noch einholen.
If you hurry, you will still catch (up with) him.

§38. IDIOMATIC USES OF THE PAST

A. The use of the past for the English past perfect. The German simple past is often used to denote an action begun at some previous time and continuing up to the time referred to in the past. This past context may be supplied by a verbal phrase or an adverbial phrase (usually **schon**, or **seit** plus dative, or both).

Er **wartete** schon anderthalb Stunden auf mich, als ich kam.
*He **had been waiting** an hour and a half for me when I came.*

(i.e., he began to wait for me at some time in the past and was still waiting for me when I came.)

Er **kannte** mich schon seit vielen Jahren.
*He **had known** me for many years.*

Wir **waren** schon lange Freunde.
*We **had been** friends for a long time.*

B. The use of the past to denote a customary occurrence in the past. The simple past in German, usually reinforced by such adverbs as **früher, immer,** and **gewöhnlich,** may be used to express a recurring or habitual action.

Früher **rauchte** er viel.
*Formerly he **used to smoke** (or he smoked) a great deal.*

Er **stand gewöhnlich** um sieben Uhr auf.
*He **used to get up** (or he usually got up) at seven o'clock.*

Wenn er bei mir war, **sprach** er immer über seine Zukunftspläne.
*Whenever he was at my house, he **would talk** (or he always talked) about his plans for the future.*

Pflegen (*to be accustomed or used to*) with a dependent infinitive is a common equivalent of the above construction:

Er pflegte viel zu rauchen.
Er pflegte um sieben Uhr aufzustehen.
Er pflegte über seine Zukunftspläne zu sprechen.

§39. IDIOMATIC USE OF THE FUTURE AND FUTURE PERFECT WITH *WOHL*

A. The German future tense, usually with **wohl,** may be used to express *present probability*.

Er wird es wohl verstehen.
He doubtless understands it.
or: *He'll understand it.*

Sie wird wohl wissen, was das bedeutet.
She doubtless knows what that means.
or: *She'll know what it means.*

B. The German future perfect is chiefly used, generally with **wohl,** to express *past probability*.

Mein Freund wird wohl krank gewesen sein.
My friend was probably sick.
Er wird wohl zu viel gegessen haben.
He probably ate too much.

CHAPTER 13

Personal Pronouns

§40. FORMS OF THE PERSONAL PRONOUNS

Listed below are the personal pronouns, singular and plural, for all cases. Genitive forms are rarely used today.

SINGULAR

NOM.	ich (*I*)	du (*you*)	er (*he*)	sie (*she*)	es (*it*)	Sie (*you*)
GEN.	(meiner)	(deiner)	(seiner)	(ihrer)	(seiner)	(Ihrer)
DAT.	mir	dir	ihm	ihr	ihm	Ihnen
ACC.	mich	dich	ihn	sie	es	Sie

PLURAL

NOM.	wir (*we*)	ihr (*you*)	sie (*they*)	Sie (*you*)
GEN.	(unser)	(euer)	(ihrer)	(Ihrer)
DAT.	uns	euch	ihnen	Ihnen
ACC.	uns	euch	sie	Sie

§41. USES OF THE PERSONAL PRONOUNS

A. Since German preserves grammatical gender, the pronouns of the third person will not always be directly translated into English; rather, their idiomatic equivalents must be sought.

Wo ist der Bleistift?   **Er** ist auf dem Tisch.
Where is the pencil?   *It is on the table.*

Wo ist die Feder?   **Sie** ist auf dem Tisch.
Where is the pen?   *It is on the table.*

Wo ist das Buch?   **Es** ist auf dem Tisch.
Where is the book?   *It is on the table.*

Ich sah ein Mädchen.   **Es** ging in den Wald.
I saw a girl.   ***She** went into the forest.*

B. There are four pronouns for the second person (*you*). **Sie,** singular and plural, is the conventional form of address. **Du,** singular, and **ihr,** plural, are the familiar forms, used with children, parents, close friends, animals, and God.[1]

Karl, was schreibst **du**?	Kinder, was schreibt **ihr**?
Carl, what are you writing?	*Children, what are you writing?*
Herr Schmidt, was schreiben **Sie**?	Meine Herren, was wollen **Sie**?
Mr. Smith, what are you writing?	*Gentlemen, what do you wish?*

C. The indefinite pronoun **es** is used idiomatically in the following common constructions:

Es sind dreißig Schüler in dieser Klasse.
***There are** thirty pupils in this class.*

Es waren meine Freunde.	Ich bin **es**.	Ist er **es**?
***They** were my friends.*	***It** is I.*	*Is **it** he?*

§42. USES OF THE GENITIVE OF PERSONAL PRONOUNS

A. With certain verbs, adjectives, and numerals. The genitive form of the personal pronouns, though rare in modern German, is found with certain verbs, adjectives, and numerals. Note the alternative construction with the accusative in (2).

(1) Schone **meiner**!   Erbarmen Sie sich **meiner**!
    Spare me.   *Pity me.*

(2) Gedenke **seiner**!
    Erinnere dich **seiner**!
    Erinnere dich **an ihn**!
    Remember him.

(3) Er wurde **seiner** gewahr.   Wir waren **unser** drei.
    He perceived him.   *There were three **of us**.*

B. With certain prepositions. The genitive of the personal pronouns is also found with prepositions governing the genitive case, particularly in combinations with **wegen** (*on account of*), **um ... willen** (*for the sake of*), and **halb(en)** (*on account of*). As explained in §32, pronouns thus used assume a form in –t instead of –r:

    meinetwegen, *on my account*   um meinetwillen, *for my sake*
    seinetwegen, *on his account*   Ihrethalben, *on your account*

---

[1]The strictness of this rule in modern Germany is hard to measure. The familiar **ihr** has always been used in addressing even a stranger as a representative rather than as an individual: **Wie macht ihr das in Amerika?** *How do you Americans do that?* Young people, especially in the German Democratic Republic, use the familiar form in violation of the rule to assert their egalitarianism.

§43. PRONOUNS OF DIRECT ADDRESS IN LETTERS

In letters all pronouns of direct address are capitalized. This applies also to the corresponding possessive forms:

> Meine liebe Rose!
> Lange habe ich nichts von **Dir** gehört. Vielleicht ist **Dein** letzter Brief verlorengegangen.
>
> > Dein **Dich** liebender Fritz.

CHAPTER 14

Interrogatives

§44. *WER, WAS, WO*-FORMS; *WELCHER* AND *WAS FÜR EIN*

A. The interrogative pronouns **wer** and **was** have the following declension:

	MASCULINE AND FEMININE	NEUTER
NOM.	wer	was
GEN.	wessen	(wessen, wes) (*rare*)
DAT.	wem	———
ACC.	wen	was

While **wer** and **was** have no plural forms, they may be followed by a plural form of the verb *to be*:

> Was **sind** die Dinge da?
> *What* **are** *those things?*

Was is found almost exclusively in the nominative and accusative. The genitive is extremely rare and is confined chiefly to such adverbial combinations as **weshalb** and **weswegen.**

The missing dative of **was** is supplied by **wo–** in such combinations as **womit, worauf.** The accusative **was** is quite rare after prepositions and is also usually replaced by **wo**-forms. **Um was** instead of **worum,** however, is quite common in such a sentence as:

> Um was handelt es sich?
> *What is it (all) about?*

The following sentences exemplify the use of these interrogative pronouns.

(1)   The nominative case:

> **Wer** ist die Dame?   **Wer** sind die Damen?
> **Who** *is the lady?*   **Who** *are the ladies?*

> **Was** ist das?
> **What** *is that?*

79

(2) The genitive case:

Wessen Buch ist das?   **Wessen** Bücher sind das?
Whose book is that?   *Whose books are those?*

Weshalb (*or* **wes**wegen) haben Sie die Stadt verlassen?
Why did you leave the city?

(3) The dative case:

Wem haben Sie die Briefe gegeben?
To whom did you give the letters?

Mit **wem** hat er einen Spaziergang gemacht?
With whom did he take a walk?

Womit schreiben Sie?   but: Mit wem sprechen Sie?
With what are you writing?   *With whom are you speaking?*

(4) The accusative case:

Wen haben Sie heute gesehen?
Whom did you see today?

An **wen** denken Sie?
Of whom are you thinking?

Worauf warten Sie?   but: Auf wen warten Sie?
For what are you waiting?   *For whom are you waiting?*

Was hat er gefunden?
What did he find?

Er wußte nicht, **was** er tun sollte.
He didn't know what to do.

B.   The interrogative adjective **welcher** and adjective phrase **was für ein** are exemplified by the following sentences:

Welcher Mann ist zu Hause?
Which man is at home?

Mit **was für einem** Bleistift schreiben Sie?
With what kind of (a) pencil are you writing?

Note that **für** in **was für ein** is not a preposition and does not determine the case of a following noun. The plural of **was für ein** is simply **was für**:

Was für Bücher haben Sie?
What kind of books do you have?

Was für ein is used in exclamations without interrogative force:

Was für ein Unglück!   **Was für** Leute!
What a misfortune!   *What people!*

Both **welcher** and **was für ein** may be used without following nouns, i.e., as interrogative pronouns:

Welcher ist zu Hause, der Professor oder sein Sohn?
Which one (pron.) *is at home, the professor or his son?*

Was für einen haben Sie gekauft?
What kind (*of one*) (used as pron.) *did you buy?*

CHAPTER 15

Relative Pronouns

§45. THE RELATIVES *DER* AND *WELCHER*

There are two common relative pronouns in German, **der** and **welcher**. Observe in the following paradigm that the declension of the relative **der** is (except for the forms in boldface) the same as that of the definite article; and that **welcher** has no genitive forms.

	SINGULAR			PLURAL
	MASC.	FEM.	NEUT.	ALL GENDERS
NOM.	der (welcher)	die (welche)	das (welches)	die (welche)
GEN.	**dessen**	**deren**	**dessen**	**deren**
DAT.	dem (welchem)	der (welcher)	dem (welchem)	**denen** (welchen)
ACC.	den (welchen)	die (welche)	das (welches)	die (welche)

The following sentences illustrate the use of the relatives **der** and **welcher**. The relative pronoun always agrees with its antecedent in *gender* and *number;* its *case* is determined by its use in the relative clause.

A. Singular number.

    (1) The nominative case:

        (*a*) Der reiche Mann, **der** (or **welcher**) sein Geld verloren hatte, war unehrlich.

            *The rich man **who** had lost his money was dishonest.*

        (*b*) München ist eine Stadt, **die** (or **welche**) durch ihre Schönheit berühmt ist.

            *Munich is a city **which** is famous for its beauty.*

        (*c*) Das deutsche Buch, **das** (or **welches**) auf dem Tische liegt, gehört meinem Bruder.

            *The German book **which** is lying on the table belongs to my brother.*

The relative **der** is used much more frequently than **welcher,** especially in conversation. **Welcher,** however, is often used to avoid a repetition of some form of **der.** In the following sentence **der** would occur successively in three forms—the demonstrative, the relative, and the definite article—if **welcher** were not used:

> Die Freude war groß, denn der, **welcher** der Familie am liebsten war, war heimgekehrt.
> *The joy was great, for the one **who** was dearest to the family had returned home.*

(2) The genitive case:

(*a*) Ein Witwer ist ein Mann, **dessen** Frau gestorben ist.
*A widower is a man **whose** wife is dead.*

(*b*) Eine Witwe ist eine Frau, **deren** Mann gestorben ist.
*A widow is a woman **whose** husband is dead.*

(*c*) Eine Waise ist ein Kind, **dessen** Eltern gestorben sind.
*An orphan is a child **whose** parents are dead.*

Whose is always genitive, but particular care must be taken to have it agree with its antecedent and *not* with the noun following:

> Er ist der Mann, **dessen** Frau krank ist.
> *He is the man **whose** wife is ill.*

Here **dessen** is masculine singular to agree with **Mann.**

(3) The dative case:

(*a*) Der Herr, **dem** (or **welchem**) ich das Buch gegeben habe, ist mein bester Freund.
*The gentleman **to whom** I gave the book is my best friend.*

(*b*) Leipzig ist eine Handelsstadt, **in der** (or **welcher**) jährliche Messen stattfinden.
*Leipzig is a commercial city **in which** annual fairs are held.*

(*c*) Das Haus, **in dem (in welchem** or **worin)** wir jetzt wohnen, gefällt mir nicht.
*I do not like the house **in which** we now live.*

A **wo**-form is frequently used instead of a preposition and a relative, provided the antecedent is a *thing*.

(4) The accusative case:

(*a*) Er ist der Mann, **den** (or **welchen**) ich gestern besucht habe.
*He is the man **whom** I visited yesterday.*

(*b*) Wo ist die Feder, **die** (or **welche**) ich heute gekauft habe?
*Where is the pen **(that)** I bought today?*

(*c*) Das ist das Buch, **das** (or **welches**) ich gestern gelesen habe.
*That is the book **(that)** I read yesterday.*

Contrary to English usage, *the relative pronoun is never omitted in German.*

B. **Plural number.**

   (1)   The nominative case:

     Das sind die Männer (die Frauen, die Kinder), **die** (or **welche**) uns gegenüber wohnen.
     Those are the men (the women, the children) **who** *live opposite us.*

   (2)   The genitive case:

     Das sind die Männer (die Frauen, die Kinder), **deren** Bücher wir jetzt lesen.
     Those are the men (the women, the children) **whose** *books we are now reading.*

   (3)   The dative case:

     Das sind die Männer (die Frauen, die Kinder), **denen** (or **welchen**) wir das Geld gegeben haben.
     Those are the men (the women, the children) **to whom** *we gave the money.*

   (4)   The accusative case:

     Das sind die Männer (die Frauen, die Kinder), **die** (or **welche**) wir letztes Jahr besucht haben.
     Those are the men (the women, the children) **whom** *we visited last year.*

Note:

(*a*)   All relative clauses are set off by commas.

(*b*)   Since all relative clauses are subordinated to the main clause of the sentence, the inflected verb must be moved to the end of the sentence.

§46. THE RELATIVE *WAS*

The relative **was** is used, instead of **das** or **welches**, if the antecedent is (1) an indefinite neuter form such as **alles, nichts, vieles, etwas, manches,** or a neuter superlative; or (2) really the *thought* or *content* of the preceding clause. It may not be used if the antecedent is a noun (see example **H**).

A.   **Alles, was** er sagt, ist wahr.
     *All (**that**) he says is true.*

B.   **Nichts, was** sie tat, ist ihr gelungen.
     *Nothing (**that**) she did turned out well for her.*

C.   Es gibt **vieles, was** mir fehlt.
     *There is **much that** I lack.*

D. Das ist **etwas, was** sie noch nicht weiß.
*That is **something (that)** she does not yet know.*

E. Er hat **manches** vergessen, **was** er in der Schule gelernt hat.
*He has forgotten **much** (or **many a thing**) **that** he learned in school.*

F. **Das Beste, was** ich habe, gebe ich dir.
*I am giving you **the best (that)** I have.*

G. Er sagte, **es gehe ihm gut, was** mich sehr freute.
*He said **he was well, which** made me very happy.*

H. Das ist **das Buch, das** (or **welches**) ich zweimal gelesen habe.
*That is **the book (that)** I read twice.*

§47. THE RELATIVE *WO*

Wo as a relative equivalent to *in which,* but often translated by *where,* requires the verb at the end of the clause:

Das ist **der Ort, wo** meine Wiege stand.
*That is **the place where** I was born (lit. where my cradle stood).*

Relative **wo** is not to be confused with interrogative **wo,** which requires the inverted word order:

Wo stand Ihre Wiege?
Where were you born?

*At the time **when** is often rendered by **zur Zeit, als** (da *or* wo) with the dependent word order:

Zur Zeit, **als** (da *or* wo) er im Lande war, gab es keine Eisenbahnen.
*There were no railroads (at the time) **when** he was in the country.*

§48. THE GENERAL (OR INDEFINITE) RELATIVES *WER* AND *WAS*

The general or indefinite relatives **wer** and **was** (not to be confused with the interrogatives) *never have an antecedent.*

A. **Wer** nicht für mich ist, (der) ist gegen mich.
***Whoever** is not for me is against me.*

B. **Was** nicht gut ist, (das) ist schlecht.
***Whatever** is not good is bad.*

§49. THE EXTENDED MODIFIER VS. THE RELATIVE CLAUSE

In German the written language provides a participial (and, less frequently, adjectival) construction which may be substituted for a relative clause. Since English makes no equivalent provision, these *extended modifiers* must be rendered as relative clauses. The extended modifier is stylistically stuffy and may always be avoided in writing German. The following sentences illustrate this construction and show the corresponding relative clause in each case:

> **Ein** von allen Zeitungen gelob**ter Sänger** ist heute angekommen.
> Ein Sänger, den alle Zeitungen gelobt haben, ist heute angekommen.
> *A singer whom all the newspapers have praised arrived today.*

> **Ein** altes ursprünglich nicht zu Schulzwecken bestimm**tes Gebäude** stand an der Ecke.
> Ein altes Gebäude, das ursprünglich nicht zu Schulzwecken bestimmt war, stand an der Ecke.
> *An old building, which was not originally intended for school purposes, stood on the corner.*

> Das Dach **des** schon seit dem Dreißigjährigen Kriege von der Familie Wagner bewohn**ten Hauses** ist neulich umgebaut worden.
> Das Dach des Hauses, das die Familie Wagner schon seit dem Dreißigjährigen Kriege bewohnt, ist neulich umgebaut worden.
> *The roof of the house that the Wagner family has occupied since the Thirty Years' War, has recently been rebuilt.*

The extended modifier is readily recognized, when encountered, by the break in syntax, the absurdity (from the point of view of a native speaker of English, who is used to reading from left to right) of an article followed by a preposition, an adverb, or an uninflected adjective.

The reader must learn to collect and reserve the information imparted in the modifier until the noun phrase is complete. If a written translation is required, this material will have to be presented as a relative clause: (1) If the last element in the extended modifier is a participle, it must be changed to a verb; (2) if the last element is an adjective, the verb *to be* must be added.

A simple variation of this use of the participle is to be found at the end of letters:

> Dein Dich liebender Vater, *your loving father*
> Deine Dich liebende Mutter, *your loving mother*

§50. PERSONAL PRONOUNS FOLLOWED BY A RELATIVE

The relative **der** follows a personal pronoun. If the antecedent is a personal pronoun of the first or second person, it is usually repeated after the relative.

If the pronoun is not repeated, the verb of the relative clause is in the third person.

> **Ich, der ich** selber krank war, konnte nicht mitgehen.
> *I, **who** was ill myself, could not go along.*
> or: *Being ill myself, I could not go along.*

> **Wir, die wir** selber krank waren, konnten nicht mitgehen.
> *We, **who** were ill ourselves, could not go along.*

> **Du, der du** selber krank warst, konntest nicht mitgehen.
> *You, who were ill yourself, could not go along.*

> **Ich, der** schon so viel gelitten hat, verlor noch mein Vermögen.
> *I, **who** have suffered so much already, lost my fortune besides.*

§51. CONCESSIVE CLAUSES WITH *WER AUCH, WAS AUCH, WO AUCH,* ETC.

Normal word order is used in a clause following one of concessive force introduced by **wer auch** (*whoever*), **was auch** (*whatever*), **wo auch** (*wherever*), etc. The combinations with **auch** are used if *nevertheless* may be supplied as introducing the second clause.

A. **Wer auch** (*whoever*):

> **Wer** er **auch** sein mag, ich werde ihm helfen.
> *Whoever he may be, I will help him.*

B. **Was auch** (*whatever*):

> **Was** sie **auch** tun mag, er wird sie lieben.
> *Whatever she may do, he will love her.*

C. **Wo auch** (*wherever*):

> **Wo** er **auch** sein mag, man wird ihn finden.
> *Wherever he may be, he will be found.*

CHAPTER 16

Possessives; Demonstratives Indefinite Pronouns and Adjectives

§52. POSSESSIVE ADJECTIVES

The sentences under **A** below illustrate the possessive adjectives **mein, dein, sein, ihr, unser, euer,** and **Ihr.** The sentences under **B** show these possessive adjectives with their corresponding personal pronouns. Compare the following list:

PERSONAL PRONOUN	POSSESSIVE ADJECTIVE	PERSONAL PRONOUN	POSSESSIVE ADJECTIVE
ich	mein (*my*)	wir	unser (*our*)
du	dein (*your*)	ihr	euer (*your*)
er	sein (*his*)		
sie	ihr (*her*)	sie	ihr (*their*)
es	sein (*its*)		
		Sie	Ihr (*your*)

A. (1) **Mein** lieber Bruder ist zu Hause.
My dear brother is at home.

(2) **Dein** alter Väter hat eine lange Reise gemacht.
Your old father took a long trip.

(3) **Sein** jüngster Sohn ist aufs Land gegangen.
His youngest son has gone to the country.

(4) **Ihr** reicher Onkel ist auf dem Lande.
Her rich uncle is in the country.

(5) **Unser** bester Freund hatte ihn gesehen.
Our best friend had seen him.

(6) Kinder, wo ist **euer** kleiner Hund?
*Children, where is **your** little dog?*

(7) Wo ist **ihr** lieber Vater?
*Where is **their** dear father?*

(8)   Wo ist **Ihr** neues Buch?
      Where is your new book?

B. (1)   Ich habe **meinen** Bleistift verloren.
      I have lost my pencil.

(2)   Du hast **deinen** Bleistift verloren.
      You have lost your pencil.

(3)   Er hat **seinen** Bleistift verloren.
      He has lost his pencil.

(4)   Sie hat **ihren** Bleistift verloren.
      She has lost her pencil.

(5)   Es (*e.g.,* das Kind) hat **seinen** Bleistift verloren.
      It has lost its pencil.

(6)   Wir haben **unsere** Freunde besucht.
      We have visited our friends.

(7)   Ihr habt **eure** Freunde besucht.
      You have visited your friends.

(8)   Sie haben **ihre** Freunde besucht.
      They have visited their friends.

(9)   Sie haben **Ihre** Freunde besucht.
      You have visited your friends.

There are numerous duplications in the forms for possessive adjectives in German. **Ihr** (not capitalized unless it heads a sentence) may mean either *her* or *their,* and when it refers to an inanimate object or to an abstract noun which is grammatically feminine in German, **ihr** must be translated by *its*:

Die Sache hat **ihre** gute Seite.
The affair *has **its** good* (or *bright*) *side.*

Sein may be translated as either *his* or *its*, depending upon whether it refers to a masculine or neuter noun. In a few instances it must be translated by *her*, if the noun is feminine in English:

Das Mädchen hat **sein** Buch.
The girl *has **her** book.*

As implied above, the German equivalent of *its* may be either **sein** or **ihr**:

Jeder Staat hat **seine** Vorzüge.
Each state *has **its** advantages.*

Die Stadt ist durch **ihre** Museen berühmt.
The city *is famous for **its** museums.*

Das Kind liebt **seinen** Vater.
The child *loves **its** father.*

§53.   AGREEMENT OF THE POSSESSIVE ADJECTIVE

The possessive in German may be thought of as part pronoun and part adjective: choice of possessive is determined by the antecedent, while choice of ending is determined by the noun modified. Thus, in the phrase **seine kleine Schwester,** *his little sister,* **sein-** is chosen because the gender of the possessor is masculine, the ending **–e** because **Schwester** is nominative singular and feminine.

> **Ihr** kleiner Bruder liest das Buch.
> *Her little brother is reading the book.*
>
> **Seine** kleine Schwester lernt Deutsch.
> *His little sister is studying German.*
>
> Er hat **seine** Bücher.
> *He has his books.*

§54.   POSSESSIVE PRONOUNS

Possessive adjectives are **ein**-words, i.e., they take the same endings as **ein** and **kein.** When any **ein**-word is used without a following noun it functions as a pronoun and takes **der**-word endings.

Mein Buch ist auf dem Tisch.	Wo ist **Ihres**?
My book is on the table.	*Where is yours?*
Mein Vater ist in der Stadt.	**Seiner** ist in Deutschland.
My father is in the city.	*His is in Germany.*
Wessen Bleistift ist das?	Es ist mein**er**.
Whose pencil is that?	*It is mine.*
Wessen Buch ist das?	Es ist mein**es**.
Whose book is that?	*It is mine.*

A possessive pronoun in the predicate, other than **ihr** and **Ihr,** does not take an ending if the subject of the sentence is a noun.

Das Buch ist mein.	Der Bleistift ist dein.
The book is mine.	*The pencil is yours.*
Das Buch ist ihr**es**.	Der Bleistift ist Ihr**er**.
The book is hers (or *theirs*).	*The pencil is yours.*

Instead of the verb *to be* followed by a possessive, **gehören** with the dative is commonly used:

> Das Buch gehört mir.
> *The book is mine* (lit. *belongs to me*).

§55. POSSESSIVES WITH VARIOUS FORMS OF THE IMPERATIVE

The sentences below indicate that **dein** is used with the singular familiar imperative; **euer,** with the plural familiar; and **Ihr,** with the formal imperative. Observe that the plural familiar imperative has the same form as the second person plural of the present indicative (but without the personal pronoun).

> **Karl,** lies **deine** Aufgabe!   **Kinder,** lest **eure** Aufgabe!
> *Carl, read your lesson.*   *Children, read your lesson.*

> Bitte, **lesen Sie Ihre** Aufgabe!
> *Please read your lesson.*

§56. LONG FORMS OF THE POSSESSIVE PRONOUN

The so-called long forms of the possessive pronoun are:

	MASCULINE	FEMININE	NEUTER
NOM.	der meine	die meine	das meine
GEN.	des meinen, *etc.*	der meinen, *etc.*	des meinen, *etc.*
or			
NOM.	der meinige	die meinige	das meinige
GEN.	des meinigen, *etc.*	der meinigen, *etc.*	des meinigen, *etc.*

These long forms are met with chiefly in books and are to be avoided in conversation and composition. They cannot be used with nouns. The following, therefore, are the three possible translations of *Where is mine?* (referring to some masculine noun such as **der Bleistift**):

> Wo ist **meiner?**
> Wo ist **der meine?**
> Wo ist **der meinige?**

§57. THE DEMONSTRATIVES *DIESER, JENER, DERSELBE,* AND *DERJENIGE*

A *demonstrative* is a word that points out, e.g., *this* or *that.* It may precede a noun: *This street is closed;* or it may stand alone: *No, this is mine and that is yours.*

The sentences under **A** and **B** show that **dieser** (*this*) and **jener** (*that*) are declined alike; the paradigm resembles that of the definite article **der,** i.e., **dieser** and **jener** are **der-**words.

A. Dieser (*this*):

   (1) **Dieser** Junge ist mein Bruder, **jener** (*or* der andere da) ist mein Vetter.
      *This boy is my brother, **that one** is my cousin.*

   (2) **Dieses** Buch gefällt mir.   **Diese** Bücher gefallen mir.
      *I like **this** book.*   *I like **these** books.*

B. Jener (*that*):

   (1) **Jener** Berg (*or* der Berg da) ist der Brocken.
      That mountain is the Brocken.

   (2) **Jene** Häuser (*or* die Häuser da) wurden im Mittelalter gebaut.
      Those houses were built in the Middle Ages.

In modern German **jener** is generally restricted in use to a specific contrast with **dieser**. In such contrastives **dieser** is often translated by *the latter* and **jener** by *the former*.

The demonstratives **derselbe** and **derjenige** are written as one word, but the first element is declined like the definite article while the second takes weak adjective endings:

NOM. SING.	derselbe	derjenige
GEN. SING.	desselben, *etc.*	desjenigen, *etc.*
NOM. PLUR.	dieselben, *etc.*	diejenigen, *etc.*

C. Derselbe (*the same*):

   (1) Er ist **derselbe** Mann, den ich gestern gesehen habe.
      *He is **the same** man whom I saw yesterday.*

   (2) Die beiden Schwestern sind an **demselben** Tag geboren.
      *The two (or Both) sisters were born on **the same** day.*

   (3) Ich hatte **denselben** Lehrer, wie mein Bruder.
      *I had **the same** teacher as my brother.*

Derselbe (unstressed) is often used—particularly in the written language—instead of a personal pronoun:

     Er hat viele Schulden aber er will **dieselben** nicht bezahlen.
     *He has many debts but he does not want to pay **them**.*

D. Derjenige (*that, the one*):

   (1) Das ist nicht mein Buch, sondern **dasjenige** meiner Schwester.
      *That is not my book but **my sister's**.*
  lit.:   *That is not my book but **that** of my sister.*

(2) **Dasjenige** im roten Einband habe ich schon gelesen.
*I have already read **the one** with a red cover.*

(3) **Diejenigen,** die das nicht verstehen, sollen Fragen stellen.
***Those** who do not understand that are to ask questions.*

The three sentences above show how **derjenige** may precede a genitive construction (1), a prepositional phrase (2), or a relative clause (3).

§58. THE DEMONSTRATIVE *DER*

The demonstrative **der** may function in two ways, as an adjective and as a pronoun, and is declined according to two different paradigms.

A. The demonstrative **der** (which is much more common in conversation than **jener**) is stressed; in print, this stress is often indicated by spacing the letters: **d e r.**

> **D e r** Mann ist klug.
> *That man is clever.*
> **D e r** ist immer auf dem Lande.
> *He is always in the country.*

B. As an adjective, the demonstrative **der** is declined like the definite article. When used as a pronoun, i.e. without a following noun, **der** is declined like the relative pronoun:

> Tut Gutes **denen,** die euch hassen!
> *Do good **to those** who hate you.*

C. The genitive plural of the demonstrative pronoun is **deren;** but, when the pronoun comes before the noun or pronoun upon which it depends, another form, **derer,** is employed.

> Nimm diese Äpfel, es gibt **deren** genug.
> *Take these apples; there are plenty **of them.***
> Das ist die Schuld **derer,** die nicht mitgeholfen haben.
> *That is the fault **of those** who did not help.*

D. The genitive singular **dessen** exists in combinations, of which the following are characteristic:

> **infolgedessen** (= deshalb), *consequently, as a result*
> **währenddessen** (= inzwischen), *in the meantime*
> **dessenungeachtet** (= trotzdem), *in spite of that*

§59. THE USE OF *SOLCHER*

If **solch** is uninflected, the following adjective takes strong endings, see **A**(1). If **solch** has strong endings, the following adjective is weak (i.e., **solch,** when inflected, is a **der**-word), see **A**(2).

A. (1)   **Solch schönes** Wetter haben wir nicht im Winter.

(2)   **Solches schöne** Wetter haben wir nicht im Winter.
We do not have such beautiful weather in winter.

B.   Er ist **kein solcher** Narr.
*He is **no such** fool.*

No such is rendered by **kein solch-.** See also §6, **N** (3).

§60. INDEFINITE PRONOUNS AND ADJECTIVES

The indefinite pronouns **man** (*one, they, people, you*), **jemand** (*somebody, someone*), **jedermann** (*everybody*), **niemand** (*nobody, no one*), **etwas** (*something, some*), and **nichts** (*nothing*) occur only in the singular, and govern a third person singular verb.

A. (1)   **Man** (sometimes **einer**) is used only in the nominative. The other cases are supplied by the forms **eines, einem,** and **einen.**

Man tut das nicht.	Es tut **einem** weh.
That is not done.	*It hurts **one.***
lit.: ***One*** *does not do that.*	

(2)   When **man** is used with reflexive verbs, **sich** serves both as dative and accusative reflexive pronoun:

Damals konnte **man sich** (dat.) so etwas nicht leisten.
At that time one couldn't afford such a thing.

Man gewöhnt **sich** (acc.) endlich an alles.
One finally gets used to everything.

(3)   **Man** and **er** cannot be used interchangeably; if **man** is used, it must be retained throughout the sentence:

Wenn **man** etwas nicht weiß, soll **man** (not **er**) nichts sagen.
If one doesn't know, he should say nothing.

B.   **Jemand (niemand)** hat das gesagt.
***Someone (nobody)** said that.*

Er hat **niemand** (or **keiner**) gesehen.
*He saw **no one.***

Hat **irgend jemand** das Buch gefunden?
*Did **anyone** find the book?*

Haben Sie **jemand anders** (or **sonst jemand**) besucht?
*Did you visit **someone else?***

(1) **Jemand** and **niemand** have a genitive in –(e)s. The dative and accusative of these pronouns usually occur without endings, although datives in –em and accusatives in –en are also found.

(2) **Keiner** is often used for **niemand**.

C. **Jedermann** (or **jeder**) weiß das.   **Alle** geben es zu.
Everybody knows that.   *All admit it.*

(1) **Jedermann** has a genitive ending in –s but its dative and accusative are like the nominative.

(2) **Alle** is used as the plural of **jedermann**.

(3) **Jeder** is often used for **jedermann**.

D. (1) Hat er **etwas** gesagt?
*Did he say **something?***

Nichts, etwas, allerlei, and **ein paar** are indeclinable.

(2) Haben Sie **etwas** Interessantes gefunden?
*Did you find **something** interesting?*

(*a*) Neuter adjectives are capitalized when used as nouns following **etwas, nichts, viel, wenig**, and **allerlei**. The adjective has the strong ending –es. The word **anderes**, however, is not capitalized:

> **etwas anderes**, *something else*
> **nichts anderes**, *nothing else*

(*b*) **Alles** usually requires the following adjective to be capitalized. The adjective has the weak ending –e.

but:
> **alles Gute**, *everything good, all good things*
> **alles mögliche**, *everything possible*
> **alles übrige**, *all the rest*
> **alles andere**, *all else*

(3) Sie hat **etwas** Brot gekauft.
*She bought **some** bread.*

Er hat **einige** Bücher mitgebracht.
*He brought **some** books along.*

Some is ordinarily rendered by **etwas** when followed by a singular noun; by **einige** when followed by a plural noun.

(4) Ich vermisse **irgend etwas**.
*I miss **something (or other)**.*

(a) **Irgend** (*any, some,* etc.) is rarely used alone, but appears in various combinations:

> **irgend jemand,** *anyone* (emphatic)
> **irgend etwas,** *something or other*
> **irgendein** (adj.), *some, other*
> **irgendeiner,** *someone* (emphatic)
> **irgendwie,** *somehow, anyhow*
> **irgendwo,** *somewhere, anywhere*

(b) **Nirgend(s)** is the negative of **irgend:**
> **nirgendwo,** *nowhere, not anywhere*

E.   Viel(e) and **wenig(e)** have both singular and plural forms:

(1)   Er hat **wenig** Geld bei sich.
*He has **little** money with him.*

Haben Sie **viel** Geld verloren?
*Did you lose **much** money?*

Distinguish between **klein,** *little* (in size), and **wenig,** *little* (in quantity):

> ein **kleines** Geldstück, *a small coin*
> but: **wenig** Geld, *little (i.e., not much) money*

(2)   Er hat **wenige** Freunde.
*He has **few** friends.*

Ich habe **viele** Schulden.
*I have **many** debts.*

(3)   Ich weiß **wenig** Gutes über ihn zu erzählen.
*I know **little** good to relate about him.*

Sie hat **viel** Gutes getan.
*She has done **much** good.*

(4)   Man kann **vieles** lernen und doch nicht viel wissen.
*One can learn **many things** and still not know much.*

The form **vieles** is very often equivalent to the English *many things.*

CHAPTER 17

Reflexive
and Impersonal Verbs

§61. REFLEXIVE VERBS

Compare the sentences in the parallel columns below. In **A,** the direct objects (**Kind, Kleid,** etc.) do not refer to the subject of the sentence while in column **B** the direct objects (**mich, dich,** etc.) are pronouns referring to the subject. Such pronouns are called *reflexive pronouns;* verbs regulary used with such reflexives may be loosely termed *reflexive verbs.*

A. (1) Ich wasche das Kind.
       I wash the child.

B. (1) Ich wasche **mich.**
       I wash myself.

    (2) Du wäsch(e)st das Kleid.
       You wash the dress.

    (2) Du wäsch(e)st **dich.**
       You wash yourself.

    (3) Sie wäscht das Handtuch.
       She washes the towel.

    (3) Sie wäscht **sich.**
       She washes herself.

    (4) Wir waschen die Strümpfe.
       We wash the stockings.

    (4) Wir waschen **uns.**
       We wash ourselves.

    (5) Ihr wascht die Kleider.
       You wash the clothes.

    (5) Ihr wascht **euch.**
       You wash yourselves.

    (6) Sie waschen die Taschentücher.
       They wash the handkerchiefs.

    (6) Sie waschen **sich.**
       They wash themselves.

    (7) Haben Sie die Tischtücher
       gewaschen?
       Did you wash the tablecloths?

    (7) Haben Sie **sich**
       gewaschen?
       Did you wash yourself?

The form of the reflexive is the same as the personal pronoun in the first and second persons, singular or plural; for the third person, singular or plural, it is **sich.**

No verb is inherently reflexive. Many are used almost exclusively with reflexive pronouns, others rarely, and verbs conjugated with the auxiliary **sein** never.

C. Idiomatic expressions with reflexive verbs. It is not to be expected that all verbs used reflexively in German will have a similar English usage. As so often in translating, one must seek, not literal correspondences, but idiomatic equivalents.

Er interessiert sich **für** die Musik.
*He is interested **in** music.*

Sie fürchtet sich **vor** Mäusen.
*She is afraid **of** mice.*

Ich werde mich **um** die Stellung bewerben.
*I shall apply **for** the position.*

Wir freuten uns **auf** die Ferien.
*We were looking forward with pleasure **to** the vacation.*

Ich muß mich daran gewöhnen.
*I must get used **to** it.*

Kümmern Sie sich nicht da**rum**!
*Don't bother **about** it.*

D. Common reflexives. The verbs listed below are generally used with reflexive pronouns. The prepositions given are used with the verb as indicated.

sich **amüsieren,** to have a good time
sich **ankleiden** (*or* **anziehen**), to dress (oneself)
sich **ärgern über** (*w. acc.*), to be provoked (*or* vexed) at
sich **ausruhen,** to rest
sich **ausziehen,** to undress (oneself)
sich **bedanken bei** (einer Person) **für** (etwas), to thank (a person) for (something)
sich **beeilen,** to hurry
sich **befinden,** to be feel
sich **benehmen** (*or* **betragen**), to behave (oneself)
sich **bewegen,** to move (oneself)
sich **bewerben um,** to apply for
sich **bücken,** to stoop
sich (*dat.*) **denken** (**einbilden** *or* **vorstellen**), to imagine
sich **empfehlen,** to take (one's leave)
sich **entschließen,** to decide
sich **erbarmen** (*w. gen. or* **über** *and acc.*), to pity
sich **erholen von,** to recover (*or* recuperate) from
sich **erinnern** (*w.* **an** *and acc.*) to remember
sich **erkälten,** to catch cold
sich **erkundigen nach,** to make inquiries about
sich **freuen,** to be glad
sich **freuen auf** (*w. acc.*), to look forward with pleasure to

sich **freuen über** (*w. acc.*), to be happy about, rejoice at
sich **fürchten vor** (*w. dat.*), to be afraid of
sich **gewöhnen an** (*w. acc.*), to get used to
sich **grämen über** (*w. acc.*), to grieve over
sich **hüten vor** (*w. dat.*), to guard against
sich **interessieren für,** to be interested in
sich **irren,** to be mistaken
sich **kümmern um,** to trouble (*or* concern) oneself about, worry (*or* bother) about
sich **legen,** to lie down
sich (*dat.*) **leisten,** to afford
sich **nähern** (*w. dat.*), to approach
sich **rächen an** (*w. dat.*), to take revenge on
sich **rühren,** to stir, move; bestir oneself
sich **schämen** (*w. gen. or* **über** *and acc.*), to be ashamed of
sich (*dat.*) **schmeicheln,** to flatter oneself
sich **sehnen nach,** to long for
sich **setzen,** to sit down, seat oneself
sich (*dat.*) **Sorgen machen um,** to worry (*or* be anxious) about
sich **üben,** to practice
sich **verbeugen vor** (*w. dat.*), to bow to
sich **verirren,** to get lost
sich **verlassen auf** (*w. acc.*), to rely (*or* depend) on
sich **waschen,** to wash (oneself)
sich (*dat.*) **weh tun,** to hurt oneself
sich **wundern über** (*w. acc.*), to be surprised at

E. Reflexives instead of the passive. German frequently employs a reflexive verb instead of the passive voice.

Das macht sich leicht.	Das läßt sich nicht tun.
That is easily done.	*That can't be done.*
Es wird sich bald zeigen.	Alles hat sich aufgeklärt.
It will soon be seen.	*Everything has been cleared up.*
Es versteht sich.	So etwas lernt sich bald.
It is understood.	*Such things are soon learned.*

F. Dative reflexives. As shown in **D** above, certain reflexive verbs—e.g., *sich einbilden, sich vorstellen, sich denken, sich Sorgen machen um, sich leisten, sich schmeicheln,* and *sich weh tun*—take a dative instead of an accusative reflexive object.

So etwas hätte ich **mir** nie vorgestellt (*or* eingebildet).
I should never have imagined such a thing.

Ich mache **mir** Sorgen um meine Geschwister.
I am worrying about my brothers and sisters.

Kannst du **dir** das leisten?	Schmeich(e)le **dir** nicht!
Can you afford that?	*Don't flatter yourself.*

Ich habe **mir** weh getan.
I hurt myself.

Note: **Sich, uns,** and **euch** serve both as accusative and dative reflexive pronouns, but **mich** and **dich** become **mir** and **dir** with dative reflexive verbs.

G. The intensives *selbst* and *selber*. In translating *myself, himself,* etc., one must distinguish carefully between reflexives and intensives. **Selbst** and **selber,** when used as intensives, follow (but not always immediately) the personal pronoun, reflexive pronoun, or noun which they emphasize:

(1) Ich setzte **mich** (refl.).	Ich **selbst** (or **selber**) habe es gesehen.
I sat down.	or: Ich habe es **selbst** (intens.) gesehen.
lit.: *I seated **myself**.*	*I saw it **myself**.*

Selbst and **selber** never change their forms.

(2) Sie lobt **sich selbst** (o**ɟ** **selber**).
*She praises **herself**.*

Here **selbst** strengthens the reflexive. The reflexive, however, cannot be omitted.

(3) Sie ist die Freundlichkeit **selbst**.
She is friendliness personified.
lit.: *She is friendliness **itself**.*

Here **selbst** emphasizes the noun.

(4) **Selbst** er hat das verstanden.
Even he understood that.

Selbst in the sense of *even* precedes a noun or pronoun.

(5) **Selbst** occurs in a number of compounds: **selbst**verständlich, *self-understood (it goes without saying)*; **selbst**gebackenes Brot, *homemade bread;* das **Selbst**gespräch, *monologue, soliloquy;* die **Selbst**steuerung, *automatic control;* etc.

H. The reciprocal pronoun *einander.*   The reciprocal pronoun **einander** is often used for the dative and accusative plural of the reflexive pronouns—i.e., instead of **uns, euch,** and **sich. Einander** never changes its form.

(1) Wir sehen **einander** (*or* uns) bald wieder.
We shall soon see each other again.

(2) Sie loben **einander** (*or* sich).
They praise each other.

(3) (*a*) **Einander** occurs in combinations with prepositions: **an**einander, **auf**einander, **aus**einander, **bei**einander, **durch**einander, **mit**einander, **nach**einander, **neben**einander, **von**einander, and **zu**einander:

Sie kümmern sich nicht **um**einander.
They aren't concerned about each other.

(*b*) These forms, whose meaning varies with that of the preposition, are in turn combined with numerous verbs: aneinander**binden,** *to tie together* (lit. *to tie to each other*); aufeinander**folgen,** *to follow each other;* etc.

§62. IMPERSONAL VERBS

Verbs that require impersonal **es** as their subject are known as *impersonal verbs.* They are used *only* in the third person singular and have neither passive nor imperative. Except for the type of verbs explained in **A** and **B** following, there are comparatively few German verbs that are *always* impersonal. Quite common, however, is the verb **geschehen** (*to happen*), which can only be used impersonally—i.e., it cannot have as subject a noun or pronoun referring to a person. It cannot, therefore, be used in such a sentence as:

He *happened to be* at home.
Er **war zufällig** zu Hause.
Zufälligerweise war er zu Hause.

A. Impersonal verbs denoting natural phenomena. As in English, verbs denoting phenomena of nature are regularly impersonal:

Es regnet.	*It is raining.*	Es hagelt.	*It is hailing.*
Es schneit.	*It is snowing.*	Es friert.	*It is freezing.*
Es blitzt.	*It is lightening.*	Es tagt.	*It is dawning.*
Es donnert.	*It is thundering.*	Es dämmert.	*It is getting dark* (if dusk) or *light* (if dawn)

B. Impersonal verbs denoting mental or physical states.   Some impersonal verbs denoting mental or physical states take the accusative, others the dative.

(1) **Ihn** schläfert.   (2) **Mir** schwindelt.

or: Er ist schläfrig.   or: Mir ist schwind(e)lig.

He is sleepy.   *I am dizzy.*

(3) **Mir** graut.

I shudder.

Impersonal **es** is the understood subject of the verb in the above examples. Impersonal verbs often omit the **es** in inverted word order: **Mir graut** for **Mir graut es** (or less commonly, **Es graut mir**).

C. Es gibt and **es ist** (pl. **es sind**).

(1) **Es gibt** weiße Mäuse.

There are white *mice.*

i.e.,   *It is a fact that there are white mice.*

Es gibt keinen Winter in jenem Lande.

There is no winter in that country.*

Es gibt is used in a general sense, is always singular, and must be followed by the accusative case.

(2) **Es sind** zwei weiße Mäuse in diesem Zimmer.

There are (not pointing) *two white mice in this room.*

Es ist (pl. **sind**) is more specific and definite than **es gibt**.

(3) **Da sind** zwei weiße Mäuse.

There (pointing) ***are*** *two white mice.*

Da serves as a demonstrative.

D. Impersonal use of certain verbs in the passive.   Note that the impersonal subject (**man**) of active sentences is omitted entirely in the corresponding passive sentences. Personal subjects (e. g., **er**) become agents (**von** + dative).

Active voice:	Passive voice:
(1) Man tanzt viel.	Es wird viel getanzt.
There is much dancing.	*There is much dancing.*
(2) Er hilft mir.	Mir wird von ihm geholfen.
He helps me.	*I am helped by him.*

(3) Man folgte ihnen nicht.   Ihnen wurde nicht gefolgt.
     They (lit. *one*) *did not follow them.*   *They were not followed.*

(4) Der Arzt riet mir, in die Berge   Mir wurde von dem Arzt ge-
     zu gehen.   raten, in die Berge zu gehen.
     The physician advised me to go to   *I was advised by the physician to*
     the mountains.   *go to the mountains.*

All verbs that take the dative—e.g., **helfen, folgen, raten, glauben,** etc.—keep the dative in the passive voice and are used impersonally with **es,** expressed or understood. If inverted word order is used in this construction, **es** must be omitted; If **es** is expressed, it comes at the head of a sentence: **Es** wurde mir von dem Arzt geraten, in die Berge zu gehen.

CHAPTER 18

Word Order

§63. NORMAL WORD ORDER

It is usual to differentiate *normal* from *inverted* word order. Both are used for independent (as opposed to dependent, i.e., subordinate) clauses, and both have the inflected verb in second position.

The sequence in normal word order is: (1) the complete subject, (2) the inflected verb, and (3) predicate modifiers and verbal elements.

A. Die Sonne geht um sechs Uhr auf.
The sun rises at six o'clock.

B. Der Apfel ist reif.
The apple is ripe.

C. Mein Freund ist müde geworden.
My friend has become tired.

D. Die Dame, die mich jetzt besucht, ist meine Freundin.
The lady who is visiting me now is my friend.

E. Er arbeitet nie.   Sie spielt immer.
He never works.   *She always plays.*

Contrary to English usage, an adverb cannot come between subject and verb.

F. Coordinating conjunctions require normal word order. The most common are: **und** (*and*), **aber** (*but*), **oder** (*or*) and **sondern** (*but rather*). **Denn** (*for, because*) is to be noted particularly, since it must not be confused with **dann** (*then*), an adverb requiring inverted word order:

Er ist nicht hier, **denn er ist** krank.
*He is not here **because he is** sick.*

Dann ist er zu nach Hause geblieben.
Then he stayed home.

§64. INVERTED WORD ORDER

The sequence in inverted word order is: (1) any word or phrase except the subject or a conjunction, or (in the case of a direct question) nothing at all; (2) the inflected verb; (3) the subject; and (4) the rest of the clause. The introductory element which displaces the complete subject may be any of those shown in **A–J**. Even an infinitive or participle may take first position where (as in **E** and **G**) it gets added emphasis.

A. **An interrogative.**

Wann **geht die Sonne** auf?
When does the sun rise?

B. **The inflected verb.**

Ist der Apfel reif?
Is the apple ripe?

C. **An adverb or adverbial phrase.**

Heute morgen **machte ich** einen Spaziergang.
This morning I took a walk.

D. **A prepositional phrase.**

Nach dem Spaziergang **ging ich** nach Hause.
After the walk, I went home.

E. **A direct object.**

Den Hut **hatte ich** vergessen.
I had forgotten my hat.

F. **An indirect object.**

Dem alten Manne **hatte er** die Bücher gegeben.
He had given the old man the books.

G. **A predicate adjective.**

Schön **ist sie** nicht.
She is not beautiful.

H. A direct quotation.

„Ich werde mitkommen," **sagte er.**
"I shall come along," he said.

I. A conjunctive adverb.

Er war krank, darum **ging er** zum Arzt.
He was ill; therefore he went to a doctor.

Dann **ging er** nach Hause.
Then he went home.

J. A dependent clause.

Als ich in die Schule ging, **regnete es.**
As I was going to school, it was raining.

Weil er gestern nicht gearbeitet hat, **wird er** heute doppelt fleißig.
Since he didn't work yesterday, he will be twice as industrious today.

The dependent clause is equivalent to an adverb or other part of speech. Even in the presence of an introductory dependent clause, the inverted independent clause may begin with an adverb:

Wenn er Zeit hat, **so** wird er bei uns ein Bier trinken.
If he has time he'll drink a beer at our house.

K. Exceptions.

(1) The insertion of a comma after ordinal conjunctions derived from numerals removes the necessity for inverting subject and verb.

Zweitens, er bespricht alles sehr genau.
In the second place, he discusses everything in great detail.

(2) The insertion of a comma after **nun** has the same effect, and changes the meaning of **nun:**

Nun, wir werden doch fortfahren.
Well, we shall nevertheless continue.

but: **Nun** werden wir fortfahren.
Now we shall continue.

(3) A direct quotation is not inverted if preceded by an introductory clause (often called the "governing clause"). They are treated as separate sentences.

Er sagte: „Meine Freundin hat mich verlassen."
He said, "My girlfriend left me."

Karl fragt: „Wann kommt sie zurück?"
Carl asks, "When is she coming back?"

§65. DEPENDENT (TRANSPOSED) WORD ORDER

A clause subordinated to (i.e., dependent upon) another has *the inflected verb in final position.* Such clauses are introduced by some subordinating element (e.g., a relative pronoun), and may come before, in the middle of, or after the independent clause.

A. Als ich in Deutschland **war,** besuchte ich meine Freunde.
When I was in Germany, I visited my friends.

B. Hunde, die viel **bellen,** beißen nicht.
Dogs that bark a great deal do not bite.

C. Wenn er die Tür **aufmacht,** wird es zu kühl im Zimmer sein.
If he opens the door, it will be too cool in the room.

Verbs with separable prefixes are not separated in dependent clauses.

D. Wenn ich Zeit gehabt **hätte,** so hätte ich ihn besucht.
If I had had time, I would have visited him.

The auxiliary, since it is the inflected verb in compound tenses, comes at the end of the dependent clause, displacing the past participle.

E. Das ist ein Rätsel, das er nicht **hat** lösen können.
That is a riddle which he has been unable to solve.

In a dependent clause having the double infinitive construction, the inflected verb (the auxiliary) must *precede* that construction. This is an exception to the rule given in **D** immediately above.

F. **Je** mehr ich Goethe lese, **desto** mehr bewundere ich ihn.
The more I read Goethe, the more I admire him.

Je reicher er wird, **desto** unverschämter benimmt er sich.
The richer he becomes, the more insolently he behaves.

(1) Clauses with **je** and **desto,** both followed by a comparative, take dependent word order in the first clause and inverted word order in the second.

(2) **Um so** may be used instead of **desto:**

Je mehr er hat, **um so** mehr will er haben.
The more he has, the more he wants.

G. Er fragte mich, ob ich ihn verstanden **hätte.**
He asked me whether I had understood him.

Ich fragte ihn, wer das gesagt **hätte.**
I asked him who had said that.

Er fragte mich, wo ich gewesen **wäre**.
He asked me where I had been.

H. Subordinating conjunctions. Subordinating conjunctions are those
which introduce subordinate (or dependent) clauses. The most common are:
als, als ob, bis, da, damit, daß, ehe (or **bevor**), **falls, indem, nachdem, ob,
obgleich, obwohl, obschon, seitdem, sobald, solange, sooft, während,
weil, wenn.**

A preposition followed by a relative or interrogative pronoun may function
as a subordinating conjunction to introduce a dependent clause:

Das ist das Haus, **in dem** er früher **wohnte**.
That is the house in which he formerly lived.

Ich fragte ihn, **von wem** er das gehört **hätte**.
I asked him from whom he had heard that.

§66. SPECIAL POINTS ABOUT WORD ORDER

A. Omission of *daß*. If **daß** is omitted, the normal word order is
required:

Er sagte, **er hätte** ihn gesehen.
but: Er sagte, daß er ihn gesehen hätte.
He said that he had seen him.

B. Omission of *wenn*. If **wenn** is omitted, the inverted word order is
required:

Hätte ich Geld, so würde ich reisen.
but: Wenn ich Geld hätte, so würde ich reisen.
If I had money, I would travel.

C. Position of unemphatic pronoun objects. Unemphatic—i.e., unstressed—pronoun objects often come between verb and subject, contrary to
the rule for inverted word order:

Heute **hat mich niemand** besucht.
Nobody called on me today.

Wann **gab dir dein reicher Onkel** das Segelboot?
When did your rich uncle give you the sailboat?

D. Position of adverbs of time, manner, and place. Adverbs (or
adverbial phrases) of time precede adverbs of manner, and both precede adverbs
of place:

Er geht jetzt nach Hause.
He is going home now.

Er fährt mit dem Zug nach Berlin.
He's going to Berlin by train.

Sie geht jeden Morgen langsam an dem Hotel vorbei.
Every morning she walks slowly past the hotel.

If there is more than one adverb or adverbial phrase of the same type in a clause, the general precedes the specific:

Jeden Nachmittag um drei treibt Ursula Gymnastik.
Every afternoon at three Ursula does gymnastics.

E. Position of direct and indirect object. Unless the direct object is a personal or reflexive pronoun, the indirect object precedes it:

Er zeigte dem Freunde das Bild.	Er zeigte es dem Freunde.
He showed his friend the picture.	*He showed it to his friend.*
Er zeigte ihm das Bild.	Er zeigte es ihm.
He showed him the picture.	*He showed it to him.*

Der König zeigte sich dem Volke.
The king showed himself to the people.

F. Position of pronoun objects. These precede adverbs:

Er hatte es gestern nicht.
He did not have it yesterday.

G. Negation. The position of negatives (**nicht, nie,** etc.) is fully explained in §7.

CHAPTER 19

Conjunctions

§67. COORDINATING CONJUNCTIONS

Conjunctions which join clauses of equal rank, i.e., independent clauses, are termed *coordinating conjunctions*. Clauses so joined continue to have normal word order. The more common coordinating conjunctions, illustrated below, are: **und** (*and*), **aber** (*but*), **sondern** (*but*), **denn** (*for*), **oder** (*or*), **sowohl . . . als auch** (*both . . . and*), and other correlatives.

A. Und:

Das Auto hält, **und** wir steigen ein.
*The auto stops **and** we get in.*

B. Aber:

(1) Er sah mich, **aber** ich sah ihn nicht.
*He saw me, **but** I did not see him.*

(2) Er war nicht zu Hause, **aber** sein Bruder war da.
*He was not at home, **but** his brother was there.*

When **aber** is used in the sense of *however* not equivalent to *but*, it may not head a clause and is not set off by commas:

(3) Der alte Mann **aber** wollte es nicht zugeben.
*The old man, **however,** did not want to admit it.*

C. Sondern:

Er ging nicht in die Stadt, **sondern** er blieb auf dem Lande.
*He did not go to the city **but** remained in the country.*

Sondern is used only after a negative, and means *on the contrary* when it connects two clauses having a common subject. Whereas **aber** merely modifies a previous statement, **sondern** introduces a statement which excludes or contradicts that of the preceding clause.

D. Denn:

Sie konnte nicht kommen, **denn** sie hatte Besuch.
*She could not come, **for** she had guests.*

Denn must not be confused with **dann** (*then*) an adverbial of time which causes inversion.

E. Oder:

Tue deine Pflicht, **oder** du wirst es später bereuen!
*Do you duty, **or** you will regret it later.*

F. The combination **sowohl ... als auch** (*both ... and*) also requires normal word order:

Sowohl die Reichen **als auch** die Armen haben gelitten.
Both rich and poor suffered.

G. Other correlatives:

(1) **Entweder** er **oder** sein Freund wird uns helfen.
Either he or his friend will help us.

Entweder du bleibst, **oder ich** bleibe.
Either you stay, or I stay.

(2) **Weder** er **noch** seine Frau konnte das Auto fahren.
Neither he nor his wife could drive the car.

(3) **Nicht nur** die Kinder **sondern auch** die Eltern wollten die Ausstellung besuchen.

Not only the children but also the parents wanted to visit the exposition.

(*a*) Correlatives such as **entweder ... oder** (*either ... or*), **weder ... noch** (*neither ... nor*), and **nicht nur ... sondern auch** (*not only ... but also*) take normal word order when they connect different subjects of the same verb, or when the subjects are emphasized.

(*b*) These correlatives otherwise use inverted word order:
Weder kann **noch** will er es tun.
He neither can, nor wants to do it.

Inverted order may be avoided, however, by placing the emphatic word first:

Entweder **du** machst die Arbeit, oder ich rufe deine Mutter.
Either you will do the work, or I shall call your mother.

§68. SUBORDINATING CONJUNCTIONS

Conjunctions which subordinate one clause to another (i.e., make one clause dependent upon another for completion) are called *subordinating conjunctions*. Clauses introduced by such conjunctions will have verb-last (sometimes called *dependent* or *transposed*) word order.

Some of the more common subordinating conjunctions are illustrated below.

A. Als:

Als wir gestern nach Hause kamen, regnete es.
When we came home yesterday, it was raining.

When may be translated by **als, wann,** or **wenn,** with the following distinctions:

(1)   **Als** refers to a single, definite past action.

(2)   **Wann** is used only in questions, both direct and indirect:

Wann ist er nach Hause gekommen?
When did he come home?

Ich fragte ihn, **wann** er nach Hause gekommen wäre.
*I asked him **when** he had come home.*

(3)   **Wenn** is often used in the sense of *whenever* to express a customary or habitual action, either with the present or with the simple past tense:

Wenn ich ihn besuchte, war er immer beschäftigt.
*When (**ever**) I visited him, he was always busy.*

Wenn is commonly rendered by *if* in conditional sentences (Chapter 23).

B. Als ob:

(1)   Er tat, **als ob** er krank **wäre**.
*He acted **as if** he were ill.*

(2)   Sie sehen aus, **als ob** Sie nicht geschlafen hätten.
*You look **as if** you had not slept.*

Als ob may be shortened to **als,** causing *inverted* word order, without change of meaning.

Er tat, **als** wäre er müde.
Er tat, **als ob** er müde wäre.
*He acted **as if** he were tired.*

C. Bis:

Er arbeitete, **bis** es dunkel wurde.
*He worked **until** it became dark.*

D. Da:

Er konnte nicht arbeiten, **da** der Lärm zu groß war.
*He could not work **because** the noise was too great.*

E. Damit:

Ich sage es dir, **damit** du es weißt.
*I am telling you **so that** you may know it.*

(1) **Damit** is very often followed by the indicative in modern German:

Er trägt das Geld auf die Bank, **damit** es Zinsen bringt.
*He takes his money to the bank **so that** it may bear interest.*

(2) **Um zu** with the infinitive is often used instead of **damit** to denote purpose, provided there is no change of subject:

Das Geld wird auf die Bank getragen, **um** Zinsen **zu** bringen.
*Money is taken to the bank **in order that** it may bear interest.*

F. Daß:

Wir wissen, **daß** die Erde rund ist.
*We know **that** the earth is round.*

G. Ehe (or bevor):

Er wird mich besuchen, **ehe** (or **bevor**) er nächsten Monat abreist.
*He will visit me **before** he leaves next month.*

Note the distinction between **bevor, vor,** and **vorher,** all meaning *before:*

(1) **Bevor** (like **ehe**) is a conjunction.

(2) **Vor** is a preposition:

Das ist vor Weihnachten geschehen.
That happened before Christmas.

(3) **Vorher** is an adverb:

Das war vorher geschehen.
That had happened before.

H. Falls:

Falls er kommen sollte, würden wir ihn freundlich empfangen.
In case he should come, we would welcome him cordially.

I. Nachdem:

Nachdem er angekommen war, besuchte er seine Freunde.
After he had arrived, he visited his friends.

Note the distinction between **nachdem, nach,** and **nachher,** all meaning *after:*

(1)   **Nachdem** is a conjunction.

(2)   **Nach** is a preposition:

> Nach dem Tanz gingen sie nach Hause.
> *After the dance, they went home.*

(3)   **Nachher** is an adverb:

> Sie tanzten nacher.
> *They danced afterwards.*

J.   Ob:

> Er fragte mich, **ob** ich ihn verstanden hätte.
> *He asked me **whether** I had understood him.*

K.   Obgleich (obwohl or obschon):

> Er ist nicht glücklich, **obgleich** er reich ist.
> *Although he is rich, he is not happy.*

L.   Seitdem:

> **Seitdem** sie uns vor fünf Jahren besucht hat, haben wir sie nicht gesehen.
> *We have not seen her **since** (the time that) she visited us five years ago.*

Note the distinction between **seitdem, seit,** and **seither:**

(1)   As a subordinating conjunction **seitdem** calls for verb-last word order. **Seitdem** also serves as an adverb:

> Seitdem ist er krank.
> *Since then (or that time) he has been sick.*

The conjunctions **da** and **seitdem,** both translating *since*, should not be confused; **da** is causative (= *because*), **seitdem** is temporal (= *ever since, since the time*).

(2)   **Seit** is a preposition:

> Er ist schon seit einem Monat hier.
> *He has been here for a month.*

(3)   **Seither** is an adverb (less commonly used than **seitdem**).

M.   Sobald:

> **Sobald** sie angekommen war, ließ sie einen Arzt holen.
> *As soon as she had arrived, she sent for a doctor.*

N.   Solange:

> **Solange** ich krank war, ist er bei mir geblieben.
> *He stayed with me **as long as** I was sick.*

O.   Sooft:

> **Sooft** Sie mich bitten, werde ich Ihnen helfen.
> *As often as you ask me, I shall help you.*

P.   Während (or indem):

(1)   **Während** ich krank war, konnte ich nicht arbeiten.
   I could not work, while (during the time that) I was sick.

(2)   **Indem** sie das sagte, trat sie ins Zimmer herein.
   While (as) she was saying that, she entered the room.

Indem indicates simultaneous action in both clauses. The clause introduced with **indem** is often equivalent to the English present participle:

> Er grüßte den König, **indem er sich tief verbeugte.**
> *Bowing deeply, he saluted the king.*

Q.   Weil:

> Er trägt einen Überrock, **weil** es kalt ist.
> *He wears an overcoat **because** it is cold.*

Do not confuse the conjunctions **weil** (= *because*) and **während** (= *while*).

R.   Wenn:

(1)   **Wenn** ich Zeit habe, so werde ich ihn besuchen.
   If I have time, I shall visit him.

Note the distinction between **wenn** and **ob,** both translated by *if:*

   (*a*)   **Wenn** is commonly rendered by *if* in conditional sentences.

   (*b*)   **Ob** may be translated by *if,* but is used only in indirect questions in the sense of *whether.*

(2)   **Wenn** man heutzutage reist, benutzt man das Flugzeug.
   When(ever) one travels nowadays, one uses the airplane.

(3)   **Wenn** er **auch** sehr schwer gearbeitet hat, so hat er doch nicht viel
   Geld gespart.
   Even though he has worked very hard, he has nevertheless not saved much money.

The combination **wenn ... auch** (*even though*) also requires the dependent word order.

S.   Interrogatives such as **wann, seit wann, warum, wo, woher, wohin, womit, worauf,** etc., take inverted word order in direct questions. But when used in indirect questions, they function as subordinating conjunctions and, therefore, require that the verb stand at the end of the dependent clause:

Direct: „Woher wissen Sie das?"
             How do you know that?

Indirect: Ich fragte ihn, woher er das wisse (*or* wüßte).
             I asked him how he knew that.

Direct: „Warum haben Sie das getan?"
             Why did you do that?

Indirect: Ich fragte ihn, warum er das getan hätte.
             I asked him why he had done that.

T. Two conjunctions may not come together in German as permitted in English: *She said that if it had rained, she would not have come.* To avoid the juxtaposition of **daß** and **wenn,** translate in one of the following ways:

Sie sagte, daß sie nicht gekommen wäre, wenn es geregnet hätte.
Sie sagte, sie wäre nicht gekommen, wenn es geregnet hätte.
Sie sagte, wenn es geregnet hätte, wäre sie nicht gekommen.

U. *Da*-**form** + *daß*-**clause or infinitive phrase.** Attention has already been called to the three prepositions **ohne, um,** and **(an)statt,** which require **zu** with a dependent infinitive (see §27). Other prepositions in similar constructions require **da**-forms (dar**auf,** da**mit,** dar**an,** *etc.*), which serve to anticipate a **daß**-clause or an infinitive. A **daß**-clause is usually used when there is a change of subject (sentences 1–5 below); an infinitive, when there is no such change (sentences 6–8). An **ob**-clause (like a **daß**-clause) is shown in example (9). Note, too, that **da**-forms vary according to the idiom.

(1)   Ich verlasse mich **darauf, daß** Sie mir helfen.
      I count on your helping me.

(2)   Ich habe nichts **dagegen, daß** Sie Klavier spielen.
      I have no objection to your playing the piano.

(3)   Er ist schuld **daran, daß** ich arm bin.
      He is to blame for my being poor.

(4)   Das kommt **davon, daß** Sie zu viel rauchen.
      That comes from (your) smoking too much.

(5)   Das Buch unterscheidet sich **darin, daß** es viele Beispiele enthält.
      The book is distinguished by the fact that it contains many examples.

(6)   Er besteht **darauf,** die beiden Fahrpreise **zu bezahlen.**
      He insists on paying both fares.

(7)   Er hat nie **daran** gedacht, so etwas **zu tun.**
      He never thought of doing such a thing.

(8)   **Daran** ist nicht **zu denken.**
      That is not to be thought of.

(9)   Es handelt sich **darum, ob** er der erste gewesen ist.
      It is a question of whether he was the first.

As the sentences above illustrate, a **da**-form followed by a subordinate **daß** clause or infinitive phrase is required when the verb of the independent clause is used with a preposition whose object is not expressible in one word. The **da**- anticipates the true object, replacing it to satisfy the grammatical requirements of the independent clause.

Er dachte an seine Mutter.
He thought about his mother.

Er dachte daran, daß seine Mutter immer noch schön wäre.
He recollected that his mother was still beautiful.

or: *He thought about the fact that his mother was still beautiful.*

CHAPTER 20

Verbal Prefixes:
Inseparable
and Separable

§69. INSEPARABLE PREFIXES

The conjugation of verbs with inseparable prefixes is shown in the following table. Such verbs are stressed on the root syllable and only rarely take the perfective **ge–** in the past participle (see **H**).

PRESENT

Er besucht mich.
He is visiting me.

PAST

Er besuchte mich.
He visited me.

PERFECT

Er hat mich besucht.
He visited me.

PAST PERFECT

Er hatte mich besucht.
He had visited me.

FUTURE

Er wird mich besuchen.
He will visit me.

FUTURE PERFECT

Er wird mich besucht haben.
He will have visited me.

The inseparable prefixes with examples of each are listed below. The meanings of these prefixes, and the effect they have on the verbs to which they are joined, are explained fully in §91 **B**.

A. Be–:

Tiefer Schnee **be**deckte die Erde.
Deep snow covered the earth.

Ich bin ihm auf der Straße **be**gegnet.
I met him on the street.

Was **be**deutet das Wort?
What does the word mean?

Wo **be**fand er sich?
Where was he?

117

B. Emp–:

Sie hat mich freundlich **emp**fangen.
She welcomed me cordially (or in friendly fashion).

Er hatte mir diese Firma **emp**fohlen.
He had recommended this firm to me.

Ich habe es peinlich **emp**funden.
It pained me.

Er läßt sich Ihrem Herrn Vater **emp**fehlen.
He wants to be remembered to your father.

C. Ent–:

Kolumbus hat Amerika **ent**deckt.   **Ent**schuldigen Sie mich!
Columbus discovered America.   *Pardon (or excuse) me.*

Er wird den unehrlichen Diener **ent**lassen.
He will discharge the dishonest servant.

Der Rhein **ent**springt in der Schweiz.
The Rhine has its source in Switzerland.

D. Er–:

Erklären Sie die Aufgabe!   Ich habe mich **er**kältet.
Explain the lesson.   *I have caught cold.*
          or: *I have a cold.*

Sie hatte mir diese Geschichte **er**zählt.
She had told me this story.

Der Sage nach ist Friedrich Barbarossa in einem Fluß **er**trunken.
According to legend, Friedrich Barbarossa drowned in a river.

E. Ge–:

Wie **ge**fällt Ihnen das Buch?   Es **ge**hört meiner Schwester.
How do you like the book?   *It belongs to my sister.*

Er mußte dem Vater **ge**horchen.
He had to obey his father.

Wir haben die schöne Musik **ge**nossen.
We enjoyed the beautiful music.

Es ist mir noch nicht **ge**lungen, meinen Plan auszuführen.
I have not yet succeeded in carrying out my plan.

F. Ver–:

Er hatte sein Geld **ver**loren.   Ich **ver**misse meine alten Freunde.
He had lost his money.   *I miss my old friends.*

Er hat den ersten Zug **ver**paßt (*or* **ver**säumt).
He missed the first train.

Verstehen Sie diesen Satz?
Do you understand this sentence?

G. Zer–:

Der Wolf **zer**fleischte ihn.   Er wurde in Stücke **zer**rissen.
The wolf mangled him.   *He was torn to pieces.*

Er hatte seine Füllfeder **zer**brochen.
He had broken his fountain pen.

Der Feind wird die Stadt **zer**stören.
The enemy will destroy the city.

H. Miß–:

Sie haben mich **miß**verstanden.   Man **miß**handelte ihn.
You misunderstood me.   *He was mistreated.*

Es ist ihm völlig **miß**lungen.   Es **miß**fällt mir.
He failed completely.   *I am not pleased with it.*

Er **miß**deutete meine Worte.
He misconstrued my words.

(1) Although most inseparable prefix verbs do not form their past
participle with **ge–**, common exceptions are **mißge**bildet and **mißge**staltet
(both meaning *misshapen* or *deformed*), and **mißge**stimmt (*discordant,* or *fig.,*
depressed, in ill humor).

(2) Certain verbs with the prefix **miß–** admit a participial form with
ge–: **miß**handelt (*or* **gemiß**handelt), *mistreated;* **miß**traut (*or* **gemiß**traut),
mistrusted. The prefix, however, is never written separately from the verb.
Its accent varies—before an unaccented prefix it is stressed (*e.g.,* **miß**verstehen); in most other verbs it is either not at all, or just slightly, stressed.

I. Prefixes that are usually inseparable.

(1) **Voll–:**

Der Bildhauer hat das große Werk **voll**bracht.
The sculptor has completed the great work.

Verbs compounded with the prefix **voll–** are inseparable when they denote
completion: **voll**bringen, **voll**enden, **voll**führen, etc. When the literal meaning
is preserved, the verb is separable: **voll**pfropfen and **voll**stopfen (*to stuff full*),
vollmachen (*to make full*), etc.

(2) **Hinter–:**

Er hat seinen Kindern viel Geld **hinter**lassen.
He left (or bequeathed) his children much money.

(3) **Wider–:**

    Widersprechen Sie mir nicht!
    Don't contradict me.

§70. SEPARABLE PREFIXES

The conjugation of verbs with separable prefixes is shown in the following table. Such a prefix is really separable only in independent clauses in the present, simple past, and imperative; otherwise it is prefixed to the verb, either directly or linked by the perfective –**ge**– or the infinitive marker –**zu**–. In separable prefix verbs, the prefix receives the stress.

PRESENT	PAST PERFECT
Ich stehe früh **auf**.	Ich war früh **auf**gestanden.
I rise early.	*I had risen early.*

PAST	FUTURE
Ich stand früh **auf**.	Ich werde früh **auf**stehen.
I rose early.	*I shall rise early.*

PERFECT	FUTURE PERFECT
Ich bin früh **auf**gestanden.	Ich werde früh **auf**gestanden sein.
I have risen early.	*I shall have risen early.*

A. (1) Heute reist er **ab**.   Er kehrt bald **zurück**.
          He is leaving today.   *He will return soon.*

       (2) Wenn er die Tür **zu**macht, wird es zu warm im Zimmer sein.
          If he closes the door, it will be too warm in the room.

B.   Er machte die Tür **zu**.
       He closed the door.

C.   Wann ist er **an**gekommen?   Er war früh **fort**gegangen.
       When did he arrive?   *He had left early.*

D.   Er wird das Buch **auf**machen.
       He will open the book.

E. (1) Er will **fort**gehen.   (2) Er wünscht **fort**zugehen.
          He wants to go away.   *He desires to go away.*

    Zu is omitted in (1) because the infinitive depends on a modal auxiliary.

F.   Stehen Sie schnell **auf**!   Drehen Sie das Licht **an**!
       Get up quickly.   *Turn on the light.*

Drehen Sie das Wasser **ab**!
Turn off the water.

G.   Common separable prefixes.   Most verbal prefixes not listed in §69 are separable. It is very important to sense the meaning of separable prefixes (which usually have the force of adverbs), since they are used to form a great number of German verbs. Some of the more common separable prefixes are listed below. Their meanings are by no means limited to those given here.

ab, *off, down:*   abnehmen, *to take off;* absteigen, *to come down from*
an, *at, on:*   ansehen, *to look at;* anziehen, *to put on*
auf, *up:*   aufstehen, *to get up*
aus, *out:*   ausführen, *to carry out, execute*
bei, *by with:*   beistehen, *to render aid, assist*
ein, *into:*   eintreten, *to enter*
empor, *up:*   emporsteigen, *to climb up*
entzwei, *in two:*   entzweibrechen, *to break in two*
entgegen, *toward:*   entgegeneilen, *to hasten toward*
fort, *away:*   fortgehen, *to go away*
heim, *home:*   heimgehen, *to go home;* heimkommen, *to come home*
her, *hither:*   herkommen, *to come hither* (toward the speaker)

In addition to being a separable prefix, **her** may also be used to indicate *past time*. It is often used with the present tense where the English idiom requires the past: Das **ist** schon lange her = *That **was** (a) long (time) ago.*

hin, *thither:*   hingehen, *to go there* (away from the speaker)
los, *loose:*   loslassen, *to release*
mit, *with, along:*   mitbringen, *to bring along*
nach, *after:*   nachlaufen, *to run after*
nieder, *down:*   sich niederlegen, *to lie down*
vor, *before:*   vorgehen, *to precede; be fast* (of a clock)
weg, *away:*   weggehen, *to go away*
zu, *to:*   zuhören, *to listen to*
zurück, *back:*   zurückkehren, *to turn (or come) back, return*
zusammen, *together:*   zusammenbringen, *to bring together*

H.   Verbs compounded with *her* and *hin*.

(1)   Many verbs are compounded with the prefixes **her** and **hin**. These prefixes are always separable; if the verb already has a separable prefix, it becomes linked to **hin** or **her**:

herkommen: Kommen Sie **her**!
                                         Come here.

herauskommen: Kommen Sie **heraus**!
                                         Come out here.

In all such compounds **her** denotes *motion toward,* whereas **hin** denotes *motion away from* the speaker or observer. Therefore, it is highly important to determine *the observer's position*:

Der Hund springt zum Fenster **her**ein. (The observer is inside.)
but: Der Hund springt zum Fenster **hin**ein. (The observer is outside.)
The dog jumps (in) through the window.

Here the English translation is the same for both sentences, but fails to bring out the difference of viewpoint clearly indicated by **her**ein and **hin**ein.

(2)   Verbs of motion with prepositional prefixes expressing locality— *e.g.,* **aus**gehen, **auf**gehen, etc.—denote motion of a *general and indefinite* nature; when compounded with the prefixes **her** and **hin**, such verbs denote motion of a *definite* nature. In English the distinction is less strongly perceived than in German.

(*a*)   Sie geht immer gern **aus.**   but: Sie geht **hinaus.**
She always likes to go out.   *She goes out.*

The first sentence is a general statement and indicates no direction of the motion; in the second, the motion is definitely away from the speaker or observer.

(*b*)   Die Sonne geht **auf.**   but: Er geht die Treppe **hinauf.**
The sun rises.   *He goes upstairs.*

In the first sentence a general upward direction is indicated; in the second, definite motion away from the observer.

(*c*)   Das kommt oft **vor.**
That often happens.
but: Er kam aus seinem Versteck **hervor.**
He came forth from his hiding place.

In the first sentence the verb **kommt** is used figuratively; in the second, **kam** is used literally to denote motion of a definite nature toward the speaker.

(*d*)   Similarly: **unter**gehen, *to set* (of the sun and moon) and **hinunter**gehen, *to go down* (*e.g.,* a mountain); **ein**kommen, *to come in, be collected* (*e.g.,* of money) and **herein**kommen, *to come in, enter* (*e.g.,* a room), etc.

§71. MIXED PREFIXES

Certain prefixes, of which the more common are illustrated below, may function as both separable and inseparable.[1] Generally, when used in a *figurative* sense they are *inseparable,* with stress on the root syllable and no **ge**– in the past participle. When they are used in a *literal* sense they are *separable,* with stress on the prefix and interposed –**ge**– in the past participle.

A. Durch:

    (1) Ich fuhr **durch.**
         I drove through.

    (2) Der Blitz durch**fuhr** die Luft.
         Lightning pierced the air.

B. Um:

    (1) Er hat sich **um**gekleidet.
         He has changed clothes.

    (2) Er hat seine Gedanken mit schönen Worten um**kleidet.**
         He has clothed his thought(s) in beautiful language.

C. Über:

    (1) Er hat mich **über**gesetzt.
         He ferried me across.

    (2) Er hat den Satz über**setzt.**
         He translated the sentence.

D. Unter:

    (1) Er stellt sich bei der Bushaltestelle **unter.**
         He takes cover at the bus stop.

    (2) Er unter**stellt** ihm eine Lüge.
         He accuses him of a lie.

E. Wieder:

    (1) Holen Sie das Buch **wieder!**
         Go get the book (back).

    (2) Wieder**holen** Sie den Satz!
         Repeat the sentence.

---

[1] Adverbs and prepositions must not be confused with verbal prefixes:

    Oben ist die Decke.   Die Decke ist **über** uns.
    Unten ist der Fußboden.   Er ist **unter** uns.
    Vorn ist der Tisch.   Der Tisch ist **vor** uns.
    Hinten ist die Tafel.   Die Tafel ist **hinter** uns.

CHAPTER 21

The Passive Voice

§72. ACTIVE AND PASSIVE FORMS

The sentences below show that the direct object of a verb used actively becomes the subject of the same verb used in the passive voice, and that *the past participle occurs in each tense of the passive voice.* Other characteristics of the passive in German are:

1. The auxiliary is **werden.**
2. **Worden** follows the past participle in the three perfect tenses.
3. The future tense ends in **werden.**
4. **Sein** is always used to form the three perfect tenses.
5. *By* becomes **von,** which is followed by the dative case.

A. The active voice:

   (1) PRESENT

      Er lobt den Jungen.
      He praises (is praising, does praise) the boy.

   (2) SIMPLE PAST

      Er lobte den Jungen.
      He praised (was praising) the boy.

   (3) PERFECT (COMPOUND PAST)

      Er hat den Jungen gelobt.
      He (has) praised the boy.

B. The passive voice:

   (1) PRESENT

      Der Junge **wird** von ihm **gelobt.**
      The boy is (being) praised by him.

   (2) SIMPLE PAST

      Der Junge **wurde** von ihm **gelobt.**
      The boy was (being) praised by him.

   (3) PERFECT (COMPOUND PAST)

      Der Junge **ist** von ihm **gelobt worden.**
      The boy has been (or was) praised by him.

(4) PAST PERFECT

Er hatte den Jungen gelobt.
He had praised the boy.

(4) PAST PERFECT

Der Junge **war** von ihm
gelobt worden.
The boy had been praised by him.

(5) FUTURE

Er wird den Jungen loben.
He will praise the boy.

(5) FUTURE

Der Junge **wird** von ihm
gelobt werden.
The boy will be praised by him.

(6) FUTURE PERFECT

Er wird den Jungen gelobt
haben.
He will have praised the boy.

(6) FUTURE PERFECT

Der Junge **wird** von ihm
gelobt worden sein.
The boy will have been praised by him.

C. Additional examples of the passive voice.

Er wird von dem Barbier rasiert.
He is being shaved by the barber.

Das Bild wurde von dem Maler gemalt.
The picture was being painted by the artist.

Alles ist von dem Feinde verwüstet worden.
Everything was (lit. *has been*) *laid waste by the enemy.*

Er war von seiner Tante erzogen worden.
He had been reared by his aunt.

Mein Auto wird morgen repariert werden.
My car will be repaired tomorrow.

§73. ACTIONAL AND STATAL PASSIVES

The *actional (real* or *true) passive,* formed with **werden** and the past participle, denotes an action that is going on at the time indicated by the tense of the verb.

The *statal* (or *apparent) passive,* formed with the verb *to be,* **sein,** and the past participle functioning as a predicate adjective, denotes a state or condition that has already resulted from some previous action.

A. The actional passive:

(1) Die Tür **wird** zugemacht.
The door is being closed.

(2) Die Kleider **werden** gewaschen.
The clothes are being washed.

B. The statal passive:

(1) Die Tür **ist** zugemacht.
The door is closed.

(2) Die Kleider **sind** gewaschen.
The clothes are washed.

(3) Das Haus **wird** grün ange-
    strichen.
    *The house **is being** painted
    green.*

(3) Das Haus **ist** grün ange-
    strichen.
    *The house **is** painted green.*

(4) Der Zaun **wurde** aus kleinen
    Brettern gemacht.
    *The fence **was** (**being**) made of
    small boards.*

(4) Der Zaun **war** aus kleinen
    Brettern gemacht.
    *The fence **was** made of small
    boards.*

§74. ADDITIONAL FEATURES OF THE PASSIVE

A.   Customary occurrence.   The passive voice is often used to denote a customary occurrence:

> Die Tür **wird** um zehn Uhr **geschlossen.**
> *The door is closed* (regularly) *at ten o'clock.*
>
> Kaffee **wird** um fünf Uhr **getrunken.**
> *We have coffee* (regularly) *at five o'clock.*

B.   *Wurde, ist geboren.*   To express *was born,* the passive **wurde geboren** is used for the dead; **ist geboren,** for the living:

> Schiller **wurde** im Jahre 1759 **geboren.**
> *Schiller was born in* 1759.
>
> Wann **sind** Sie **geboren?**
> *When were you born?*

C.   Means or instrument.   In the passive voice, means or instrument is usually expressed by **durch** with the accusative:

> Die Bretter wurden **durch** einen Nagel zusammengehalten.
> *The boards were held together by a nail.*
>
> Der Löwe wurde **durch** einen Schuß getötet.
> *The lion was killed by a shot.*

D.   Intransitive verbs used impersonally in the passive.   For the impersonal use of intransitive verbs in the passive, see §62 **D.**

E.   The passive imperative.   The passive imperative is usually formed with **sein** (as in examples 1, 2, and 3 below) but sometimes with **werden** (example 4). The present Subjunctive I is used for the third person; **lassen** with a dependent infinitive is a common equivalent to this construction in the second person (example 5).

(1) Es **sei** ferner erwähnt, daß andere Gründe vorliegen.
It is furthermore to be noted that there are other reasons.

(2) **Seien** Sie gegrüßt!   (3) Der Herr **sei** gelobt!
Be greeted.   *May the Lord be praised.*

(4) Er **werde** hereingeführt!
Have him brought in.

(5) **Lassen** Sie sich nicht ţäuschen!
Don't be deceived.

§75. SUBSTITUTE CONSTRUCTIONS FOR THE PASSIVE

A. The active voice with *man*. A common equivalent of the passive voice is the active voice with **man.**

Man tut das nicht.	Man muß es tun.
That is not done.	*It must be done.*
Wie buchstabiert man das Wort?	Man gab ihm die Gelegenheit.
How is that word spelled?	*He was given the opportunity.*

In the last sentence, the subject *he* could not be rendered by **er.** But a passive verb might be used with **Gelegenheit** as subject:

Die Gelegenheit wurde ihm gegeben.
or: Ihm wurde die Gelegenheit gegeben.
The opportunity was given (to) him.

B. Reflexive verbs. For the common use of a reflexive verb instead of the passive, see §61 **E.**

C. The active infinitive preceded by *zu*. After the verb **sein,** the active infinitive preceded by **zu** is equivalent to the passive:

Er ist telefonisch nicht zu erreichen.
He cannot be reached by telephone.
*He is not **to be reached** by telephone.*

D. *Lassen* with a dependent infinitive. The verb **lassen** with a dependent infinitive is equivalent to the passive:

Ich habe mir das Haar schneiden lassen.
I had my hair cut.

E. Verbs equivalent to the English passive. The following German verbs in their active voice are equivalent to English passives: **dürfen** (*to be allowed*), **sollen** (*to be said*), **heißen** (*to be called*), **ertrinken** or **ersaufen** (*to be drowned*, i.e., *to drown* used intransitively), and **erschrecken** (*to be frightened*):

Das Kind **darf nicht** auf der Straße spielen.
*The child **is not allowed** to play on the street.*

Er **soll** sehr klug sein.   Wie **heißt** es?
*He **is said** to be very clever.*   *What **is it called?***

Er **ist ertrunken.**   Sie **erschrak.**
*He **was drowned.***   *She **was frightened.***

CHAPTER 22

The Subjunctive in
Indirect Discourse and
Independent Sentences

§76. INDIRECT STATEMENTS

Before examining the uses of the subjunctive, reference should be made to the paradigms in §§102–109 in the Appendix. It will be seen that although the indicative has six tenses, the subjunctive has only four: present, past, future, and future perfect. There are, however, two sets of subjunctive tenses, called Subjunctive I and Subjunctive II; the future and future perfect Subjunctive II forms are also called the Conditional.

While Subjunctive I forms are encountered in written German, modern usage favors Subjunctive II forms. With infrequent exceptions, the user may always employ Subjunctive II for indirect discourse (statements, questions, and commands).

Formation of the subjunctive is simply stated: To the stem of the present infinitive (for present Subjunctive I) and to the stem of the simple past (for present Subjunctive II), add the endings –e, –est, –e, –en, –et, –en. Strong verbs and modal auxiliaries (except **sollen** and **wollen**) are umlauted in Subjunctive II. The verb **sein** is normal except for the loss of final –e in the first and third persons singular: **ich sei, er sei.**

The following sentences illustrate the use of the subjunctive for indirect statements. Column **A** shows the original direct statement, Column **B** the indirect statement. Note that:

1. The Subjunctive II forms are given in parentheses.
2. If the indirect statement is introduced by the subordinating conjunction **daß**, the inflected verb is moved to final position; if not, normal word order prevails.
3. The tense of the indirect statement is always the same as that of the original direct statement, and is unaffected by the tense of the introductory (or governing) clause.

A. Direct statement:

(1) Er sagte: „Ich **habe** Glück."
He said: "I am lucky."

(2) Er sagte: „Ich **hatte**
Glück."
He said: "I was lucky."
Er sagte: „Ich **habe** Glück
gehabt."
He said: "I have been lucky."
Er sagte: „Ich **hatte** Glück
gehabt."
He said: "I had been lucky."

(3) Er sagte: „Ich **werde**
Glück **haben.**"
He said: "I shall be lucky."

(4) Er sagte: „Ich **werde**
Glück **gehabt haben.**"
*He said: "I shall have been
lucky."*

B. Indirect statement:

(1) Er sagte, er **habe** (or **hätte**)
Glück.
Er sagte, daß er Glück
habe (or **hätte**).
He said that he was lucky.

(2) Er sagte, er **habe** (or **hätte**)
Glück **gehabt.**
Er sagte, daß 'er Glück **ge-
habt habe** (or **hätte**).
He said that he had been lucky.

(3) Er sagte, er **werde** (or
würde) Glück **haben.**
Er sagte, daß er Glück
haben werde (or **würde**).
He said that he would be lucky.

(4) Er sagte, er **werde** (or
würde) Glück **gehabt
haben.**
*He said that he would have
been lucky.*

C. Changes of tense from direct to indirect statement. In translating
an English indirect statement into German it is best to return to the original
direct statement, for from the tense of its verb the tense of the subjunctive verb
is most easily determined:

1. A present indicative in the direct statement becomes a present Subjunctive I or II.
2. *Any* past indicative (past, perfect, or past perfect) becomes a past
Subjunctive I or II.
3. A future indicative becomes a future Subjunctive I or a present Conditional.
4. A future perfect indicative becomes a future perfect Subjunctive I or
a past Conditional.

It is usual to employ the Subjunctive I forms of **sein,** the three singular
persons of the modals, the third person singular of **haben** and **werden,** and the
third person singular of strong and weak verbs: these forms are all clearly dis-

tinct from the present indicative—**er sei, ich könne, er habe, er werde, er schlage, er lebe.** But otherwise Subjunctive II and the Conditional are used for indirect discourse.

D.   Verbs of knowing or averring followed by the indicative.   Verbs such as **wissen** (*to know*), **sehen** (*to see*), and phrases such as **es ist klar** (*it is clear*), **es ist nicht zu leugnen** (*it cannot be denied*) are followed by the indicative. This use of the indicative is particularly common after the first person present of such verbs as **wissen.** Verbs of knowing emphasize, support, or endorse the truth of what follows—thus giving to the sentence as a whole the force of a direct statement—and the indicative, as the mood of fact, is used to express this certainty:

Wir **wissen** alle, daß Sie recht **haben.**
We all know that you are right.

Ich **weiß**, daß er morgen **abfährt.**
I know that he will leave tomorrow.

Es ist nicht zu leugnen, daß der Blitz manchmal **einschlägt.**
It cannot be denied that lightning often strikes.

Similarly, verbs of averring such as **sagen**, particularly in the present tense, first person, are frequently followed by the indicative:

Ich **sage** Ihnen, daß der Mann unschuldig **ist.**
I tell you that the man is innocent.

Ich **sage** Ihnen nochmals, daß ich furchtbar müde **bin.**
I tell you again (or repeat) that I am terribly tired.

E.   Verbs that introduce indirect statements.   Indirect statements are introduced by verbs of saying, thinking, and feeling such as: **sagen** (*to say, tell*), **erzählen** (*to tell, relate*), **schreiben** (*to write*), **antworten** (*to answer*), **berichten** (*to report*), and **fürchten** (*to fear*):

Er sagte, er würde mich um acht Uhr besuchen.
He said (that) he would call on me at eight o'clock.

Sie schrieb mir, die ganze Familie hätte einen Ausflug ins Gebirge gemacht.
She wrote me that the whole family had taken a trip to the mountains.

Die Zeitung berichtete, daß ein berühmter europäischer Schauspieler angekommen wäre.
The newspaper reported that a famous European actor had arrived.

F.   Change of pronouns and possessives from direct to indirect statement.   In changing sentences from the direct to the indirect form, care must be taken to change not only the verb but also pronouns and possessives. Note particularly changes in reflexive forms:

Karl sagte: „Ich habe **mein** Buch verloren."

INDIR.:   Karl sagte, **er** hätte **sein** Buch verloren.
Carl said (that) he had lost his book.

Sie schrieb mir: „Ich bin bei **meiner** Tante."

INDIR.:   Sie schrieb mir, **sie** wäre bei **ihrer** Tante.
She wrote me that she was at her aunt's house.

Er sagte zu mir: „Ich kann es **mir** nicht leisten."

INDIR.:   Er sagte mir, **er** könnte es **sich** nicht leisten.
He told me that he could not afford it.

Zu after **sagen** is dropped in an indirect statement.

G.   Subjunctives in the direct statement.   If the direct statement contains a subjunctive, it is retained in the indirect statement:

Er meinte: „Wenn ich die Universität besuchte, würde ich eine bessere Stelle finden können."
He thought, "If I were to go to college I would be able to find a better job."

Er meinte, wenn er die Universität besuchte, würde er eine bessere Stelle finden können.
He thought that if he went to college he would be able to find a better job.

H.   Dependent clauses in the direct statement.   If the direct statement contains a dependent clause, it too becomes subjunctive in the indirect statement:

Er berichtete: „Karl, der jeden Tag spät ankommt, gewinnt den Preis."
Er berichtete, daß Karl, der jeden Tag spät ankäme, den Preis gewänne.
He reported that Karl, who came late every day, won the prize.

§77.   INDIRECT QUESTIONS

The sentences in **A** and **B** below show that indirect questions are formulated in the same way as indirect statements. Note that:

1. Indirect questions always begin with an interrogative; if the direct question had no interrogative, the subordinating conjunction **ob** must be supplied:

   Er fragte: „War sie krank?"
   Er fragte, ob sie krank gewesen wäre.

2. Indirect questions are always dependent clauses, with verb-last word order.

A. Direct question:

(1) Ich fragte ihn: „Was **haben Sie** in der Hand?"
I asked him: "What have you in your hand?"

(2) Ich fragte ihn: „Wo **waren Sie** heute morgen?"
I asked him: "Where were you this morning?"

(3) Ich fragte ihn: „**Haben** die Leute das **verstanden?**"
I asked him: "Did the people understand that?"

(4) Ich fragte ihn: „**Werden** Ihre Freunde **mitkommen?**"
I asked him: "Will your friends come along?"

B. Indirect question:

(1) Ich fragte ihn, was **er** in der Hand **habe** (or **hätte**).
I asked him what he had in his hand.

(2) Ich fragte ihn, wo **er** heute morgen **gewesen sei** (or **gewesen wäre**).
I asked him where he had been this morning.

(3) Ich fragte ihn, ob die Leute das **verstanden hätten**.
I asked him whether the people had understood that.

(4) Ich fragte ihn, ob seine Freunde **mitkommen würden**.
I asked him whether his friends would come along.

C. The indicative in indirect questions.   After an introductory clause in the present tense, and after an imperative, the indirect question is in the indicative.

Er fragt, ob sie noch **schläft**.
He asks whether she is still asleep.

Erzählen Sie mir, was geschehen **ist**!
Tell me what happened.

§78. INDIRECT COMMANDS

The indirect command in German, as the sentences in **A** and **B** show, is formulated much in the same way as the indirect statement. Note especially that:

1. Direct commands in German have an exclamation mark; indirect commands have a period.
2. An indirect command is customarily expressed by the present Subjunctive I or II of **sollen** and a dependent present infinitive.
3. The English infinitive often represents an indirect command. The German infinitive cannot be used in this way.

*He told me **to come.***

also: *He told me that I should come.*

Er sagte mir, daß ich kommen sollte.

A.   Direct command:

(1)   Er sagte zu mir: „**Stehen Sie auf!**"
He said to me: "Get up."

(2)   Ich sagte zu ihm: „**Vergessen Sie** das nicht!"
I said to him: "Don't forget that."

(3)   Wir sagten zu ihr: **Lesen Sie** das deutsche Buch!"
We said to her: "Read the German book."

B.   Indirect command:

(1)   Er sagte mir, ich **solle** (or **sollte**) **aufstehen.**
or: Er sagte mir, daß ich **aufstehen solle** (or **sollte**).
He told me to get up (or that I should get up).

(2)   Ich sagte ihm, er **solle** (or **sollte**) das nicht **vergessen.**
or: Ich sagte ihm, daß er das nicht **vergessen solle** (or **sollte**).
I told him not to forget (or that he should not forget) that.

(3)   Wir sagten ihr, sie **solle** (or **sollte**) das deutsche Buch **lesen.**
or: Wir sagten ihr, daß sie das deutsche Buch **lesen solle** (or **sollte**).
We told her to read (or that she should read) the German book.

§79.   INDEPENDENT SENTENCES

The subjunctive may also be used in independent sentences to express *wish, command, possibility, doubt,* etc.

A.   The subjunctive in wishes.

(1)   Es **lebe** die Freiheit!
May freedom live.
Seine Seele **ruhe** in Frieden!
May his soul rest in peace.
Möge das neue Jahr Ihnen viel Glück bringen!
May the new year bring you much good fortune.

Gott **gebe** es!
(May) God grant it.

The present Subjunctive I is used—chiefly in set phrases, prayers, and formal greetings—to express a wish that may be fulfilled. The present Subjunctive I of **mögen** with a dependent infinitive is also used in this construction.

(2) **Wäre** ich nur reich!	**Hätte** er doch Geduld!
or: Wenn ich nur reich **wäre**!	or: Wenn er doch Geduld **hätte**!
If only I were rich!	*If only he had patience!*
or: *Would that I were rich.*	or: *Would that he had patience.*

The present Subjunctive II is used to express a wish that is equivalent to a present contrary-to-fact condition of which the conclusion is to be supplied. This form is used both when a wish is incapable and when it is capable of fulfillment, although the idea of unreality may be obvious at the time a wish is expressed:

Wenn ich nur Flügel **hätte**!	Wenn der Zug nur **käme**!
Hätte ich nur Flügel!	**Käme** der Zug nur!
If only I had wings!	*If only the train would come!*

The present Subjunctive II (used in wishes and otherwise) may indicate impatience on the part of the speaker (**Hätte er doch Geduld!**); it may also convey modesty, when the statement concerns the speaker:

> **Möchte** es mir nur bald gelingen!
> or: **Gelänge** es mir nur bald!
> or: Wenn es mir nur bald **gelänge**!
> *May I succeed soon!*

(3) **Wäre** er nur hier **gewesen**!
or: Wenn er nur hier **gewesen wäre**!
Would that he had been here.
or: *If he had only been here!*

Hätte sie mir doch **geschrieben**!
or: Wenn sie mir doch **geschrieben hätte**!
Would that she had written me.
or: *If she had only written me!*

The past Subjunctive II is used to express a wish that is equivalent to a past contrary-to-fact condition of which the conclusion is to be supplied. The present or past Subjunctive II, when used to express a wish, is usually accompanied by **doch** or **nur**.

B. The subjunctive in commands.

(1) Since the imperative exists only for the second person, singular and plural, the present Subjunctive I is used to express commands for the third singular and first and third plural. The first person plural is used with inversion:

Lesen wir jetzt weiter!   **Fangen** wir jetzt **an**!
Let us continue reading.   *Let us begin now.*

Reden wir nicht mehr davon!   **Vergessen** wir das nicht!
Let us talk no more about it.   *Let us not forget that.*

(2)   The third person singular may have either normal or inverted word order:

„Edel **sei** der Mensch."   Er **komme**! (or **Komme** er!)
Let man be noble.   *Let him come.*

Jeder **kehre** vor seiner Tür!
Mind your own business.

lit.   *Let each one sweep before his (own) door.*

Man **beachte** die Vorschriften!
Let everybody (lit. *one*) *observe the rules.*

(3)   The third person plural is infrequently used:

Alle **setzen** sich!
(Let) all be seated.

(4)   The second person singular and plural formal address, identical in form to the third plural, is frequently used. While, strictly speaking, it is present Subjunctive I in form, because of its frequency and because it is always identical to the third plural indicative, it is thought of and listed as an imperative. The exceptional form **seien** betrays its true origin:

Herr Doktor, **seien** Sie ruhig!
Be quiet, doctor.

(5)   Far more common than the constructions explained in (1), (2), or (3) is the imperative of **lassen** with a dependent present infinitive. Note that the subject of the subjunctive command becomes the object of **lassen**.

Laß (**laßt** or **lassen Sie**) uns gehen!
Let us go.

Laß (**laßt** or **lassen Sie**) ihn kommen!
Let him come.

C.   The subjunctive to express possibility and doubt.

(1)   The present Subjunctive II is used to express possibility and doubt, especially in modest, mild, polite, or diplomatic terms.

Wie **wäre** es mit einer Partie Schach?
How would you like to play a game of chess?
How about a game of chess?

Wäre es möglich, daß Fritz das Schachbrett **verlegt hätte**?
Is it possible that Fred misplaced the chessboard?

Nicht daß ich **wüßte.**   Das **wäre** schade!
Not that I am aware of.   *That would be a pity.*

(2)   The modal auxiliaries are frequently employed in the same sense.

Wo **könnte** (or **dürfte**) es wohl sein?
Where might it possibly be?

Sie **dürften** sich geirrt haben.
You may possibly have made a mistake.

Das **sollte** ich doch meinen!
I should think so!

Dürfte ich Sie um Ihr Opernglas bitten?
Might I ask you for your opera glasses?

Es **möchte** wohl besser sein, wenn wir es unterließen.
It would probably be better if we did not do it.

§80. CONCESSIVE CLAUSES

Subjunctive I may be used to express concession. The second clause is not inverted because both clauses were originally independent.

A.   **Sei** die Gefahr auch noch so groß, ich werde mich nicht fürchten.
Die Gefahr **sei** auch noch so groß, ich werde mich nicht fürchten.
Be the danger ever so great, I shall not be afraid.
Although the danger be ever so great, I shall not be afraid.

B.   **Sei** es früh, **sei** es spät, er ist immer auf seinem Posten.
(Be it) early or (be it) late, he is always at his post.

Concession may be expressed in several ways without the subjunctive. For example, the first clause of **A** above might read:

Mag die Gefahr auch noch so groß sein, . . .
Die Gefahr mag auch noch so groß sein, . . .
Ist die Gefahr auch noch so groß, . . .

CHAPTER 23

Conditional Sentences

§81. CONDITIONAL SENTENCES WITH THE INDICATIVE

The indicative mood is used in both clauses of a conditional sentence, *provided nothing in the if-clause is contrary to fact.*

A.
Wenn er Zeit **hat,** (so) **wird** er mich **besuchen.**
Hat er Zeit, so **wird** er mich **besuchen.**
Er **wird** mich **besuchen,** wenn er Zeit **hat.**
If he has time, he will visit me.
He will visit me if he has time.

B.
Wenn es stark **regnet,** (so) **wird** er zu Hause **bleiben.**
Regnet es stark, so **wird** er zu Hause **bleiben.**
Er **wird** zu Hause **bleiben,** wenn es stark **regnet.**
If it rains hard, he will stay at home.
He will stay at home if it rains hard.

(1)   The use of **so** (not to be translated but felt as a weak suppressed *then*) may introduce a main clause, provided an *if*-clause precedes; **so** is usually used if **wenn** is omitted in the preceding clause. **So** in such sentences serves to sum up the thought of a preceding clause. It is required in short sentences having the inverted word order in both main and dependent clauses, provided the meaning is not clear otherwise:

Muß er, so kommt er.
If he has to, he will come.

(2)   **So** as connective is used chiefly after clauses of *condition* (see first sentences under **A** and **B** above) or *concession:*

Wenn er auch viel geleistet hat, so ist er doch nicht zufrieden.
Even though he has accomplished much, he is nevertheless not satisfied.

138

§82. CONTRARY-TO-FACT CONDITIONS

Conditions that are contrary to fact (i.e., not true) may refer both to the *present* and to the *past*.

A. Present contrary-to-fact conditions. In the sentences below, the *if*-clauses (the condition clauses) are contrary to fact; thus it follows that the *then*-clauses are incapable of fulfillment. In (1), for example, he does not have the money, so cannot give it away.

(1)   Wenn er das Geld **hätte**, (so) **würde** er es mir **geben**.
     Wenn er das Geld **hätte**, (so) **gäbe** er es mir.
     Hätte er das Geld, so **würde** er es mir **geben**.
     Hätte er das Geld, so **gäbe** er es mir.
     If he had the money, he would give it to me.

(2)   Wenn er hier **wäre**, (so) **würde** er ins Theater **gehen**.
     Wenn er hier **wäre**, (so) **ginge** er ins Theater.
     Wäre er hier, so **würde** er ins Theater **gehen**.
     Wäre er hier, so **ginge** er ins Theater.
     If he were here, he would go to the theater.

These *if*-clauses refer to present time, and both English and German use a present subjunctive verb; in English, this form is largely identical to the simple past indicative; German employs the Subjunctive II. Note that:

1. If a condition is contrary to fact in present time, the present Subjunctive II must be used in the *if*-clause.
2. In the same case, the main (*then*- or conclusion clause) may have its verb in either the present Subjunctive II or the present Conditional (this latter is more common in everyday German).

B. Past contrary-to-fact conditions. Sentences expressing conditions contrary to fact in the past time use past Subjunctive II in the *if*-clause and either past Subjunctive II or past Conditional in the main clause.

(1)   Wenn er das Geld **gehabt hätte**, (so) **hätte** er es mir **gegeben**.
     Wenn er das Geld **gehabt hätte**, (so) **würde** er es mir **gegeben haben**.
     Hätte er das Geld **gehabt**, so **hätte** er es mir **gegeben**.
     Hätte er das Geld **gehabt**, so **würde** er es mir **gegeben haben**.
     If he had had the money, he would have given it to me.

(2)   Wenn er hier **gewesen wäre**, (so) **wäre** er ins Theater **gegangen**.
     Wenn er hier **gewesen wäre**, (so) **würde** er ins Theater **gegangen sein**.
     Wäre er hier **gewesen**, so **wäre** er ins Theater **gegangen**.
     Wäre er hier **gewesen**, so **würde** er ins Theater **gegangen sein**.
     If he had been here, he would have gone to the theater.

C.   Mixed contrary-to-fact conditions.

Wenn Sie die Tür nicht **zugemacht hätten,** (so) **wäre** es jetzt nicht so warm im Zimmer.

If you had not closed the door, it would not be so warm in the room now.

The tenses of the two clauses in a contrary-to-fact condition do not always have to agree. Here, **zugemacht hätten** is past because it refers to the past, while **wäre,** speaking of the present, is present.

D.   *Als ob* clauses with implied contrary-to-fact ideas.   The Subjunctive II is often used in clauses introduced by **als ob.** If **als ob** is shortened to **als,** inverted word order is required.

(1)   Sie kleidet sich, **als ob** sie reich **wäre.**
Sie kleidet sich, **als wäre** sie reich.
She dresses as if she were rich.

(2)   Sie taten, **als ob** sie es nicht **verstanden hätten.**
Sie taten, **als hätten** sie es nicht **verstanden.**
They acted as if they had not understood it.

E.   *Hätte können* and *hätte sollen* indicating past contrary-to-fact conditions.   Constructions with *could have* and *should have* (with a dependent infinitive) require the subjunctive, since contrary-to-fact ideas are involved. Note that the past Subjunctive II is used, since there is reference to the past.

Er **hätte** es **tun können,** wenn er das Geld gehabt hätte.
He could have done it, if he had had the money.

Ich **hätte** nach Hause **gehen sollen.**
I should have gone home.

Wenn er es **hätte tun können,** (so) hätte er es mir gesagt.
If he could have done it, he would have told me so.

Können and **sollen** are used instead of **gekonnt** and **gesollt,** because they are used with dependent infinitives.

CHAPTER 24

Modal Auxiliaries
and the
Dependent Infinitive

§83. THE MODALS WITH AND WITHOUT
A DEPENDENT INFINITIVE

The six modal auxiliaries are:

können, konnte, hat gekonnt, er kann	*to be able, can, could, etc.*
müssen, mußte, hat gemußt, er muß	*to have to, must, etc.*
dürfen, durfte, hat gedurft, er darf	*to be allowed*
mögen, mochte, hat gemocht, er mag	*to like to, care for*
wollen, wollte, hat gewollt, er will	*to want, desire*
sollen, sollte, hat gesollt, er soll	*to be (required) to*

The development of the modals in German has yet to be completely explained. At an older stage, strong verbs in German had different roots for the singular and plural in the past. The past tense of these verbs came to be used as presents. Then a new past, analogous to the weak verb past, was derived. Sometime later a past participle identical to the infinitive came into use (perhaps on the model of **lassen, liess, lassen**—the **ge–** prefix was not always added in the older language). And finally another past participle, a projection of the new simple past form, was devised.

This brief survey explains away much of the anomalous nature of the modals. Their important features are:

1. The present singular and the present plural (except **sollen**) have different roots; and the present singular is inflected like the simple past of strong verbs.

2. The modals have two past participles:
   (*a*) The weak form (e.g., **gekonnt**) is employed when there is no dependent infinitive.
   (*b*) The form similar to the infinitive (e.g., **können**) appears in conjunction with a dependent infinitive; its similarity to the present infinitive is reflected in the term *double infinitive*.

Several other verbs (e.g., **lassen, sehen, hören**) share this characteristic with the modals (see §84).

3. Whereas English modals are defective, German modals have acquired complete paradigms over the years. This results in problems of translation: **Ich muss gehen** = *I must go*. But: **Ich musste gehen** = *I had to go*. **Ich kann schreiben** = *I can write*. But: **Ich hatte schreiben können** = *I had been able to write*.

The following sentences illustrate the use of the modals absolutely (in column **A**) and with dependent infinitives (in column **B**).

A. Modals without an infinitive:

(1) **Können:**

Er kann es.
He can.

Er konnte es.
He could.

Er hat es **gekonnt.**
He has been able to.

Er hatte es **gekonnt.**
He had been able to.

Er wird es können.
He will be able to.

Er wird es **gekonnt** haben.
He will have been able to.

(2) **Müssen:**

Wir müssen es.
We must.

Wir mußten es.
We had to.

Wir haben es **gemußt.**
We have had to.

Wir hatten es **gemußt.**
We had had (or been obliged) to.

Wir werden es müssen.
We shall have to.

Wir werden es **gemußt** haben.
We shall have had (or been obliged) to.

B. Modals with an infinitive:

(1) **Können:**

Er kann es tun.
He can do it.

Er konnte es tun.
He could do it.

Er hat es tun **können.**
He has been able to do it.

Er hatte es tun **können.**
He had been able to do it.

Er wird es tun können.
He will be able to do it.

Er wird es haben tun **können.**
He will have been able to do it.

(2) **Müssen:**

Wir müssen es tun.
We must do it.

Wir mußten es tun.
We had to do it.

Wir haben es tun **müssen.**
We have had to do it.

Wir hatten es tun **müssen.**
We had had (or been obliged) to do it.

Wir werden es tun müssen.
We shall have to do it.

Wir werden es haben tun **müssen.**
We shall have had (or been obliged) to do it.

(3) **Dürfen:**

Er darf es.
He may.

Er hat es **gedurft.**
He has been allowed to.

(4) **Mögen:**

Er mag es.
He likes to.

Er hat es **gemocht.**
He has liked to.

(5) **Wollen:**

Ich will es.
I want to.

Ich habe es **gewollt.**
I have wanted to.

(6) **Sollen:**

Ich soll es.
I am to.

Ich habe es **gesollt.**
I have been required (or *called upon*) *to.*

(3) **Dürfen:**

Er darf es tun.
He may do it.

Er hat es tun **dürfen.**
He has been allowed to do it.

(4) **Mögen:**

Er mag es tun.
He likes to do it.

Er hat es tun **mögen.**
He has liked to do it.

(5) **Wollen:**

Ich will es tun.
I want to do it.

Ich habe es tun **wollen.**
I have wanted to do it.

(6) **Sollen:**

Ich soll es tun.
I am to do it.

Ich habe es tun **sollen.**
I have been required (or *called upon*) *to do it.*

From the foregoing it may be observed that:

1. All modal auxiliaries are conjugated with **haben.**
2. As independent transitive verbs, German modals may take their own direct objects.
3. Contrary to English usage, German may retain a direct object (particularly **es** or **das**) with a modal used as an independent transitive verb.

Kann er das beweisen? Er kann **es.** (or: **Das** kann er.)
Can he prove that? *He can.*

Here **es** and **das** are direct objects of the verb **beweisen,** which is understood.

4. Modal auxiliaries take dependent infinitives without the infinitive marker **zu.**
5. When used with a dependent infinitive the weak past participles (**gekonnt,** etc.) are replaced by the strong forms (**können,** etc.). The past participle comes at the end of the clause, directly *preceded by the dependent infinitive.*

6. In the future perfect tense, the auxiliary **haben** precedes the double infinitive. Similarly, in a subordinate clause, the auxiliary is displaced from final position by the double infinitive:

> Er glaubte, dass er die Hausarbeit nicht hätte schreiben müssen.
> *He believed that he hadn't had to do the homework.*

§84. DOUBLE INFINITIVE CONSTRUCTION WITH VERBS OTHER THAN MODALS

The sentences below illustrate some of the more common verbs which, like modal auxiliaries, take dependent infinitives without **zu** and which may be used in double infinitive constructions.

A. Lassen:

(1) Er läßt den Arzt holen.   Er hat den Arzt holen **lassen.**
He sends for the doctor.   *He sent for the doctor.*

(2) Ich lasse mir das Haar schneiden.
I am having my hair cut.

Ich habe mir das Haar schneiden **lassen.**
I had my hair cut.

(3) Sie läßt sich ein neues Kleid machen.
She is having a new dress made.

Sie hat sich ein neues Kleid machen **lassen.**
She had a new dress made.

B. Sehen:

Ich sehe ihn kommen.   Ich habe ihn kommen **sehen.**
I see him coming.   *I saw him coming.*

C. Heißen:

Er heißt mich gehen.   Er hat mich gehen **heißen.**
He orders me to go.   *He ordered me to go.*

D. Helfen:

Ich helfe das Geschäft begründen.
I am helping to establish the business.

Ich habe das Geschäft begründen **helfen.**

or: Ich habe geholfen, das Geschaft zu begründen.
I helped to establish the business.

E. Hören:

Hören Sie die Dame singen?
Do you hear the lady singing?

Haben Sie die Dame singen **hören**?
Did you hear the lady sing?

F. Lernen:

Er lernt fliegen.
He is learning to fly.

Ich habe ihn gestern kennen**gelernt** (or kennen**lernen**).
I made his acquaintance yesterday.

G. Lehren:

Ich lehre ihn schreiben.
I am teaching him to write.

Ich habe ihn schreiben **lehren** (or **gelehrt**).
I taught him to write.

§85. VERBS OTHER THAN MODALS REQUIRING A DEPENDENT INFINITIVE WITHOUT *ZU*

The sentences below illustrate verbs which take a dependent infinitive without **zu**, but may not be used in double infinitive constructions.

A. (1) Gehen:

Er **geht** spazieren.
He goes walking.

(2) **Reiten** (or **fahren**):

Wir **reiten** (or **fahren**) spazieren.
We are going riding (or *driving*).

B. (1) Stehenbleiben:

Sie **bleibt** stehen.
She stops.

Sie **blieb** stehen.
She stopped.

(2) **Sich schlafen legen:**

Er **legt sich** schlafen.
He lies down to sleep.

After a verb of motion German sometimes employs the *past participle* (instead of the present infinitive as in the above sentences) *with present sense,* where the English idiom requires the present participle:

Er kam **gelaufen.**
*He came **running.***

Sie kommt **gesprungen.**
*She comes **jumping** along.*

§86. MODAL AUXILIARIES WITH PASSIVE FORMS

Modal auxiliaries have no passive voice, but may be followed by a *passive infinitive*.

<table>
<tr><td>Das kann gemacht werden.</td><td>Eine Brücke soll gebaut werden.</td></tr>
<tr><td>That can be done.</td><td>A bridge is to be built.</td></tr>
</table>

Das muß **gesagt werden.**
That must be said.

Das Radarsignal konnte sofort **identifiziert werden.**
The radar signal could be identified at once.

An alternative construction with the active infinitive would be:

Man muß das sagen.
That must be said.

Cannot be is often rendered by **sein** followed by **nicht zu** and an active infinitive:

<table>
<tr><td>Es ist nicht zu leugnen.</td><td>Er ist telefonisch nicht zu errei-</td></tr>
<tr><td>It cannot be denied.</td><td>chen.</td></tr>
<tr><td></td><td>He cannot be reached by telephone.</td></tr>
</table>

§87. IDIOMATIC USES OF MODAL AUXILIARIES

The idiomatic uses of modal auxiliaries are illustrated in **A–F.** Some of the literal meanings of modals have been included for comparison. It is important to study the explanatory notes following each section.

A. Sollen:

(1) Was **soll** ich tun?
*What **am** I **to** (or **shall** I) do?*

(2) Sie **sollen** arbeiten.
*You **are to** work.*

(3) Sie **sollten** arbeiten.
*You **should** (or **ought to**) work.*

(4) Er **soll** sehr arm sein.
*He **is said** to be very poor.*

(5) Du **sollst** nicht stehlen.
*Thou **shalt** not steal.*

(6) Er **hätte** zu Hause **bleiben sollen.**
*He **should have stayed** at home.*

Note:

(*a*) **Sollen** may not be used for English *shall* to denote future time; **werden** is the auxiliary for the future in German.

(*b*) English *should* (or *ought to*) is rendered by the present Subjunctive II of **sollen,** denoting unaccomplished possibility.

(*c*) The past indicative, identical in form to the present Subjunctive II, may be illustrated by such a sentence as:

> Gestern **sollte** ich abfahren, aber leider mußte ich in der Stadt bleiben.
> *Yesterday I **was** (supposed) **to** leave, but unfortunately I had to stay in the city.*

B. Wollen:

(1) Er **will** morgen abfahren.
*He **intends** to leave tomorrow.*

(2) Er **will** es getan haben.
*He **claims** to have done it.*

(3) Sie **will** einen reichen Onkel haben.
*She **professes** to have a rich uncle.*

(4) Was **wollen** Sie damit **sagen**?
*What do you **mean** by that?*

(5) **Wir wollen** (or **Wollen wir**) nicht mehr davon **sprechen.**
*Let's not **talk** any more about it.*

(6) **Wollen Sie** Tee oder Kaffee?
*Will **you take** tea or coffee?*

Note:

(*a*) German **will** is not to be used for English *will* to denote future time.

(*b*) **Wollen,** in present Subjunctive I but with normal word order permitted, is commonly used in conversation with the force of an imperative (see sentence 5 above).

C. Mögen:

(1) Er **mag** das Essen nicht.
*He does not **like** the food (or meal).*

(2) Das **mag** (or kann) sein.
*That **may** be.*

(3) Er **möchte** (gern) ins Theater gehen.
*He **would like** to go to the theater.*

(4) **Möchten Sie** mit?
Would you like to go along?

(5) Er **mochte wohl** dreißig Jahre alt sein.
He was probably thirty years old.

(6) Das Buch **mag** auch noch so schwer sein, er wird es lesen.
or: **Mag** das Buch auch noch so schwer sein, er wird es lesen.
Although the book be ever so difficult, he will read it.

(7) **Möge** Gott dir helfen!
May God help you.

Note:

(*a*) English *would* (or *should*) *like* is commonly rendered by the present Subjunctive II of **mögen.**

(*b*) **Mögen** is frequently used to express *probability* (sentence 5) and *concession* (sentence 6).

D. Können:

(1) Letzten Monat **konnte** ich ihn nicht besuchen.
I could not (i.e., *was unable to*) *visit him last month.*

(2) Ich **könnte** ihn jetzt besuchen, wenn ich Zeit **hätte.**
I could (i.e., *should be able to*) *visit him now if I had time.*

(3) Er **kann** nichts dafür.   Was **kann** ich dafür?
It is not his fault.   *How can I help it?*
He can't help it.

(4) Ich **konnte nicht umhin,** ihm die Wahrheit zu sagen.
I couldn't help telling him the truth.

(5) Er **kann** Deutsch.
He knows German.

(6) Das **kann** (or mag) sein.
That may be.

(7) Es **könnte** nützlich sein.
It might be useful.

(8) Sie **hätten** ein deutsches Buch lesen **können.**
You could have read a German book.

Note:

(*a*) If English *could* is the equivalent of *was able,* it is rendered by the past indicative **konnte.** If it is the equivalent of *should be able* or *would be able,* it is rendered by the present Subjunctive II **könnte.**

(*b*) Such a sentence as *He could have written it* must *not* be translated by: **Er könnte es geschrieben haben** (i.e., *It might be that he wrote it*). Rather use: **Er hätte es schreiben können.**

(*c*)   The phrase **nicht umhin können** takes a dependent infinitive with **zu** (see example 4).

E.   Dürfen:

(1)   Das **dürfen** Sie **nicht** tun.
       *You **must not** do that.*

(2)   **Dürfte** ich Sie um das Buch bitten?
       ***Might** I ask you for the book?*
       Darf ich Sie um das Brot bitten?
       ***May** I ask you for the bread?*

(3)   Es **dürfte** (*or* könnte) sein.
       *It **might** (**possibly**) be.*

(4)   Er **durfte** es tun.
       *He **was allowed** to do it.*

(5)   Sie **dürften** ihn mißverstanden haben.
       *You **may possibly** have misunderstood him.*

Note:

(*a*)   Used negatively, **dürfen** is far more forceful than **müssen**. In common usage, **nicht dürfen** is the opposite of **müssen,** and **nicht müssen** simply means that one is *not obliged to* do something.

F.   Müssen:

(1)   Ich **muß** gleich an die Arbeit (gehen).
       *I **must** go to work at once.*

(2)   Er **mußte** die Miete bezahlen.
       *He **had to** pay the rent.*

(3)   Wir **haben** es tun müssen.
       *We **were compelled** to do it.*

(4)   Er **hatte** es tun **müssen.**
       *He **had been obliged** to do it.*

(5)   Er **hätte** es tun **müssen.**
       *He **would have been obliged** to do it.*

(6)   Er **muß** es **getan haben.**
       *He **must have done** it.*

Note:

(*a*)   When the inference is that the action implied in a sentence took place, **muss** with the past infinitive is required.

(*b*)   *Not to have to* in the sense of *not to need to* is rendered by **brauchen** with **nicht zu** and a dependent infinitive:

Ich **brauche** es **nicht zu** tun.
I don't have (i.e., *need*) *to do it.*

In conversational German, **brauchen** often appears with a dependent infinitive without the marker **zu**:

Du brauchst nicht gehen.
You don't have to go.

CHAPTER 25

Idioms

§88. GERMAN IDIOMS AND THEIR ENGLISH EQUIVALENTS

Translation is an exercise, not in recording exact correspondences, but in finding suitable equivalents. If **Er steht an dem Tisch** means *He stands at the table,* does **Er denkt an ihn** mean *He thinks at him?*

Listed below are the more frequently used idiomatic expressions. Since all or almost all of them have been encountered and explained in the previous chapters, this list may serve as a review of the book. In studying these idioms, particular attention should be paid to the use of prepositions.

1. Er denkt an ihn. *He thinks of him.*
2. Ich warte auf den Mann. *I am waiting for the man.*
3. Er ist stolz auf den Sohn. *He is proud of his son.*
4. Er geht in die Schule. *He goes to school.*
5. Er ist in der Schule. *He is in school.*
6. Nach der Schule spielt er Ball. *He plays ball after school.*
7. Hat er recht oder unrecht? *Is he right or wrong?*
8. Wie geht es Ihnen? *How are you?*
9. (*a*) Ich lese gern. *I like to read.*
   (*b*) Ich habe es gern. *I like it.*
10. (*a*) Er liest lieber. *He prefers to read.*
    (*b*) Er hat es lieber. *He prefers it.*
11. (*a*) Sie liest am liebsten. *She likes best to read.*
    (*b*) Sie hat es am liebsten. *She likes it best.*
12. Er ist auf dem Lande. *He is in the country.*
13. Er geht aufs Land. *He is going to the country.*
14. Sie ist zu Hause. *She is at home.*
15. Sie geht nach Hause. *She is going home.*
16. Es wird immer heißer. *It is getting hotter and hotter.*
17. Was fehlt Ihnen? *What is the matter with you?*
18. Es tut mir leid. *I am sorry.*

151

19. Er bittet mich um den Bleistift. *He asks me for the pencil.*

20. Je öfter ich das Buch lese, desto besser gefällt es mir. *The oftener I read the book, the better I like it.*

21. Er sprach vor sich (*acc. refl.*) hin. *He spoke to himself.*

22. Er hat gar nichts. *He has nothing at all.*

23. Ich verstehe es gar nicht. *I do not understand it at all.*

24. Er kommt, nicht wahr? *He is coming, is he not?*

25. Es tut mir weh. *It hurts me.*

26. Das geht Sie nichts an. *That does not concern you.*

27. Erinnern Sie sich an den Jungen? *Do you remember the boy?*

28. Auf Wiedersehen! *Goodbye.*

29. Leben Sie wohl! *Farewell.*

30. Er ist noch nicht da. *He has not yet come.*

31. Er hat ein Paar Schuhe. *He has a pair of shoes.*

32. Er hat ein paar Bücher. *He has several books.*

33. Geben Sie mir noch ein Buch! *Give me another (i.e., an additional) book.*

34. Geben Sie mir ein anderes Buch! *Give me another (i.e., a different) book.*

35. Wir lernten ihn kennen. *We made his acquaintance.*

36. Er soll sehr reich sein. *He is said to be very rich.*

37. Sie denkt sich (*dat. refl.*) das. *She imagines that.*

38. Er ist es los. *He is rid of it.*

39. Kümmern Sie sich nicht um ihn! *Don't worry (or bother) about him.*

40. Er fürchtet sich vor dem Hunde. *He is afraid of the dog.*

41. Sie ist toll vor Schmerz. *She is frantic with pain.*

42. Er ist außer sich vor Zorn. *He is beside himself with anger.*

43. Sie ging auf und ab. *She walked up and down (or to and fro).*

44. Es ist mir nicht gelungen, ihn zu überzeugen. *I didn't succeed in convincing him.*

45. Er bleibt stehen. *He stops.*

46. Ich kann es mir nicht leisten. *I can't afford it.*

47. Fahren Sie mit dem Dampfer oder mit der Eisenbahn? *Are you going by steamer or by rail?*

48. Heute über acht Tage wird er kommen. *He will come a week from today.*

49. Schreiben Sie das auf deutsch! *Write that in German.*

50. Nehmen Sie sich in acht! *Be careful (or Take care).*

51. Es geschah vor acht Tagen. *It happened a week ago.*

52. Ich freue mich auf den Besuch. *I am looking forward with pleasure to the visit.*

53. Ich freue mich über Ihren Erfolg. *I am happy about your success.*

54. Es kommt darauf an. *That depends.*

55. Um so besser. *All the better.*

56. (*a*) Er ist bei mir. *He is at my house.*
    (*b*) Ich habe kein Geld bei mir. *I have no money with me.*

57. Er klopft an die Tür. *He is knocking at the door.*

58. Ich wollte gerade gehen. *I was on the point of going.*

59. Er tat es auf diese Weise. *He did it in this manner.*
60. Das Haus besteht aus sechs Zimmern. *The house consists of six rooms.*
61. Man machte ihn zum Führer. *They made him (or He was made) leader.*
62. Man gewöhnt sich an alles. *One gets used to everything.*
63. Ich ärgere mich über ihn. *I am provoked at him.*
64. Es macht mir Freude. *It gives me pleasure.*
65. Sie lachten ihn aus. *They laughed at him.*
66. Er verliebte sich in das Mädchen. *He fell in love with the girl.*
67. Er verlobte sich mit dem Mädchen. *He became engaged to the girl.*
68. Er antwortet auf meine Frage. *He answers my question.*
69. Ich habe mich erkältet. *I have caught cold (or I have a cold).*
70. Was wird aus ihm werden? *What will become of him?*
71. (*a*) Ich bin es. *It is I.*
    (*b*) Ist er es? *Is it he?* Er ist es. *It is he.*
72. Ich wohne ihm gegenüber. *I live opposite him.*
73. Er ließ mich holen. *He sent for me.*
74. Sie wohnte in meiner Nähe. *She lived near me.*
75. Er setzte sich an den Tisch. *He sat down at the table.*
76. Ich schrieb einen Brief an meinen Vetter. *I wrote my cousin a letter.*
77. Der wievielte ist heute? *What is today's date?*
78. Um wieviel Uhr kommt er? *At what time is he coming?*
79. Es geschieht ihm recht. *It serves him right.*
80. Ich habe ihm einen großen Gefallen getan. *I did him a great favor.*
81. Es freut mich. *I am glad.*
82. (*a*) Die Reihe ist an mir (or Ich bin an der Reihe). *It is my turn.*
    (*b*) Ich bin an die Reihe gekommen. *My turn has come.*
83. Der Stuhl gefällt mir. *I like the chair.*
84. Auf einmal begann es zu regnen. *Suddenly it began to rain.*
85. (*a*) Meine Uhr geht vor. *My watch is fast.*
    (*b*) Meine Uhr geht nach. *My watch is slow.*
86. Wir hoffen auf günstiges Wetter. *We are hoping for favorable weather.*
87. Er hat entweder eine Feder oder einen Bleistift. *He has either a pen or a pencil.*
88. Er hat weder das eine noch das andere. *He has neither the one nor the other.*
89. Sowohl sein Vater als auch seine Mutter sind gekommen. *Both his father and his mother came.*
90. Passen Sie auf! *Pay attention.*
91. Es hat noch nicht geklingelt. *The bell has not yet rung.*
92. Amüsieren Sie sich! *Have a good time.*
93. Er hat Kopfweh. *He has a headache.*
94. Das macht nichts aus. *That makes no difference.*
95. Er arbeitet in der Nacht. *He works at night.*
96. Er schläft am Tage. *He sleeps in the daytime.*
97. Er geht auf einen Monat aufs Land. *He is going to the country for a month.*

98. Was gibt's Neues? *What's new?*
99. Gehen Sie ins Theater? *Are you going to the theater?*
100. Was ißt er zum Frühstück? *What does he eat for breakfast?*
101. Er sieht zum Fenster hinaus. *He is looking out of the window.*
102. Ich gehe an ihm vorbei. *I pass him.*
103. Sie spricht von ihm. *She is speaking about him.*
104. Sie setzt (sich) den Hut auf. *She is putting on her hat.*
105. Sie zieht sich die Handschuhe an. *She is putting on her gloves.*
106. Er ist Student auf der Universität. *He is a student at the university.*
107. Er ist Professor an der Universität. *He is a professor at the university.*
108. (*a*) Es ist nicht der Mühe (*gen.*) wert.
     (*b*) Es lohnt sich nicht der Mühe (*gen.*). *It is not worth while* (or *does not pay*).
109. Ich bin derselben Meinung (*gen.*). *I am of the same opinion.*
110. Er möchte eine Reise (einen Spaziergang) machen. *He would like to take a trip (a walk).*
111. Er fährt lieber zweiter Klasse. *He prefers to travel second class.*
112. Wir haben viel Schönes gesehen. *We saw many beautiful things.*
113. Er ist auf einen Baum geklettert. *He climbed a tree.*
114. (*a*) Seien Sie nicht grausam gegen den Hund! *Don't be cruel to the dog.*
     (*b*) Er ist gegen jeden Menschen freundlich (gütig, höflich, kalt). *He is friendly (kind, polite, cold) to every human being.*
115. Seien Sie nicht böse auf mich! *Don't be angry with me.*
116. Das Land ist reich (arm) an Wäldern. *The country is rich (poor) in forests.*
117. Besten Gruß an Ihren Bruder. *Best regards to your brother.*
118. Fangen Sie von vorn an! *Begin at the beginning.*
119. Er erhielt viele schöne Geschenke zum Geburtstag (zu Weihnachten). *He received many beautiful gifts for his birthday (for Christmas).*
120. Köln ist durch den Dom (*or* wegen des Domes) berühmt. *Cologne is famous for its cathedral.*
121. Sie wird den Brief auf die Post bringen. *She will mail the letter.*
122. Lernen Sie das Gedicht auswendig! *Learn the poem by heart.*
123. Er benimmt sich schlecht. *He behaves badly.*
124. Das Pferd ist blind auf beiden Augen. *The horse is blind in both eyes.*
125. (*a*) Das schmeckt nach saurer Milch. *That tastes of sour milk.*
     (*b*) Es riecht nach frischem Heu. *It smells of fresh hay.*
126. Er wird es nicht tun, es sei denn, daß sie ihn darum bitten. *He will not do it unless they ask him to.*

Word Formation and Cognates

§89. COMPOUND NOUNS

The German language comprises a very large percentage of compounded words, which abound not only in technical and scientific but also in common parlance: der **Handschuh** (*glove*), der **Fingerhut** (*thimble*), der **Maulkorb** (*muzzle*), etc. Students should acquire the habit of analyzing compounded words into their component parts. With a comparatively small number of root words and a knowledge of prepositions, adverbs, prefixes, and suffixes, one can usually determine the meaning of a long compounded word without the help of a dictionary.

A. Formation of compound nouns. German forms compounds chiefly from simpler German words rather than coining words with Latin and Greek roots, as English so frequently does: das **Bindewort** (*conjunction*), die **Ausnahme** (*exception*), der **Wasserstoff** (*hydrogen*), die **Rolltreppe** (*escalator*).

B. Gender of compound nouns. Compound nouns have the gender of their *last* component:

> der Hausschlüssel (= das Haus + der Schlüssel), *housekey*
> die Eisenbahn (= das Eisen + die Bahn), *railroad*
> der Birnbaum (= die Birne + der Baum), *pear tree*
> das Vaterland (= der Vater + das Land), *native land*
> die Raumkapsel (= der Raum + die Kapsel), *space capsule*
> die Kernenergie (= der Kern + die Energie), *nuclear energy*
> die Feuerversicherungsgesellschaft (= das Feuer + die Versicherung + die Gesellschaft), *fire insurance company*

Note:

(1) A connective –(**e**)**s**– often appears in the compound, irrespective of the gender of a noun:

> der Geburtstag (= die Geburt + der Tag), *birthday*

155

das Hochzeitskleid (= die Hochzeit + das Kleid), *wedding dress*
die Jahreszeit (= das Jahr + die Zeit), *season*

(2)   A connective –(e)n– is also common in compounds: der Hirtenknabe (= der Hirt + der Knabe), *shepherd boy*. This connective sometimes shows the old genitive form of certain feminine nouns, which otherwise rarely occurs in modern German:

der Sonnenstrahl (= die Sonne + der Strahl), *sunbeam*

§90. SUFFIXES

Originally most suffixes and prefixes were independent words; in modern German, however, they have lost their independent identity and become affixed to other words.

A. Noun suffixes.   Noun suffixes occur in all three genders; some of the more common ones are listed below.

(1)   Feminine noun suffixes: **–e, –ei, –heit, –keit, –kunft, –in, –schaft, –ung, –ion,** and **–tät.**

(*a*)   **–e:**   This suffix forms from adjectives abstract nouns denoting *quality, state,* or *condition.* Note the umlaut on the root vowel:

die Güte, *goodness* or *kindness*   (from gut, *good*)
die Kürze, *shortness* or *brevity*   (from kurz, *short*)

(*b*)   **–ei:**   This suffix forms from nouns of occupation nouns denoting (*place of*) *business* or *trade:*
die Bäckerei, *bakery* (from der Bäcker, *baker*)
die Druckerei, *printing office* (from der Drucker, *printer*)
die Brauerei, *brewery* (from der Brauer, *brewer*)

(*c*)   **–heit** and **–keit:**   These suffixes form from adjectives and nouns abstract nouns denoting *state, condition, quality,* or *character:*
die Schönheit, *beauty* (from schön, *beautiful*)
die Fruchtbarkeit, *fruitfulness* or *fertility* (from fruchtbar, *fertile*)
die Folgsamkeit, *obedience* (from folgsam, *obedient*)
die Leitfähigkeit, *conductivity* (from leitfähig, *conductive*)

Note: The suffix **–heit** is often equivalent to the English suffix **–*hood:*** die Kindheit, *childhood.*

The suffix **–keit** (rather than **–heit**) is usually appended to adjectives ending in **–bar, –lich, –sam, –er,** and **–ig.**

(*d*)   **–kunft:**   This suffix forms from prepositions and adverbs of motion nouns denoting *coming:*

die Ankunft, *arrival* (from an, *at* or *to*)
die Zukunft, *future* (from zu, *to* or *towards*)

Note: The suffix **–kunft** was formerly a noun meaning *coming* and is etymologically related to the verb **kommen,** as its modern German compounds indicate.

(*e*) **–in:** This suffix forms feminine nouns—usually with umlaut—from masculine nouns:

die Gräfin, *countess* (from der Graf, *count*)
die Lehrerin, *woman teacher* (from der Lehrer, *teacher*)
die Amerikanerin, *American woman* (from der Amerikaner)
die Königin, *queen* (from der König, *king*)

(*f*) **–schaft:** This suffix forms from nouns abstract and collective nouns denoting *state, condition,* or *quality; office, dignity,* or *profession.* It is often equivalent to the English suffix *–ship.*

die Freundschaft, *friendship* (from der Freund, *friend*)
die Feindschaft, *enmity* (from der Feind, *enemy*)
die Mannschaft, *crew* or *team* (from der Mann, *man*)
die Herrschaft, *dominion* (from der Herr, *master* or *ruler*)

(*g*) **–ung:** This suffix forms from verbal roots nouns denoting an *action* or the *result of an action:*

die Erfindung, *discovery* (from erfinden, *to discover*)
die Erziehung, *education* (from erziehen, *to educate*)
die Spaltung, *cleavage, splitting* (from spalten, *to cleave* or *split up*); *cf.* Kernspaltung, *nuclear fission.*

Note: The suffix **–ung** is often equivalent to the English suffix *–ing:* die Warnung, *warning;* die Endung, *ending.*

(*h*) **–ion:** This suffix occurs with nouns of foreign origin, many of which occur in English in about the same form: die Million, *million;* die Religion, *religion;* die Nation, *nation;* die Lektion, *lesson;* die Erdrotation, *rotation of the earth.*

(*i*) **–tät:** This suffix occurs with nouns of foreign origin and is often equivalent to English *-ty:* die Universität, *university;* die Elektrizität, *electricity;* die Qualität, *quality;* die Quantität, *quantity;* die Relativität, *relativity;* die Radioaktivität, *radioactivity.*

(2)   Neuter noun suffixes: **–chen, –lein, –nis, –sal,** and **–tum.**

(*a*) **–chen** and **–lein:** These suffixes form from nouns *diminutives* and nouns denoting *endearment,* usually with umlaut:

das Bächlein, *little brook* or *brooklet* (from der Bach, *brook*)
das Bäumchen, *little tree* (from der Baum, *tree*)
das Blümlein, *little flower* from die Blume, *flower*)

das Mütterchen, *dear mother* (from die Mutter, *mother*)

das Väterchen, *dear father* (from der Vater, *father*)

das Körperchen, *corpuscle* or *particle* (from der Körper, *body*)

Note: The suffix –**chen** is equivalent to the English suffix –***kin***: das Lämmchen, *lambkin.*

The suffix –**lein** originated in South Germany, where it is still used in preference to –**chen** in ordinary conversation and various dialect forms.

(*b*) –**nis**: This suffix forms from verbal roots neuter (and sometimes feminine) nouns, usually with umlaut, denoting the *result* or *object of an activity* implied in the verbal stem of a compound:

das Ergebnis, *result* (from sich ergeben, *to result*)

das Verständnis, *understanding* (from verstehen, *to understand*)

das Vermächtnis, *testament* or *legacy* (from vermachen, *to bequeath*)

Note: The suffix –**nis** is sometimes equivalent to the English suffix –***ness,*** as in *darkness.*

Two common feminines formed with –**nis** are:

die Erlaubnis, *permission* (from erlauben, *to permit*)

die Kenntnis, *knowledge* (from kennen, *to know*)

(*c*) –**sal**: This suffix forms from verbal roots nouns similar to those ending in –**nis** but often more comprehensive and forceful:

das Schicksal, *fate* (from schicken, *to send*)

das Wirrsal, *confusion* (from wirren, *to entangle*)

(*d*) –**tum**: This suffix forms from noun, adjective, and verbal roots neuter nouns (with only two exceptions) denoting *dignity* or *rank, condition* or *state,* or *a collective idea:*

das Königtum, *royalty* or *kingship* (from der König, *king*)

das Siechtum, *state of poor health* (from siech, *sickly*)

das Bürgertum, *citizenry* (from der Bürger, *citizen*)

Note: The suffix –**tum** is often equivalent to the English suffix –***dom,*** as in *martyrdom* (Märtyrtum).

Two *masculine* nouns are formed with –**tum**:

der Reichtum, *riches* (from reich, *rich*)

der Irrtum, *error* (from irr(e), *in error*)

(3) Masculine nouns suffixes: –**er,** –**el,** and –**ling.**

(*a*) –**er**: This suffix, identical in English, forms from verbal roots masculine nouns denoting *the personal agent;* from noun stems, nouns of *nationality*. The umlaut is often present:

der Räuber, *robber* (from rauben, *to rob*)

der Maler, *painter* (from malen, *to paint*)

der Arbeiter, *worker* or *workman* (from arbeiten, *to work*)

der Diener, *servant* (from dienen, *to serve*)

der Engländer, *Englishman* (from England, *England*)

der Spanier, *Spaniard* (from Spanien, *Spain*)

der Sender, *sender, transmitter, broadcasting station* (from senden, to send)

Note: Nouns denoting the personal agent are sometimes formed with the suffixes –ler or –ner:

der Künstler, *artist* (from die Kunst, *art*)

der Kellner, *waiter* (from der Keller, *cellar*)

(*b*) **–el:** This suffix forms from verbal roots nouns—usually masculine—denoting *instrument*:

der Schlüssel, *key* (from schließen, *to close* or *lock*)

der Deckel, *lid* (from decken, *to cover*)

der Zügel, *rein* (from ziehen, *to draw*)

(*c*) **–ling:** This suffix forms, from adjective, noun, and verbal roots, masculine nouns denoting people or animals who appear *young, small,* or *contemptible.* Umlaut is usual:

der Jüngling, *young man* or *youth* (from jung, *young*)

der Feigling, *coward* (from feig, *cowardly*)

der Emporkömmling, *upstart* (from empor, *up* + kommen, *to come*)

der Spößling, *scion* or *descendant* (from der Sproß, *sprout*)

Note: Compare the English suffix *–ling,* as in *duckling, foundling,* etc.

B. Adjective suffixes. Some of the more common adjective suffixes are: **–er, –(e)n** and **–ern, –haft, –bar, –isch, –lich, –ig, –los, –sam, –reich,** and **–voll.**

(1) **–er:** This suffix forms from names of cities indeclinable adjectives:

eine Münch(e)ner Zeitung, *a Munich newspaper* (from München)

das Heidelberger Schloß, *Heidelberg Castle* (from Heidelberg)

(2) **–(e)n** and **–ern:** These suffixes form from nouns adjectives of *material,* sometimes with umlaut. The English suffix *–en* is often equivalent:

hölzern, *wooden* (from das Holz, *wood*)

ledern, *of leather* (from das Leder, *leather*)

bleiern, *of lead* or *leaden* (from das Blei, *lead*)

stählern, *of steel* (from der Stahl, *steel*)

(3) **–haft:** This suffix (related linguistically to **haben**) forms from nouns adjectives that denote *having the nature of:*

knabenhaft, *boyish* (from der Knabe, *boy*)

schmerzhaft, *painful* (from der Schmerz, *pain*)

meisterhaft, *masterly* (from der Meister, *master*)

fabelhaft, *fabulous* (from die Fabel, *fable*)

vorteilhaft, *advantageous, profitable* (from der Vorteil, *advantage, profit*)

(4) **–bar:** This suffix, equivalent to English *–able* or *–ible,* forms from verbal and noun roots adjectives denoting *ability, fitness,* or *worthiness:*

lesbar, *legible* (from lesen, *to read*)

eßbar, *edible* (from essen, *to eat*)

denkbar, *thinkable* or *conceivable* (from denken, *to think*)

sichtbar, *visible* (from sehen, *to see*)

Note: The negative prefix **un–** is frequently used with adjectives ending in **–bar:** unlesbar (*illegible*), undenkbar (*unthinkable*), unauflösbar, *insoluble.*

(5) **–isch:** This suffix, comparable to English *–ish,* forms from nouns and proper names adjectives that denote *belonging to* or *of the nature of:*

kindisch, *childish* (from das Kind, *child*)

teuflisch, *devilish* (from der Teufel, *devil*)

himmlisch, *heavenly* (from der Himmel, *heaven*)

regnerisch, *rainy* (from der Regen, *rain*)

englisch, *English* (from England, *England*)

römisch, *Roman* (from Rom, *Rome*)

französisch, *French* (from der Franzose, *Frenchman*)

Do not confuse the following forms: **kindisch,** *childish* and **kindlich,** *childlike;* **weibisch,** *womanish* (i.e., *unmanly* or *effeminate*) and **weiblich,** *womanly.*

(6) **–lich:** This suffix forms from nouns adjectives denoting *full of* or *like in appearance, manner,* or *nature:*

göttlich, *godly* or *divine* (from der Gott, *God*)

gefährlich, *dangerous* (from die Gefahr, *danger*)

schädlich, *harmful* (from der Schaden, *harm*)

Note: The suffix **–lich** is usually equivalent to the English suffixes *–ly, –ous,* and *–ful.*

(7) **–ig:** This suffix forms from nouns adjectives denoting *full of, characterized by,* or *pertaining to.* English equivalents are *–y, –ful,* and *–ous.* There are many cognates in **–ig** equivalent to English final *y:*

schmutzig, *dirty* (from der Schmutz, *dirt*)

hungrig, *hungry* (from der Hunger, *hunger*)

blutig, *bloody* (from das Blut, *blood*)

mutig, *courageous* (from der Mut, *courage*)

freudig, *joyful* (from die Freude, *joy*)

(8) **–los:** This suffix, usually equivalent to the English suffix *–less,* forms from nouns adjectives denoting *lack of:*

> endlos, *endless* (from das Ende, *end*)
> grundlos, *groundless* or *bottomless* (from der Grund, *ground* or *bottom*)
> zahllos, *countless* (from die Zahl, *number*)
> hilflos, *helpless* (from die Hilfe, *help*)

(9) **–sam:** This suffix (sometimes equivalent to the English suffix *–some*) forms adjectives that denote *causing,* or *a considerable degree of:*

> mühsam, *troublesome* or *toilsome* (from die Mühe, *trouble* or *toil*)
> langsam, *slow* (from lang, *long*)
> biegsam, *flexible* (from biegen, *to bend*)
> wirksam, *effective, operative* (from wirken, *to effect, to operate*)

(10) **–reich:** This suffix forms from nouns adjectives denoting *full of, rich* (or *abounding*) *in:*

> silberreich, *rich in silver* (from das Silber, *silver*)
> liebreich, *loving* or *affectionate* (from die Liebe, *love*)
> ideenreich, *rich in ideas* (from die Ideen, *ideas*)

Note: There is a difference in meaning, depending on stress, between **stein**reich (accented on the first syllable) = *stony* and stein**reich** (stressed on the second syllable) = *very rich.*

Similarly, when **–arm** is used as a suffix, **blut**arm = *of poor blood;* blut**arm** = *very poor.*

(11) **–voll:** This suffix forms from nouns adjectives denoting *full of:*

> gefahrvoll, *full of danger* or *risky* (from die Gefahr, *danger*)
> liebevoll, *loving* or *affectionate* (from die Liebe, *love*)

C. Verbal suffixes. Some of the more common verbal suffixes are: **–eln, –igen, –en, –ern, –ieren,** and **–zen.**

(1) **–eln:** This suffix forms from adjectives, nouns, and other verbs, verbs denoting a *diminutive idea* or the *repetition* of an activity:

> säuseln, *to rustle* (from sausen, *to roar,* as wind)
> handeln, *to trade* (from die Hand, *hand*)

Note: Sometimes the verb combines both senses of diminution and iteration: kränkeln, *to be sickly* (from krank, *sick*).

In the case of verbs derived from nouns ending in **–el,** the verbal suffix **–eln** can hardly be said to have any meaning other than to convert the noun into a verb:

> gurgeln, *to gargle* (from die Gurgel, *throat*)
> prügeln, *to fight* or *thrash* (from der Prügel, *cudgel* or *stick*)

(2) **–igen:** This suffix forms verbs from adjectives and nouns:

> steinigen, *to stone* (from der Stein, *stone*)
>
> befestigen, *to fasten* or *make secure* (from fest, *firm*)

(3) **–en:** This suffix forms factitive verbs from the positive or comparative of adjectives to which it is affixed. A factitive verb indicates accomplishment of the state denoted by the adjective:

> zähmen, *to tame* (from zahm, *tame*)
>
> heizen, *to heat* (from heiß, *hot*)
>
> wärmen, *to warm* (from warm, *warm*)

A number of weak verbs ending in **–nen** are derived from nouns or adjectives in **–en:**

> regnen, *to rain* (from der Regen, *rain*)
>
> trocknen, *to dry* (from trocken, *dry*)
>
> zeichnen, *to draw* or *sketch* (from das Zeichen, *sign, mark*)

(4) **–ern:** This suffix forms from verbs and nouns intensives, iteratives, and factitives:

> klappern, *to rattle* (from klappen, *to clap* or *clatter*)
>
> räuchern, *to (expose to) smoke* (from der Rauch, *smoke*)
>
> steigern, *to raise, strengthen,* or *enhance* (from steigen, *to mount*)

(5) **–ieren:** This suffix forms derivatives which are usually of foreign origin. They are always weak and do not form their past participle in **ge:**

> ich amüsiere mich, *I enjoy myself*
>
> ich habe mich amüsiert, *I enjoyed myself*

(6) **–zen:** This suffix forms verbs that mean *to utter the word or sound* of the root word:

> duzen, *to address with* du (from du, *you*)

§91. PREFIXES

A. Noun and adjective prefixes. A few of the more common noun and adjective prefixes are: **ge–, ur–, un–,** and **erz–.**

(1) **ge–:** This prefix forms from noun stems nouns denoting *collectivity;* from verbal roots, nouns denoting the *action of the verb:*

> das Gebirge, *mountain range* or *mountainous region* (from der Berg, *mountain*)
>
> das Gebüsch, *bushes* (from der Busch, *bush*)
>
> der Geschmack, *taste* (from schmecken, *to taste*)
>
> der Geruch, *smell* (from riechen, *to smell*)

Note: The prefix **ge–** is often equivalent to the English prefix **com–**:

>   der Gefährte, *comrade* or *fellow traveler* (from fahren, *to travel*)
>   der Geselle, *companion,* lit. *roommate* (from der Saal, *room*)

Observe the plural forms **Gebrüder** = *brothers,* and **Geschwister** = *brothers and sisters.*

(2)   **ur–:**   This prefix forms from nouns and adjectives nouns and adjectives denoting *primitive, original,* or *very ancient:*

>   uralt, *very old, ancient* (from alt, *old*)
>   der Urgroßvater, *great-grandfather* (from der Großvater, *grandfather*)
>   die Ururgroßmutter, *great-great-grandmother* (from die Großmutter, *grandmother*)
>   der Urwald, *primeval forest* (from der Wald, *forest*)
>   die Ursache, *the (first) cause* (from die Sache, *thing* or *cause*)
>   der Urzustand, *original condition* (from der Zustand, *condition*)
>   das Urgestein, *primitive rock, mother* or *igneous rock* (from das Gestein, *rock*)

(3)   **un–:**   This prefix *negates* the meaning of the original noun or adjective. English equivalents are ***un–, in–,*** and ***im–.***

>   unmöglich, *impossible* (from möglich, *possible*)
>   unverständlich, *unintelligible* or *incomprehensible* (from verständlich, *comprehensible*)
>   der Undank, *ingratitude* (from der Dank, *thanks*)
>   eine Unzahl, *a great* (i.e. *un*countable) *number* (from die Zahl, *number*)
>   unbemannt, *unmanned* (from bemannt, *manned*)
>   unverdünnt, *undiluted* (from verdünnt, *diluted*)

Note: Sometimes the prefix **un–** may negate or intensify the original meaning: **die Untiefe** (from die Tiefe, *depth*) may mean either *shallowness* or *great depth.*

(4)   **erz–:**   This prefix forms from nouns, nouns denoting *chief, principal,* or *master;* from adjectives, adjectives in which the meaning of the original has been intensified. The English equivalent is ***arch–.***

>   der Erzengel, *archangel* (from der Engel, *angel*)
>   der Erzbischof, *archbishop* (from der Bischof, *bishop*)
>   erzfaul, *extremely lazy* (from faul, *lazy*)

B.   Verbal prefixes.   Verbal prefixes may be either *separable* or *inseparable.* For separable verbal prefixes, see §70. For sentences with inseparable prefixes, see §69.

Inseparable verbal prefixes originally had certain fundamental meanings which are still preserved in some verbs although lost in many others. Only the meaning of **zer**– has remained constant. The inseparable prefixes are: **be**–, **ent**– (or **emp**–), **er**–, **ge**–, **ver**–, and **zer**–.

(1) **be**–: This prefix serves to make a verb transitive (i.e., a verb formed with it may take a direct object): bedienen, *to serve;* bekommen, *to receive;* beantworten, *to answer.*

(2) **ent**– (or **emp**–): This prefix denotes the *beginning of an action* or *separation:* entstehen, *to arise* (or *come into existence*); entzünden, *to inflame;* entlassen, *to dismiss;* entgehen, *to escape;* entlaufen, *to run away;* entsäuern, *to deacidify, to neutralize.*

(3) **er**–: This prefix denotes *origin* or *accomplishment:* erblühen, *to blossom;* erwachen, *to wake;* erleben, *to experience;* erreichen, *to attain;* erraten, *to guess correctly.*

(4) **ge**–: This prefix (which is used to form the past participle) denotes *result* or *completeness* and often *successful action:* gelangen, *to arrive at;* genesen, *to get well;* gewinnen, *to gain.*

The prefix **ge**– originally denoted *with* or *together* (*cf.* noun prefix **ge**– in **A** (1) above) and had perfective force equivalent to the Latin prefix **con**–, as in "*conficere,*" *to accomplish.*

(5) **ver**–: This prefix often denotes that the action of a verb *miscarried:* verführen, *to lead astray;* verspielen, *to lose money in playing;* verkennen, *to misjudge;* verlegen, *to misplace;* sich verschlafen, *to oversleep;* verdrehen, *to distort.*

(6) **zer**–: This prefix is the most constant in meaning of any of the inseparable prefixes. It regularly denotes *going asunder, apart,* or *in pieces;* or *destruction* or *damage* resulting from the action of the original verb: zer**reißen**, *to tear to pieces* (*damage by tearing*); zer**brechen**, *to break to pieces;* zer**schneiden**, *to cut to pieces;* zer**fallen**, *to fall to pieces;* zer**legen**, *to take apart;* zer**streuen**, *to scatter;* zer**knallen**, *to explode.*

§92. COGNATES

The ability to recognize English-German cognates (i.e., words etymologically related) enables a student to understand words which might otherwise be unintelligible to him without the aid of a dictionary.

A. Changes in form and meaning of cognates.   Since English and German both belong to the Indo-European language family, there are, as one might expect, many cognate words. Certain cognates are identical in both form and meaning (Arm, *arm;* Hand, *hand*), others differ slightly in form but have the same meaning (Distel, *thistle*), and some differ in both form and meaning (Stube, *stove*). Orthographic changes follow definite laws of phonology; thus if the

English cognates of **D**istel and **D**urst are *thistle* and *thirst*, we may look for a similar correspondence in many other words—e.g., Leder and *leather*.

B.   Common cognates.   A full study of cognates is beyond the scope of this book. The following are merely some of the more common English-German cognates classified according to *consonant* changes. The symbol > meaning *becomes* is used because the English consonant system antedates Modern German.

(1)   English *p* > German **f, ff,** or **pf**:

sharp, scharf	*open,* offen
up, auf	*ship,* Schiff
leap, laufen	*plant,* Pflanze
deep, tief	*penny,* Pfennig

(2)   English *t* > German **z** or **ß**:

twig, Zweig	*ten,* zehn
to, zu	*curt,* kurz
timber, Zimmer	*foot,* Fuß

(3)   English *k* > German **ch**:

week, Woche	*make,* machen
lark, Lerche	*sake,* Sache
token, Zeichen	*book,* Buch

(4)   English *d* > German **t**:

day, Tag	*word,* Wort
deal, Teil	*God,* Gott
wide, weit	*blade,* Blatt
side, Seite	*deer,* Tier
old, alt	*fodder,* Futter

(5)   English *th* > German **d**:

thou, du	*earth,* Erde
three, drei	*brother,* Bruder
thine, dein	*seethe,* sieden

(6)   English *v* or *f* > German **b**:

silver, Silber	*evil,* übel
harvest, Herbst	*deaf,* taub

(7)   English *y* > German **g**:

day, Tag	*holy,* heilig
way, Weg	*yester(day),* gestern
fly, fliegen	*yawn,* gähnen

APPENDIX II

Declensions
and Paradigms

§93   THE DEFINITE ARTICLE

	SINGULAR			PLURAL
	MASCULINE	FEMININE	NEUTER	ALL GENDERS
Nom.	der	die	das	die
Gen.	des	der	des	der
Dat.	dem	der	dem	den
Acc.	den	die	das	die

§94.   THE DEMONSTRATIVE *DIESER*

	SINGULAR			PLURAL
	MASCULINE	FEMININE	NEUTER	ALL GENDERS
Nom.	dieser	diese	dieses	diese
Gen.	dieses	dieser	dieses	dieser
Dat.	diesem	dieser	diesem	diesen
Acc.	diesen	diese	dieses	diese

Note: All **der**-words are declined like **dieser** (see §8).

§95.   THE INDEFINITE ARTICLE

	SINGULAR		
	MASCULINE	FEMININE	NEUTER
Nom.	ein	eine	ein
Gen.	eines	einer	eines
Dat.	einem	einer	einem
Acc.	einen	eine	ein

Note: **Ein** has no plural forms.

§96. THE POSSESSIVE *MEIN*

	SINGULAR			PLURAL
	MASCULINE	FEMININE	NEUTER	ALL GENDERS
Nom.	mein	meine	mein	meine
Gen.	meines	meiner	meines	meiner
Dat.	meinem	meiner	meinem	meinen
Acc.	meinen	meine	mein	meine

Note: All **ein**-words are declined like **mein** (see §10).

§97. THE DEMONSTRATIVE *DERSELBE*

	SINGULAR			PLURAL
	MASCULINE	FEMININE	NEUTER	ALL GENDERS
Nom.	derselbe	dieselbe	dasselbe	dieselben
Gen.	desselben	derselben	desselben	derselben
Dat.	demselben	derselben	demselben	denselben
Acc.	denselben	dieselbe	dasselbe	dieselben

Note: **Derjenige** is declined like **derselbe**.

§98. NOUN DECLENSION

A. **The strong declension:**

Class I: Plural in –, with frequent umlaut.

SINGULAR

Nom.	der Vater	der Onkel	die Mutter	das Mädchen
Gen.	des Vaters	des Onkels	der Mutter	des Mädchens
Dat.	dem Vater	dem Onkel	der Mutter	dem Mädchen
Acc.	den Vater	den Onkel	die Mutter	das Mädchen

PLURAL

Nom.	die Väter	die Onkel	die Mütter	die Mädchen
Gen.	der Väter	der Onkel	der Mütter	der Mädchen
Dat.	den Vätern	den Onkeln	den Müttern	den Mädchen
Acc.	die Väter	die Onkel	die Mütter	die Mädchen

Class I comprises:

(1) Masculine and neuter nouns ending in –el, –en, and –er, except mixed nouns such as der Bauer, and der Vetter, (see **C** below).

(2) Two feminine nouns: die Mutter (pl. Mütter), *mother* and die Tochter (pl. Töchter), *daughter.*

(3) Neuter diminutives in –**chen** and –**lein**.

(4) Neuter nouns with the prefix **ge**– and ending in –**e**: das Gebäude, *building;* das Gebirge, *mountain range* (or *mountainous region*).

Class II: Plural in –**e,** with frequent umlaut.

SINGULAR

Nom.	der Baum	der Arm	die Hand	der König	das Ereignis
Gen.	des Baumes	des Armes	der Hand	des Königs	des Ereignisses
Dat.	dem Baume	dem Arme	der Hand	dem König	dem Ereignis
Acc.	den Baum	den Arm	die Hand	den König	das Ereignis

PLURAL

Nom.	die Bäume	Arme	Hände	Könige	Ereignisse
Gen.	der Bäume	Arme	Hände	Könige	Ereignisse
Dat.	den Baümen	Armen	Händen	Königen	Ereignissen
Acc.	die Bäume	Arme	Hände	Könige	Ereignisse

Class II comprises:

(1) Monosyllables:

(*a*) Many masculines, which usually take umlaut: der Sohn (pl. Söhne).

Exceptions: The following common nouns, do *not* take umlaut: der Arm, der Dom, der Hund, der Laut, der Mond, der Park, der Schuh, der Tag.

(*b*) Some feminines, which always take umlaut: die Wand (pl. Wände).

(*c*) Some neuters, which do not take umlaut: das Jahr (pl. Jahre).

Exceptions: das Floß (pl. Flöße), *raft;* das Chor (pl. Chöre), *choirloft.*

(2) Polysyllables (usually without umlaut):

(*a*) Masculine nouns ending in –**ig** and –**ling**: der Honig (pl. Honige), *honey;* der Frühling, *spring.*

(*b*) Nouns ending in –**nis** and –**sal** (usually neuter but sometimes feminine): das Erlebnis, *experience;* die Erlaubnis, *permission;* das Schicksal, *fate;* die (*or* das) Trübsal, *affliction.*

Note: Nouns in –**nis** double the final **s** before an ending: das Ereignis (die Ereignisse), *event.*

(*c*) Neuters with the prefix **ge**–: das Gedicht, *poem;* das Gesetz, *law.*

(*d*) Words of foreign origin accented on the last syllable: der Vokal, *vowel;* das Papier, *paper.*

Class III: Plural in –**er**, with umlaut wherever possible.

SINGULAR

Nom.	der	Mann	das	Haus	das	Eigentum
Gen.	des	Mannes	des	Hauses	des	Eigentums
Dat.	dem	Manne	dem	Hause	dem	Eigentum
Acc.	den	Mann	das	Haus	das	Eigentum

PLURAL

Nom.	die Männer	die Häuser	die Eigentümer
Gen.	der Männer	der Häuser	der Eigentümer
Dat.	den Männern	den Häusern	den Eigentümern
Acc.	die Männer	die Häuser	die Eigentümer

Note: There are no feminine nouns in Class III.

Class III comprises:

(1)   Many neuter nouns of one syllable, and some polysyllabic neuters with the prefix **ge–**: das Gesicht, *face;* das Gespenst, *ghost.*

(2)   A few masculines of one syllable.

(3)   Neuters ending in –**tum,** and two masculines: der Reich**tum,** *riches* and der Irr**tum,** *error.*

B.   The weak declension:

SINGULAR

Nom.	der Junge	die Frau	der Student	die Feder
Gen.	des Jungen	der Frau	des Studenten	der Feder
Dat.	dem Jungen	der Frau	dem Studenten	der Feder
Acc.	den Jungen	die Frau	den Studenten	die Feder

PLURAL

Nom.	die Jungen	die Frauen	die Studenten	die Federn
Gen.	der Jungen	der Frauen	der Studenten	der Federn
Dat.	den Jungen	den Frauen	den Studenten	den Federn
Acc.	die Jungen	die Frauen	die Studenten	die Federn

Note: There are no weak neuter nouns. In the weak declension there is never an umlaut in the plural.

The weak declension comprises:

(1)   All feminine nouns of more than one syllable except: die Mutter (pl. Mütter), die Tochter (pl. Töchter), and a few feminine nouns ending in –**nis** and –**sal.**

(2)   Many feminines of one syllable.

(3)   Masculine nouns of one syllable denoting living beings: der Herr, *gentleman, master, Mr.,* or *lord*; der Bär, *bear;* der Mensch, *man.*

(4)   Masculine nouns of more than one syllable ending in –e and denoting living beings: der Junge, *boy;* der Neffe, *nephew;* der Ochse, *ox;* der Affe, *ape* or *monkey.*

(5)   Masculine nouns of foreign origin accented on the last syllable: der Soldat, *soldier;* der Elefant, *elephant;* der Präsident, *president;* der Student, *student.*

C.   The mixed (or irregular) declension:

SINGULAR

Nom.	der Staat	der Professor	das Auge
Gen.	des Staates	des Professors	des Auges
Dat.	dem Staate	dem Professor	dem Auge
Acc.	den Staat	den Professor	das Auge

PLURAL

Nom.	die Staaten	die Professoren	die Augen
Gen.	der Staaten	der Professoren	der Augen
Dat.	den Staaten	den Professoren	den Augen
Acc.	die Staaten	die Professoren	die Augen

The mixed (or irregular) declension comprises:

(1)   A few native German or naturalized nouns: der Schmerz, *pain;* der Staat, *state;* das Auge, *eye;* das Bett, *bed;* das Ende, *end;* das Hemd, *shirt;* das Ohr, *ear;* der Vetter, *male cousin;* der Bauer,[1] *peasant* (or *farmer*).

(2)   Masculine nouns of foreign origin ending in –**or,** in which the short o becomes long in the plural by a shift in syllabic stress, e.g., der Proféssor, pl. die Professóren.

(3)   Neuter nouns in –**um** of foreign (mostly Latin) origin, with the plural in –**en**:

	SINGULAR	PLURAL
Nom.	das Gymnasium	die Gymnasien
Gen.	des Gymnasiums	der Gymnasien
Dat.	dem Gymnasium	den Gymnasien
Acc.	das Gymnasium	die Gymnasien

Other neuter nouns of this type are: Datum (pl. Daten), *date;* Museum, *museum;* Observatorium, *observatory;* Partizipium, *participle;* Territorium, *territory.*

---

[1]Der **Bauer** often has weak endings (–n) in the singular.

(4)   Foreign neuters in –il and –al with the plural in –ien: das Fossil (des Fossils, die Fossilien), *fossil;* das Mineral (des Minerals, die Mineralien), *mineral.*

(5)   Foreign nouns with plural forms in –s in all cases: das Hotel (des Hotels, die Hotels), *hotel;* das Sofa (des Sofas, die Sofas), *sofa;* das Auto (des Autos, die Autos), *auto;* das Kino, (des Kinos, die Kinos), *cinema;* das Radio (des Radios, die Radios), *radio;* der Tee (des Tees, die Tees), *tea;* das Echo (des Echos), *echo.*

(6)   A few foreign nouns ending in –s have the same form throughout the singular and plural, e.g., das Relais (*relay*), a word now common in technical vocabulary, especially in compounded forms: der Funk-Relais-Satellit (*radio-relay satellite*).

§99.   ADJECTIVE DECLENSION

A.   The strong declension:

SINGULAR

Nom.	guter Tee	rote Seide	kaltes Bier
Gen.	guten Tees	roter Seide	kalten Bieres
Dat.	gutem Tee	roter Seide	kaltem Biere
Acc.	guten Tee	rote Seide	kaltes Bier

PLURAL

Nom.	treue Freunde	schöne Freuen	reiche Länder
Gen.	treuer Freunde	schöner Frauen	reicher Länder
Dat.	treuen Freunden	schönen Frauen	reichen Ländern
Acc.	treue Freunde	schöne Frauen	reiche Länder

B.   The weak declension:

SINGULAR

Nom.	der gute Freund	die liebe Tochter	das große Haus
Gen.	des guten Freundes	der lieben Tochter	des großen Hauses
Dat.	dem guten Freunde	der lieben Tochter	dem großen Hause
Acc.	den guten Freund	die liebe Tochter	das große Haus

PLURAL

Nom.	die guten Freunde	die lieben Töchter	die großen Häuser
Gen.	der guten Freunde	der lieben Töchter	der großen Häuser
Dat.	den guten Freunden	den lieben Töchtern	den großen Häusern
Acc.	die guten Freunde	die lieben Töchter	die großen Häuser

Note: The weak adjective declension occurs after any **der**-word (see §8).

C. The mixed declension:

SINGULAR

Nom.	ein	kleiner Stuhl	eine	rote Rose	ein	kleines Zimmer
Gen.	eines	kleinen Stuhles	einer	roten Rose	eines	kleinen Zimmers
Dat.	einem	kleinen Stuhle	einer	roten Rose	einem	kleinen Zimmer
Acc.	einen	kleinen Stuhl	eine	rote Rose	ein	kleines Zimmer

Note:

(1) The mixed declension uses the masculine and neuter nominative singular and the neuter accusative singular of the strong declension; it takes all other forms, singular and plural, from the weak declension.

(2) The mixed declension occurs after **ein**-words.

§100. DECLENSION OF PROPER NAMES

Nom.	Goethe	Amerika	Karl der Große
Gen.	Goethes	Amerikas	Karls des Großen
Dat.	Goethe	Amerika	Karl dem Großen
Acc.	Goethe	Amerika	Karl den Großen

Nom.	König Friedrich	der König Friedrich
Gen.	König Friedrichs	des Königs Friedrich
Dat.	König Friedrich	dem König Friedrich
Acc.	König Friedrich	den König Friedrich

§101. DECLENSION OF PRONOUNS

A. Personal pronouns:

SINGULAR

Nom.	ich (*I*)	du (*you*)	er (*he*)	sie (*she*)	es (*it*)	Sie (*you*)
Gen.	(meiner)	(deiner)	(seiner)	(ihrer)	(seiner)	(Ihrer)
Dat.	mir	dir	ihm	ihr	ihm	Ihnen
Acc.	mich	dich	ihn	sie	es	Sie

PLURAL

Nom.	wir (*we*)	ihr (*you*)	sie (*they* [all genders])	Sie (*you*)
Gen.	(unser)	(euer)	(ihrer)	(Ihrer)
Dat.	uns	euch	ihnen	Ihnen
Acc.	uns	euch	sie	Sie

Note: The genitive forms are given in parentheses because they are rare.

B. **Interrogative pronouns:**

	MASCULINE AND FEMININE	NEUTER
Nom.	wer	was
Gen.	wessen	(wes, wessen)
Dat.	wem	———
Acc.	wen	was

C. **Demonstrative pronouns:**

(1) **Dieser** and **jener** are declined like the definite article (see paradigm in §94).

(2) For the declension of **derselbe** and **derjenige,** see §97.

(3) **Der** as demonstrative pronoun is declined like the relative pronoun **welcher** see **D** below).

(*a*) **Dieser, jener, derselbe, derjenige,** and **der** are also demonstrative adjectives.

(*b*) As demonstrative adjective, **der** is declined like the definite article.

D. **Relative pronouns:**

	SINGULAR			PLURAL
	MASCULINE	FEMININE	NEUTER	ALL GENDERS
Nom.	der, welcher	die, welche	das, welches	die, welche
Gen.	dessen	deren	dessen	deren
Dat.	dem, welchem	der, welcher	dem, welchem	denen, welchen
Acc.	den, welchen	die, welche	das, welches	die, welche

Note: As relative pronouns, **wer** and **was** are declined like the interrogatives **wer** and **was** (see §101 **B**).

§102. THE AUXILIARY VERBS: *HABEN, SEIN, WERDEN*

A. **The indicative mood:**

(1) PRESENT (*I have; I am; I become*)

ich habe	ich bin	ich werde
du hast	du bist	du wirst
er hat	er ist	er wird
wir haben	wir sind	wir werden
ihr habt	ihr seid	ihr werdet
sie haben	sie sind	sie werden

(2) SIMPLE PAST (*I had* or *have had; I was* or *have been; I became* or *have become*)

ich hatte	ich war	ich wurde
du hattest	du warst	du wurdest
er hatte	er war	er wurde
wir hatten	wir waren	wir wurden
ihr hattet	ihr wart	ihr wurdet
sie hatten	sie waren	sie wurden

(3) COMPOUND PAST (*same as* SIMPLE PAST)

ich habe gehabt	ich bin gewesen	ich bin geworden
du hast gehabt	du bist gewesen	du bist geworden
er hat gehabt	er ist gewesen	er ist geworden
wir haben gehabt	wir sind gewesen	wir sind geworden
ihr habt gehabt	ihr seid gewesen	ihr seid geworden
sie haben gehabt	sie sind gewesen	sie sind geworden

(4) PAST PERFECT (*I had had; I had been; I had become*)

ich hatte gehabt	ich war gewesen	ich war geworden
du hattest gehabt	du warst gewesen	du warst geworden
er hatte gehabt	er war gewesen	er war geworden
wir hatten gehabt	wir waren gewesen	wir waren geworden
ihr hattet gehabt	ihr wart gewesen	ihr wart geworden
sie hatten gehabt	sie waren gewesen	sie waren geworden

(5) FUTURE (*I shall have; I shall be; I shall become*)

ich werde haben	ich werde sein	ich werde werden
du wirst haben	du wirst sein	du wirst werden
er wird haben	er wird sein	er wird werden
wir werden haben	wir werden sein	wir werden werden
ihr werdet haben	ihr werdet sein	ihr werdet werden
sie werden haben	sie werden sein	sie werden werden

(6) FUTURE PERFECT (*I shall have had; I shall have been; I shall have become*)

ich werde
du wirst
er wird
wir werden } gehabt haben   gewesen sein   geworden sein
ihr werdet
sie werden

B.   The subjunctive mood:

(1)   PRESENT SUBJUNCTIVE I

ich habe	ich sei	ich werde
du habest	du seiest	du werdest
er habe	er sei	er werde
wir haben	wir seien	wir werden
ihr habet	ihr seiet	ihr werdet
sie haben	sie seien	sie werden

(2)   PRESENT SUBJUNCTIVE II

ich hätte	ich wäre	ich würde
du hättest	du wärest	du würdest
er hätte	er wäre	er würde
wir hätten	wir wären	wir würden
ihr hättet	ihr wäret	ihr würdet
sie hätten	sie wären	sie würden

(3)   PAST SUBJUNCTIVE I

ich habe	gehabt	ich sei	gewesen	ich sei	geworden
du habest	gehabt	du seiest	gewesen	du seiest	geworden
er habe	gehabt	er sei	gewesen	er sei	geworden
wir haben	gehabt	wir seien	gewesen	wir seien	geworden
ihr habet	gehabt	ihr seiet	gewesen	ihr seiet	geworden
sie haben	gehabt	sie seien	gewesen	sie seien	geworden

(4)   PAST SUBJUNCTIVE II

ich hätte	gehabt	ich wäre	gewesen	ich wäre	geworden
du hättest	gehabt	du wärest	gewesen	du wärest	geworden
er hätte	gehabt	er wäre	gewesen	er wäre	geworden
wir hätten	gehabt	wir wären	gewesen	wir wären	geworden
ihr hättet	gehabt	ihr wäret	gewesen	ihr wäret	geworden
sie hätten	gehabt	sie wären	gewesen	sie wären	geworden

(5)   FUTURE SUBJUNCTIVE I

ich werde	haben	ich werde	sein	ich werde	werden
du werdest	haben	du werdest	sein	du werdest	werden
er werde	haben	er werde	sein	er werde	werden
wir werden	haben	wir werden	sein	wir werden	werden
ihr werdet	haben	ihr werdet	sein	ihr werdet	werden
sie werden	haben	sie werden	sein	sie werden	werden

(6) FUTURE PERFECT SUBJUNCTIVE I

ich werde ⎫
du werdest ⎪
er werde ⎪
              ⎬ gehabt haben   gewesen sein   geworden sein
wir werden ⎪
ihr werdet ⎪
sie werden ⎭

C. The conditional mood:

(1) PRESENT

ich würde ⎫
du würdest ⎪
er würde ⎪
              ⎬ haben   sein   werden
wir würden ⎪
ihr würdet ⎪
sie würden ⎭

(2) PAST

ich würde ⎫
du würdest ⎪
er würde ⎪
              ⎬ gehabt haben   gewesen sein   geworden sein
wir würden ⎪
ihr würdet ⎪
sie würden ⎭

D. The imperative mood:

	SINGULAR	
habe!	sei!	werde!
haben Sie!	seien Sie!	werden Sie!
	PLURAL	
habt!	seid!	werdet!
haben Sie!	seien Sie!	werden Sie!

E. Infinitives:

(1) PRESENT: haben, sein, werden.
(2) PAST: gehabt haben, gewesen sein, geworden sein.

F. Participles:

(1) PRESENT: habend, seiend, werdend. (These forms are rarely used.)
(2) PAST: gehabt, gewesen, geworden.

§103. THE WEAK CONJUGATION

The weak verb **lernen** (**lernte, hat gelernt**) is conjugated as follows:

A. The indicative mood: **B. The subjunctive mood:**

(1) PRESENT (*I learn, am*   (1) PRESENT SUBJ. I
      learning, do learn)

    ich lerne   ich lerne
    du lernst   du lernest
    er lernt   er lerne
    wir lernen   wir lernen
    ihr lernt   ihr lernet
    sie lernen   sie lernen

(2) SIMPLE PAST (*I learned, have*   (2) PRESENT SUBJ. II
      learned)

    ich lernte   ich lernte
    du lerntest   du lerntest
    er lernte   er lernte
    wir lernten   wir lernten
    ihr lerntet   ihr lerntet
    sie lernten   sie lernten

(3) COMPOUND PAST (*same*   (3) PAST SUBJ. I
      as SIMPLE PAST)

    ich habe gelernt   ich habe gelernt
    du hast   gelernt   du habest gelernt
    er hat   gelernt   er habe gelernt
    wir haben gelernt   wir haben gelernt
    ihr habt gelernt   ihr habet gelernt
    sie haben gelernt   sie haben gelernt

(4) PAST PERFECT (*I had*   (4) PAST SUBJ. II
      learned)

    ich hatte   gelernt   ich hätte   gelernt
    du hattest gelernt   du hättest gelernt
    er hatte   gelernt   er hätte   gelernt
    wir hatten gelernt   wir hätten gelernt
    ihr hattet gelernt   ihr hättet gelernt
    sie hatten gelernt   sie hätten gelernt

(5) FUTURE (*I shall learn*)

ich werde   lernen
du wirst   lernen
er   wird   lernen

wir werden lernen
ihr werdet lernen
sie werden lernen

(5) FUTURE SUBJ. I

ich werde   lernen
du werdest lernen
er   werde   lernen

wir werden lernen
ihr werdet lernen
sie werden lernen

(6) FUTURE PERFECT (*I shall have learned*)

ich werde   gelernt haben
du wirst   gelernt haben
er   wird   gelernt haben

wir werden gelernt haben
ihr werdet gelernt haben
sie werden gelernt haben

(6) FUTURE PERF. SUBJ. I

ich werde   gelernt haben
du werdest gelernt haben
er   werde   gelernt haben

wir werden gelernt haben
ihr werdet gelernt haben
sie werden gelernt haben

C.   The conditional mood:

(1) PRESENT

ich würde   lernen
du würdest lernen
er   würde   lernen

wir würden lernen
ihr würdet lernen
sie würden lernen

(2) PAST

ich würde   gelernt haben
du würdest gelernt haben
er   würde   gelernt haben

wir würden gelernt haben
ihr würdet gelernt haben
sie würden gelernt haben

D.   The imperative mood:

SINGULAR	PLURAL
lerne!	lernt!
lernen Sie!	lernen Sie!

E.   Infinitives:

(1) PRESENT: lernen
(2) PAST: gelernt haben

F.   Participles:

(1) PRESENT: lernend
(2) PAST: gelernt

Note: For passive forms (of the verb **sehen**) see §108.

§104. THE STRONG CONJUNGATION

A. Sehen. The strong verb **sehen** (**sah, hat gesehen**) is conjugated as follows:

(1) **The indicative mood:**

    (*a*) PRESENT (*I see, I am seeing, I do see*)

ich sehe
du siehst
er sieht
wir sehen
ihr seht
sie sehen

    (*b*) SIMPLE PAST (*I saw, I have seen*)

ich sah
du sahst
er sah
wir sahen
ihr saht
sie sahen

    (*c*) COMPOUND PAST (*same as* SIMPLE PAST)

ich habe gesehen
du hast   gesehen
er hat   gesehen
wir haben gesehen
ihr habt gesehen
sie haben gesehen

    (*d*) PAST PERFECT (*I had seen*)

ich hatte gesehen
du hattest gesehen
er hatte gesehen
wir hatten gesehen
ihr hattet gesehen
sie hatten gesehen

(2) **The subjunctive mood:**

    (*a*) PRESENT SUBJ. I

ich sehe
du sehest
er sehe
wir sehen
ihr sehet
sie sehen

    (*b*) PRESENT SUBJ. II

ich sähe
du sähest
er sähe
wir sähen
ihr sähet
sie sähen

    (*c*) PAST SUBJ. I

ich habe gesehen
du habest gesehen
er habe gesehen
wir haben gesehen
ihr habet gesehen
sie haben gesehen

    (*d*) PAST SUBJ. II

ich hätte gesehen
du hättest gesehen
er hätte gesehen
wir hätten gesehen
ihr hättet gesehen
sie hätten gesehen

(e) FUTURE (*I shall see*)   (e) FUTURE SUBJ. I

ich werde sehen   ich werde sehen
du wirst   sehen   du werdest sehen
er wird   sehen   er werde   sehen

wir werden sehen   wir werden sehen
ihr werdet sehen   ihr werdet sehen
sie werden sehen   sie werden sehen

(f) FUTURE PERFECT   (f) FUTURE PERF. SUBJ. I
     (*I shall have seen*)

ich werde gesehen haben   ich werde   gesehen haben
du wirst   gesehen haben   du werdest gesehen haben
er wird   gesehen haben   er werde   gesehen haben

wir werden gesehen haben   wir werden gesehen haben
ihr werdet gesehen haben   ihr werdet gesehen haben
sie werden gesehen haben   sie werden gesehen haben

(3) **The conditional mood:**

(a) PRESENT   (b) PAST

ich würde sehen   ich würde   gesehen haben
du würdest sehen   du würdest gesehen haben
er würde   sehen   er würde   gesehen haben

wir würden sehen   wir würden gesehen haben
ihr würdet sehen   ihr würdet gesehen haben
sie würden sehen   sie würden gesehen haben

(4) **The imperative mood:**

SINGULAR   PLURAL

sieh!   seht!
sehen Sie!   sehen Sie!

(5) **Infinitives:**

(a) PRESENT: sehen
(b) PAST: gesehen haben

(6) **Participles:**

(a) PRESENT: sehend
(b) PAST: gesehen

Note: Passive forms of the verb **sehen** are given in §108.

B. Kommen. The strong verb **kommen (kam, ist gekommen)** is conjugated as follows:

(1) **The indicative mood:**   (2) **The subjunctive mood:**

(*a*) PRESENT (*I come, etc.*)

ich komme
du kommst
er kommt
wir kommen
ihr kommt
sie kommen

(*a*) PRESENT SUBJ. I

ich komme
du kommest
er komme
wir kommen
ihr kommet
sie kommen

(*b*) SIMPLE PAST (*I came, have come*)

ich kam
du kamst
er kam
wir kamen
ihr kamt
sie kamen

(*b*) PRESENT SUBJ. II

ich käme
du kämest
er käme
wir kämen
ihr kämet
sie kämen

(*c*) COMPOUND PAST
(*same as* SIMPLE PAST)

ich bin gekommen
du bist gekommen
er ist gekommen
wir sind gekommen
ihr seid gekommen
sie sind gekommen

(*c*) PAST SUBJ. I

ich sei gekommen
du seiest gekommen
er sei gekommen
wir seien gekommen
ihr seiet gekommen
sie seien gekommen

(*d*) PAST PERFECT (*I had come*)

ich war gekommen
du warst gekommen
er war gekommen
wir waren gekommen
ihr wart gekommen
sie waren gekommen

(*d*) PAST SUBJ. II

ich wäre gekommen
du wärest gekommen
er wäre gekommen
wir wären gekommen
ihr wäret gekommen
sie wären gekommen

(*e*) FUTURE (*I shall come*)

ich werde kommen
du wirst kommen
er wird kommen

(*e*) FUTURE SUBJ. I

ich werde kommen
du werdest kommen
er werde kommen

wir werden kommen	wir werden kommen
ihr werdet kommen	ihr werdet kommen
sie werden kommen	sie werden kommen

(*f*) FUTURE PERFECT (*I shall have come*)   (*f*) FUTURE PERF. SUBJ. I

ich werde gekommen sein	ich werde gekommen sein
du wirst gekommen sein	du werdest gekommen sein
er wird gekommen sein	er werde gekommen sein
wir werden gekommen sein	wir werden gekommen sein
ihr werdet gekommen sein	ihr werdet gekommen sein
sie werden gekommen sein	sie werden gekommen sein

(3) **The conditional mood:**

(*a*) PRESENT   (*b*) PAST

ich würde kommen	ich würde gekommen sein
du würdest kommen	du würdest gekommen sein
er würde kommen	er würde gekommen sein
wir würden kommen	wir würden gekommen sein
ihr würdet kommen	ihr würdet gekommen sein
sie würden kommen	sie würden gekommen sein

(4) **The imperative mood:**

SINGULAR	PLURAL
komme!	kommt!
kommen Sie!	kommen Sie!

(5) **Infinitives:**   (6) **Participles:**

(*a*) PRESENT: kommen   (*a*) PRESENT: kommend
(*b*) PAST: gekommen sein   (*b*) PAST: gekommen

§105. SEPARABLE VERBS

The separable verb **anfangen (fing an, hat angefangen)** is conjugated as follows:

A. The indicative mood: **B. The subjunctive mood:**

(1) PRESENT (*I begin, etc.*)   (1) PRESENT SUBJ. I

   ich fange an   ich fange an
   du fängst an, *etc.*   du fangest an, *etc.*

(2) SIMPLE PAST (*I began, etc.*)   (2) PRESENT SUBJ. II

   ich fing an, *etc.*   ich finge an, *etc.*

(3) COMPOUND PAST (*same as*   (3) PAST SUBJ. I
    SIMPLE PAST)

    ich habe angefangen   ich habe   angefangen
    du hast angefangen, *etc.*   du habest angefangen, *etc.*

(4) PAST PERFECT (*I had begun*)   (4) PAST SUBJ. II

    ich hatte angefangen, *etc.*   ich hätte angefangen, *etc.*

(5) FUTURE (*I shall begin*)   (5) FUTURE SUBJ. I

    ich werde anfangen   ich werde   anfangen
    du wirst anfangen, *etc.*   du werdest anfangen, *etc.*

(6) FUTURE PERFECT (*I shall*   (6) FUTURE PERFECT SUBJ. I
    have begun)

    ich werde angefangen haben   ich werde   angefangen
    du wirst angefangen haben   haben
    etc.   du werdest angefangen
                                          haben, *etc.*

C. The conditional mood:

(1) PRESENT: ich würde   (2) PAST: ich würde angefangen
    anfangen, *etc.*   haben, *etc.*

D. Imperatives:

SINGULAR   PLURAL
fange an!   fangt an!
fangen Sie an!   fangen Sie an!

E. Infinitives: ## F. Participles:

(1) PRESENT: anfangen   (1) PRESENT: anfangend
(2) PAST: angefangen haben   (2) PAST: angefangen

§106. INSEPARABLE VERBS

The inseparable verb **beginnen (begann, hat begonnen)** is conjugated as
follows:

A. The indicative mood: ## B. The subjunctive mood:

(1) PRESENT (*I begin, etc.*)   (1) PRESENT SUBJ. I

    ich beginne   ich beginne
    du beginnst, *etc.*   du beginnest, *etc.*

(2) SIMPLE PAST (*I began, etc.*)
ich begann, *etc.*

(2) PRESENT SUBJ. II
ich begönne (*or* begänne), *etc.*

(3) COMPOUND PAST
ich habe begonnen
du hast begonnen, *etc.*

(3) PAST SUBJ. I
ich habe   begonnen
du habest begonnen, *etc.*

(4) PAST PERFECT (*I had begun*)
ich hatte begonnen, *etc.*

(4) PAST SUBJ. II
ich hätte begonnen, *etc.*

(5) FUTURE (*I shall begin*)
ich werde beginnen
du wirst beginnen, *etc.*

(5) FUTURE SUBJ. I
ich werde   beginnen
du werdest beginnen, *etc.*

(6) FUTURE PERFECT (*I shall have begun*)
ich werde begonnen haben
du wirst begonnen haben
etc.

(6) FUTURE PERFECT SUBJ. I
ich werde   begonnen haben
du werdest begonnen haben
etc.

C. The conditional mood:

(1) PRESENT: ich würde beginnen, *etc.*

(2) PAST: ich würde begonnen haben, *etc.*

D. The imperative mood:

SINGULAR
beginne!
beginnen Sie!

PLURAL
beginnt!
beginnen Sie!

E. Infinitives:

(1) PRESENT: beginnen
(2) PAST: begonnen haben

F. Participles:

(1) PRESENT: beginnend
(2) PAST: begonnen

§107. REFLEXIVE VERBS

A. Direct reflexives. The direct reflexive verb **sich setzen (setzte sich, hat sich gesetzt)** is conjugated as follows:

(1) **The indicative mood:**

(*a*) PRESENT (*I sit down, etc.*)

ich setze   mich
du setzt   dich
er setzt   sich

wir setzen uns
ihr setzt   euch
sie setzen sich

(*b*) SIMPLE PAST (*I sat
    or have sat down*)

ich setzte   mich
du setztest dich
er setzte   sich

wir setzten uns
ihr setztet euch
sie setzten sich

(*c*) COMPOUND PAST (*same
    as* SIMPLE PAST)

ich habe mich gesetzt
du hast dich gesetzt, *etc.*

(*d*) PAST PERFECT (*I had sat
    down*)

ich hatte mich gesetzt, *etc.*

(*e*) FUTURE (*I shall sit down*)

ich werde mich setzen
du wirst dich setzen, *etc.*

(*f*) FUTURE PERFECT (*I shall
    have sat down*)

ich werde mich gesetzt haben
du wirst dich gesetzt haben
etc.

(2) **The subjunctive mood:**

(*a*) PRESENT SUBJ. I

ich setze   mich
du setzest dich
er setze   sich

wir setzen uns
ihr setzet euch
sie setzen sich

(*b*) PRESENT SUBJ. II

ich setzte   mich
du setztest dich
er setzte   sich

wir setzten uns
ihr setztet euch
sie setzten sich

(*c*) PAST SUBJ. I

ich habe   mich gesetzt
du habest dich gesetzt, *etc.*

(*d*) PAST SUBJ. II

ich hätte mich gesetzt, *etc.*

(*e*) FUTURE SUBJ. I

ich werde   mich setzen
du werdest dich setzen, *etc.*

(*f*) FUTURE PERF. SUBJ. I

ich werde   mich gesetzt
haben
du werdest dich gesetzt
haben, *etc.*

(3) **The conditional mood:**

(*a*) PRESENT: ich würde mich
    setzen, *etc.*

(*b*) PAST: ich würde mich
    gesetzt haben, *etc.*

(4) **The imperative mood:**

SINGULAR	PLURAL
setze dich!	setzt euch!
setzen Sie sich!	setzen Sie sich!

(5) **Infinitives:**

   (*a*) PRESENT: sich setzen

   (*b*) PAST: sich gesetzt haben

(6) **Participles:**

   (*a*) PRESENT: sich setzend

   (*b*) PAST: sich gesetzt

B. **Reflexives that take the dative.** The reflexive verb **sich schaden (schadete sich, hat sich geschadet)** is conjugated as follows:

(1) **The indicative mood:**

   (*a*) PRESENT (*I hurt myself*)

ich schade   mir
du schadest dir
er schadet sich

wir schaden uns
ihr schadet euch
sie schaden sich

   (*b*) SIMPLE PAST: (*I hurt or have hurt myself*)

ich schadete mir, *etc.*

   (*c*) COMPOUND PAST (*same as* SIMPLE PAST)

ich habe mir geschadet
du hast dir geschadet, *etc.*

   (*d*) PAST PERFECT: (*I had hurt myself*)

ich hatte mir geschadet, *etc.*

   (*e*) FUTURE (*I shall hurt myself*)

ich werde mir schaden
du wirst dir schaden, *etc.*

   (*f*) FUTURE PERFECT (*I shall have hurt myself*)

ich werde mir geschadet haben
du wirst dir geschadet haben
etc.

(2) **The subjunctive mood:**

   (*a*) PRESENT SUBJ. I

ich schade mir
du schadest dir
er schade sich

wir schaden uns
ihr schadet euch
sie schaden sich

   (*b*) PRESENT SUBJ. II

ich schadete mir, *etc.*

   (*c*) PAST SUBJ. I

ich habe mir geschadet
du habest dir geschadet

   (*d*) PAST SUBJ. II

ich hätte mir geschadet, *etc.*

   (*e*) FUTURE SUBJ. I

ich werde mir schaden
du werdest dir schaden, *etc.*

   (*f*) FUTURE PERF. SUBJ. I

ich werde mir geschadet haben
du werdest dir geschadet haben, *etc.*

(3) **The conditional mood:**

    (*a*) PRESENT: ich würde mir   (*b*) PAST: ich würde mir
        schaden, *etc.*   geschadet haben, *etc.*

(4) **The imperative mood:**

    SINGULAR   PLURAL

    schade dir!   schadet euch!
    schaden Sie sich!   schaden Sie sich!

(5) **Infinitives:**   (6) **Participles:**

    (*a*) PRESENT: sich schaden   (*a*) PRESENT: sich schadend
    (*b*) PAST: sich geschadet   (*b*) PAST: sich geschadet
                haben

§108. THE PASSIVE VOICE

The passive of **sehen (sah, hat gesehen)** is conjugated as follows:

A. The indicative mood: **B. The subjunctive mood:**

(1) PRESENT [*I am (being)*   (1) PRESENT SUBJ. I
    seen, etc.]:

    ich werde gesehen   ich werde gesehen
    du wirst gesehen   du werdest gesehen
    er wird gesehen   er werde gesehen
    wir werden gesehen   wir werden gesehen
    ihr werdet gesehen   ihr werdet gesehen
    sie werden gesehen   sie werden gesehen

(2) SIMPLE PAST [*I was (being)*   (2) PRESENT SUBJ. II
    seen]

    ich wurde gesehen   ich würde gesehen
    du wurdest gesehen   du würdest gesehen
    er wurde gesehen   er würde gesehen
    wir wurden gesehen   wir würden gesehen
    ihr wurdet gesehen   ihr würdet gesehen
    sie wurden gesehen   sie würden gesehen

(3) COMPOUND PAST (*same*   (3) PAST SUBJ. I
    as SIMPLE PAST)

    ich bin gesehen worden   ich sei   gesehen worden
    du bist gesehen worden   du seiest gesehen worden
    er ist gesehen worden   er sei   gesehen worden

wir sind gesehen worden   wir seien gesehen worden
ihr seid gesehen worden   ihr seiet gesehen worden
sie sind gesehen worden   sie seien gesehen worden

(4) PAST PERFECT (*I had been*   (4) PAST SUBJ. II
seen*)

ich war   gesehen worden   ich wäre   gesehen worden
du warst gesehen worden   du wärest gesehen worden
er war   gesehen worden   er wäre   gesehen worden

wir waren gesehen worden   wir wären gesehen worden
ihr wart   gesehen worden   ihr wäret gesehen worden
sie waren gesehen worden   sie wären gesehen worden

(5) FUTURE (*I shall be seen*)   (5) FUTURE SUBJ. I

ich werde gesehen werden   ich werde gesehen werden
du wirst   gesehen werden   du werdest gesehen werden
er wird   gesehen werden   er werde   gesehen werden

wir werden gesehen werden   wir werden gesehen werden
ihr werdet gesehen werden   ihr werdet gesehen werden
sie werden gesehen werden   sie werden gesehen werden

(6) FUTURE PERFECT (*I shall* (6) FUTURE PERFECT SUBJ. I
have been seen)

ich werde ⎫   ich werde ⎫
du wirst ⎪   du werdest⎪
er wird   ⎬ gesehen worden sein   er werde   ⎬ gesehen worden sein
wir werden⎪   wir werden⎪
ihr werdet⎪   ihr werdet⎪
sie werden⎭   sie werden⎭

C. The conditional mood:

(1) PRESENT   (2) PAST

ich würde ⎫   ich würde ⎫
du würdest⎪   du würdest⎪
er würde ⎬ gesehen werden   er würde ⎬ gesehen worden sein
wir würden⎪   wir würden⎪
ihr würdet⎪   ihr würdet⎪
sie würden⎭   sie würden⎭

D. The imperative mood:

SINGULAR   PLURAL

sei (*or* werde) gesehen!   seid (*or* werdet) gesehen!
seien (*or* werden) Sie gesehen! seien (*or* werden) Sie gesehen!

Note: The passive imperative is quite rare. See §74 **E** for examples.

E. Infinitives:

    (1) PRESENT: gesehen werden
    (2) PAST: gesehen worden sein

F. Participles:

    (1) PRESENT: —
    (2) PAST: gesehen

§109. THE MODAL AUXILIARIES

The modals **können, wollen, müssen, mögen, dürfen,** and **sollen** are conjugated as follows:

A. The indicative mood:

    (1) PRESENT:

	KÖNNEN	WOLLEN	MÜSSEN	MÖGEN	DÜRFEN	SOLLEN
ich	kann	will	muß	mag	darf	soll
du	kannst	willst	mußt	magst	darfst	sollst
er	kann	will	muß	mag	darf	soll
wir	können	wollen	müssen	mögen	dürfen	sollen
ihr	könnt	wollt	müßt	mögt	dürft	sollt
sie	können	wollen	müssen	mögen	dürfen	sollen

    (2) SIMPLE PAST: ich konnte, wollte, mußte, mochte, durfte, sollte

    (3) COMPOUND PAST: ich habe gekonnt, gewollt, gemußt, gemocht, gedurft, gesollt

Note: Participles assume the form of an infinitive when used with dependent infinitives.

    (4) PAST PERFECT: ich hatte gekonnt, gewollt, gemußt, gemocht, gedurft, gesollt

    (5) FUTURE: ich werde können, wollen, müssen, mögen, dürfen, sollen

    (6) FUTURE PERFECT: ich werde gekonnt haben, gewollt haben, gemußt haben, gemocht haben, gedurft haben, gesollt haben

B. The subjunctive mood:

    (1) PRESENT I: ich könne, wolle, müsse, möge, dürfe, solle

    (2) PRESENT II: ich könnte, wollte, müsste, möchte, dürfte, sollte

(3) PAST I: ich habe   gekonnt, gewollt, gemusst, *etc.*

(4) PAST II: ich hätte   gekonnt, gewollt, *etc.*

(5) FUTURE I: ich werde   können, wollen, müssen, *etc.*

(6) FUTURE PERFECT I: ich werde   gekonnt haben, gewollt haben, gemusst haben, *etc.*

C. The conditional mood. The conditional of modals is quite rare and should be avoided.

D. The imperative mood:

SINGULAR	PLURAL
wolle!	wollt!
wollen Sie!	wollen Sie!

Note: **Wollen** is the only modal having imperative forms.

E. Infinitives:

(1) PRESENT: können, wollen, müssen, mögen, dürfen, sollen.

(2) PAST: gekonnt haben, gewollt haben, gemußt haben, gemocht haben, gedurft haben, gesollt haben.

F. Participles:

(1) PRESENT: könnend, wollend, müssend, mögend, dürfend, sollend.

(2) PAST: gekonnt, gewollt, gemußt, gemocht, gedurft, gesollt.

Note: The present participle of modals is very rarely used.

§110. IRREGULAR WEAK VERBS AND THE PRESENT INDICATIVE OF *WISSEN*

A. Irregular weak verbs:

INFINITIVE	PAST INDICATIVE	COMP. PAST INDICATIVE	PRESENT INDICATIVE	PRESENT SUBJ. II	IMPERATIVE (sing. fam.)	
brennen	brannte	hat gebrannt	er brennt	brennte	brenn(e)	*to burn*
rennen	rannte	ist gerannt	er rennt	rennte	renn(e)	*to run*
kennen	kannte	hat gekannt	er kennt	kennte	kenn(e)	*to know*
nennen	nannte	hat genannt	er nennt	nennte	nenn(e)	*to name*
senden	sandte (sendete)	hat gesandt (gesendet)	er sendet	sendete	send(e)	*to send*
wenden	wandte (wendete)	hat gewandt (gewendet)	er wendet	wendete	wend(e)	*to turn*
denken	dachte	hat gedacht	er denkt	dächte	denk(e)	*to think*
bringen	brachte	hat gebracht	er bringt	brächte	bring(e)	*to bring*
wissen	wußte	hat gewußt	er weiß	wüßte	wisse	*to know*

B. Present indicative of *wissen*. Although not a modal auxiliary, **wissen** resembles modals in the conjugation of its present indicative:

SINGULAR	PLURAL
ich weiß	wir wissen
du weißt	ihr wißt
er weiß	sie wissen

§111. PRINCIPAL PARTS OF STRONG AND IRREGULAR VERBS

INFINITIVE	PAST INDICATIVE	COMP. PAST INDICATIVE	PRESENT INDICATIVE	PRESENT SUBJ. II	IMPERATIVE (sing. fam.)	
backen	buk	hat gebacken	er bäckt	büke	back(e)	to bake
befehlen	befahl	hat befohlen	er befiehlt	beföhle	befiehl	to command
beginnen	begann	hat begonnen	er beginnt	begönne (begänne)	beginn(e)	to begin
beißen	biß	hat gebissen	er beißt	bisse	beiß(e)	to bite
bergen	barg	hat geborgen	er birgt	bürge (bärge)	birg	to hide
bersten	barst	ist geborsten	er birst	börste (bärste)	birst	to burst
betrügen	betrog	hat betrogen	er betrügt	betröge	betrüg(e)	to deceive
bewegen	bewog	hat bewogen	er bewegt	bewöge	beweg(e)	to induce (= to move, is weak)
biegen	bog	hat gebogen	er biegt	böge	bieg(e)	to bend
bieten	bot	hat geboten	er bietet	böte	biet(e)	to offer
binden	band	hat gebunden	er bindet	bände	bind(e)	to bind
bitten	bat	hat gebeten	er bittet	bäte	bitte	to ask
blasen	blies	hat geblasen	er bläst	bliese	blas(e)	to blow
bleiben	blieb	ist geblieben	er bleibt	bliebe	bleib(e)	to remain
braten	briet	hat gebraten	er brät	briete	brat(e)	to roast
brechen	brach	hat gebrochen	er bricht	bräche	brich	to break
dringen	drang	hat gedrungen	er dringt	dränge	dring(e)	to press
dürfen	durfte	hat gedurft	er darf	dürfte	—	to be allowed
einladen (see laden)						

empfehlen	empfahl	hat empfohlen	er empfiehlt	empföhle (empfähle)	empfiehl	*to recommend*
erlöschen	erlosch	ist erloschen	er erlischt	erlösche	erlisch	*to go out, become extinguished*
erschrecken	erschrak	ist erschrocken	er erschrickt	erschräke	erschrick	*to be frightened (= to frighten, trans., is weak)*
essen	aß	hat gegessen	er ißt	äße	iß	*to eat*
fahren	fuhr	ist gefahren	er fährt	führe	fahr(e)	*to drive, ride, go*
fallen	fiel	ist gefallen	er fällt	fiele	fall(e)	*to fall*
fangen	fing	hat gefangen	er fängt	finge	fang(e)	*to catch*
fechten	focht	hat gefochten	er ficht	föchte	ficht	*to fight*
finden	fand	hat gefunden	er findet	fände	find(e)	*to find*
flechten	flocht	hat geflochten	er flicht	flöchte	flicht	*to braid*
fliegen	flog	ist geflogen	er fliegt	flöge	flieg(e)	*to fly*
fliehen	floh	ist geflohen	er flieht	flöhe	flieh(e)	*to flee*
fließen	floß	ist geflossen	er fließt	flösse	fließ(e)	*to flow*
fressen	fraß	hat gefressen	er frißt	fräße	friß	*to eat* (of animals)
frieren	fror	hat gefroren	er friert	fröre	frier(e)	*to freeze*
gebären	gebar	hat geboren	sie gebiert	gebäre	gebier	*to bear, give birth to*
geben	gab	hat gegeben	er gibt	gäbe	gib	*to give*
gedeihen	gedieh	ist gediehen	er gedeiht	gediehe	gedeih(e)	*to thrive*
gehen	ging	ist gegangen	er geht	ginge	geh(e)	*to go*
gelingen	gelang	ist gelungen	es gelingt	gelänge	—	*to succeed*
gelten	galt	hat gegolten	er gilt	gölte (gälte)	gilt	*to be worth*
genesen	genas	ist genesen	er genest	genäse	genese	*to recover*
genießen	genoß	hat genossen	er genießt	genösse	genieß(e)	*to enjoy*

INFINITIVE	PAST INDICATIVE	COMP. PAST INDICATIVE	PRESENT INDICATIVE	PRESENT SUBJ. II	IMPERATIVE (sing. fam.)	
geschehen	geschah	ist geschehen	es geschieht	geschähe	—	to happen
gewinnen	gewann	hat gewonnen	er gewinnt	gewönne (gewänne)	gewinn(e)	to win, gain
gießen	goß	hat gegossen	er gießt	gösse	gieß(e)	to pour
gleichen	glich	hat geglichen	er gleicht	gliche	gleich(e)	to be like, resemble
gleiten	glitt	ist geglitten	er gleitet	glitte	gleit(e)	to glide
graben	grub	hat gegraben	er gräbt	grübe	grab(e)	to dig
greifen	griff	hat gegriffen	er greift	griffe	greif(e)	to seize
haben	hatte	hat gehabt	er hat	hätte	hab(e)	to have
halten	hielt	hat gehalten	er hält	hielte	halt(e)	to hold
hangen	hing	hat gehangen	er hängt	hinge	hang(e)	to hang (intr.)
hauen	hieb	hat gehauen	er haut	hiebe	hau(e)	to hew
heben	hob	hat gehoben	er hebt	höbe (hübe)	heb(e)	to lift
heißen	hieß	hat geheißen	er heißt	hieße	heiß(e)	to be called
helfen	half	hat geholfen	er hilft	hülfe (hälfe)	hilf	to help
kennen	kannte	hat gekannt	er kennt	kennte	kenne	to know
klingen	klang	hat geklungen	er klingt	klänge	kling(e)	to sound
kommen	kam	ist gekommen	er kommt	käme	komm(e)	to come
können	konnte	hat gekonnt	er kann	könnte	—	to be able
kriechen	kroch	ist gekrochen	er kriecht	kröche	kriech(e)	to creep
laden	lud (ladete)	hat geladen	er ladet (lädt)	lüde (ladete)	lad(e)	to invite (usually **ein**laden)
lassen	ließ	hat gelassen	er läßt	ließe	laß	to let
laufen	lief	ist gelaufen	er läuft	liefe	lauf(e)	to run

Infinitive	Preterite	Konjunktiv	Present	Perfect	Imperative	Meaning
leiden	litt	litte	er leidet	hat gelitten	leid(e)	to suffer
leihen	lieh	liehe	er leiht	hat geliehen	leih(e)	to lend
lesen	las	läse	er liest	hat gelesen	lies	to read
liegen	lag	läge	er liegt	hat gelegen	lieg(e)	to lie
lügen	log	löge	er lügt	hat gelogen	lüg(e)	to (tell a) lie
meiden	mied	miede	er meidet	hat gemieden	meid(e)	to avoid
messen	maß	mäße	er mißt	hat gemessen	miß	to measure
mögen	mochte	möchte	er mag	hat gemocht	—	to like; may
müssen	mußte	müßte	er muß	hat gemußt	—	to have, to must
nehmen	nahm	nähme	er nimmt	hat genommen	nimm	to take
pfeifen	pfiff	pfiffe	er pfeift	hat gepfiffen	pfeif(e)	to whistle
preisen	pries	priese	er preist	hat gepriesen	preis(e)	to praise
quellen	quoll	quölle	er quillt	ist gequollen	quill	to gush forth
raten	riet	riete	er rät	hat geraten	rat(e)	to advise; guess
reiben	rieb	riebe	er reibt	hat gerieben	reib(e)	to rub
reißen	riß	risse	er reißt	hat gerissen	reiß(e)	to tear
reiten	ritt	ritte	er reitet	ist geritten	reit(e)	to ride
riechen	roch	röche	er riecht	hat gerochen	riech(e)	to smell
rufen	rief	riefe	er ruft	hat gerufen	ruf(e)	to call
saufen	soff	söffe	er säuft	hat gesoffen	sauf(e)	to drink (of animals)
schaffen	schuf	schüfe	er schafft	hat geschaffen	schaff(e)	to create (= to work, is weak)
scheiden	schied	schiede	er scheidet	ist geschieden	scheid(e)	to part
scheinen	schien	schiene	er scheint	hat geschienen	schein(e)	to seem, shine

INFINITIVE	PAST INDICATIVE	COMP. PAST INDICATIVE	PRESENT INDICATIVE	PRESENT SUBJ. II	IMPERATIVE (sing. fam.)	
schelten	schalt	hat gescholten	er schilt	schölte (schälte)	schilt	*to scold*
schieben	schob	hat geschoben	er schiebt	schöbe	schieb(e)	*to shove*
schießen	schoß	hat geschossen	er schießt	schösse	schieß(e)	*to shoot*
schlafen	schlief	hat geschlafen	er schläft	schliefe	schlaf(e)	*to sleep*
schlagen	schlug	hat geschlagen	er schlägt	schlüge	schlag(e)	*to strike*
schleichen	schlich	ist geschlichen	er schleicht	schliche	schleich(e)	*to creep*
schließen	schloß	hat geschlossen	er schließt	schlösse	schließ(e)	*to shut*
schleifen	schliff	hat geschliffen	er schleift	schliffe	schleif(e)	*to whet*
schmelzen	schmolz	ist geschmolzen	er schmilzt	schmölze	schmilz	*to melt*
schneiden	schnitt	hat geschnitten	er schneidet	schnitte	schneid(e)	*to cut*
schreiben	schrieb	hat geschrieben	er schreibt	schriebe	schreib(e)	*to write*
schreien	schrie	hat geschrie(e)n	er schreit	schriee	schrei(e)	*to cry*
schreiten	schritt	ist geschritten	er schreitet	schritte	schreit(e)	*to stride*
schweigen	schwieg	hat geschwiegen	er schweigt	schwiege	schweig(e)	*to be silent*
schwellen	schwoll	ist geschwollen	er schwillt	schwölle	schwill	*to swell*
schwimmen	schwamm	ist geschwommen	er schwimmt	schwömme (schwämme)	schwimm(e)	*to swim*
schwinden	schwand	ist geschwunden	er schwindet	schwände	schwind(e)	*to vanish (usually* **verschwinden**)
schwingen	schwang	hat geschwungen	er schwingt	schwänge	schwing(e)	*to swing*
schwören	schwur (schwor)	hat geschworen	er schwört	schwüre	schwör(e)	*to swear*
sehen	sah	hat gesehen	er sieht	sähe	sieh	*to see*
sein	war	ist gewesen	er ist	wäre	sei	*to be*

Infinitive	Preterite	Present (3rd)	Perfect	Subjunctive	Imperative	Meaning
sieden	sott (siedete)[1]	es siedet	hat gesotten	sötte	sied(e)	*to boil*
singen	sang	er singt	hat gesungen	sänge	sing(e)	*to sing*
sinken	sank	er sinkt	ist gesunken	sänke	sink(e)	*to sink*
sinnen	sann	er sinnt	hat gesonnen	sönne (sänne)	sinn(e)	*to think*
sitzen	saß	er sitzt	hat gesessen	säße	sitz(e)	*to sit*
sollen	sollte	er soll	hat gesollt	sollte	—	*to be (required) to; should, ought to*
speien	spie	er speit	hat gespie(e)n	spiee	spei(e)	*to spit*
spinnen	spann	er spinnt	hat gesponnen	spönne (spänne)	spinn(e)	*to spin*
sprechen	sprach	er spricht	hat gesprochen	spräche	sprich	*to speak*
sprießen	sproß	es sprießt	ist gesprossen	sprösse	sprieß(e)	*to sprout*
springen	sprang	er springt	ist gesprungen	spränge	spring(e)	*to jump*
stechen	stach	er sticht	hat gestochen	stäche	stich	*to prick*
stehen	stand	er steht	hat gestanden	stände (stünde)	steh(e)	*to stand*
stehlen	stahl	er stiehlt	hat gestohlen	stöle (stähle)	stiehl	*to steal*
steigen	stieg	er steigt	ist gestiegen	stiege	steig(e)	*to climb*
sterben	starb	er stirbt	ist gestorben	stürbe	stirb	*to die*
stieben	stob	er stiebt	ist gestoben	stöbe	stieb(e)	*to scatter*
stoßen	stieß	er stößt	hat gestoßen	stieße	stoß(e)	*to push*
streichen	strich	er streicht	hat gestrichen	striche	streich(e)	*to stroke*
streiten	stritt	er streitet	hat gestritten	stritte	streit(e)	*to contend*
tragen	trug	er trägt	hat getragen	trüge	trag(e)	*to carry*

[1] The weak form usually occurs in figurative use, e.g., *seethed* with rage.

INFINITIVE	PAST INDICATIVE	COMP. PAST INDICATIVE	PRESENT INDICATIVE	PRESENT SUBJ. II	IMPERATIVE (sing. fam.)	
treffen	traf	hat getroffen	er trifft	träfe	triff	to meet; hit
treiben	trieb	hat getrieben	er treibt	triebe	treib(e)	to drive
treten	trat	ist getreten	er tritt	träte	tritt	to step
trinken	trank	hat getrunken	er trinkt	tränke	trink(e)	to drink
tun	tat	hat getan	er tut	täte	tu(e)	to do
verderben[1]	verdarb	hat verdorben	er verdirbt	verdürbe	verdirb	to ruin, spoil
vergessen	vergaß	hat vergessen	er vergißt	vergäße	vergiß	to forget
verlieren	verlor	hat verloren	er verliert	verlöre	verlier(e)	to lose
verschwinden	(see schwinden)					
verzeihen	verzieh	hat verziehen	er verzeiht	verziehe	verzeih(e)	to pardon
wachsen	wuchs	ist gewachsen	er wächst	wüchse	wachs(e)	to grow
waschen	wusch	hat gewaschen	er wäscht	wüsche	wasch(e)	to wash
weichen	wich	ist gewichen	er weicht	wiche	weich(e)	to recede
weisen	wies	hat gewiesen	er weist	wiese	weis(e)	to show
werben	warb	hat geworben	er wirbt	würbe	wirb	to woo
werden	wurde (ward)	ist geworden	er wird	würde	werd(e)	to become
werfen	warf	hat geworfen	er wirft	würfe	wirf	to throw
wiegen	wog	hat gewogen	er wiegt	wöge	wieg(e)	to weigh
winden	wand	hat gewunden	er windet	wände	wind(e)	to wind
wollen	wollte	hat gewollt	er will	wollte	wolle	to wish
ziehen[2]	zog	hat gezogen	er zieht	zöge	zieh(e)	to pull
zwingen	zwang	hat gezwungen	er zwingt	zwänge	zwing(e)	to force

[1]As an intransitive verb, **verderben** is conjugated with the auxiliary **sein.**
[2]As an intransitive verb, **ziehen** (*to move*) is conjugated with **sein.**

§112. VERBS THAT ARE SIMILAR IN SOUND AND SPELLING

The following verbs are commonly confused because of similarity in sound or spelling:

A. beten, bieten, and bitten:

beten	betete	hat gebetet	*to pray*
bieten	bot	hat geboten	*to offer*
bitten	bat	hat gebeten	*to ask, request*

B. danken and denken:

danken	dankte	hat gedankt	*to thank*
denken	dachte	hat gedacht	*to think*

C. brechen and bringen:

brechen	brach	hat gebrochen	*to break*
bringen	brachte	hat gebracht	*to bring*

D. kennen, können, and wissen (see §16 B):

kennen	kann	hat gekannt	*to know* (a person or thing)
können	konnte	hat gekonnt	*to know* (by study)
wissen	wußte	hat gewußt	*to know* (a fact)

E. legen, liegen, and lügen:

legen	legte	hat gelegt	*to lay*
liegen	lag	hat gelegen	*to lie*
lügen	log	hat gelogen	*to tell a lie*

Note: **sich legen** means *to lie down.*

F. reisen, reißen, and reizen:

reisen	reiste	ist gereist	*to travel*
reißen	riß	hat gerissen	*to tear*
reizen	reizte	hat gereizt	*to excite, irritate*

G. setzen and sitzen:

setzen	setzte	hat gesetzt	*to set*
sitzen	saß	hat gesessen	*to sit*

Note: **sich setzen** means *to sit down.*

H. lassen and lesen:

lassen	ließ	hat gelassen	*to let*
lesen	las	hat gelesen	*to read*

I.   fallen, gefallen, and fällen:

fallen	fiel	ist gefallen	*to fall*
gefallen	gefiel	hat gefallen	*to please*
fällen	fällte	hat gefällt	*to fell*

J.   reiten, raten, and retten:

reiten	ritt	ist geritten	*to ride (on horseback)*
raten	riet	hat geraten	*to advise; guess*
retten	rettete	hat gerettet	*to save, rescue*

K.   fliegen and fliehen:

fliegen	flog	ist geflogen	*to fly*
fliehen	floh	ist geflohen	*to flee*

L.   erschrecken (transitive and intransitive):

erschrecken	erschrak	ist erschrocken	*to be(come) frightened* (intr.)
erschrecken	erschreckte	hat erschreckt	*to frighten* (tr.)

M.   schneien and schneiden:

schneien	schneite	hat geschneit	*to snow*
schneiden	schnitt	hat geschnitten	*to cut*

N.   fahren and führen:

fahren	fuhr	ist gefahren	*to ride, travel*
führen	führte	hat geführt	*to lead*

O.   lernen and lehren:

lernen	lernte	hat gelernt	*to learn, study*
lehren	lehrte	hat gelehrt	*to teach*

P.   leiden and leiten:

leiden	litt	hat gelitten	*to suffer*
leiten	leitete	hat geleitet	*to lead*

Q.   wachsen and waschen:

wachsen	wuchs	ist gewachsen	*to grow*
waschen	wusch	hat gewaschen	*to wash*

R.   ziehen and zeigen:

ziehen	zog	hat gezogen	*to draw, pull*
zeigen	zeigte	hat gezeigt	*to show*

S.   reichen, riechen, and rauchen:

reichen	reichte	hat gereicht	*to reach*
riechen	roch	hat gerochen	*to smell*
rauchen	rauchte	hat geraucht	*to smoke*

§113. NOUN PECULIARITIES

A. Nouns used only in the plural. Some of the more common nouns used only in the plural are: Eltern (*parents*), Leute (*people*), Gebrüder (*brothers*), Geschwister (*brothers and sisters*), Ferien (*vacation*), Masern (*measles*), Insignien (*insignia*). Weihnachten (*Christmas*) and Pfingsten (*Whitsuntide*) occur as plurals and also as neuter and feminine singulars. Ostern (*Easter*) may be either plural or neuter singular.

B. Nouns used only in the singular. Some of the more common nouns used only in the singular are:

der Adel, –s, *nobility*	der Hafer, –s, *oats*
die Beute, –, *booty*	das Publikum, –s, *public*
der Bodensatz, –es, *sediment, dregs*	die Mathematik, –, *mathematics*
das Elend, –(e)s, *misery*	die Musik, –, *music*

C. Nouns having irregular compound plural forms. A number of abstract and collective nouns have compound forms in the plural. These plural forms are often derivatives in which the singular noun functions as a component part. Some of the more common nouns of this type are:

SINGULAR	PLURAL
der Atem, *breath*	Atemzüge
der Dank, *thanks*	Danksagungen, *expressions of gratitude*
das Glück, *luck*	Glücksfälle, *pieces of good fortune*
der Rat, *advice*	Ratschläge, *counsels*
der Regen, *rain*	Regenfälle (*or* Niederschläge)
der Streit, *dispute*	Streitigkeiten
der Tod, *death*	Todesfälle
das Unglück, *misfortune*	Unglücksfälle
die Vorsicht, *precaution*	Vorsichtsmaßregeln, *precautionary measures*

§114. PUNCTUATION

Rules for punctuation in German differ in many respects from those in English and should be noted carefully.

A. Punctuation marks. The more common punctuation marks used in German are:

,	= das Komma, *comma*
.	= der Punkt, *period*

:   = der Doppelpunkt, *colon*
;   = das Semikolon, *semicolon*
!   = das Ausrufungszeichen, *exclamation mark*
?   = das Fragezeichen, *question mark*
"   " = Anführungszeichen (pl.), *quotation marks*
—   = der Gedankenstrich, *dash*
-      = der Bindestrich, *hyphen*
( )   = runde Klammern (pl.), *parentheses*

B. The comma.   Commas are used:

(1) To set off dependent (*or* subordinate) clauses:

Die Dame, die uns jetzt besucht, ist sehr reich.
The lady who is visiting us now is very rich.

(2) Before **ohne . . . zu, um . . . zu,** and **(an) statt . . . zu** (all of which are followed by an infinitive):

Er ging an mir vorbei, ohne etwas zu sagen.
He passed me without saying anything.

Note: Phrases with **zu** are also preceded by a comma when the following infinitive has modifiers, and when **zu** is the equivalent of **um . . . zu:**

Gewöhne dich daran, immer früh aufzustehen.
Accustom yourself to early rising.

Es lebt ein Gott, zu strafen und zu rächen.
There is (lit. *lives*) *a God, to punish and take revenge.*

but: Es fing an zu regnen.
It began to rain.

(3) Before the coördinating conjunctions **und** and **oder,** provided the following clause contains both subject and verb:

Die Luft ist blau, und die Felder sind grün.
The air is blue and the fields are green.

but: Er legte sich hin und schlief sogleich ein.
He lay down and fell asleep at once.

(*a*) Contrary to English usage, **aber** meaning *however* is not set off by commas:

Der alte Mann aber verlor den Mut nicht.
The old man, however, did not lose courage.

(*b*) Contrary to English usage, no comma is used before **und** or **oder** in a series:

Karl, Fritz und Johann sind meine besten Freunde.
Carl, Fred, and John are my best friends.

C. The period.   Periods are used when the endings of ordinals have been omitted:

> den 4. (= 4ten *or* vierten) März, *March 4.*
> Friedrich II. (= der Zweite), *Frederick II*

D.   Exclamation marks are used:

(1)   Usually after the salutation in letters:
   Lieber Vater! *Dear Father*

(2)   Regularly after emphatic commands:
   Folgen Sie mir! *Follow me.*

E.   Question marks are used at the end of interrogative sentences, as in English:

> Haben Sie ihn gesehen?
> *Did you see him?*

Indirect questions, however, end with a period:

> Er fragte mich, ob ich den Mann gesehen hätte.
> *He asked me whether I had seen the man.*

F.   Quotation marks are used to enclose a direct quotation, as in English:

> Der Fuchs sprach: „Die Trauben sind mir zu sauer."
> *The fox said, "The grapes are too sour for me."*

(1)   In German, opening quotation marks are written *below* the line; close quotes, *above* the line.

(2)   The open quotation mark is preceded in German by a colon.

G.   Hyphens are used:

(1)   To divide words at the end of a line.
(2)   To indicate the omission of the last component common to two or more compounds in a series:

> Haupt- und Nebensatz, *main and dependent clause*
> Feld- und Gartenfrüchte, *field and garden fruits*

(3)   Rarely, to form compound nouns.

§115.   CAPITALIZATION

Capitalization is far more frequent in German than in English, and has important grammatical significance. The conditions under which it occurs should therefore be noted very carefully.

A. Words that *must* be capitalized.   Capitalization is required by:

(1) Neuter adjectives used as nouns after **etwas** (*something*), **viel** (*much*), **nichts** (*nothing*), **alles** (*all*), **allerlei** (*all kinds* or *sorts of*), and **wenig** (*little, not much*):

> etwas Schönes, *something beautiful*
> viel Wichtiges, *much of importance*
> nichts Schlechtes, *nothing bad*
> alles Gute, *all good things* (or *all that is good*)
> allerlei Unverständliches, *all kinds of unintelligible things*
> wenig Nützliches, *little of use*

(2) Words of all kinds used as nouns:

der Arme, *the poor man*	eine Fünf, *a (figure) five*
Gutes und Böses, *good and evil*	Altes und Neues, *old and new*
jedem das Seine, *to each his own*	
Das Lesen fällt ihm schwer. *Reading is difficult for him.*	Die Armen haben nichts zu essen. *The poor have nothing to eat.*

(3) The pronoun of formal address **Sie** (*you*), and its corresponding adjective **Ihr** (*your*):

> Haben Sie Ihr Buch?
> *Have you your book?*

(*a*) The reflexive **sich** is *not* capitalized:

> Setzen Sie sich! *Sit down.*

(*b*) **Du, dein, ihr,** and **euer** are *not* capitalized unless used in direct address in letters:

Karl, hast du dein Buch?	Kinder, was tut ihr?
Carl, have you your book?	*Children, what are you doing?*

but: Lieber Karl!

> Hoffentlich hast Du Dich nicht erkältet.
> Dein Dich liebender Fritz.

(4) The first word of a direct quotation (following a quotation mark preceded by a colon):

> Der Schüler sagte: „Jetzt verstehe ich diesen Satz.“
> *The pupil said, "Now I understand this sentence."*

(*a*) If a direct quotation is interrupted, the word resuming the quotation is *not* capitalized:

> „Die Trauben,“ sprach der Fuchs, „sind mir zu sauer.“

(*b*)   The word directly after a question mark or an exclamation mark is *not* capitalized if what follows completes the sentence:

„Was wollen Sie?“ fragte der Mann.
"What do you wish?" asked the man.

„Karl, mache deine Aufgabe!“ sagte der Lehrer.
"Carl, do your lesson!" said the teacher.

B.   Words that are *not* capitalized.   Capitalization does *not* occur in:

(1)   Combinations with **heute, morgen,** and **gestern:**

heute morgen, *this morning*
gestern morgen, *yesterday morning*
gestern abend, *yesterday evening* (or *last night*)

(2)   Proper adjectives such as *German, English, French,*—unless they are used in titles:

Wo ist Ihr deutsches (englisches, französisches) Buch?
Where is your German (English, French) book?

but: das Deutsche Reich, the German empire

(*a*)   Observe the absence of capitalization in the phrase **auf deutsch,** *in German.* Similarly:

auf englisch, *in English*   auf französisch, *in French*

(*b*)   Observe the use of **Deutsch** as noun:

Studieren Sie **Deutsch?**
Are you studying German?

(3)   The following common pronouns and numerals are not capitalized: **man,** *one;* **jemand,** *someone;* **niemand,** *no one;* **jedermann,** *everyone;* **derselbe,** *the same one;* **einer,** *one;* **keiner,** *no one;* (ein) **jeder,** *each one;* **zwei,** *two;* **beide** (**die beiden** or **alle beide**), *both;* **der eine . . . der andere,** *the one . . . the other;* **drei,** *three;* **alle drei,** *all three;* **das andere,** *the rest;* **alles anders,** *all else;* **die anderen,** *the others;* **alle anderen,** *all others;* **nichts anderes,** *nothing else;* **das übrige,** *the rest;* **alles übrige,** *all else;* **die übrigen,** *the others;* **alle übrigen,** *all others;* **der erste . . . der letzte,** *the first . . . the last;* **einige,** *some;* **alle,** *all;* **viele,** *many;* **etwas,** *something;* **nichts,** *nothing;* **viel,** *much;* **mehr,** *more;* **das meiste,** *the most;* **das mindeste,** *the least;* **der einzelne,** *the individual;* **einzelne,** *individuals;* **alles mögliche,** *everything possible.*

(4)   The following boldfaced words in verbal idioms are not capitalized:

Er ist **schuld** daran.   Es tut mir **leid.**
He is to blame for that.   *I am sorry.*

Tut es Ihnen **weh**?   (Das ist) **schade**!
Does it hurt you?   *That is too bad.*

Nehmen Sie sich in **acht**!   Er nimmt daran **teil**.
Take care (or *be careful*).   *He takes part (in it).*

Sind Sie **imstande,** das zu tun?   Jetzt geht er **heim**.
Can you do that?   *He is going home now.*

Wann findet die Vorstellung **statt**?
When will the performance take place?

Exercises

The exercises cover the material discussed in §§1-88 of the text. For explanation and review, refer back to the pertinent sections as required.

§§1–2. Principles of Case

A. Supply the missing endings.

1. Er liest d— Satz.
2. Sie ist mein— Freundin.
3. Ich werde d— Mann etwas Geld geben.
4. D— Eltern hatten d— Kind auf der Straße gesehen.
5. Er gibt d— Frau— (*pl.*) d— Bücher.
6. Haben Sie d— Kinder gehört?
7. Sie zeigte d— Vater d— Bild.
8. Wo ist d— Mutter d— Mädchen— (*sing.*)?
9. D— Arzt war gestern auf dem Lande.
10. Wer ist d— Lehrer d— Jung— (*sing.*)?
11. Wie heißen d— Kinder d— Frau?
12. D— Häuser sind sehr alt.
13. Ich hatte mein— Freund, d— Zahnarzt, ein— Brief geschrieben.
14. Schreiben Sie mi— bald, Herr Müller!
15. Haben Sie d— Rhein gesehen?

B. Rewrite in the plural sentences 1, 2, 3, 8, and 10 of the preceding exercise.

C. Translate into German:

1. She loves her brother.
2. The children were visiting their parents.
3. He gave the woman some money.
4. Did you see the boy?

5. She showed the man the watch.
6. He will close the door.
7. The children had shown their parents the pictures.
8. He gave the horse something to eat.
9. That village is in Germany.
10. His sister's friends are in the country.
11. He is my friend.
12. The children's parents were poor.
13. Please write me a letter, Mr. Brown.
14. He will visit his friend, the lawyer.
15. She had shown her brother the flowers.
16. He has given his sister the pencil.

§§3–5. Principles of Tense

A. Complete the following sentences with the verb forms indicated.

1. Mein Bruder —— das Buch ——. (*has read*)
2. —— er einen Brief ——? (*will write*)
3. Er —— den Vater. (*is visiting*)
4. Was —— er ——? (*had seen*)
5. Er —— Ball auf der Straße. (*was playing*)
6. Ich —— meinen Freund ——. (*shall visit*)
7. Wann —— Sie ——? (*did arrive*)
8. Das Kind —— mit dem Hund. (*is playing*)
9. Gestern —— ich den Knaben ——. (*saw*)
10. Mein Freund —— um zwei Uhr in Berlin ——. (*had arrived*)
11. Ich —— eine interessante Geschichte. (*was reading*)
12. Er —— ihn ——. (*will have visited*)
13. Ich —— (*went*) in die Stadt, —— (*visited*) meinen Freund und ——
    (*came*) um elf Uhr nach Hause.
14. Gestern —— er seinen Freund ——. (*visited*)
15. Heute —— er um acht Uhr nach Hause ——. (*came*)

B. Translate into German.

1. He had written a letter.
2. Have you read it?
3. The boy is playing ball.
4. She was coming home.
5. Have you seen her?
6. They had never visited me.
7. When will they read the book?
8. He is visiting his parents.

9. Have they arrived?
10. He will have read the story.
11. She is arriving early.
12. He will come home late.
13. He had never read the poem.
14. He went to the country, played ball, and came home tired.
15. She went to the city, visited a friend, and came home at ten o'clock.

§6. Definite and Indefinite Articles

A. Complete the following sentences. (A few are correct without any additions.)

1. Zürich und Luzern sind Städte in —— Schweiz.
2. Letzten Sommer war ich in —— Deutschland.
3. Waren Sie jemals in —— Türkei oder in —— Tschechoslowakei?
4. Meine beiden Vettern waren nie in —— Vereinigten Staaten oder in —— Niederlanden.
5. —— Kunst ist lang, —— Leben kurz.
6. —— Schreiben fällt (*is*) meinem kleinen Bruder schwerer als —— Lesen.
7. Sie setzt sich —— Hut auf.
8. Was hat das kleine Mädchen in —— Hand?
9. Er wohnt in —— Kehlerstraße.
10. Dieser faule Junge kommt immer zu spät in —— Schule.
11. Sein älterer Bruder war schon in —— Schule.
12. Nach —— Schule läuft er schnell nach Hause.
13. —— (*In*) Winter laufen wir Schlittschuh (*we skate*).
14. —— Juli ist das Wetter oft sehr heiß.
15. —— Montag werde ich ins Theater gehen.
16. Ich besuchte ihn immer dreimal —— Woche.
17. Das Fleisch kostet eine Mark —— Pfund.
18. —— Bruder und —— Schwester waren beide zu Hause.
19. Ist sein Vater —— Arzt oder —— Advokat?
20. Er ist —— (*a good*) Arzt.
21. —— solch— Gewitter haben wir nie erlebt.
22. Solch——Gewitter haben wir nie erlebt.
23. Welch— Stadt!
24. Heute haben wir Obst —— Frühstück.
25. —— meisten Knaben spielen gern Ball.
26. —— (*As a*) Regel spielt Karl nach —— Schule.
27. Man machte ihn —— Präsidenten.
28. —— klein— Karl wollte seine Aufgaben nicht machen.

29. Karl d— Groß— besiegte die Sachsen.
30. Als wir in Potsdam waren, sahen wir die Bibliothek Friedrich— d— Groß—.
31. König Friedrich— Schloß hieß Sanssouci.
32. Viele Bekannte d— König— Friedrich waren Künstler.

B.   Translate into German.

1. Switzerland is a republic.
2. I was never in Switzerland, but two years ago I was in Germany.
3. Last summer my brother was in Turkey and Czechoslovakia.
4. Last winter my friend was in England, France, and Spain.
5. Life is short.   Art is long.   Man is mortal.
6. The old lady was putting on her gloves.
7. She had already put on her hat.
8. What has that little boy got in his hand?
9. Reading is easier than writing.
10. Summer is here (*i.e.,* has come).   Winter is over (vorüber).
11. In January we usually have cold weather.
12. At what time do you go to school?
13. After school I usually take a long walk.
14. It costs three marks a pound.
15. He is a famous physician.
16. What a man!   What a class!   What a building!
17. Is he a teacher or a dentist?   He is a good dentist.
18. Before breakfast I always take a short walk.
19. After supper I read the paper.
20. Is dinner ready?
21. As a rule I study in the evening.
22. Most girls like to dance.
23. Do you have a headache?
24. Little Fred is already in bed.
25. What did you have for breakfast this morning?
26. Many artists lived at the court of Frederick the Great.
27. Voltaire was King Frederick's guest.

§7.   Negation with *nicht, nie, niemals*

A.   Rewrite the following as negative sentences with **nicht.**

1. Mein guter Freund wird kommen.
2. Er ist gekommen.
3. Sein kleiner Bruder ist klug.
4. Sein reicher Onkel ist Arzt.

5. Das kleine Kind hatte im Walde gespielt.
6. Er ging nach Hause.
7. Sein Vater ist hier.
8. Sie wird es ansehen.
9. Sehen Sie es an!
10. Er wird mitkommen.
11. Ich möchte fliegen.

B. Translate:

1. My dear friend was not at home.
2. He is never at home.
3. Our old physician is not here.
4. That little boy does not have the book.
5. The little children had not found their German books.
6. Carl is never sick.
7. He will not see him.
8. He is not a teacher.
9. She does not have a pencil.
10. They have not received my letter.
11. He is not in school today.
12. Don't look at him.
13. He was not looking at her.
14. Don't do it.
15. She is not looking at me.
16. The work is not easy but hard.

§§8–12. Adjective Declension

A. Supply the correct endings.
1. Haben Sie d— deutsch— Zeitung gelesen?
2. Der Wolf ist ein wild— Tier.
3. Gut— Morgen! Gut— Nacht!
4. Das ist ein gut— Witz.
5. Er gibt mir immer gut— Rat.
6. D— arm— Frau hatte kein Geld.
7. Lieb— Kind, was fehlt dir?
8. Ihr gut— Freund war nicht zu Hause.
9. Im Klassenzimmer hängt ein— groß— Wandkarte von Deutschland.
10. Er ist ein Mann von hoh— Gestalt.
11. Sagen Sie mir d— ganz— Wahrheit!
12. D— klein— Kinder spielen auf der Straße.
13. Er hatte nur ein Stück trocken— Brot.
14. Dieser gut— alt— Mann ist mein best— Freund.

15. Ich habe ein deutsch— Buch.
16. Er besitzt ein groß— Vermögen.
17. D— alt— Mann ist plötzlich verschwunden.
18. Unser reich— Freund wird uns bald besuchen.
19. Er hat d— erst— Zug verpaßt.
20. Wo liegt die Vaterstadt d— beid— Freunde?
21. Was hat er d— arm— Leut— gegeben?
22. Er hat ein— gut— Vater und ein— gut— Mutter.
23. Das war ein groß— Unglück.
24. Er trägt ein— schwer— Überrock.
25. Das Buch liegt auf d— klein— Tisch.
26. Was haben Sie in d— link— Tasche?
27. Er ist ein gut— Schüler.
28. Sie ist ein gut— klein— Mädchen.
29. Haben Sie d— Leipzig— Messe besucht?
30. Er hat all— deutsch— Zeitungen gelesen.
31. Ich lasse all— gut— Freunde grüßen.
32. Welcher klug— Mann! Welch klug— Mann!
33. Er hat viel— treu— Freunde.
34. Das Buch gehört d— klein— Jungen (*sing.*).
35. Wir werden d— alt— Stadt Rothenburg besuchen.
36. Die Eltern d— klein— Jungen (*sing.*) sind auf dem Lande.
37. Lieb— Mädchen, was fehlt dir?
38. Sie ist ein— schön— Frau mit kurz— Haar.
39. Haben Sie frisch— Brot gekauft?
40. Er hat mehrere wichtig— Dinge vergessen.
41. Unser freundlich— Arzt hatte ein— München— Zeitung gekauft.
42. Wenig— ehrlich— Leute würden das tun.
43. Das ist ein klein— alt— Haus.
44. Alle deutsch— Bücher habe ich zu Hause.
45. Kinder, wo ist euer lieb— Onkel?
46. Ich habe viele gut—Freunde.
47. Unser reich— Onkel ist nicht zu Hause.
48. Der Rhein ist ein berühmt— deutsch— Strom.
49. Er hat alles, was zu ein— bequem— Leben gehört.

B. Translate into German.

1. Our dear friend (*masc.*) is in the country this week.
2. Yesterday I visited my best friend.
3. Berlin is the largest city in (of) Germany.
4. He is carrying a long cane.
5. The lady has a beautiful voice.

6. Those boys go to the same school.

7. The old men were in the same school, when they were boys.

8. Have you seen the beautiful castles on the Rhine?

9. He is a famous German singer.

10. He is wearing a new coat.

11. She will take a long trip.

12. He had always given me good advice.

13. Have you ever seen a German city hall?

14. We shall pass (bestehen) this easy examination.

15. She was showing the little boy a beautiful picture.

16. The lion is a wild animal.

17. The dog is a domesticated animal.

18. I gave him many good reasons.

19. Our old friend is a good physician.

20. When did you see that little boy?

21. He had bought a new house.

22. He had given his little sister a beautiful book.

23. She was showing her older brother an interesting picture.

24. Where did you buy your new hat?

25. Write these short sentences in (w. acc.) your notebook.

26. If you don't understand, raise your (the) right hand.

27. I have learned one German poem by heart.

28. That is a very tall building.

29. We have a large classroom.

30. He has many good friends.

31. She will sing a well-known German folksong.

32. Have you read that interesting story?

33. That is a beautiful old village.

34. All diligent pupils have written the short sentences.

35. I have learned many German poems by heart.

36. Give me other important reasons.

37. Did you help the little children?

38. He has several valuable books in his library.

39. I bought a Berlin newspaper.

40. Few poor people wear such clothes.

41. He will attend (besuchen) the Leipzig fair.

42. My rich uncle lives in a suburb.

43. Write with black ink.

44. She has red hair.

45. Good morning.   Good evening.   Good night.

46. Today we are having beautiful weather.

47. To whom do these German books belong?

48. Do you belong to the German glee club?

§13. Nouns

A.   Rewrite the following sentences in the plural.
1. Das Dienstmädchen wird das große Zimmer reinigen.
2. Der Schüler hat das deutsche Buch verloren.
3. Der Kellner hat das gute Trinkgeld gern.
4. Der Dieb schwimmt über den breiten Fluß.
5. Das Mädchen spitzte den stumpfen Bleistift.
6. Der kluge Junge antwortet auf jede Frage.
7. Hast du das hohe Gebäude in der Stadt gesehen?
8. Siehst du den schönen Baum in jenem tiefen Tal?
9. Ich bewundere das alte Schloß auf dem hohen Berg.
10. Der Junge hat diesen großen Fehler gemacht.
11. Mein Onkel hat mir das scharfe Messer gegeben.
12. Die kurze Geschichte gefällt der Tochter.
13. Dieser kleine Vogel ist durch das offene Fenster geflogen.
14. Die Mutter ist mit der kleinen Tochter fortgegangen.
15. Der berühmte Arzt hat dem Mann sehr geholfen.
16. Mein Freund hatte mir diesen langen Brief geschrieben.
17. Die Katze fängt die graue Maus.
18. Wo hat die Dame diesen kostbaren Hut gekauft?
19. Wie heißt deine Nachbarin?
20. Lerne diesen idiomatischen Ausdruck auswendig!
21. Er hat den allerschönsten Hof.
22. Ich habe meine gute Freundin besucht.
23. Die gute Frau wird die alte Burg bewundern.
24. Die Schwester hatte ihrem Bruder diese interessante Geschichte erzählt.
25. Mein reicher Vetter hat das große Auto gekauft.
26. Ich warte schon lange auf den alten Doktor.
27. Das Bild an der Wand ist sehr schön.
28. Mein älterer Bruder besucht das Gymnasium.
29. Er mußte jedes Hindernis überwinden.

B.   Translate.
1. The Germans are very proud of (stolz auf *w. acc.*) their beautiful forests.
2. Did you visit the beautiful city of Munich?
3. The porter will carry my heavy suitcase through the railroad station.
4. My dear friend had seen the old castles on the Rhine.
5. That little girl has a beautiful face.
6. I gave the tall (lang) waiter a good tip.
7. That little boy always gives good answers to (auf *w. acc.*) my questions.
8. He had written me that long letter.

9. She will give them those German books.
10. Did she sing that well-known folksong?
11. She entered the large room and sat down on the sofa.
12. The servant girl had broken (zerbrechen) many good plates.
13. The fastest German steamers were formerly the (die) Europa and the (die) Bremen.
14. The flyers were hoping for favorable weather.
15. Did you see the President when you were in the capital?
16. Our English teacher will give us a very easy examination.
17. Wait a moment. I shall give you a better book.
18. That little bird flew through an open window.
19. Those rich women live in a beautiful suburb.
20. How long have you been waiting for that train?
21. How many idiomatic expressions did you learn by heart?
22. The President delivered (halten) a short speech.
23. At what time will you go to school tomorrow?
24. The dog sees its own shadow in the water.
25. Last summer I often went to the theater.
26. With what kind of (a) pen are you writing?
27. Yesterday the little children took a long walk.
28. In the fall the trees have beautiful leaves.
29. Last month the old man visited his youngest daughter.
30. The waiter will bring you another cup of coffee.
31. Tell me the whole truth.
32. The singers (*fem.*) do not earn so much money this year.
33. That man will easily overcome all obstacles.

§§14–17. Verbs

A. Rewrite the following sentences in the simple past, compound past, past perfect, and future tenses.

1. Ich warte auf meinen lieben Freund.
2. Er studiert zu Hause.
3. Fritz liebt die Mutter sehr.
4. Ich beantworte die erste Frage.
5. Sie macht die Tür auf.
6. Marie buchstabiert das lange Wort.
7. Ich amüsiere mich.
8. Er redet nicht gern.
9. Sie sagt nichts Gutes über ihn.
10. Heinrich macht seine Aufgabe.
11. Das Kind gehorcht der Mutter.
12. Ich vermisse dich sehr.

13. Mein reicher Vetter fährt um zehn Uhr ab.
14. Er geht nach Hause.
15. Wir kommen um halb neun in die Schule.
16. Frau Schmidt trägt einen neuen Hut.
17. Sie sieht müde aus.
18. Er gibt mir immer guten Rat.
19. Sie liest nicht gern.
20. Es wird heiß.
21. Klara schneidet das Brot.
22. Wir stehen um sechs Uhr auf.
23. Er kommt immer zu spät an.
24. Sie nimmt das deutsche Buch in die Hand.
25. Die Mutter ruft das kleine Mädchen.
26. Ich schreibe den kurzen Satz.
27. Er nimmt den Hut ab.
28. Das wilde Tier läuft in den Wald.
29. Er ißt langsam.
30. Ich denke an dich.
31. Er brennt vor Ungeduld.
32. Er kennt meinen besten Freund.
33. Ich weiß es.
34. Sie kann Französisch.
35. Das bringt Glück.
36. Das Kind rennt schnell zu der Mutter.
37. Ich nenne ihn Fritz.
38. Er sendet ihn zu mir.
39. Warum wendest du ihm den Rücken zu?
40. Er schläft nicht.
41. Er schläft schnell ein.
42. Er steht an der Tafel.
43. Er steht langsam auf.
44. Der Vogel fliegt auf das Dach.
45. Wir gehen aufs Land.
46. Wir kommen bald zurück.
47. Es gelingt mir nicht, das zu tun.
48. Meine Eltern bleiben auf dem Lande.

B. Translate into German.

1. He did not hear me.
2. She is answering (beantworten) the second question.
3. My older brother was traveling through Switzerland.
4. My brother was studying his lesson.
5. She had never loved him.
6. When did you telephone me?

    7. They were having a good time.

    8. Why did you not open the door?

    9. When did you buy that house?

  10. He was sitting down on the sofa.

  11. How long did you stay in the country?

  12. Those little boys looked very tired.

  13. He had written a long letter to his old parents.

  14. She was taking off her hat.

  15. When does school begin?

  16. They always arrived late.

  17. Were they singing a German folksong?

  18. He had given the old men some money.

  19. The little dog was lying under a chair.

  20. When did that famous man die?

  21. They were going home. (*Rewrite in the past perfect tense.*)

  22. He knows German.

  23. She knows Schiller's works.

  24. Do you know where he lives?

  25. The child ran quickly to its father.

  26. Why did he turn his back on me?

  27. I do not know that old man.

  28. Why did you stay in the city this summer?

  29. My best friends had gone to the country.

  30. They have not yet returned.

  31. How long did you sleep?

  32. When did you fall asleep?

  33. When did you get up this morning?

  34. He had fallen into the water.

  35. What has happened?

  36. Carl, give me your book.

  37. Marie, take the chalk in your hand.

  38. Henry, tell the truth.

  39. Children, help your mother.

  40. William, take off your hat.

  41. Children, go to sleep.

  42. Fred, go to sleep.

  43. Marie, don't eat so fast.

§§18–20. Numerals

  A. Complete the following sentences. All numerals should be spelled out.

    1. Zwei Bleistifte liegen auf dem Tisch. —— (*One*) gehört mir.

    2. Ich habe zwei Bücher gelesen. —— (*One*) war sehr interessant.

3. —— Bleistift und —— Buch liegen auf dem Tisch.

4. —— Tisch ist in diesem Zimmer, —— ist im Nebenzimmer.

5. „Wie viele Tische sind hier?" „Nur —— (*one*)."

6. —— Zimmer ist groß, —— ist klein.

7. „Wie viele Zimmer hat der Student?" „—— (*One*)."

8. D— ein— Stuhl gefällt mir.

9. Er hat —— (*a hundred*) Briefmarken gekauft.

10. Er hat viele —— (*hundreds*) in seiner Briefmarkensammlung.

11. Es waren —— (*a thousand*) Menschen da.

12. Viele —— (*thousands*) klatschten in die Hände.

13. Wie viele —— (*million*) Einwohner hat die Stadt Berlin?

14. Ist das —— (*an eight*) oder —— (*a zero*)?

15. Er hat —— (*sixteen*) Bücher, aber nur —— (*six*) davon hat er gelesen.

16. Das kleine Kind kann noch nicht gehen.   Es kriecht auf allen —— (*fours*).

17. Mein Geburtstag ist am —— (*30th*) April.

18. Heute haben wir d— —— (*17th*) Dezember.   Heute ist d— —— (*17th*) Dezember.

19. Meine Schwester ist am —— (*20th*) Mai geboren.

20. Schiller wurde am —— (*10th*) November —— (*1759*) geboren.

21. Er starb in Weimar am —— (*9th*) Mai —— (*1805*).

22. Karl ist d— —— (*16th*) Schüler in der Klasse.

23. Fritz sitzt in d— —— (*6th*) Reihe.

24. Heinrich, lies d— —— (*20th*) Satz!

25. Aus zweierlei Gründen bin ich nicht nach Europa gereist: —— (*in the first place*) war ich krank, —— (*in the second place*) hatte ich kein Geld.

26. Wir mußten d— —— (*30th*) Satz —— (*ten times*) schreiben.

27. Der Satz hatte eine —— (*threefold*) Bedeutung.

28. Nach —— (*an hour and a half*) erschien er.

29. Bitte, geben Sie mir —— (*half a cup of*) Kaffee.

30. Hat der Mann —— (*a third*) oder —— (*a fourth*) seines Vermögens verloren?

31. Welches von den —— (*two*) Mädchen ist deine Freundin?

B.   Translate into German.

1. Today is the 30th of January.   (*Translate in two ways.*)

2. Washington was born on February 22, 1732.

3. The 22nd of February is Washington's birthday.

4. He died on the 14th of December 1799.

5. The 16th of June is my birthday.

6. I saw a hundred autos this morning.

7. Hundreds of (von) people were looking at them.

8. It cost a thousand dollars.
9. The city has about eight million inhabitants.
10. One son will go to the country, one will remain in the city.
11. His one son does not yet go to school.
12. I cannot take a walk today: in the first place, I'm too tired; in the second place, it's raining.
13. He had read that interesting book three times.
14. Give me half a pound of tea.
15. There were (es gab) two types of questions.
16. It is a quarter after twelve.
17. He had eaten half an orange.
18. Those goods have a fourfold value.
19. After an hour and a half he came.
20. Which one of the two sisters was interested in music?

§§21–22. Comparison of Adjectives and Adverbs

A.   Form sentences according to the following model:

Die Mutter, der Vater, der Großvater; *alt* sein.
Die Mutter ist **alt**.   Der Vater ist **älter**.   Der Großvater ist **am ältesten**.

1. Das Dienstmädchen, die Tochter, die Mutter; *fleißig* sein.
2. Die Stunde, die Minute, die Sekunde; *kurz* sein.
3. Das Haus, die Kirche, der Berg; *hoch* sein.
4. Das Auto, der Schnellzug, das Flugzeug; *schnell* fahren.
5. Dieses Jahr, letztes Jahr, vorletztes Jahr; *warm* sein.
6. Karl, Fritz, Johann; *gern* lesen.
7. Eine Taschenuhr, ein Fernsehapparat, ein Mercedes 450 SEL; *kostspielig* sein.

B.   Supply comparative and superlative forms according to the model:

Er ist ein kluger Junge.   Sein Bruder ist ein **klügerer** Junge.
Fritz ist der **klügste** Junge.

1. Heute ist ein kalter Tag.   Gestern war ein —— Tag.   Vorgestern war der —— Tag des ganzen Winters.
2. Das war ein harter Schlag.   Das war ein —— Schlag.   Das war der —— Schlag, den er dem Weltmeister gegeben hat.
3. Ein langer Weg liegt vor mir.   Ein —— Weg liegt vor mir.   Der —— Weg liegt vor mir.
4. Das ist ein scharfes Messer.   Das ist ein —— Messer.   Das ist das —— Messer, das ich je gekauft habe.

C. Complete the sentences.

1. Sie wurde —— (*weaker and weaker*).
2. Die Nacht wird —— (*darker and darker*).
3. Sie sang —— (*most beautifully*).   *aufs schönste*
4. Von allen Damen sang sie —— (*most beautifully*).
5. Sie war —— (*the most beautiful of all*).   *die schönste von allen*
6. —— (*The most beautiful*) Dame sang das Lied.

D. Translate into German.

1. He works most diligently when he is alone.
2. She likes to read.   She prefers to talk.   She likes best to dance.
3. She is a charming woman.   Her sister is more charming.   Her friend is most charming.
4. He likes tea.   (*Use* gern.)   She prefers coffee.   We like beer best.
5. Which month was coldest?
6. Have you ever seen a more beautiful village?
7. He will visit the most famous cities in Germany.
8. That is most (*use a form of* hoch) interesting.
9. Formerly the Woolworth Building was the tallest in New York.
10. The Rhine is one of the most beautiful rivers in Europe.
11. This week we are having warmer weather.
12. That is the longest lesson we ever had.
13. In what season are the days shortest?
14. She always speaks more clearly than her sister.
15. He usually speaks as clearly as she.
16. Last winter he saw the largest cities in Germany.
17. The weather is becoming colder and colder.
18. The most diligent boy in the class was reading the sentence.
19. He was the most diligent of all.
20. Most boys like to play ball.
21. Last month my older brother was in the country.
22. My youngest brother does not yet go to school.
23. He writes better than his sister.
24. She does not write as well as her brother.
25. My friend likes to travel alone.   That can be *very* dangerous.

§§23–25. Expression of Time and Date

A. Complete:

1. Letzt— Jahr war ich in Deutschland.
2. Nächst— Sommer werde ich nach Europa reisen.

3. Vorig— Woche war ich im Theater.
4. Er ist a— 15. Mai 1905 geboren.
5. Ein— Morgen— erhielt ich einen langen Brief von ihm.
6. „D— 18. Juni" stand oben auf der ersten Seite des Briefes.
7. Nächst— Montag muß ich diesen Brief beantworten.
8. D— wie— ist heute?
9. D— wie— haben wir heute?
10. Es ist —— (*half past twelve*).
11. Es ist —— (*a quarter to nine*).
12. Es ist —— (*a quarter after three*).
13. Der Vater wird —— (*at*) zwei Uhr kommen.
14. —— (*Tomorrow morning*) werde ich aufs Land gehen.
15. —— (*Yesterday evening*) war ich in der Oper.
16. —— (*This morning*) habe ich einen Spaziergang gemacht.
17. —— (*In*) Frühling blühen die Obstbäume.
18. —— (*In*) Winter fällt der Schnee.
19. D— ganz— Sommer habe ich mich herrlich amüsiert.
20. Jed— Herbst bewundere ich die schönen Farben der Blätter.
21. —— Tage arbeiten wir.   Arbeiten Sie d— ganz— Tag?
22. —— (*At*) Nacht scheint der Mond.
23. Mein Freund ist —— 10. März geboren.
24. Ein— Tag— begegnete ich meinem alten Freund auf der Straße.
25. —— (*On the*) 11. September fängt die Schule an.
26. Dies— Sommer werde ich auf dem Lande sein.
27. Der Sturm war am heftigsten —— (*toward*) Morgen.
28. Wir gehen —— zwei Monat— in die Berge.
29. Heute —— acht Tag— wird der Flieger in Berlin ankommen.
30. —— acht Tag— (*A week ago*) war ich bei meinem Vetter.
31. Wir frühstücken —— (*about*) halb acht.

B. Translate:

1. Every Saturday I go to the theater.
2. Last Saturday my dear friend was in the movies.
3. Next week I shall see him.
4. Next year she will go to Germany.
5. At the top of (oben auf) the first page of the letter I wrote: "June 16."
6. Goethe was born on the 28th of August 1749.
7. Goethe died on the 22nd of March 1832.
8. This morning I wrote my parents a long letter.
9. Next week I shall receive an answer.
10. Tomorrow morning he will visit me.
11. Yesterday morning I was not at home.
12. Tomorrow afternoon we shall go to the country.

13. Yesterday afternoon we were at my friend's house.
14. Last night I did not sleep well (gut).
15. Did you see him day before yesterday?
16. Day after tomorrow we shall read those German stories.
17. Winter begins in December.
18. He likes to swim in summer.
19. One summer I visited my rich uncle.
20. What is today's date?
21. What is tomorrow's date?
22. It is half past one.
23. It is a quarter after two.
24. It is a quarter to three.
25. His younger sister usually studies in the forenoon.
26. In the afternoon I always take a long walk.
27. Last Thursday we played ball.
28. Some day we shall travel to Turkey.
29. Next month we shall win (siegen).
30. Every day we must work hard.
31. The performance (Die Vorstellung) begins at about eight o'clock.
32. I saw my old friend a week ago.
33. A week from today I shall go to the beach.
34. The storm was most violent toward evening.
35. We are going to the country for a month.

§§26–32. Prepositions

A.   Complete the following sentences:

1. Ein kleiner Vogel ist auf d— hoh— Baum geflogen.
2. Er geht an d— Fenster.
3. Er sitzt an d— Fenster.
4. Während d— Sommer— war ich auf dem Lande.
5. Er wohnt bei sein— älter— Schwester.
6. Er bereitet sich auf sein— nächst— Prüfung vor.
7. Sie sehnte sich nach d— alt—Heimat.
8. Tun Sie es mein— Sohn—wegen!
9. —wegen (*On your account*) werde ich es tun.
10. Das Kind hat mit d— Ball gespielt.
11. Kümmern Sie sich nicht um ih—!
12. Der Junge war dreimal um d— Haus gelaufen.
13. Der Flieger wartet auf günstig— Wetter.
14. Trotz d— Hitze arbeitete er auf d— Feld.
15. Berlin liegt an d— Spree.

16. Er war nach —— (*him*) gelaufen.
17. Der Boxer kämpfte gegen d— Weltmeister.
18. Man trinkt Kaffee aus ein— Kaffeetasse.
19. Der Apfelbaum steht neben d— Haus.
20. Außer d— Mutter war niemand da.
21. Anstatt ein— König— hat das Land jetzt einen Präsidenten.
22. Mein Freund ist seit ein— Woche krank.
23. Der Bleistift liegt auf d— Tisch.
24. Ich lege den Bleistift auf d— Tisch.
25. Er begleitete mich bis an d— Tür.
26. Was haben Sie gegen mi—?
27. Bayern liegt diesseits d— Alpen.
28. Jenseits d— Gebirg— liegt die Schweiz.
29. Gehen Sie hinter mi—!
30. Sie stand hinter mi—.
31. Er bleibt bis zu— nächst— Monat in Bonn.
32. Ich habe an mein— alt— Freund gedacht.
33. Sie hatte einen Brief von ihr— best—Freundin erhalten.
34. Innerhalb ein— Jahr— hat mein Freund viele Länder besucht.
35. Früher hat er außerhalb d— Stadt gewohnt.
36. Ich setzte mich neben d— klein— Jung— (*sing.*).
37. Ich saß neben d— klein— Jung— (*sing.*).
38. Das ist gegen d— Wunsch seiner Mutter.
39. Der Vater hat ein Geschenk für sein— jüngst— Sohn gekauft.
40. Meine Schwester wohnt in d— Stadt.
41. Gestern sind meine Freunde in d— Stadt gekommen.
42. Er sagt zu d— Mädchen: „Du solltest nach Europa reisen."
43. Sie wohnt d— alt— Kirche gegenüber.
44. Das Luftschiff schwebt über unser— Haus.
45. Gestern ist das Luftschiff über uns— Haus geflogen.
46. Ich halte ihn für ein— ehrlich— Mann.
47. Man darf nicht gegen d— Strom schwimmen.
48. —— (*In*) Sommer sind die Tage heiß.
49. Er wird über ei— interessant— Buch sprechen.
50. Um Gott— willen!
51. D— Sage nach kommen die Hexen in d— Walpurgisnacht nach d— Brocken.
52. Wohnen Sie bei Ihr— Eltern?
53. Er hatte sich zwischen d— beid— Brüder geworfen.
54. Er stand zwischen d— beid— Brüder—.
55. Nach d— Regen schien die Sonne.
56. Der Dom ist jenseits d— Strom—.
57. Während welch— Monate haben Sie Ferien?

58. Die deutschen Kinder gehen durch d— schön— Wald spazieren.
59. Viele Leute standen um d— jung— Mann.
60. Die Kinder traten vor d— groß— Haustür.
61. Vor d— groß— Haustür stand die Mutter.
62. Was ist aus Ihr— alt— Freund geworden?
63. Seit d— groß— Krieg hat er mich nicht besucht.
64. Er wird es um sein—willen tun.
65. Stecken Sie das Taschentuch in d— link— Tasche!
66. Das Taschentuch ist schon in d— link— Tasche.
67. Ohne Ihr— Hilfe bin ich verloren.
68. Das ist unter mein— Würde.
69. Er tauchte unter d— Wasser.
70. Nach d— Abendessen liest er die deutsche Zeitung.
71. Er winkte mir mit d— Hand.
72. Ein Wasserfall ist oberhalb d— klein— Gasthaus—.
73. Unterhalb d— schön— Wasserfall— ist ein großer Wald.
74. Das Buch wird von d— Schüler gelesen werden.
75. Früher wohnte sie d— deutsch— Theater gegenüber.
76. Bayreuth ist durch d— Vorstellungen der Wagneropern berühmt.
77. Er sagte zu d— klein— Kinder—: „Seid fleißig!“
78. Wir setzten uns unter d— schön— Lindenbaum.
79. Köln liegt an d— (or a—) Rhein.
80. Das Haus wird von d— alt—Zimmermann gebaut.
81. Deutschland liegt zwischen d— Meer und d— Alpen.
82. Ist das für —— (*him*) oder für —— (*her*)?
83. Er setzte sich —— (*without saying anything*).
84. Er geht in die Schule —— (*in order to learn German*).
85. —— (*Instead of working*), spielte er immer.
86. „—— [*From (i.e., out of) what*] trinkt er?“   „Aus d—Tasse.“
87. Er trinkt —— [*from (i.e., out of) it*].
88. „—— (*With what*) schreibt er?“   „Mit d— Feder.“
89. Er schreibt —— (*with it*).
90. „—— (*Of what*) spricht er?“   „Von d— Wetter.“
91. Ich spreche —— (*of it*). Er spricht —— (*of him*).
92. Gehen Sie —— Hause? Mein Bruder ist schon —— Hause.
93. Das Pult ist —— Holz.
94. Das Gedicht ist —— Goethe.

B. Rewrite the following sentences:

(1) As questions with the proper **wo**-form.
(2) As declarative sentences with the proper **da**-form.

Model: Man sieht **mit** den Augen.

Wo-form: Wo**mit** sieht man?
Da-form: Man sieht da**mit**.

1. Er denkt **an** die Vergangenheit.
2. Die Bücher lagen **auf** dem Tisch.
3. Er wird **über** die Geschichte sprechen.
4. Er hat sich **nach** der Heimat gesehnt.
5. Die Kinder waren **durch** das Zimmer gelaufen.
6. Sie hat dem Mann **für** das Buch gedankt.

C. Translate:

1. The little children had run through the large house.
2. The brown dog was lying under the table.
3. It (*i.e.,* the dog) ran under a small chair.
4. With whom will he travel this summer?
5. In spite of the bad weather, she had come to school.
6. What have you against them?
7. He will come out of the house at half past nine.
8. On what days do you not go to school?
9. He accompanied me as far as Berlin.
10. Have you any money with you?
11. At whose house do you live now?
12. He will buy a gift for his best friend.
13. He entered the room; then he sat down.
14. He sat down beside her.
15. He was sitting beside her.
16. During the night it had rained hard.
17. "Shall (Soll) I open the window?" "Yes, for all I care."
18. After breakfast he will take a long walk.
19. For two hours she has been reading that French book.
20. In most classes the pupils sit according to the alphabet.
21. I have not seen him since day before yesterday.
22. What did he want of me?
23. After school I must go home quickly.
24. She never worries about him.
25. Many people are standing around her.
26. He will jump over the small table.
27. Over the table (there) was a beautiful picture.
28. It happened a week ago.
29. He was talking about (über) his interesting experiences.
30. She is standing before the pupils.
31. She steps in front of the pupils.
32. We now live opposite the beautiful park.

33. Yesterday I received a long letter from my old grandmother.
34. Today I am going to my brother's (house).
35. He passed me without saying a word.
36. We eat in order to live. We do not live in order to eat.
37. Instead of going away at once, he remained five weeks.
38. For heaven's sake!
39. Does he now live outside of the city?
40. "With what was he writing?" "He was writing with a pen." "He was writing with it."
41. By whom was the house built?
42. For whom were you working?

§33. Uses of the Genitive Case[1]

A. Complete the following sentences, as necessary:

1. Ein— Morgen— begegnete ich ihm auf der Straße.
2. Ein— Tag— wird er mich besuchen.
3. Er war sich sein— Schuld bewußt.
4. Sind Sie d— Leben— müde?
5. Sie ist ihr— Sache gewiß.
6. Ich hatte sechs Pfund frisch— Fleisch— gekauft.
7. Er bestellte zehn Glas —— Bier für die Gesellschaft.
8. Ein Gast wollte ein Glas hell— Bier—.
9. Ist das eine neue Art —— Telefon?
10. Jetzt bin ich —— (it) los. Ich war —— (it) müde.
11. Es ist nicht d— Mühe wert, die Geschichte zu lesen.
12. Ein— Abend— werde ich einen langen Spaziergang machen.
13. Fahren Sie gewöhnlich erst— oder zweit— Klasse?
14. Sind Sie —— (of the same) Meinung?
15. Ist er ein— solch— Tat fähig?
16. Er ist Ihr— Hilfe würdig.
17. Er beraubte ih— sein— Vermögen—.
18. Sie wird nie ihr— Leben— froh.
19. Er wurde d— Verrat— (treason) angeklagt.
20. Erst jetzt werde ich mein— Irrtum— gewahr.
21. Er schämt sich sein— arm— Eltern nicht.
22. Ich war mein— Sinn— (pl.) nicht mächtig.
23. Er rühmt sich sein— Glück—.
24. Sind Sie d— Geld— bedürftig?
25. Erinnern Sie sich —— unser Versprechen?
26. Haben Sie ihn d— Lüge beschuldigt?

---

[1]It should be remembered that most of the genitive uses in these exercises are avoided or replaced in Modern *spoken* German.

27. Bedürfen Sie ein— Arzt—?
28. Gedenke dein— Versprechen—!
29. Leicht— Herz— (*sing.*) liefen die Kinder nach Hause.
30. Heute ist er gut— Laune.
31. Mein— Wissen— ist er heute nicht hier.
32. Sie wohnt link— vom Walde.
33. Laß mich mein— Weg— ziehen!

B.   Translate into German:

1. Please give me three pounds of meat.
2. He is not ashamed of his friends.
3. The city of Hamburg is (liegt) on the Elbe.
4. There are still two pounds of fresh butter at home.
5. Some day I shall visit him.
6. One evening the little children took a long walk.
7. She is not capable of such a deed.
8. He is rid of it.   He was tired of it.
9. He wanted a cup of hot coffee.
10. He never travels third class.
11. She is of the same opinion.
12. That is not worth while.
13. Remember your promise!
14. He needs a doctor.
15. He was not conscious of any injustice.
16. Avail yourself (*or* make use) of his advice.
17. He always boasts of his success.
18. They were not in (control of) their senses.
19. He was accused of theft.
20. They robbed him of all his money.
21. She is worthy of your help.
22. He was charged with (*or* accused of) the lie.
23. I am by no means satisfied.
24. Are you in good humor today?
25. With a heavy heart she went to work.
26. As far as I know, nobody is absent today.
27. They live to the right of (von) the church.
28. Let her go her way.
29. In any case, I am sure of his help.

§34.   Uses of the Dative Case

A.   Complete the following sentences:

1. Antworten Sie d— alt— Mann!
2. Antworten Sie —— dies— Frage!

3. D— jünger— Tochter ist d— Vater ähnlich.
4. Dies— kurz— Geschichte ist mi— gar nicht bekannt.
5. We— sind Sie auf d— Straße begegnet?
6. Haben Sie d— gut— Frau geholfen?
7. Ich werde es mi— bequem machen.
8. Was fehlt d— klein— Jung— (*sing.*)?
9. D— jung— Männer sind uns all— fremd.
10. Seien Sie —— (*them*) freundlich!
11. We— gehören dies— deutsch— Bücher?
12. Die Ferien kommen d— klein— Kind— (*pl.*) gelegen.
13. Ihr Besuch ist mein— älter— Bruder stets angenehm.
14. D— jüngst— Kind gleicht d— Mutter.
15. Glauben Sie —— (*them*)? Glauben Sie —— (*it*)?
16. Das war —— (*her*) nie eingefallen.
17. Ist dies— kurz— Prüfung d— Schüler— (*pl.*) schwer?
18. Ich gratuliere —— (*you*) zum Geburtstag.
19. Es ist —— (*us*) all— sehr lieb, daß Sie das sagen.
20. Langsam näherte er sich d— alt— Dorf.
21. Er befahl mi—, bald zurückzukehren.
22. Das war —— (*them*) ein Rätsel.
23. Er hatte —— (*his*) Hände gewaschen.
24. Sie setzte —— (*her*) Hut auf.
25. Wir haben —— (*ourselves*) nicht geschmeichelt. Schmeicheln Sie
    —— (*yourself*) nicht!
26. Diese Speise wird dein— Gesundheit nicht schaden.
27. Wie gefällt —— (*you*) dies— lang— Geschichte?
28. Der Polizist ist d— Dieb gefolgt.
29. Es ist mi— ganz gleich, was er sagt. Ich glaube —— (*it*) nicht.
30. Widersprich d— Eltern nicht!
31. Ihr Wort genügt mi—.
32. Er hat d— arm— Frau viel Geld gegeben.
33. Sie war ihr— Vater stets dankbar.
34. Das Dorf liegt mein— Vaterstadt nahe.
35. Seien Sie —— (*him*) nicht böse!
36. Wozu haben Sie —— (*her*) geraten?
37. Es ist mi— noch nicht gelungen, diesen Plan auszuführen.

B. Translate:

1. How do you like this new book?
2. That will not hurt her health.
3. It was all the same to me what he said. I saw it myself.
4. She had given the poor children some apples.
5. Show those little boys the interesting pictures.

6. That was a riddle to her.
7. He is putting on his hat.
8. Don't flatter yourself.
9. Don't contradict that old man.
10. Finally it occurred to me.
11. This short examination was easy for them.
12. Is writing difficult for you?
13. They are slowly approaching the city of Fulda.
14. Formerly we lived near them (*i.e.*, in their vicinity).
15. We were helping our dear friends.
16. "Did you answer him?" "No, I did not answer his questions."
17. Do you believe him?   Do you believe it?
18. The older brother resembles his mother.
19. That serves you right!
20. I met that famous man on the street today.
21. She will obey her mother.
22. To whom do these interesting pictures belong?
23. They are all strangers (*use adj.* fremd) to me.
24. What is the matter with those young men?
25. I shall always be grateful to him.
26. What (in the world) do you mean?
27. Of what use is that to you?

§35. Uses of the Accusative Case

A.   Complete the following sentences:

1. Wir werden d— ganz— Sommer in Europa sein.
2. Er hatte mi— sein— best— Freund genannt.
3. —— Hut in d— Hand, trat er in d— Zimmer.
4. Jed— Samstag gehe ich in— Theater.
5. Nächst— Sommer werde ich —— Hause bleiben.
6. D— ganz— Monat war ich auf dem Lande.
7. Ein— Tag— wurde ich krank.
8. Das Band war ein— Finger breit.
9. Sie lehrte mi— d— schön— Lied.
10. Die Wand war ein— Fuß dick.
11. Er hatte —— (*him*) ein— Narren gescholten.
12. Das Buch kostete —— (*her*) ein— Dollar.
13. Ich bin d— Frühaufstehen nicht gewöhnt.
14. Langsam ging er d— Straße entlang.
15. Das Brett ist nur ein— Fuß lang.
16. Endlich bin ich d— Sache los.

17. Fritz ist ein— Kopf größer als sein jüngerer Bruder.
18. Beantworten Sie mein— erst— Frage!
19. Antworten Sie —— mein— erst— Frage!
20. Ein— ganz— Tag verfolgte er mi—.
21. Ich träumte ein— schön— Traum.
22. Jed— Winter bleibe ich in d— Stadt.
23. Ein— Morgen— hatten wir viel Schnee.
24. Es ist kein— Mark wert.
25. Die Arbeit kostete mi— viel Mühe.

B. Translate:

1. Next winter my best friend will visit me.
2. Every Sunday I take a long walk.
3. We shall be in Germany the whole summer.
4. With his cane in his hand, he walked through the village.
5. I had called him my friend.
6. He is going along the street.
7. It is worth a mark.
8. They were not used to hard work.
9. Were you working all morning?
10. Last summer I visited my best friend.
11. My little brother played ball all afternoon.
12. The thief followed me through the dark street.
13. He pursued me for a whole hour.
14. Why didn't you answer my question?
15. The water is a foot deep.
16. I am tired of it.   At last I am rid of it.
17. He walked slowly along the river.
18. The work cost me much trouble.
19. I was frightened.   I frightened him.
20. The tall trees were falling.   They were felling the tall trees.
21. She disappears.   She never squanders her money.

§§36–39. Special Uses of Tense

A. Translate into idiomatic English:

1. Wie lange ist Herr Schmidt schon in Amerika?
2. Wir waren schon eine Viertelstunde im Hotel, als er kam.
3. Sie wartet schon eine Stunde auf mich.
4. Sie wird wohl wissen, warum ich zu spät komme.
5. Seit wann ist Ihr alter Freund auf dem Lande?
6. Er wird wohl gewußt haben, warum ich ihn letzten Sommer nicht besuchen konnte.

7. Ich wohne erst seit zwei Tagen in diesem Haus.
8. Der Winter ist bald da (*here*).
9. Wenn Sie sich nicht warm anziehen, so werden Sie sich erkälten.
10. Wie lange ist der Mann schon da?
11. Der Mann wird wohl zu viel getrunken haben.
12. Wir waren schon lange Freunde.
13. Ich werde es wohl verlegt haben.
14. Er pflegte früh aufzustehen.

B. Translate into German.   Consider the tense very carefully.

1. Since when has your rich uncle been living in this small village?
2. He doubtless knows why I am here.
3. I have been waiting an hour and a half for him.
4. She had been there half an hour when I came.
5. How long has your dear friend been in the country?
6. I have been here since half past eight.
7. Her little brother is probably in school.
8. For four days I have been looking for my fountain pen.
9. I probably misplaced it.
10. Spring will soon be here (da).
11. She has been living in this city for only one month.
12. I had known her for many years.
13. She probably has a headache.
14. She probably studied too hard.
15. He used to speak about his experiences.

§§40–43. Personal Pronouns

A. Complete the following sentences. Use the conventional, formal *you*, unless otherwise indicated.
1. Bitte, geben Sie —— (*me*) das Buch!
2. Wird er —— [*you* (fam. sing.)] heute besuchen?
3. Sie hat —— (*me*) heute auf der Straße gesehen.
4. Das wird —— [*you* (fam. sing.)] nicht schaden.
5. Ich hatte —— (*him*) nicht verstanden.
6. Kinder, hat die Mutter —— (*you*) geholfen?
7. Ich gab —— (*him*) die Feder.
8. Wir werden —— (*her*) nächsten Monat besuchen.
9. Sie hat —— (*us*) nicht erkannt.
10. Gefällt di— das Buch?
11. Gefällt ih— die Geschichte? (*Complete in three ways.*)
12. Er folgte —— (*us*).
13. Was fehlt —— (*you*)?

14. Er kannte —— (*them*).
15. Er begegnete —— (*me*) in der Stadt.
16. Er hat —— (*me*) auf dem Lande getroffen.
17. Gehört das Buch —— (*her*) oder —— (*him*)?
18. Er hatte —— (*her*) nicht gehört.
19. Er hat —— (*me*) befohlen aufzustehen.
20. Der Hund wird —— (*him*) nicht beißen.
21. Bitte, tun Sie das —— (*on my account*)!
22. Ich werde —— (*you*) die Bücher geben.
23. Nächste Woche werde ich —— (*you*) besuchen.
24. Frau Schmidt, man muß —— (*you*) loben.
25. Meine Damen, man muß —— (*you*) loben.
26. Der Stuhl ist schön. —— (*It*) gehört —— (*her*).
27. Die Prüfung ist nicht schwer. —— (*It*) ist leicht.
28. Das Kleid ist schön. —— (*It*) gefällt mi—.
29. Zeigen Sie es —— (*them*)!
30. Ich werde es —— (*you*) zeigen.

B.   Translate:

1. "Where is my trunk?"   "It is in the station."
2. Please give me the ink.   Is it black or red?
3. My old friend was visiting me.
4. He will help me.
5. I have not forgotten him.
6. I shall write him a long letter.
7. Do you like the books?   (*Translate three ways, using* gefallen)
8. Our old physician had not believed them.
9. My younger sister did not understand them.
10. Did you not hear me?
11. Why have you forgotten her?
12. I shall thank her for the letter.
13. When did you see him?
14. He did not recognize me.
15. He always loved her.
16. What is the matter with him?
17. When will you visit me?
18. We had not heard them.

§44.   Interrogatives

A.   Complete the following sentences:

1. —— (*Whom*) haben Sie heute besucht?
2. —— (*To whom*) hat er die Bilder gezeigt?

3. —— (*What*) hat er in der Hand?
4. —— (*With what*) wird er den Brief schreiben?
5. Mit —— (*what kind of a*) Feder schreibt er?
6. —— (*What*) Bücher lagen auf dem Tisch?
7. —— (*What*) Junge ist heute nicht hier?
8. —— (*Which one*) fehlt heute?
9. —— (*Whom*) haben Sie auf der Straße gesehen?
10. —— (*Whom*) sind Sie auf dem Lande begegnet?
11. —— (*To whom*) hatte er das Geld gegeben?
12. —— (*Whom*) hat er gestern getroffen?
13. —— (*Whose*) Arbeit ist das?
14. Er fragte mich, —— (*who*) gekommen wäre.
15. —— (*On what*) sitzen Sie?
16. —— (*With what*) hört man?
17. —— (*Whom*) hat er geschlagen?
18. —— (*To whom*) sagte er das?
19. In —— (*what kind of a*) Buch haben Sie das gelesen?
20. —— (*Of what*) denken Sie?
21. —— (*Of whom*) denken Sie?
22. —— (*Why*) haben Sie mich verlassen?
23. „Ich habe ein Buch vergessen." „—— (*Which one*) haben Sie vergessen?"
24. —— (*For what*) warten Sie?
25. —— (*For whom*) warten Sie?
26. —— (*What kind of*) wissenschaftliche Bücher haben Sie neulich gelesen?

B. Translate:

1. With whom are the little children playing?
2. With what were they playing?
3. Who is that old gentleman?   Which one is ill?
4. Who are those old gentlemen?
5. Which friend did you see today?
6. Which one (*i.e.*, friend) did you see?
7. Whose pens are those?
8. Whom did you visit yesterday?
9. For what are you waiting?
10. For whom was he waiting?
11. With what kind of (a) pen had he written the letter?
12. Which story do you like?
13. Of whom are you thinking?
14. Of what were you thinking?
15. Whom had his younger brother followed?

16. Why will he leave this beautiful city?
17. Whom did he see yesterday?
18. To whom did you give those interesting German books?

§§45–51. Relative Pronouns

A. Complete the following sentences:

1. Der alte Mann, —— er das Geld gab, war sehr arm.
2. Der Stuhl, —— in der Ecke steht, gefällt mir.
3. Der Lehrer, —— Buch ich jetzt habe, ist heute zu Hause.
4. Die schöne Stadt, —— an der Isar liegt, heißt München.
5. Die Stadt, —— Dom weltbekannt ist, heißt Köln.
6. Die Frau, —— ich die Bücher gegeben habe, wohnt in der Stadt.
7. Ein Löschblatt ist ein Blatt, —— man Tinte löscht.
8. Das Haus, —— wir gekauft haben, besteht aus zehn Zimmern.
9. Das Kind, —— Eltern arm sind, heißt Karl.
10. Der Bleistift, —— ich jetzt schreibe, ist gelb.
11. Die Bücher, —— er die Geschichten gelesen hat, sind interesant.
12. Die Freunde, —— wir besuchen wollten, waren nicht zu Hause.
13. Die Kinder, —— auf der Straße spielen, amüsieren sich.
14. Die Jungen, —— ich helfen wollte, arbeiten fleißig.
15. Die Schüler, —— Eltern reich sind, arbeiten nicht.
16. —— reich ist, (der) ist nicht immer glücklich.
17. —— sie verspricht, (das) vergißt sie immer.
18. Sie sagte, es gehe ihr gut, —— mich sehr freute.
19. Das war etwas, —— ich noch nicht wußte.
20. Alles, —— ich hatte, ist jetzt verloren.
21. Nichts, —— sie sagt, ist wahr.
22. Die Herren, mit —— ich gesprochen habe, waren Ausländer.
23. Die Künstlerin, —— Werke ich bewundert habe, ist heute abgefahren.

B. Translate:

1. The people in whose house (bei) I lived have moved (umziehen).
2. My old friends who live in the country will visit me next week.
3. The pupils whose sentences I have corrected worked very hard.
4. Those (Das) are the boys whom I helped.
5. The little girl to whom I shall give the books is at home today.
6. The letter which is (liegen) on the table consists of four pages.
7. I like the story which my little brother is reading.
8. The gentleman whom I met (begegnen) yesterday is my best friend.

9. I don't like (gefallen) the chair I bought yesterday.
10. He gave me everything he had.
11. At the time when I visited him he was ill.
12. That is something he will not understand.
13. He gave his wife the money he had earned.
14. Whoever she may be, I will help her.
15. My grandfather, whom I visited last summer, is eighty years old.
16. Nothing I have is safe.
17. The old village in which he is now living has many beautiful castle ruins.
18. That is the city I like best.
19. Whatever he says, I don't believe it.
20. Nothing he says is true.
21. We, who are ill ourselves, cannot help the others.
22. The lady whose beautiful voice I admired left (abfahren) today.
23. A coffee cup is a cup from (*i.e.,* out of) which one drinks coffee.
24. Hamburg, Bremen, and Lübeck are German cities that were formerly Hanseatic states (Hansestaaten).
25. Heidelberg is a German city which is famous for its university.
26. That is the most beautiful thing (*use neut. adj. as noun*) that I have ever (je) seen.
27. That is the best that we have.

§§52–56. Possessive Adjectives and Pronouns

A. Complete the following sentences with the correct possessive form:

1. Die Mutter liebt ―― (*her*) Kind.   Das Kind liebt ―― (*its*) Mutter.
2. Ist das Kind ―― (*hers*)?
3. Der Vater suchte ―― (*his*) Sohn.
4. Mein Sohn ist in der Schule.   Wo ist ―― (*his*)?
5. Geben Sie mir ―― (*my*) Buch!
6. Mein Buch ist auf dem Tisch.   Wo ist ―― (*yours*)?
(Rewrite sentences 1–6 in the plural.)
7. Er hat ―― (*his*) Freunden viel Geld gegeben.
8. Sie hat ―― (*her*) Bruder das Bild gezeigt.
9. Bitte, zeigen Sie mir ―― (*your*) Buch!
10. Die Schüler hatten ―― (*their*) Bücher vergessen.
11. Das Mädchen hatte ―― (*her*) Buch verloren.
12. Die Stadt ist durch ―― (*its*) Dom berühmt.
13. Dieser Stuhl ist ―― (*mine*).   Wo ist ―― (*his*)?
14. Das Buch ist ―― (*his*).   Wo ist ―― (*yours*)?
15. ―― (*Her*) Bruder ist Physiker.

B. Complete the following sentences with the proper imperative and possessive forms.

    1. Karl, —— (*eat*) —— (*your*) Suppe!
       Kinder, —— (*eat*) —— (*your*) Suppe!
       Bitte, —— (*eat*) —— (*your*) Suppe!
    2. Karl, —— (*read*) —— (*your*) Aufsatz!
       Kinder, —— (*read*) —— (*your*) Aufsatz!
       Bitte, —— (*read*) —— (*your*) Aufsatz!
    3. Fritz, —— (*break*) —— (*your*) Stock nicht!
       Meine lieben Kinder, —— (*break*) —— (*your*) Stöcke nidht!
       Herr Schmidt, bitte, —— (*break*) —— (*your*) Stock nicht!
    4. Marie, —— (*give*) mir —— (*your*) Buch!
       Marie und Luise, —— (*give*) mir —— (*your*) Bücher!
       Herr Werner, bitte, —— (*give*) mir —— (*your*) Buch!
    5. Johann, —— (*help*) —— (*your*) Freund!
       Johann und Wilhelm, —— (*help*) —— (*your*) Freund!
       Bitte, —— (*help*) —— (*your*) Freund!

C. Supply a suitable adjective for each of the direct objects in the above sentences.

D. Translate:

    1. That is my old coat.   Where is yours?
    2. Have you seen my black fountain pen?   Where is his?
    3. The father is praising his youngest daughter.
    4. Her younger son is not in school today.
    5. Tomorrow he will give me his German book.
    6. She had put (legen) her books on the little round table.
    7. Cologne is famous for its beautiful cathedral.
    8. We shall show them our new radio.
    9. They were preparing for (sich vorbereiten auf *w. acc.*) their examination.
   10. "Whose book is that?   Yours?"   "No, not mine."

§§57–59. Demonstratives

A. Complete the following sentences:

    1. Diese kurze Geschichte gefällt mir.   —— (*That one*) gefällt mir nicht.
    2. Dieses neue Haus ist viel schöner als —— (*that one*).
    3. —— (*This*) Gebäude ist nicht so hoch wie —— (*that one*).
    4. —— (*This*) Insel ist ebenso groß wie —— (*that one*).
    5. Das ist —— (*the same*) Junge, den ich gestern gesehen habe.

6. Es ist —— (*the same*) Krawatte, die ich immer getragen habe.

7. Ich habe —— (*the same*) Mann oft geholfen.

8. —— (*The same one*) hat mich heute besucht.

9. Er hatte —— (*the same*) Kindern viele schöne Geschenke gegeben.

10. Im Herbst —— (*of the same*) Jahres sind die beiden Brüder nach Amerika gekommen.

11. —— (*Those*), die den Satz nicht verstehen, sollen Fragen stellen.

12. Das sind die Namen —— (*of those*), die mitgeholfen haben.

13. Treue Freunde halte fest! Es gibt —— (*of them*) nicht viele.

14. Groß war die Freude, denn —— (*the one*), der dem Vater am liebsten war, hatte den ersten Preis gewonnen.

15. —— (*That*) Junge ist klug.

16. —— [*He* (emphatic)] arbeitet immer fleißig.

17. Karl hatte —— (*no such*) Erfolg.

18. Ich denke —— (*of that*).

19. Er wird —— (*for that*) warten.

20. Er hatte —— (*about that*) gesprochen.

21. —— (*Such a*) Hitze haben wir nie in dieser Stadt erlebt.

22. —— (*Such*) Fragen wie —— (*these*) hat er nie beantwortet.

23. Sie sprachen von —— (*this*) Jungen und von —— (*that*) Mädchen.

24. —— (*Those*) sind unsere Bücher. Fritz hat —— (*no such*) Buch.

25. Vorige Nacht hat es stark geregnet. —— (*Consequently*) sind die Straßen jetzt sehr naß.

26. —— (*In the meantime*) müssen wir zu Hause bleiben.

27. —— (*In spite of that*) werden wir später einen kurzen Spaziergang machen.

28. Ich begegnete Herrn Braun und Herrn Fischer auf der Straße. —— (*The former*) ist Mathematiker; —— (*the latter*) ist Arzt.

B. Translate:

1. This large trunk is heavier than that one.

2. This beautiful country is warmer than that one.

3. This narrow street is longer than that one.

4. That German book belongs to my sister. This one belongs to my brother.

5. I met the same men last summer in the country.

6. The two men have moved (ziehen) into the same house.

7. Those who have made mistakes must correct them.

8. Take these interesting German books. There are (es gibt) few of them (*dem.*).

9. That is the fault of those who have not paid attention.

10. My dear friend had waited for that.

11. He always speaks of that.

12. I have never read such a book.

13. Have you ever read such books?

14. He never writes with such a pen.

15. Give me another knife.   This one does not cut well.

16. The two brothers went to the same school.

17. One day we took a long walk.   Consequently we both became very tired.

18. My father has gone to Germany.   In the meantime I must stay at home.

§60.   Indefinite Pronouns and Adjectives

A.   Complete the following sentences:

1. —— (*Everybody*) sagt es.

2. —— (*No one*) ist im Zimmer.

3. Ich höre —— (*someone*) kommen.

4. —— [*People* (indef.)] glaubt ihm.

5. Sie hat —— (*some*) Butter gekauft.

6. —— (*Some*) Häuser in dieser Stadt sind sehr hoch.

7. Haben Sie etwas —— (*new*) gehört?

8. Ich habe nichts —— (*interesting*) gelesen.

9. Er hat wenig —— (*good*) getan.

10. Sie hat viel —— (*beautiful*) geschrieben.

11. —— (*Something*) gefällt ihm nicht.

12. Außer seiner Schwester war —— (*no one else*) da.

13. Hat —— (*anybody*) Karl gesehen?

14. Fehlt —— (*anyone else*) heute?

15. Haben Sie —— (*nothing*) getan?

16. Er hat —— (*little*) Geduld.

17. Mit —— (*few*) Worten hat er alles erklärt.

18. Haben Sie —— (*many*) Freunde?

19. Er wird —— (*much*) Geld verdienen.

20. Er hat —— (*no one*) geholfen.

21. Haben Sie —— (*everything possible*) getan?

22. Er hatte —— (*everything else*) vergessen.

23. Mein alter Freund wohnt —— (*somewhere*) in dieser Stadt.

24. Ich konnte ihn —— (*nowhere*) finden.

25. Das macht —— (*one*) Freude.

26. Er hat —— (*many things*) vergessen.

B.   Translate:

1. Please give me some money.

2. Tell me something interesting.

3. No one believes that.
4. People (*indef.*) had never believed him.
5. She was reading something else.
6. Nobody was in that large room.
7. My dear friends had seen no one.
8. Did you visit anyone this summer?
9. No one else understood the first sentence.
10. My little brother has little patience.
11. That old man had many enemies.
12. That gives one pleasure.
13. Here they (*indef.*) speak German.
14. My best friend lives somewhere in this old village.
15. That is something different.
16. Have you forgotten everything else?
17. I did everything possible.
18. Nowhere are there better streets than in this city.
19. He will help somebody.
20. When I was in Europe, I saw many things.
21. He read the story in some book or other.

§61.   Reflexive Verbs

A.   Complete the following sentences:

1. Erkundigen Sie sich —— d— Herrn!
2. Freuen Sie sich —— (*look forward to*) d— Reise?
3. Haben Sie sich —— d— Besuch Ihres Freundes gefreut (*be happy about*)?
4. Kann ich mich —— dies— Jungen (*sing.*) verlassen?
5. Er verbeugte sich —— d— König.
6. Er hat sich —— sein— Feind— (*pl.*) gerächt.
7. Hüten Sie sich —— jen— Mann!
8. Haben Sie sich —— all— (*everything*) gewöhnt?
9. Warum ärgern Sie sich —— dies— Frau?
10. Haben Sie sich —— —— (*him*) gewundert?
11. Kümmern Sie sich nicht —— mi—!
12. Er bewirbt sich —— d— Stellung.
13. Fürchten Sie sich —— d— Tier?
14. Erinnern Sie sich —— Ihr— Kindheit?
15. Ich kümmere —— nicht —— —— (*him*).
16. Erinnerst du —— —— (*it*)?
17. Er verläßt sich —— —— (*her*).
18. Wir machen —— Sorgen —— —— (*him*).
19. Er hat sich —— ein— schwer— Krankheit erholt.

20. Ich habe —— entschlossen, eine lange Reise zu machen.
21. Ich habe —— zu einer langen Reise entschlossen.
22. Ich interessiere —— —— d— Chemie.
23. Diesen Sommer werden wir —— herrlich amüsieren.
24. Fritz, ziehe —— schnell an!   Kinder, zieht —— schnell an!
25. Ich muß —— beeilen, sonst komme ich zu spät an.
26. Letzte Woche habe ich —— stark erkältet.
27. Marie, benimm —— anständig!
28. So etwas kann ich —— gar nicht vorstellen.
29. Schmeich(e)le —— (*yourself*) nicht!
30. Es wird —— bald zeigen, wer recht hat.

B.   Translate:

1. Did you have a good time?
2. I shall always rely on you.
3. Do you remember those interesting people we met last month?
4. I am looking forward with pleasure to your visit.
5. He will apply for the first prize.
6. They will never get used to it.
7. She had dressed quickly.
8. I am rejoicing at his great success.
9. He is always provoked at me.
10. Even a physician is sometimes mistaken.
11. They love each other.
12. She did that herself.
13. Even I understand that.
14. That is understood.
15. He will long for his old friends.
16. Have a good time.   (*Translate in three ways.*)
17. What are you interested in?
18. I have decided to take a long walk.
19. We can't imagine such a thing.
20. You must hurry; otherwise you will arrive late.
21. Fred, sit down on the bench.
22. He is not afraid of that large dog.
23. You must get used to hard work.
24. I thanked (*use* bedanken) her for the beautiful books.

§62. Impersonal Verbs

A.   Review the following sentences, then translate the exercises in **B.**

1. Es hat stark gefroren.
2. Es gibt dreibeinige Stühle.   Es sind zwei dreibeinige Stühle in diesem Zimmer.   Da ist ein dreibeiniger Stuhl.

3. Es hat lange geregnet.
4. Wird es morgen schneien?
5. Ihm graut, wenn er daran denkt.
6. Mich schläfert (*or* Ich bin schläfrig).
7. Es ist so schnell geschehen, daß er nicht wußte, um was es sich handelte.
8. Sein Vater war zufällig (*or* Zufälligerweise war sein Vater) auch da.
9. Es wurde viel getrunken.
10. Da liegt mein deutsches Buch. Es gibt nicht viele Bücher dieser Art. Es sind verschiedene deutsche Zeitschriften im Nebenzimmer.
11. Wer dies nicht versteht, dem ist nicht zu helfen.
12. Es blitzt schon seit einer Stunde.
13. Vorigen Monat hat es stark gehagelt.

B.   Translate:

1. It was thundering.
2. I think (that) it will rain tomorrow.
3. I shudder when I think of that.
4. Did it snow yesterday?
5. He is not believed.
6. They were not helped.
7. It has been raining for three hours.
8. She is dizzy.
9. She was advised by the physician to go to the mountains.
10. There was much dancing.
11. There (*pointing*) are the notebooks.
12. It happened so quickly that I didn't know what it was all about.
13. My mother happened to be there too.
14. Last month it froze hard.
15. It has been snowing for an hour and a half.
16. The men will not be able to fly, because it is snowing today.
17. There are ten German states.
18. There are six books on the table.

§§63–66. Word Order

A.   Combine the pairs into a single sentence using the conjunction in parentheses. Exercise (1) is done as a model.

1. Sie war nicht hier. Sie war krank. (denn)
   Sie war nicht hier, denn sie war krank.
2. Wir kamen ins Zimmer. Wir setzten uns. (dann)
3. Man setzt sich. Man ist müde. (wenn)
4. Ich besuchte ihn. Er war auf dem Lande. (als)

5. Er arbeitet jetzt.   Er ist schläfrig.   (obgleich)
6. Der Mann ist zu Hause.   Seine Frau ist in der Stadt.   (aber)
7. Ich war gestern in Bett.   Es regnete stark.   (als)
8. Die Leute fliehen.   Sie sind in Gefahr.   (denn)
9. Er schreibt den Satz nicht.   Er versteht ihn nicht.   (weil)
10. Antworten Sie nicht!   Er fragt Sie.   (ehe)
11. Er antwortete.   Er schrieb den Satz an die Tafel.   (dann)
12. Er ging aufs Land.   Ich hatte ihn besucht.   (nachdem)

B.   Rewrite the following sentences with the dependent clause first.

1. Es regnete stark, als er in der Schule war.
2. Sie antwortete nicht, obgleich ich sie zweimal fragte.
3. Er sagte nichts, bevor ich ihn fragte.
4. Er wird das Buch lesen, wenn es nicht zu schwer ist.
5. Eine direkte Beobachtung der Venus-Oberfläche ist unmöglich, weil die dichte, wolkenerfüllte Atmosphäre des Planeten die eigentliche Planetenoberfläche vollständig und dauernd verbirgt.

C.   Translate:

1. The sun sets at half past seven.
2. Her little brother is not in school, for he is ill.
3. She is not happy, although she is very rich.
4. The old men had become tired.
5. My dear friends who are at my house today, live in a beautiful suburb.
6. She always stays at home.
7. He never visits me.
8. This evening he will take a long walk.
9. When will you read that German book?
10. As I was reading it (*i.e.,* the book) this morning, my little sister entered the room.
11. He always speaks German.
12. After he had read the first sentence, he wrote it on the blackboard.
13. Although he wrote the sentences, he made many mistakes.
14. While I was in the country last summer, I met my old friends.
15. He had given the old men some money.
16. They were never at home when I visited them.
17. When will you take (machen) the examination?
18. I know that I shall pass (bestehen) it.
19. I cannot fail (durchfallen), for I have studied very hard.
20. If I close the door, it will be too warm in the room.
21. He is not going along, for he is too tired.
22. When will you visit her?
23. He is not going to Germany, because he has no money.

§§67–68. Conjunctions

A. Combine the following pairs of sentences using the conjunction shown in parentheses.

1. Man nimmt den Hut ab. Man grüßt eine Dame. (*when*)
2. Sie trägt eine Brille. Sie will besser sehen. (*because*)
3. Ich bin im Theater gewesen. [Ich] habe die neueste Oper gesehen. (*and*)
4. Man füllt einen Freiballon mit Helium. Es ist unverbrennbar und leichter als Luft. (*because*)
5. Er konnte nicht arbeiten. Der Lärm war zu groß. (*since,* i.e. *because*)
6. Der Junge war nicht in der Schule. Er war krank. (*for*)
7. Sie war krank. Sie ging zum Arzt. (*therefore*)
8. Besuchen Sie mich! Ich werde böse auf Sie sein. (*or*)
9. Sagen Sie es mir! Ich weiß es auch. (*so that*)
10. Er konnte nicht früher kommen. Er war sehr beschäftigt. (*for*)
11. Er ist nicht hier. Sein Bruder wird mit uns sprechen. (*but*)
12. Er schrieb den Satz an die Tafel. Er hatte ihn gelesen. (*after*)
13. Er ist viel älter als die Schwester. Er ist nicht so klug. (*but*)
14. Sein Bruder schlief. Er spielte Ball. (*while*)
15. Er ging nach Hause. Er war fertig. (*as soon as*)
16. Ich fragte sie. Sie hatte ihn gesehen. (*whether*)
17. Er besuchte mich. Er reiste ab. (*before*)
18. Das ist alles sehr schön. Ich glaube es nicht. (*but*)
19. Sie war in der Stadt. Er war auf dem Lande. (*but*)
20. Ich sah, daß sie unzufrieden war. Sie sagte nichts. (*although*)
21. Wir müssen arbeiten. Es wird dunkel. (*until*)
22. Heute morgen spielte ich Klavier. Er trat ins Zimmer. (*when*)
23. Ich amüsierte mich herrlich. Ich war auf dem Lande. (*as long as*)
24. Sie kauft Blumen. Sie geht aus. (*as often as*)
25. Wir würden uns sehr freuen. Er sollte kommen. (*in case*)
26. Sie war nie zu Hause. Ich wollte sie besuchen. (*when*)
27. Ich weiß nicht. Er ist hier. (*whether*)
28. Ich werde ihn besuchen. Er ist hier. (*if*)

B. Translate:

1. If the weather is good, we shall take a long walk.
2. Although he knew me, he did not greet me.
3. My friend wrote me that he would arrive day after tomorrow.
4. He wanted to know whether this was a good book.
5. That was all very fine (schön), but he did not believe it.
6. Not he, but she, was to blame for that.
7. The auto stopped and we got in.

8. He acted as if he had not understood it.
9. We come to school in order to learn something.
10. She could not come yesterday, for she was ill.
11. Visit me next month, or I shall be angry with you.
12. This morning I could not go along because I was too tired.
13. My old friend was always busy when I visited him.
14. While it was raining this morning, I wrote a long letter.
15. As soon as I had written the letter, I mailed it.
16. They worked until it became dark.
17. Do you know if Mr. Smith is at home?
18. If he is not at home, I shall call on him next month.
19. Both teachers and pupils were looking forward with pleasure to the vacation.
20. Neither Fred nor his sister wanted to stay at home.
21. Not only the parents but also the children had gone to the theater.
22. Mother had company; therefore she did not go along today.
23. Either she or her brother will drive the car.
24. He counts (*or* relies) on my helping him.
25. I have no objection to your opening the window.
26. That comes from (your) eating too much.
27. He always insists on paying my fare.
28. He had never thought of doing such a thing.
29. That is not to be thought of.
30. He asked to see the book.
31. It is a question of how long the trip will take (dauern).
32. If I have the money, I shall fly by jet.

C.   Translate:

1. That happened before the war.
2. What had happened before?
3. Before I go to school, I always read the German newspaper.
4. After he had read the paper, he went to school.
5. My little brother read the story afterwards.
6. After the dance, they took a long walk.
7. What has happened since (then)?
8. When I was at home this morning, my little sister was playing.
9. When I visited him, he was always busy.
10. If I have time today, I shall write him a long letter.
11. She looks as if she were tired.
12. They acted (tun) as if they had heard the story.
13. We asked them whether they had understood us.
14. Her older brother stayed at home, for he had a headache.
15. That (Das) smaller book belongs to my younger sister.

16. I know that he has read this short story.
17. They were very tired because they had worked all morning.
18. While they were working, it began to rain.
19. During the rain, they stood under a tree.
20. Have you some money in your pocket?
21. I have no money because I bought some books yesterday.
22. Without working, we cannot learn.
23. Instead of working, one little girl talked continually (fortwährend).
24. Instead of his brother, his sister appeared.
25. Where do you live?   Where are you going?
26. The more I read those short stories, the more interesting I find them.
27. What (Woran) are you thinking of?   I am thinking of it (daran).
28. What are you sitting on?   On a chair—I am sitting on it.
29. With what are you writing?   With a pen—I am writing with it.
30. Whose book have you in your hand?
31. The man whose book I have is not at home today.

§69. Inseparable Prefixes

A.   Supply the proper form of the verbs in parentheses.

1. Der Kaufmann hatte sein Geld ——. (verlieren)
2. Das Dienstmädchen hat viele Teller ——. (zerbrechen)
3. Wie —— Ihnen der neue Hut? (gefallen)
4. Gestern —— er mir auf der Straße ——. (begegnen)
5. —— Sie —— nicht! (sich erkälten)
6. Die Großmutter wird uns morgen die Geschichte ——. (erzählen)
7. Warum hat er die beiden Diener ——? (entlassen)
8. Er hatte alles ——, was er gesehen hatte. (beschreiben)
9. Sie hat es schmerzlich ——. (empfinden)
10. Wer hat Amerika ——? (entdecken)
11. Wem —— die Bücher? (gehören)
12. Das wilde Tier hat den armen Mann ——. (zerfleischen)
13. Haben Sie mich ——, als ich fort war? (vermissen)
14. Ich habe ihn ——. (mißverstehen)
15. Er hat mich sehr freundlich ——. (empfangen)
16. Wissen Sie, was das lange Wort ——? (bedeuten)
17. Haben Sie das Konzert ——? (genießen)
18. Ich habe den Zug ——. (verpassen)

B.   Translate:

1. Did you enjoy the meal?
2. Does she like (gefallen) these short stories?

3. She met her old friend on the street.
4. He recommended (empfehlen) that firm to them.
5. I have explained the third sentence.
6. We had caught cold.
7. The angry animal tore the man to pieces.
8. The enemy was destroying a small village.
9. Did you miss the first train?
10. I always miss my dear friends.
11. When did you lose your book?
12. How do you like my new hat?
13. We enjoyed the music very much.
14. She told me an interesting story.
15. What altitude did the flyer reach (erreichen)?

§§70–71. Mixed Prefixes

A. Form sentences with the following combinations in the present, past, compound past, past perfect, and future tenses.

1. Schüler —— Tür —— aufmachen.
2. Gepäckträger —— Koffer —— forttragen
3. Schule —— im September —— anfangen
4. Marie —— Treppe —— hinaufgehen
5. Onkel —— Kinder —— einladen
6. Karl —— Hut —— abnehmen
7. Fritz —— um sechs Uhr —— aufstehen
8. Er —— schnell —— sich anziehen
9. Jemand —— Treppe —— heraufkommen
10. Kind —— um sieben Uhr —— einschlafen
11. Familie —— im Oktober —— zurückkehren

B. Complete the following sentences with the proper **hin-** and **her-** words:

1. Karl (*oben*) sagt zu Fritz (*unten*):   „Komm —auf!"
2. Karl (*unten*) sagt zu Fritz (*unten*):   „Geh —auf!"
3. Karl (*unten*) sagt zu Fritz (*oben*):   „Komm —unter!"
4. Karl (*oben*) sagt zu Fritz (*oben*):   „Geh —unter!"
5. Karl (*vor der Tür*) sagt zu Fritz (*vor der Tür*):   „Geh —ein!"
6. Karl (*an der Tür*) sagt zu Fritz (*im Zimmer*):   „Komm —aus!"
7. Karl (*im Zimmer*) sagt zu Fritz (*an der Tür*):   „Komm —ein!"
8. Karl (*im Zimmer*) sagt zu Fritz (*im Zimmer*):   „Geh —aus!"

C. Translate:

1. The sun rises at six o'clock.
2. The boy gets up at half past seven.

3. The best train leaves (abfahren) at half past ten.
4. If we close the door, it will be too warm in the room.
5. Do you wish to go away?   (*Translate first with* wollen, *then* wünschen.)
6. The old lady was returning home.
7. My little brother had dressed quickly.
8. The porter is carrying away my heavy trunk.
9. The sun sets at half past six.
10. Translate the thirtieth sentence.
11. Repeat the last word, please.

§§72–75. The Passive Voice

A. Change the following sentences from the active to the passive voice. Make sure of the principal parts of a verb and that its tense is the same in the passive.

1. Der Schüler buchstabierte das Wort.
2. Der Junge hat die Geschichte gelesen.
3. Ich rufe den Kellner.
4. Er sah mich.
5. Sie wird das Buch lesen.
6. Wir hatten das Lied gesungen.
7. Sie besucht ihn.
8. Die Mutter hatte die Tochter begleitet.
9. Karl zerriß den Anzug.
10. Der alte Mann hat einen kurzen Spaziergang gemacht.
11. Sein jüngerer Bruder wird einen neuen Hut kaufen.
12. Ich binde die Krawatte.
13. Er hat viele Briefmarken gesammelt.
14. Mein alter Freund verkaufte ein großes Haus.
15. Der Barbier hat ihn heute morgen rasiert.
16. Sie verwöhnte den kleinen Jungen.
17. Die jungen Mädchen hatten die deutsche Aufgabe geschrieben.
18. Jene faulen Jungen schrieben nichts.
19. Ein berühmter Maler hat dieses Bild gemalt.
20. Unser reicher Onkel hat die beiden Freunde mitgebracht.
21. Sie (*They*) werden die Tür aufmachen.
22. Sie tadelte ihn immer.
23. Er wird den Regenschirm wohl gefunden haben.

B. Translate into German. Be careful to distinguish between actional and statal passives.

1. He was reared by his grandparents.
2. The German newspaper was being printed.

3. Many beautiful houses had been built.
4. Much tea is drunk in England.
5. The window was being closed.   The window was closed.
6. As a rule German nouns are capitalized.
7. The house is being sold.   It is sold.
8. He has been bitten by a large black dog.
9. My new car is being repaired today.
10. He will be praised by his friends.
11. The door is closed at half past nine.   It is (already) closed.
12. The little boy had been spoiled by his aunt.
13. When were you born?
14. Goethe was born in 1749.
15. My brother is now getting (or being) shaved by the barber.
16. The short sentences have been read by the whole class.
17. The door was being closed by the little girl.
18. A large house had been built by the old carpenter.
19. The notebooks will be returned (zurückgeben) tomorrow.
20. He has not been seen by his neighbors.
21. The boards are held together by a nail.

C.   The following sentences involve substitute constructions for the passive. Translate:

1. That is easily said.
2. Why were the children not allowed to play?
3. What was to be seen?
4. He is said to be a famous artist.
5. No bread was to be had.
6. That is a matter of course (or understood).
7. Those books are said to be very interesting.
8. Nothing was to be seen.
9. I was frightened.
10. Praised be God!
11. They were given the opportunity. (*Use* **man** *as subject.*)

§76. The Subjunctive in Indirect Statements

A.   Rewrite the following sentences as indirect statements —first with, then without **daß**:

1. Er sagte: „Ich war gestern im Theater.   Mein Freund Fritz blieb zu Hause."
2. Sie schrieb mir: „Wir werden morgen abfahren."
3. Die Kinder sagten: „Die Geschichte gefällt uns."
4. Der Lehrer antwortete: „Ich werde noch eine Geschichte vorlesen."

5. Mein Freund schrieb mir: „Ich war vorigen Monat sehr beschäftigt."

6. Karl sagte: „Es ist heute sehr heiß."

7. Fritz antwortete: „Es war letzte Woche noch heißer."

8. Er schrieb uns: „Ich hatte kein Glück."

9. Wir antworteten: „Es wird Ihnen das nächste Mal gelingen."

10. Die Zeitung berichtete: „Ein großes Unglück ist geschehen."

11. Er schrieb mir: „Das Gewitter war um acht Uhr am heftigsten."

12. Ich sagte zu ihm: „Ich werde nächsten Sommer eine Reise machen."

13. Der Vater telefonierte: „Ich habe den Zug versäumt. Ich komme erst morgen an."

14. Er sagte: „Ich habe kein Geld bei mir."

15. Sie sagte zu mir: „Ich interessiere mich für die Kunst."

16. Er schrieb mir: „Der Plan ist mir noch nicht gelungen."

17. Marie erzählte uns: „Die Mutter hat mir zu Weihnachten ein schönes Bilderbuch gegeben."

18. Er sagte zu mir: „Ich habe mich an alles gewöhnt."

19. Unsere Freunde schrieben uns: „Wir amüsieren uns herrlich auf dem Lande."

B. Translate the following sentences, paying particular attention to tenses and mood:

1. My friend wrote me that he had seen the tall buildings of our beautiful city.

2. She says that it is too warm in the room.

3. He said that he would write the simple sentence on the board.

4. They told us that the famous men would arrive tomorrow.

5. The old lady said that her friends had been in the country.

6. Her younger brother said that he preferred to play ball.

7. She wrote me that she took a long walk every day.

8. He said that he had been there day before yesterday.

9. They said that they would answer these easy questions.

10. She told me that she had visited those beautiful German villages.

11. He said that the little boys were not allowed to play on the street.

12. His sister wrote him that she would arrive day after tomorrow.

13. I heard that he had caught cold recently.

14. He said that he was looking forward with pleasure to the trip.

15. I told him that I could not afford it.

16. He said that his father had given him a beautiful fountain pen for Christmas.

17. She wrote us that she was recovering from a severe illness.

18. The hotelkeeper said that he had sold much beer. He added that he had only two bottles left.

19. He said that it reminded him of old times.

§77. The Subjunctive in Indirect Questions

A. Rewrite the following as indirect questions after: (1) Er fragte den Mann; (2) Er fragte die Männer; and (3) Er fragte mich:

1. „Woher haben Sie so viel Geld?"
2. „Wann sind Sie geboren?"
3. „Haben Sie schon gegessen?"
4. „Warum antworten Sie nicht auf die Frage?"
5. „Wo waren Sie gestern?"
6. „Waren Sie auf dem Lande?"
7. „Werden Sie nächstes Jahr nach Deutschland reisen?"
8. „Werden Ihre Freunde Sie heute besuchen?"
9. „Freuen Sie sich auf den Besuch?"
10. „Haben Sie sich amüsiert?"
11. „Was haben Sie getan?"
12. „In was für einem Haus wohnen Sie?"
13. „Wo spielten Ihre Kinder gestern?"
14. „Haben Sie Geld bei sich?"
15. „Woher wissen Sie das denn eigentlich?"
16. „Was wollen Sie damit sagen?"
17. „Haben Sie sich erkältet?"
18. „Worüber ärgern Sie sich so sehr?"
19. „Haben Sie sich weh getan?"
20. „Wofür interessieren Sie sich?"

B. Translate the following sentences:

1. She asked him whether he had seen her little brown dog.
2. They asked her when she would visit them.
3. He asked me whether I was hungry.
4. He asked them whether they had a house in the country.
5. I asked the little boys whether they had brought their books (along).
6. She asked him what time it was.
7. He asked me why I had not written him a letter. (*Use* kein *for* not a.)
8. I asked him how he knew that.
9. She asked him whether he was interested in music.
10. We asked the children whether they had hurt themselves.
11. They asked us whether we had caught cold.
12. He asked me why I was bothering about that.
13. She asked me whether I had had a good time.
14. I asked him why he didn't answer my question.
15. She asked me where I had seen him.

16. He asked me what I was interested in.
17. They didn't know what it was all about.
18. The technician asked us whether we had learned many new technical expressions.

§78. The Subjunctive in Indirect Commands

A. Rewrite as indirect commands, using Subjunctive II as in the model.

DIRECT: Ich sagte zu dem kleinen Jungen: „Sei fleißig!"
INDIRECT: Ich sagte dem kleinen Jungen, er sollte fleißig sein.
or: Ich sagte dem kleinen Jungen, daß er fleißig sein sollte.

1. Sie sagte zu mir: „Kommen Sie morgen wieder!"
2. Der Arzt sagte zu ihm: „Rauchen Sie nicht!"
3. Ich sagte zu den Kindern: „Geht schnell!"
4. Wir sagten zu ihnen: „Bleibt hier!"
5. Der Lehrer sagte zu uns: „Lernen Sie das deutsche Gedicht auswendig!"
6. Er sagte zu mir: „Schreiben Sie den zweiten Satz an die Tafel!"
7. Er sagte zu dem Schüler: „Setze dich!"
8. Er sagte zu mir: „Setzen Sie sich!"
9. Die Mutter sagte zu mir: „Kaufe für sechs Mark Briefmarken!"
10. Mein Freund telegrafierte mir: „Fahre mit dem ersten Schnellzug!"
11. Marie schrieb ihrer Freundin: „Komme bald aufs Land!"
12. Sie sagte zu ihr: „Amüsiere dich!"
13. Fritz schrieb mir: „Amüsiere dich!"
14. Herr Wagner schrieb uns: „Amüsieren Sie sich!"

B. Complete the following sentences:

1. Ich sagte dem Vater, daß er mir —— (*should buy a model airplane*).
2. Der Lehrer sagte uns, daß wir —— (*should learn new technical expressions*).
3. Die Mutter sagte mir, daß ich —— (*should attend scientific lectures*).

C. Translate:

1. He told me to sit down.
2. She told him to learn the poem by heart.
3. I told him to be careful.
4. She told him not to bother about it.
5. He told me to phone him at half past three.
6. We told them to have a good time.
7. Mother told my little brother to behave (sich anständig benehmen).
8. He told me not to hurry.

§§79–80. The Subjunctive in Independent Sentences and in Concessive Clauses

A.   Translate:

1. If she only had patience!
2. If they only had been here!
3. Let us work now.
4. Let him enter.
5. Let's take a walk.
6. "Did he really do that (*indic.*)?"   "Not that I am aware of."
7. Where can he possibly be?
8. Is it possible that he did such a thing?
9. That would be stupid indeed.
10. It might perhaps be in order.
11. Can he have said that? ·
12. That would be a pity.
13. Be the lesson ever so difficult, the pupils will write it.
14. Be it early or be it late, she is always working.
15. Might I ask you for the book?
16. Where might my book (possibly) be?
17. Is it possible that my little brother misplaced it?
18. Let us not forget his advice.
19. If you had only studied your lesson!
20. If I had only worked harder!

§§81–82. Conditional Sentences

A.   Complete the following sentences by supplying the proper forms of verbs in parentheses:

1. Wenn er —— (kommen), (so) werden wir ihn freundlich empfangen.
2. Wenn der Arzt hier —— (sein), (so) wäre das Kind nicht gestorben.
3. Wenn das Wetter schön —— (sein), (so) werde ich einen Spaziergang machen.
4. Wenn er das Geld —— (haben), (so) hätte er das Haus gekauft.
5. Wenn er einfacher —— (leben), (so) wäre er reich.
6. Wenn ich Zeit —— (haben), (so) werde ich einen Brief schreiben.
7. Wenn der Preis nicht so hoch wäre, (so) —— er das Buch —— (kaufen).
8. Wenn sie Geld hat, (so) —— sie dieses Jahr —— (reisen).
9. Wenn er nicht so müde gewesen wäre, (so) —— er nicht —— (einschlafen).
10. Wenn es nicht so weit wäre, (so) —— ich dorthin —— (fahren).

11. Wenn das Buch interessant ist, (so) —— ich es —— (lesen).
12. Wenn es nicht geregnet hätte, (so) —— ich nicht zu Hause ——
    (bleiben).
13. Bäte er mich um Hilfe, so —— ich ihm —— (helfen).
14. Wäre er da gewesen, so —— er das —— (wissen).
15. Hätte er mich eingeladen, so —— ich ihn —— (besuchen).
16. Wäre ich ein Vogel, so —— ich zu dir —— (fliegen).
17. Der Schüler hätte nicht so viele Fehler gemacht, wenn er aufmerksam
    —— (sein).
18. Ich würde den Arzt nicht kommen lassen, wenn ich gesund ——
    (sein).
19. Er hätte mich nicht gefragt, wenn er das —— (wissen).
20. Wenn er mehr Geduld hätte, (so) —— es ihm —— (gelingen).
21. Er —— die Sätze an die Tafel —— (*could have written*).
22. Er —— keine Fehler —— (*should have made*).
23. Wir —— zu Hause —— (*should have stayed*).
24. Ich —— die Aufgabe —— (*could have written*).
25. Sie sah aus, als ob sie müde —— (*were*).
26. Er tat, als ob er es nicht —— (*had heard*).
27. Sie tat, als ob sie es nicht —— (*had understood*).
28. Er sah aus, als ob er schläfrig —— (*were*).
29. —— (*Had*) ich nur eine gute Feder!
30. —— (*Were*) der Vater nur hier!
31. —— er es nur —— (*Had known*)!
32. —— er nur zu Hause —— (*Had stayed*)!
33. Wenn er das deutsche Buch —— (*could have read*), (so) hätte er es
    getan.
34. Wenn Sie das —— (*could have done*), (so) hätte ich mich sehr gefreut.
35. Wenn Sie das Fenster nicht zugemacht hätten, (so) —— es jetzt nicht
    so warm im Zimmer (sein).
36. Er sah aus, als ob er hungrig —— (*were*).
37. Er —— das nicht —— (*should have said*).
38. Wenn er —— (kommen), (so) hätte ich ihn gesehen.
39. Wenn mein alter Freund hier wäre, (so) —— ich ihn —— (besuchen).
40. —— (*Haben*) ich Zeit, so würde ich viele Bücher lesen.

B. Translate:

1. If I had phoned him, he would have met me at the station.
2. If they had a good airplane, they would fly to New York.
3. If I have time, I shall read an interesting German book.
4. If the book were interesting, he would read it.
5. If it had rained, my dear friends would have stayed at home.
6. If it does not rain this morning, I shall take a long walk.
7. If I do not find his new address, I shall not be able to visit him.

8. If he had had the money, he would have bought that large house.
9. If he read more German books, he would speak German better.
10. If they had been punctual, he would not have been angry.
11. If he had lived more simply, he would have become rich.
12. If our dear friend had the money, he would give it to me at once.
13. If he had the time today, he would accompany me.
14. If he had studied the grammar, he would have known the answers to these simple questions.
15. If he helped the poor men, they would thank him.
16. You should have visited me last summer.
17. He could have visited them last winter.
18. Had I only known it!
19. If he were only here!
20. If I only had more money.
21. If they had only paid attention!
22. He looked as if he were sleepy.
23. She acted as if she had not understood the last sentence.
24. They looked as if they were tired.
25. He ate as if he had not eaten anything for (seit) a week.
26. You should have read that interesting story in the German newspaper.
27. He could have taken a long trip if he had had the money.
28. His father would have given him the money if he had earned more this year.
29. He would earn more if times (die Zeiten) were not so bad (schlecht).
30. If he earns more next year, he will take a trip.
31. If you had worked harder last month, you would not be so poor now.
32. If you only had more patience!
33. You should have learned more.
34. Your younger brother could have worked harder.
35. Your older sister should have helped you.
36. If he were here, they would be happy.
37. If the old men had visited me, I should have thanked them.
38. If it rains, I shall stay at home.
39. If he had known that, he would not have gone.
40. He looked as if he had grown (werden) much older.

§§83-87 Modal Auxiliaries

A. Rewrite each of the following sentences in the future, perfect, and past perfect indicative:

1. Ich muß den ganzen Tag arbeiten.
2. Das Kind durfte nicht auf der Straße spielen.

3. Er kann nicht schlafen.
4. Er wollte Deutsch sprechen.
5. Wir hören die alte Dame sprechen.
6. Er läßt den Arzt holen.
7. Ich sah ihn kommen.
8. Ich muß gleich an die Arbeit gehen.
9. Ich kann es mir nicht leisten.
10. Mein kleiner Bruder läßt sich das Haar schneiden.
11. Seine jüngere Schwester muß zu Hause bleiben.
12. Ich sah den alten Mann arbeiten.
13. Er kann den langen Brief nicht lesen.
14. Sie wollte ins Kino gehen.
15. Ich kann den Fehler nicht finden.
16. Sein lieber Freund muß bis in die Nacht arbeiten.
17. Man darf nicht im Theater rauchen.
18. Das schöne Mädchen läßt sich ein neues Kleid machen.
19. Wir hörten den Weltbekannten Tenor singen.
20. Er will viel Geld verdienen.

B.   Rewrite the following sentences with **hätte ... können** and **hätte ...
sollen,** and translate them into English according to the following model:

Er geht aufs Land.
He goes to the country.
Er **hätte** aufs Land gehen **können.**
He could have gone to the country.
Er **hätte** aufs Land gehen **sollen.**
He should have gone to the country.

1. Mein reicher Onkel macht eine lange Reise.
2. Ich las ein deutsches Buch.
3. Er besuchte seinen alten Freund.
4. Sie gibt dem armen Mann etwas Geld.
5. Er steht früh auf.
6. Mein älterer Bruder arbeitet fleißig.

C.   Translate:

1. We have to go to school.
2. My little brother was unable to go to school today.
3. You should (*or* ought to) stay at home.
4. Yes, you are right.   I should have stayed at home.
5. Do you know German?
6. Carl does not know his lesson.
7. Those little boys never wanted to study.

8. When will your dear friend have to go home?
9. We could have gone home at half past eleven.
10. Might I ask you for your new German dictionary?
11. The little children were not allowed to play on the street.
12. Have they ever been allowed to play there?
13. He wants to visit me next month.
14. I was on the point of going out, when I received your long, interesting letter.
15. She intends to go to the country next week.
16. She claims to have seen him in the country.
17. He professes to have a rich aunt.
18. You should have visited her.
19. You could have taken a long trip.
20. Next summer you should visit your old parents.
21. Yesterday I could go.   Today I could go if I had the time.
22. Would you like to take a long walk this morning?
23. I don't like (mögen) the meal.
24. It is not her fault.
25. If he could have done it, he would have written me.
26. You should have visited those beautiful German villages.
27. My dear friend is said to be very ill.
28. He should not work so hard.
29. He should have stayed in bed.
30. What are we to do this afternoon?
31. He wants to give the little children some beautiful gifts.
32. They were about to sit down when I entered the room.
33. She claims to have read that short story.   That may be.
34. We shall not be able to give them those interesting books.
35. Last year we could do it.   This year, however, we could not do it, even if we earned twice as much money.
36. Can he understand these simple German sentences?
37. When did your older brother have his hair cut?
38. A week ago my younger sister had a beautiful dress made.
39. Why did you send for the doctor?
40. Have you ever seen that lazy boy working?
41. He will be unable to read this long letter.
42. Does your poor neighbor have to work all night?
43. He had been unable to sleep.
44. She has always wanted to earn much money.
45. Did you hear that famous tenor sing?
46. They (use man) were not allowed to smoke in the theater.
47. Were you unable (perfect tense) to find those mistakes?
48. Might I ask you for a good pencil?
49. I should like to read a good German book.

50. You should have translated these short German sentences.
51. That may be. That might (possibly) be.
52. Thou shalt not kill.
53. Will you take tea or coffee?
54. He claims to have heard him.
55. She was probably thirty years old. (*Use a modal auxiliary.*)
56. Might I ask you for another (i.e., an additional) pen?
57. Might I ask you for another (i.e., a different) chair?
58. They must have done that. (*The inference is that they did it.*)
59. They would have been obliged to do it.
60. That might be dangerous.

§88. Idioms

A.   Complete the following sentences:

1. Ich warte schon eine Stunde —— mein— lieb— Freund.
2. Er kann es —— nicht —— (*afford*).
3. —— (*A week from today*) werde ich Sie besuchen.
4. Sein Vetter war früher Professor —— d— Universität.
5. Haben Sie —— mi— gedacht?
6. Schreiben Sie diesen Satz —— (*in German*)!
7. Sein ältester Sohn ist Student —— d— Universität.
8. Die Mutter war sehr stolz —— d— klein— Mädchen.
9. Sie —— die Handschuhe —— (*was putting on*).
10. Sein kleiner Bruder geht noch nicht —— (*to school*).
11. Der kleine Junge ist —— (*in the country*).
12. Karl, —— (*be careful*)! Kinder, —— (*be careful*)! Herr Schmidt,
    —— (*be careful*)!
13. Er —— den Hut —— (*was putting on*).
14. Es geschah —— (*a week ago*).
15. Fährt er —— (*by steamer*) oder —— (*by rail*)?
16. Das kleine Mädchen ist —— (*in school*).
17. Er geht schon anderthalb Stunden —— (*up and down*).
18. —— (*After school*) wird er einen langen Spaziergang machen.
19. Sie sprach —— (*about me*).
20. Was essen Sie —— (*for breakfast*)?
21. Er klopfte —— d— Tür.
22. Ich werde es —— dieselb— Weise tun.
23. Das Essen besteht —— sechs Gäng—.
24. Er war —— (*to the country*) gegangen.
25. Ich bin außer mi— —— Zahnweh.
26. Mein Bruder ist —— (*to the*) Theater gegangen.
27. Man machte —— (*him*) König.

28. Sie ist nicht —— (*at home*).
29. Ärgern Sie sich nicht —— (*about it*)!
30. Wann wird er —— (*home*) gehen?
31. Er ist toll —— Schmerz.
32. Schlafen Sie auch —— (*in the daytime*)?
33. Das Kind fürchtet sich —— d— groß— Katze.
34. Er lachte —— (*at her*).
35. Ich kümmere —— nicht —— (*about him*).
36. Sind Sie —— (*it*) endlich los geworden?
37. Es wurde —— (*colder and colder*).
38. Was fehlt —— (*those little children*)?
39. Arbeiten Sie —— (*at night*)?
40. Ich habe —— (*a headache*).
41. Hat er sich —— d— Mädchen verliebt?
42. Er hat sich schon —— d— Mädchen verlobt.
43. Er hat —— d— Tisch gesetzt.
44. Antworten Sie —— dies— kurz— Frage!
45. Das Kind hat —— (*neither*) Vater —— (*nor*) Mutter.
46. Es tat d— alt— Mann leid.
47. Es geschieht —— (*you*) recht.
48. Ich werde —— (*him*) —— ein— gut— Bleistift bitten.
49. Tut es —— (*you*) weh?
50. Erinnern Sie sich —— d— freundlich— Leute?
51. Ich muß —— (*either*) einen Bleistift —— (*or*) eine Feder haben.
52. Wir hoffen schon lange —— gut— Wetter.
53. Das geht —— (*him*) nichts an.
54. Er hat einen Brief —— sein— alt— Freund geschrieben.
55. Er hat mi— ein— groß— Gefallen getan.
56. —— (*Both*) sein Bruder —— (*and*) seine Schwester sind zu Hause geblieben.
57. Es ist nicht d— Mühe —— (*worthwhile*).
58. Sind Sie —— (*of the same*) Meinung?
59. Wir werden es nicht tun, —— (*unless*) sie uns darum bitten.
60. Friedrich der Große war sehr stolz —— (*of his*) Flötenspiel [*flute playing* (neut.)].
61. Wir werden morgen ein— kurz— Spaziergang ——.
62. Karl, —— (*behave*) anständig!
63. Nicht alle Reichen fahren erst— Klasse.
64. Fritz, hast du vergessen, meinen Brief —— (*to mail*)?
65. Der Soldat war —— d— link— Auge blind.
66. Die Kinder mußten das Gedicht —— (*by heart*) lernen.
67. Es roch —— ein— faul— Ei.
68. Die Speise schmeckt —— Knoblauch [*garlic* (masc.)].
69. Er hat mir etwas —— (*interesting*) erzählt.

70. Haben Sie nichts —— (*new*) gehört?
71. Unsere Bibliothek ist reich —— (*books*) über Goethe.
72. Dresden ist —— sein— Museen berühmt.
73. Besten Gruß —— Ihr— lieb— Eltern.
74. Der kleine Junge —— d— Dach —— (*had climbed*).
75. Sie hat viele interessant— Bücher —— Geburtstag erhalten.
76. Er ist —— (*angry with*) sein— Nachbar.
77. Sie singt nie, —— (*unless*) man sie darum bittet.

B.   Translate:

1. I am looking forward with pleasure to the vacation.
2. My best friend will come a week from today.
3. The old man is looking out of the window.
4. That happened a week ago.
5. He stopped in front of the house.
6. I have not succeeded in finding my old umbrella.
7. She was thinking of her dear mother.
8. How long have you been waiting for me?
9. Is she right or wrong?
10. After school the little boys play ball.
11. "Will you go to the country for a week?"   "That depends."
12. Fred is already in school.   His brother does not yet go to school.
13. Look out of the window.
14. Last month we were at their house.
15. Their house consists of twelve large rooms.
16. Do you live near them?
17. Do you remember those little children?
18. Their parents are said to be very poor.
19. I am sorry for them.
20. Last summer we made their acquaintance.
21. Do they still live in the country?
22. He had fallen in love with a rich girl.
23. Two months ago he became engaged to her.
24. They went to the theater yesterday evening.
25. The more I read Goethe, the more I admire him.
26. He liked to travel.
27. He was a student at the university of Leipzig.
28. Schiller was a professor at the university of Jena.
29. She likes to read.   She prefers to sing.   She likes best to dance.
30. Do you like it?   Do you prefer it?   Do you like it best?   (*Use* gern.)
31. They had sent for a good physician.
32. Put on your hat and gloves.
33. Did you pass those old houses?
34. He was speaking of his friends.

35. What do you eat for breakfast?
36. In the daytime we must all work hard.
37. I don't like to work at night. (*Use* gern.)
38. That makes no difference.
39. Suddenly he stopped.
40. We can't afford it.
41. I shall travel either by steamer or by rail.
42. He never worries about the future.
43. Why should he worry about it?
44. You will visit me next winter, will you not?
45. He has been walking up and down for an hour and a half.
46. Have a good time when you are in the country.
47. I have a headache. I am frantic with pain.
48. "When did you catch cold?" "A week ago."
49. We caught cold last month when we were at their house.
50. (*a*) "Is it he (him)?" "It's he (him)."
    (*b*) "Is it they (them)?" "It's they (them)."
    (*c*) "Is it you?" "It's I (me)."
51. Our dear friend was on the point of going home.
52. We shall get used to it.
53. It gives the little boy pleasure.
54. What will become of those lazy children?
55. What time is it?
56. What is today's date?
57. It serves you right.
58. He did me a great favor.
59. It is your turn.
60. Most children are afraid of the dark.
61. Are you (*perf. of* werden) finally rid of it?
62. I like this pencil. Bring me another one.
63. I don't like this pen. Bring me another one.
64. She bought a pair of gloves.
65. Several books are (lying) on the table.
66. "Farewell." "Goodbye."
67. It hurts me. I am sorry.
68. What is the matter with that old lady?
69. She is talking to herself.
70. She is very proud of her grandson.
71. Both the grandfather and the grandmother are over a hundred years old.
72. They never take a walk unless we ask them to.
73. They always say, "It isn't worthwhile."
74. They are both of the same opinion.

75. Perhaps they are right.
76. Would you like to take a long trip to Europe?
77. The little child was behaving badly.
78. Do you usually travel second class?
79. I shall learn that short poem by heart.
80. Please mail this letter.
81. We had seen many beautiful things.   (Use *the adjective as noun.*)
82. Heidelberg is famous for its old university.
83. The fox had climbed a tall tree.
84. Did you receive many beautiful gifts for Christmas?
85. Don't be angry with him.
86. Please begin at the beginning.
87. Best regards to your charming sister.
88. The country is rich in coal.
89. It tastes of onions.
90. The whole hall smells of roses.
91. In which eye is the poor animal blind?
92. He never does it unless he has to (*supply* es).
93. They have done nothing at all for her.
94. He just imagines that.
95. The old hotelkeeper is said to be very rich.
96. Don't bother about it.
97. Is he happy about it?
98. He will never get used to it.
99. When did the bell ring?
100. He was always friendly to his neighbors.

LIST OF ABBREVIATIONS

abbr.	= abbreviation		*lit.*	= literally	
acc.	= accusative		*masc.*	= masculine	
adj.	= adjective		*neg.*	= negative	
adv.	= adverb(ial)		*neut.*	= neuter	
art.	= article		*nom.*	= nominative	
aux.	= auxiliary		*num.*	= numeral	
colloq.	= colloquial		*obj.*	= object	
comp.	= comparative		*part.*	= particle	
conj.	= conjunction		*pers.*	= person	
correl.	= correlative		*p.p.*	= past participle	
dat.	= dative		*pl.*	= plural	
decl.	= declension		*poss.*	= possessive	
def.	= definite		*prep.*	= preposition(al)	
dem.	= demonstrative		*pres.*	= present	
dep.	= dependent		*pres. p.*	= present participle	
dir.	= direct		*pret.*	= preterit	
emph.	= emphatic		*prin.*	= principal	
excl.	= exclamation		*pron.*	= pronoun	
fem.	= feminine		*ques.*	= question	
fig.	= figurative(ly)		*ref.*	= referring	
fut.	= future		*refl.*	= reflexive	
gen.	= genitive		*rel.*	= relative	
imperf.	= imperfect		*sep.*	= separable	
impers.	= impersonal		*sing.*	= singular	
indecl.	= indeclinable		*str.*	= strong	
indef.	= indefinite		*sub.*	= subordinating	
indir.	= indirect		*subj.*	= subjunctive	
inf.	= infinitive		*superl.*	= superlative	
insep.	= inseparable		*temp.*	= temporal	
intens.	= intensive		*th.*	= thing	
inter.	= interrogative		*tr.*	= transitive	
interj.	= interjection		*vb.*	= verb	
intr.	= intransitive		*w.*	= with	
invar.	= invariable		*wk.*	= weak	

German-English Vocabulary

Genitive singular and nominative plural endings are given for all nouns. Principal parts are given only for strong or irregular verbs. The auxiliary is indicated only for verbs conjugated with **sein,** e.g., **abfahren, fuhr ab, ist** *abgefahren, fährt ab;* if no auxiliary is given, the verb is conjugated with **haben.** Reflexive verbs show **sich** with the infinitive only: **sich** *ausziehen, zog aus, ausgezogen.* Separable verbs show an accent on the prefix when their principal parts are not given: **ánklagen;** inseparable verbs indicate the stress only when it is doubtful: **überráschen.**

A

der **Abend, -s, -e,** evening; **eines —s,** one evening; **gestern abend,** last night; **heute abend,** this evening, tonight

das **Abendessen, -s, -,** supper, evening meal

aber, but, however

abfahren, fuhr ab, ist abgefahren, fährt ab, to depart, leave

abholen, holte ab, abgeholt, to call (*or* come) for

abnehmen, nahm ab, abgenommen, nimmt ab, to take off; **er nimmt den Hut ab,** he takes off his hat

die **Abreise, -, -n,** departure

abreisen, reiste ab, ist abgereist, to depart, leave

abschaffen, schaffte ab, abgeschafft, to do away with, abolish

der **Abschied, -(e)s, -e,** departure

abschreiben, schrieb ab, abgeschrieben, to copy

die **Absicht, -, -en,** intention

abspielen, spielte ab, abgespielt, to play back

absteigen, stieg ab, ist abgestiegen, to come down from; **er steigt vom Pferde ab,** he dismounts

abwesend, absent

acht, eight

der **Acker, -s, ⁀,** field

der **Adler, -s, -,** eagle

die **Adresse, -, -n,** address

der **Advokat, -en, -en,** lawyer

der **Affe, -n, -n,** monkey, ape

ähnlich (*w. dat.*), similar (to), **er ist dem Vater —,** he resembles his father

alle (*pl.*), all; **auf —n vieren,** on all fours

allein (*adv.*), alone; (*conj.*), but

allerlei, all kinds of

allerschönst-, most beautiful of all

alles, everything, all; **—, was,** all that

als (*after a comp.*) than; (*conj. ref. def. past action*) when; **— ob,** as if

also, so, consequently, therefore

alt, old

das **Alter, -s, -,** age

amerikanisch, American

sich **amüsieren,** to have good time

an (*prep. w. dat. or acc.*), at, on, to, **Professor an der Universität,** professor at the university

ander-, other

ändern, to change

anders, differently, otherwise

anderthalb, one and a half

der **Anfang, -(e)s, ⁀e,** beginning

anfangen, fing an, angefangen, fängt an, to begin

angehen, ging an, hat (*or* ist) angegangen, to concern; **das geht ihn nichts an,** that does not concern him

angenehm (*w. dat.*), pleasant, agreeable

die **Angst, -, ⸚e,** fear

ánklagen (*w. acc. of the pers. & gen. of the th.*), to accuse of

ankommen, kam an, ist angekommen, to arrive

annehmen, nahm an, angenommen, nimmt an, to accept

ansehen, sah an, angesehen, sieht an, to look at

der **Anspruch, -(e)s, ⸚e** (*w.* auf *and acc.*), claim

anständig, decent, proper

(an)statt (*prep. w. gen.*), instead of

die **Antwort, -, -en,** answer

antworten, to answer; **man antwortet einer Person** (*dat.*), **man antwortet auf eine Frage** (*acc.*)

anwesend, present

anziehen, zog an, angezogen, to put on; (*refl*) **sie zieht sich an,** she dresses (herself); (*w. dat.*) **du solltest dir ein neues Kleid —,** you should put on a new dress

der **Anzug, -(e)s, ⸚e,** suit of clothes

der **Apfel, -s, ⸚,** apple

der **Apfelbaum, -(e)s, ⸚e,** apple tree

der **Appetit, -(e)s, -e** appetite

die **Arbeit, -, -en,** work

arbeiten, to work; **fleißig (schwer** *or* **tüchtig) —,** to work hard

der **Arbeiter, -s, -,** laborer

ärgerlich, vexed, provoked

sich **ärgern über** (*w. acc.*), to be provoked at

arm, poor

der **Arm, -(e)s, -e,** arm

die **Armut, -,** poverty

die **Art, -, -en,** kind

der **Arzt, -es, ⸚e,** physician, doctor; **den — holen** (*or* **kommen**) **lassen,** to send for the doctor

der **Ast, -es, ⸚e,** branch

der **Astronaut, -en, -en,** astronaut

der **Astronom, -en, -en,** astronomer

astronomisch, celestial

der **Atem, -s, -züge,** breath

atmen, to breathe

die **Atmosphäre, -, -n,** atmosphere

atomisch, atomic; **das atomische Zeitalter,** the Atomic Age

auch, also, too

auf (*prep. w. dat. or acc.*), on, to; **— dem Lande,** in the country; **Student auf der Universität,** student at the university; **— einmal,** suddenly; **—s Land,** to the country

die **Aufgabe, -, -n,** lesson, assignment, task, exercise, homework; **er macht seine —n,** he does his lessons

aufgeben, gab auf, aufgegeben, gibt auf, to give up

aufhalten, hielt auf, aufgehalten, hält auf, to·stop, check

aufheben, hob auf, aufgehoben, hebt auf, to pick up

aufhören, hörte auf, aufgehört, to stop, cease

aufmachen, machte auf, aufgemacht, to open

aufmerksam, attentive

die **Aufnahme, -, -n,** photograph

der **Aufsatz, -es, ⸚e,** composition, essay

aufsetzen, setzte auf, aufgesetzt, to put on (*as hat or glasses*); **setze (dir) den Hut auf!** put on your hat

aufstehen, stand auf, ist aufgestanden, to (a)rise, get up

aufsteigen, stieg auf, ist aufgestiegen, to rise, ascend

der **Aufstieg, -s, -e,** ascent

das **Auge, -s, -n,** eye

der **Augenblick, -(e)s, -e,** moment

aus (*prep. w. dat.*), out (of), from; **— welchem Grunde?** for what reason?

ausbessern, besserte aus, ausgebessert, to repair, mend

der **Ausdruck, -(e)s, ⸚e,** expression

ausführen, führte aus, ausgeführt, to execute, carry out

der **Ausländer, -s, -,** foreigner

sich **ausruhen, ruhte aus, ausgeruht,** to rest

aussehen, sah aus, ausgesehen, sieht aus, to look, appear

außen, outside; outwardly

außer (*prep. w. dat.*), besides; except; **ich bin — mir vor Freude,** I am beside myself with joy

außerdem, besides, moreover

außerhalb (*prep. w. gen.*)., outside of

aussetzen, setzte aus, ausgesetzt, to expose

aussprechen, sprach aus, ausgesprochen, spricht aus, to pronounce

auswendig, by heart; **— lernen,** to learn by heart

sich **ausziehen, zog aus, ausgezogen,** to undress

das **Auto, -s, -s,** auto, car

automatisch, automatic, self-acting

B

der **Bach, -(e)s, ⁼e,** brook

backen, buk, gebacken, bäckt, to bake

der **Bäcker, -s, -,** baker

die **Bäckerei, -, -en,** bakery

das **Bad, -(e)s, ⁼er,** bath

baden, to bathe

die **Bahn, -, -en,** road, track

der **Bahnhof, -(e)s, ⁼e** station

der **Ball, -(e)s, ⁼e,** ball

der **Ballon, -s, -e** (*or* -s), balloon

der **Band, -(e)s, -e,** volume

das **Band, -(e)s, ⁼er,** ribbon

die **Bank, -, ⁼e,** bench

die **Bank, -, -en,** bank (*monetary*)

der **Bär, -en, -en,** bear

der **Barbier, -s, -e,** barber

der **Bart, -(e)s, ⁼e,** beard

bauen, to build

der **Bauer, -s** (*or* -n), -n, farmer, peasant

der **Baum, -(e)s, ⁼e,** tree

Bayern, -s (*neut.*), Bavaria

der **Beamte, -n, -n,** official; **ein —r** (*w. adj. decl.*)

beantworten (*w. acc.*), to answer

sich **bedanken,** to thank; **sich bei einer Person für etwas —,** to thank a person for something

bedeuten, to mean

die **Bedeutung, -, -en,** meaning, importance

bedienen, to serve

sich **bedienen** (*w. gen.*), to make use of

bedürfen (*w. gen.*), to need

bedürftig (*adj. w. gen.*), in need of

sich **beeilen,** to hurry

sich **befassen mit,** to concern oneself with, occupy oneself with

befehlen, befahl, befohlen, befiehlt (*w. dat.*), to order, command

sich **befinden, befand, befunden,** to be, fare, feel

begegnen, begegnete, ist begegnet (*w. dat.*), to meet

beginnen, begann, begonnen, to begin

begleiten, to accompany

begraben, begrub, begraben, begräbt, to bury

behalten, behielt, behalten, behält, to retain, keep

behandeln, to treat

behaupten, to maintain, assert

bei (*prep. w. dat.*), next to, with, at (the house of); **— mir,** at my house; **das Geld, das ich — mir hatte,** the money I had with me

beide, both; **—** (*or* **die —n**) **Brüder,** the two (*or* both) brothers

das **Bein, -(e)s, -e,** leg

das **Beispiel, -(e). ., -e,** example; **zum —** (*abbr.* **z.B.**), for example

beißen, biß, gebissen, to bite

beistehen, stand bei, beigestanden (*w. dat.*), to render aid, assist

bekannt, (well-)known

der **Bekannte, -n, -n,** acquaintance; **ein —r** (*w. adj. decl.*)

sich **beklagen über** (*w. acc.*), to complain about

bekommen, bekam, bekommen, to receive

beliebt, beloved; favorite, popular

bellen, to bark

belohnen, to reward

bemannt, manned

bemerken, to notice

sich **benehmen, benahm, benommen, benimmt,** to behave

benutzen, to use, utilize, employ, take advantage of, avail, profit

beobachten, to observe

die **Beobachtung, -, -en,** observation, study

bequem, comfortable; **mache es dir —!** make yourself at home

berauben (*w. acc. of the pers. & gen. of the th.*), to rob

bereit, ready, prepared

bereiten, to prepare

bereits, already

der **Berg, -(e)s, -e,** mountain

berichten, to report

berühmt famous; **— durch** (*w. acc.*) [*or* **wegen** (*w. gen.*)] famous for

beschäftigt, busy

beschreiben, beschrieb, beschrieben to describe

beschuldigen (*w. acc. of the pers. & gen. of the th.*), to accuse

der **Besen, -s, -,** broom

besiedeln, to settle

besiegen, to conquer

besitzen, besaß, besessen, to possess
besonders, especially
besser (*comp. of* gut), better
bestehen, bestand, bestanden, to pass (*an examination*); — aus, to consist of
bestellen, to order
bestimmt, certain(ly), sure(ly); determined, destined
bestrafen, to punish
der Besuch, -(e)s, -e, visit
besuchen, to visit
beten, to pray
betrachten, to observe
sich betragen, betrug, betragen, beträgt, to behave
betrügen, betrog, betrogen, to deceive
das Bett, -(e)s, -en, bed
betteln, to beg
bevor (*conj.*), before
beweisen, bewies, bewiesen, to prove
sich bewerben, bewarb, beworben, bewirbt (*w.* um *& acc.*), to apply for
bewundern, to admire
bewußt (*adj. w. gen.*), aware of
bezahlen, to pay
bezug: in — (*or* Bezug) auf (*w. acc.*), with reference to, with regard to
die Bibliothek, -, -en, library
biegen, bog, gebogen, to bend
die Biene, -, -n, bee
das Bier, -(e)s, -e, beer
bieten, bot, geboten, to offer
das Bild, -(e)s, -er, picture
bilden, to form
die Bildung, -, education
binden, band, gebunden, to tie
die Birne, -, -n, pear
bis (*prep. w. acc.*), to, as far as; (*conj.*) until; (*often w. other preps.*) — an das Fenster, up to the window
bisher, until now
bitte, (if you) please; you are welcome
bitten, bat, gebeten, to ask; um etwas (*acc.*) —, to ask for something
bitter, bitter
blasen, blies, geblasen, bläst, to blow
blaß, pale
das Blatt, -(e)s, -er, leaf; sheet
blau, blue
das Blei, -(e)s, -e, lead
bleiben, blieb, ist geblieben, to remain, stay; er bleibt stehen, he stops

der Bleistift, -(e)s, -e, pencil
der Blick, -(e)s, -e, glance, look
blicken, to look
blind, blind; — auf (*w. dat.*), blind in
blitzen, to glitter, sparkle; es blitzt, it is lightening
bloß, bare; mit bloßem Auge, with the naked eye
blühen, to bloom
die Blume, -, -n, flower
das Blut, -(e)s, blood
der Boden, -s, ⁎(*or* -), floor
der Bogén, -s, - (*or* ⁎), arch; bow; sheet of paper
das Boot, -(e)s, -e, boat
die Börse, -, -n, purse; stock exchange
böse, angry; — sein auf (*w. acc.*), to be angry with
der Boxer, -s, -, boxer, pugilist
braten, briet, gebraten, brät, to roast
brauchen, to need
braun, brown
die Braut, -, ⁎e, fiancée
brechen, brach, gebrochen, bricht, to break
breit, wide, broad; einen Fuß —, a foot wide
brennen, brannte, gebrannt, to burn; er brennt vor Ungeduld, he burns with impatience
das Brett, -(e)s, -er, board
der Brief, -(e)s, -e, letter
die Briefmarke, -, -n, stamp
die Briefmarkensammlung, -, -en, stamp collection
die Brille, -, -n, (eye)glasses, spectacles; eine — tragen, to wear glasses
bringen, brachte, gebracht, to bring
das Brot, -(e)s, -e, bread
die Brücke, -, -n, bridge
der Bruder, -s, ⁎, brother
die Brust, -, ⁎e, breast
das Buch, -(e)s, ⁎er, book
buchstabieren, to spell
sich bücken, to stoop
bunt, variegated, many-colored
die Burg, -, -en, castle
der Bürger, -s, -, citizen
der Bürgermeister, -s, -, mayor
der Bursche, -n, -n, fellow; lad; student
die Butter, -, butter

C

der Charákter, -s, Charaktére, character
die Chemie, -, chemistry

der **Chemiker, -s, -,** chemist
chemisch, chemical
die **Cousine, -, -n,** (*female*) cousin

D

da (*adv.*) there; (*conj.*) since, as
dabei, thereby; while doing it
das **Dach, -(e)s, ⁼er,** roof
dafür, for it
dagegen, on the other hand; against it
daheim, at home
daher, therefore
damals, at that time, then
die **Dame, -, -n,** lady
damit (*adv.*), with it; (*conj.*) in order that
der **Dampfer, -s, -,** steamer
das **Dampfschiff, -(e)s, -e,** steamship
der **Dank, -(e)s,** thanks
dankbar (*w. dat.*), thankful, grateful
danken (*w. dat*), to thank; **ich danke Ihnen für das Buch,** I thank you for the book
dann, then, at that time; — **und wann,** now and then
darauf, thereupon, after that; upon it (that *or* them)
darauffolgend, following, later
darin, therein; in it (that *or* them)
darum, therefore
daß (*conj.*), that
das **Datum, -s, Daten,** date
dauernd, continually, constantly
davon, of (*or* about) it (*or* them)
dazu, for that; in addition
die **Decke, -, -n,** ceiling; cover
decken, to cover
dein, deine, dein (*poss. ädj.*), your
denken, dachte, gedacht, to think; — **an** (*w. acc.*), to think of
denn (*conj.*) for, because, then; **warum hat er es — getan?,** why then did he do it?; (*adv.*) in that case; **es sei denn, daß,** unless, except
derselbe, dieselbe, dasselbe, the same
deshalb, therefore
dessen (*masc. & neut. sing.*), **deren** (*fem. sing.*), **deren** (*pl.*) (*gen. forms of the rel. pron.* **der, die, das**), whose
desto: je... desto, the ... the; **je höher er steight, — kälter wird es,** the higher he climbs, the colder it gets
deutlich, distinct(ly)

deutsch (*adj.*), German; **auf —,** in German
Deutsch (*noun*), German; **lernen Sie —?** are you studying German?
der **Deutsche, -n, -n** (*w. adj. decl.*), German, native of Germany; **ein —r,** a German (man)
Deutschland, -s (*neut.*), Germany
dicht, dense, compact
der **Dichter, -s, -,** poet
dick, thick; **einen Fuß —,** a foot thick
der **Dieb, -(e)s, -e,** thief
dienen (*w. dat.*), to serve
der **Diener, -s, -,** servant
der **Dienstag, -(e)s, -e,** Tuesday
das **Dienstmädchen, -s, -,** maid, servant
dieser, -e, -es (*adj.*), this; (*pron.*) this one
diesseits (*prep. w. gen.*), on this side of
das **Ding, -(e)s, -e,** thing
direkt, direct
doch, still, however, yet
der **Doktor, -s, -en,** doctor, physician
der **Dom, -(e)s, -e,** cathedral
donnern, to thunder
der **Donnerstag, -(e)s, -e,** Thursday
doppelt, double, doubly
das **Dorf, -(e)s, ⁼er,** village
der **Dorn, -(e)s, -en (-e** *or* **⁼er),** thorn
dort, there (*in that place*)
dorthin, there (*to that place*), thither
draußen, outside
drehen (*often refl.*), to turn
drei, three
dreibeinig, three-legged
dreifach, threefold, triple
dreimal, three times
drinnen, inside
dritt (*num. adj.*), third
drohen (*w. dat.*), to threaten
drüben, over there
dumm, stupid
die **Dummheit, -, -en,** stupidity
dunkel, dark
dünn, thin
durch (*prep. w. acc.*), through, by
durchführen, führte durch, durchgeführt, to carry out, perform, accomplish
dürfen, durfte, gedurft, darf, to be allowed; **das — Sie nicht tun,** you must not do that; **dürfte ich Sie darum bitten?** might I ask you for that?
der **Durst, -es,** thirst
durstig, thirsty
das **Dutzend, -s, -e,** dozen

E

eben, even; just

ebenso, just as; — groß wie, just as large as

das Echo, -s, -s, echo

echt, genuine

die Ecke, -, -n, corner

edel, noble

ehe (*conj.*), before

die Ehre, -, -n, honor

ehrlich, honest

das Ei, -(e)s, -er, egg

die Eiche, -, -n, oak

eigen (*adj.*), own

eigentlich, real(ly)

eihen (*w.* sein), to hasten

einander, each other

sich (*dat.*) einbilden, to imagine

einfach, simple

der Einfall, -(e)s, ⁓e, idea, notion

einfallen, fiel ein, ist eingefallen, es fällt ein, to occur; das war mir nie eingefallen, that had never occurred to me

einladen, lud ein, eingeladen, ladet (*or* lädt) ein, to invite

einmal, once; once upon a time; auf —, suddenly

einschlafen, schlief ein, ist eingeschlafen, schläft ein, to fall asleep

einseitig, one-sided, partial, biased

einstecken, steckte ein, eingesteckt, to put in; man hat ihn ins Gefängnis eingesteckt, they put him in prison

der Einwohner, -s, -, inhabitant

das Eis, -es, ice

das Eisen, -s, iron

die Eisenbahn, -, -en, railroad

der Elefant, -en, -en, elephant

Elsaß, -es (*neut.*) Alsace

die Eltern, - (*pl.*), parents

empfangen, empfing, empfangen, empfängt, to receive

empfinden, empfand, empfunden, to feel; er empfindet es schmerzlich, it pains him

empfindlich, susceptible, sensitive, responsive

emporsteigen, stieg empor, ist emporgestiegen, to climb up

das Ende, -s, -n, end; zu — lesen, to finish reading, read through

enden, to end

endlich, finally, at last

eng, narrow

der Engländer, -s, -, Englishman

entdecken, to discover

entfernt, distant, remote

entgegen (*prep. w. dat.*), toward, against, in face of

entlang (*w. acc.*), along

entlassen, entließ, entlassen, entläßt, to dismiss

entscheiden, entschied, entschieden, to decide; (*refl*) to make up one's mind

sich entschließen, entschloß, entschlossen, to decide, make up one's mind

entschuldigen (*w. acc.*), to excuse, pardon

die Entstehung, -, -en, origin, formation, genesis

entwickeln, to develop

entzünden, to inflame

entzweibrechen, brach entzwei, entzweigebrochen, bricht entzwei, to break in two

die Erde, -, earth, world

erfahren, erfuhr, erfahren, erfährt, to learn, experience, discover (knowledge); — über (*w. acc.*) to learn about

erfinden, erfand, erfunden, to invent

der Erfolg, -(e)s, -e, success

erfolgreich, successful

erforderlich, necessary, required, requisite

das Ergebnis, -ses, -se, result

erhalten, erhielt, erhalten, erhält, to receive

sich erholen von, to recover (*or* recuperate) from

sich erinnern (*w. gen. or* an & *acc.*), to remember

sich erkälten, to catch cold

erkennen, erkannte, erkannt, to recognize

sich erkundigen nach, to make inquiries about

erlauben (*w. dat.*), to permit

die Erlaubnis, -, -se, permission

erleben, to experience, live through

das Erlebnis, -ses, -se, experience

ernst, serious

erreichen, to reach, attain

erscheinen, erschien, ist erschienen, to appear

erschrecken, erschrak, ist erschrocken, erschrickt (*intr.*), to be frightened; (*wk. tr.*), to frighten

erst (*adj.*), first, foremost; (*adv.*), at first, first of all; not until, only

erstaunt, astonished
erwachen, erwachte, ist erwacht (*intr.*), to awake
erwarten, to expect
erweisen, erwies, erwiesen, to show, render (*e.g., honor*)
erwidern, to reply
erzählen, to tell, relate
erziehen, erzog, erzogen, to bring up, rear, educate
der **Esel, -s, -,** donkey
essen, aß, gegessen, ißt, to eat
etliche (*pl.*), some, several
etwa, perhaps
etwas, some, something, somewhat
euer, eu(e)er, euer (*poss. adj.*), your
ewig, eternal

F

das **Fach, -(e)s, ⁼er,** subject, branch, specialty
fähig (*adj. w. gen.*), capable (of)
fahren, fuhr, ist gefahren, fährt, to ride, travel, drive, go
die **Fahrkarte, -, -n,** ticket
die **Fahrt, -, -en,** trip, voyage, ride
das **Fahrzeug, -s, -e,** vehicle, vessel, craft
der **Fall, -(e)s, ⁼e,** fall; case, instance
fallen, fiel, ist gefallen, fällt, to fall; **das Schreiben fällt mir schwer,** writing is difficult for me
der **Fallschirm, -s, -e,** parachute
die **Familie, -, -n,** family
fangen, fing, gefangen, fängt, to catch
die **Farbe, -, -n,** color
fast, almost
faul, lazy; rotten
die **Feder, -, -n,** feather; pen
fehlen, to be absent; lack, miss; be the matter with; **was fehlt Ihnen?** what is the matter with you?
der **Fehler, -s, -,** mistake
feiern, to celebrate
der **Feiertag, -(e)s, -e,** holiday
fein, fine
der **Feind, -(e)s, -e** enemy
feindlich (*adj. w. dat.*), hostile; — **gesinnt,** hostile toward
das **Feld, -(e)s, -er,** field; **auf dem —e,** in the field
der **Felsen, -s, -,** rock, cliff
das **Fenster, -s, -,** window

die **Ferien, -** (*pl.*), vacation
fern, far, distant, remote
der **Fernsehapparat, -s, -e,** television set
fertig, ready, finished
festhalten, hielt fest, festgehalten, hält fest, to hold on, cling, adhere to
fett, fat
das **Feuer, -s, -,** fire
finden, fand, gefunden, to find
der **Finger, -s, -,** finger
der **Fisch, -es, -e,** fish
flach, flat, plain; shallow
die **Fläche, -, -n,** plane surface, area
die **Flamme, -, -n,** flame
die **Flasche, -, -n,** bottle, flask
das **Fleisch, -es,** meat
der **Fleiß, -es,** diligence
fleißig, diligent, industrious; — **arbeiten,** to work hard
fliegen, flog, ist geflogen, to fly
der **Flieger, -s, -,** aviator, flyer
fliehen, floh, ist geflohen, to flee
fließen, floß, ist geflossen, to flow
fließend, fluent(ly)
der **Flug, -(e)s, ⁼e,** flight
der **Flügel, -s, -,** wing
das **Flugzeug, -(e)s, -e,** airplane
der **Fluß, -(ss)es, ü(ss)e,** river
die **Folge, -, -n,** consequence, result
folgen, folgte, ist gefolgt (*w. dat.*), to follow
die **Form, -, -en,** form, shape
der **Forscher, -s, -,** investigator, scientist, researcher
die **Forschung, -, -en,** investigation, research, inquiry, study
fort, away
fortgehen, ging fort, ist fortgegangen, to go away
fortlaufen, lief fort, ist fortgelaufen, läuft fort, to run away
forttragen, trug fort, fortgetragen, trägt fort, to carry away
fortwährend, continual(ly)
die **Frage, -, -n,** question; **eine — an eine Person** (*acc.*) **stellen,** to ask a person a question
fragen, to ask, question
Frankreich, -s (*neut.*), France
der **Franzose, -n, -n,** Frenchman
französisch, French
die **Frau, -, -en,** woman; wife; Mrs.
das **Fräulein, -s, -,** young lady, Miss
frei, free
die **Freiheit, -, -en,** freedom, liberty
der **Freitag, -(e)s, -e,** Friday
fremd, strange, foreign; **er ist mir —,** he is a stranger to me

die **Freude, -, -n,** joy, happiness, pleasure; **ich bin außer mir vor —,** I am beside myself with joy; **es macht mir —,** it gives me pleasure; **ich habe meine — daran,** I take pleasure in that

freuen, to make glad; **es freut mich,** I am glad

sich **freuen,** to be glad; **er freut sich,** he is glad; **sich — auf** (*w. acc.*), to look forward with pleasure to; **sich — über** (*w. acc.*), to be happy about, be pleased with, rejoice at

der **Freund, -(e)s, -e,** (*male*) friend

die **Freundin, -, -nen,** (*female*) friend

freundlich, friendly; **seien Sie ihm —!** be friendly to him

die **Freundschaft, -, -en,** friendship

der **Friede(n), -ns,** peace

frieren, fror, gefroren, to freeze; **vorige Nacht hat es stark gefroren,** last night it froze hard

frisch, fresh

froh, glad, happy; **er wird seines Lebens nicht —,** he leads an unhappy life

fröhlich, happy, cheerful

fromm, pious

die **Frucht, -, ⁻e,** fruit

früh, early

früher, earlier; sooner; formerly

der **Frühling, -s, -e,** spring; **im —,** in spring

das **Frühstück, -(e)s, -e,** breakfast; **zum —,** for breakfast

frühstücken, frühstückte, gefrühstückt, to have breakfast

fühlen, to feel

führen, to lead

der **Führer, -s, -,** leader, guide

füllen, to fill

die **Füllfeder, -, -n,** fountain pen

für (*prep. w. acc.*), for; **— fünf Mark Zucker,** five marks worth of sugar

fürchten, to fear; **sich — vor** (*w. dat.*), to be afraid of

der **Fürst, -en, -en,** prince

der **Fuß, -es, ⁻e,** foot

der **Fußboden, -s, ⁻,** floor

füttern, to feed

G

die **Gabel, -, -n,** fork

der **Gang, -(e)s, ⁻e** course (*of a meal*); corridor

die **Gans -, ⁻e,** goose

ganz, entire(ly), all, whole

gar, quite, very; **— nicht,** not at all; **— nichts,** nothing at all

der **Garten, -s, ⁻,** garden

der **Gast, -es, ⁻e,** guest

gebären, gebar, geboren, gebiert, to give birth to

das **Gebäude, -s, -,** building

geben, gab, gegeben, gibt, to give; **es gibt** (*impers. w. acc.*), there is (*or* are)

das **Gebiet, -(e)s, -e,** territory, domain; (*fig.*) field

das **Gebirge, -s, -,** mountain range, mountainous region

geboren (*p.p of* **gebären**), born; **wurde —,** was born (*used for the dead*); **ist —,** was born (*used for the living*); **wann sind Sie —?** when were you born?

gebrauchen, to use

die **Geburt, -, -en,** birth

der **Geburtstag, -(e)s, -e,** birthday; **zum —,** for one's birthday

das **Gedächtnis, -ses, -se,** memory

der **Gedanke, -ns, -n,** thought

gedenken (*w. gen.*), to remember

das **Gedicht, -(e)s, -e,** poem

die **Geduld, -,** patience

geduldig, patient

die **Gefahr, -, -en,** danger

gefährlich, dangerous

gefallen, gefiel, gefallen, gefällt (*w. dat.*), to please; **es gefällt mir,** I like it

der **Gefallen, -s, -,** favor; **er tut mir den —,** he does me the favor

das **Gefängnis, -ses, -se,** prison

das **Gefühl, -(e)s, -e,** feeling

gegen (*prep. w. acc.*), against; toward; contrary to

die **Gegend, -, -en,** region, neighborhood

der **Gegensatz, -es, ⁻e,** contrast, opposite

gegenüber (*prep. w. dat*), opposite

die **Gegenwart, -,** the present, modern times; presence; **in meiner —,** in my presence

geheim, secret(ly)

das **Geheimnis, -ses, -se,** secret

geheimnisvoll, mysterious

gehen, ging, ist gegangen, to go; **in die Schule —,** to go to school; **wie geht es Ihnen?** how are you?

gehorchen (*w. dat.*), to obey

gehören (*w. dat. & no prep. if ownership is denoted*), to belong to; **— zu,** to be part (*or* member) of

der **Geist, -es, -er,** mind, spirit
gelangen, gelangte, ist gelangt, to attain; come to; **endlich ist er zu einem Schluße gelangt,** he finally reached a conclusion
gelb, yellow
das **Geld, -(e)s, -er,** money
gelegen (*adj. w. dat.*), opportune
die **Gelegenheit, -, -en** opportunity, occasion; **bei dieser —,** on this occasion
gelingen, gelang, ist gelungen (*w. dat.*), to succeed; **es ist mir gelungen, Ihre Schrift zu entziffern,** I succeeded in deciphering your writing
gelten, galt, gegolten, gilt, to be worth (*or* of value); be meant for
das **Gemüt, -(e)s, -er,** feeling, soul, heart
gemütlich, cosy, comfortable; sociable
genau, exact(ly)
genesen, genas, ist genesen, genest, to recover (*from illness*)
genießen, genoß, genossen, genießt, to enjoy
genug, enough
genügen (*w. dat.*), to be enough; satisfy
das **Gepäck, -(e)s, -e,** baggage, luggage
der **Gepäckträger, -s, -,** porter
gerade (*adj. & adv.*), straight, direct; (*adv.*) just, exactly
geraten, geriet, ist geraten, gerät (*w. in & acc.*), to get (*or* stray) into; turn out to be
das **Gericht, -(e)s, -e,** court (of justice); dish, course
gern (lieber, am liebsten), gladly, willingly; **er hat es —,** he likes it; **er tut es —,** he likes to do it
der **Gesangverein, -(e)s, -e,** glee club, choral society
das **Geschäft, -(e)s, -e,** business; occupation
geschehen, geschah, ist geschehen, es geschieht, to happen; **es geschieht ihm recht,** it serves him right
das **Geschenk, -(e)s, -e,** gift, present
die **Geschichte, -, -n,** story; history
das **Geschlecht, -(e)s, -er,** sex, gender, race, stock, species
die **Geschwindigkeit, -, -en** speed, velocity
der **Geschwindigkeitsmesser, -s, -,** speedometer
der **Geselle, -n, -n,** fellow; journeyman

die **Gesellschaft, -, -en,** society, company
das **Gesetz, -es, -e,** law
das **Gesicht, -(e)s, -er,** face
gesinnt (*adj.*), minded, disposed; **feindlich —,** hostile toward
das **Gespräch, -(e)s, -e,** conversation
die **Gestalt, -, -en,** form, figure, stature
gestern, yesterday
gesund, well, healthy
die **Gesundheit, -, -en,** health
das **Getränk, -(e)s, -e,** drink
gewahr werden (*w. gen.*), to become aware of, perceive
die **Gewalt, -, -en,** force
gewinnen, gewann, gewonnen, to win, gain
gewiß (*adj. w. gen.*), sure, certain; (*adv.*) surely, indeed, certainly
das **Gewitter, -s, -,** (thunder)-storm
sich **gewöhnen an** (*w. acc.*), to get used to; **ich bin nicht daran gewöhnt,** I am not used to it
gewohnt, accustomed; **ich bin es** (*acc.*) **—,** I am used to it
gießen, goß, gegossen, to pour
das **Gift, -(e)s, -e,** poison
der **Gipfel, -s, -,** top, summit
glänzen, to shine, sparkle
das **Glas, -es, ⁻er,** glass
glatt, smooth
der **Glaube, -ns, -n,** belief
glauben, (*w. dat. of the pers. & acc. of the th.*), to believe; **er glaubt mir,** he believes me; **er glaubt es,** he believes it
gleich, equal; like; (= **sogleich**) immediately; **es ist mir ganz —,** it is all the same to me
gleichen (*w. dat.*), to resemble
die **Glocke, -, -n,** bell
das **Glück, -(e)s, -sfälle,** (good) luck, fortune, happiness
glücklich, happy
das **Gold, -(e)s,** gold
der **Gott, -es, ⁻er,** God
graben, grub, gegraben, gräbt, to dig
der **Graf, -en, -en,** count
sich **grämen über** (*w. acc.*), to grieve at (*or* over)
das **Gras, -es, Gräser,** grass
grau, gray
grauen (*impers.*), to shudder; **mir graut,** I shudder
greifen, griff, gegriffen, to grasp, seize, take hold of
die **Grenze, -, -n,** boundary, limit
grob, rude

groß, (größer, größt-), large, big; tall; great
großartig, grand
die Großeltern, - (*pl.*), grandparents
die Großmutter, -, ⸚, grandmother
der Großvater, -s, ⸚, grandfather
grün, green
der Grund, -(e)s, ⸚e, reason; ground, bottom; aus welchem —e? for what reason?
gründlich, thoroughly
die Gruppe, -, -n, group, troop
der Gruß, -es, ⸚e, greeting; besten Gruss an (*w. acc.*), best regards to
grüßen, to greet
günstig, favorable
gut (besser, best-), good
das Gymnasium, -s, Gymnasien, academic high school

H

das Haar, -(e)s, -e, hair
haben, hatte, gehabt, hat, to have
die Hafenstadt, -, ⸚e, seaport
der Hahn, -(e)s, ⸚e, cock, rooster
halb, half
die Hälfte, -, -n, half
der Hals, -es, Hälse, neck, throat
das Halsweh, -(e)s, sore throat
halten, hielt, gehalten, hält, to hold; eine Rede —, to deliver a speech; er hält Wort, he keeps his word; ich halte ihn für einen ehrlichen Mann, I believe he is an honest man
die Hand, -, ⸚e, hand; mit der — winken, to wave, beckon
der Handel, -s, trade
sich handeln um (*impers.*), to concern, be a question of; um was handelt es sich? what is it (all) about?
der Handschuh, -(e)s, -e, glove
hangen, hing, gehangen, hängt (*intr.*), to hang
hängen (*tr.*), to hang
hart, hard
der Hase, -n, -n, hare
hassen, to hate
häufig, frequent(ly)
das Haupt, -(e)s, ⸚er, head; chief
das Haus, -es, Häuser, house; zu Hause, at home; nach Hause, home (ward)
das Haustier, -(e)s, -e, domestic animal
die Haustür, -, -en, front door
heben, hob gehoben, hebt, to lift, raise; (*refl.*) to rise

das Heer, -(e)s, -e, army
das Heft, -(e)s, -e, notebook
heftig, violent
heilig, holy
die Heimat, -, -en, home(land)
heimlich, secret(ly)
heiraten, to marry
heiß, hot
heißen, hieß, geheißen, heißt, to be called; mean; command; call; wie — Sie? what is your name? er heißt, his name is; das heißt (*abbr. d.h.*), that is, (i.e.)
der Held, -en, -en, hero
helfen, half, geholfen, hilft (*w. dat.*), to help
hell, light, bright(ly)
das Hemd, -(e)s, -en, shirt
die Henne -, -n, hen
herabsinken, sank herab, ist herabgesunken, to (sink down), drop
der Herbst, es, -e, fall, autumn
herkommen, kam her, ist hergekommen, to come hither, approach
der Herr, -n, -en, master, lord, gentleman, sir, Mr.; meine —en, gentlemen
herrlich, glorious, magnificent; sich — amüsieren, to have a wonderful time
herrschen, to rule
der Herrscher, -s, -, ruler
das Herz, -ens, -en, heart
herzlich, cordial(ly)
der Herzog, -(e)s, -e (*or* ⸚e), duke
heute, today; — morgen, this morning; — abend, this evening, tonight
die Hexe, -, -n, witch
hier, here
die Hilfe, -, -n, help
der Himmel, -s, -, heaven, sky
hinaufgehen, ging hinauf, ist hinaufgegangen, to go up
das Hindernis, -ses, -se, obstacle, hindrance
hingehen, ging hin, ist hingegangen, geht hin, to go there (*or* to a place)
hinten (*adv.*), in the rear
hinter (*prep. w. dat. or acc.*), behind
der Hirt, -en, -en, shepherd
die Hitze, -, heat
hoch, (höher, höchst-), high; einen Fuß —, a foot high
die Hochzeit, -, -en, wedding
der Hof, -(e)s, ⸚e, yard; court; estate
hoffen auf (*w. acc.*), to hope for
die Hoffnung, -, -en, hope
höfflich, polite

die **Höhe, -, -n,** height, altitude, elevation
hohl, hollow
holen, to get, fetch; — **lassen,** to send for; **er hat den Arzt — lassen,** he sent for the doctor
das **Holz, -es, ⁼er,** wood
der **Honig, -s, -e,** honey
hören, to hear; **ich höre ihn lachen,** I hear him laughing
das **Horn, -(e)s, ⁼er,** horn
das **Hotel, -s, -s,** hotel
der **Hügel, -s, -,** hill
das **Huhn, -(e)s, ⁼er,** chicken
humoristischerweise, in a humorous manner
der **Hund, -(e)s, -e,** dog
hundert (*num. adj.*), a hundred
das **Hundert, -(e)s, -e,** hundred
hundertmal, a hundred times
der **Hunger, -s,** hunger; **ich habe —,** I am hungry
hungrig, hungry
der **Hut, -(e)s, ⁼e,** hat
sich **hüten vor** (*w. dat.*), to guard against

I

idiomatisch, idiomatic
ihr, ihre, ihr (*poss. adj.*), her; their; its
Ihr, Ihre, Ihr (*poss. adj.*), your
immer, always
in (*prep. w. dat. or acc.*), in(to)
indem, while
der **Indianer, -s, -,** Indian
Indien, -s (*neut.*), India
der **Inhalt, -(e)s,** contents
inner, inner, internal, interior
innerhalb (*prep. w. gen.*), within
die **Insel, -, -n,** island
das **Instrument, -s, -e,** instrument, device, apparatus
interessant, interesting
sich **interessieren für,** to be interested in
inzwischen, in the meantime
irgend (*used in various compounds*), any; some; — **jemand,** anybody
irgendwo, anywhere
sich **irren,** to be mistaken
der **Irrtum, -(e)s, ⁼er,** mistake

J

ja, yes; indeed
jagen, to hunt, chase

das **Jahr, -(e)s, -e,** year
die **Jahreszeit, -, -en,** season
das **Jahrhundert, -(e)s, -e,** century
je, ever; **je . . . desto,** the . . . the
jeder, jede, jedes, each, every
jedermann, everbody
jemals, ever, at any time
jemand, someone; anyone; **irgend —,** anybody
jener, jene, jenes (*dem. adj.*), that; (*dem. pron.*) that one
jenseits (*prep. w. gen.*), on that side of
jetzt, now
der **Juli, -(s), -s,** July
jung, young
der **Junge, -n, -n,** boy
der **Jüngling, -s, -e,** young man
der **Juni, -(s), -s,** June

K

der **Kaffee, -s, -s,** coffee
die **Kaffeetasse, -, -n,** coffee cup
der **Kahn, -(e)s, ⁼e,** boat
der **Kaiser, -s, -,** emperor
das **Kalb, -(e)s, ⁼er,** calf
kalt, cold
die **Kälte, -,** cold
der **Kamerad, -en, -en,** comrade, companion, chum
der **Kamm, -(e)s, ⁼e,** comb
der **Kampf, -(e)s, ⁼e,** fight, struggle
kämpfen, to fight, battle
Kanada, -s (*neut.*), Canada
der **Kanal, -s, Kanäle,** canal
karg, stingy
die **Karte, -, -n,** card; map
die **Katze, -, -n,** cat
kaufen, to buy
der **Kaufmann, -(e)s, Kaufleute,** merchant
kaum, hardly, barely, scarcely
kein, keine, kein, no, not a, not any
keiner, keine, keines (*pron.*), none, not one (*or* any)
keineswegs (*adv.*), by no means
der **Keller, -s, -,** cellar
der **Kellner, -s, -,** waiter
kennen, kannte, gekannt, to know, be acquainted with
der **Kerl, -(e)s, -e,** fellow
das **Kind, -(e)s, -er,** child
die **Kindheit, -,** childhood
das **Kinn, -(e)s, -e,** chin
das **Kino, -s, -s,** moving pictures
die **Kirche, -, -n,** church

die **Kirsche, -, -n,** cherry
das **Kissen, -s, -,** pillow, cushion
klagen, to complain
klar, clear(ly)
die **Klärung, -, -en,** clarification
die **Klasse -, -n,** class; **erster —** (*gen.*)
fahren, to travel first class
das **Klassenzimmer, -s, -,** classroom
klatschen, to clap; **in die Hände
—,** to clap one's hands
das **Klavier, -s, -e,** piano; **—** (*no art.*)
spielen, to play the piano
das **Kleid, -(e)s, -er,** dress; (*pl.*) clothes
sich **kleiden,** to dress (oneself)
klein, small, little
klettern (auf), to climb (up)
klingeln, to ring
klingen, klang, geklungen, to ring,
chime, sound
klopfen, to knock; **an die Tür —,** to
knock at the door
klug, clever, intelligent, wise, bright
der **Knabe, -n, -n,** boy
das **Knie, -s, -,** knee
der **Knopf, -(e)s, ⁼e,** button
kochen, to cook
der **Koffer, -s, -,** trunk
die **Kohle, -, -n,** coal
Köln, -s, (*neut.*), Cologne
kommen, kam, ist gekommen, to
come
der **König, -(e)s, -e,** king
können, konnte, gekonnt, kann, to
be able, can; know; **er hätte es tun
—,** he could have done it; **er kann
Deutsch,** he knows German; **er
kann nichts dafür,** it is not his fault
konstruieren, to construct, design,
build
das **Konzert, -(e)s, -e,** concert
der **Kopf, -(e)s, ⁼e,** head
das **Kopfweh, -(e)s,** headache
der **Korb, -(e)s, ⁼e,** basket
der **Körper, -s, -,** body
der **Körperbau, -s,** bodily structure, frame,
build
kostbar, expensive, precious
kosten, to cost; **es kostete mich** (*or*
mir) **einen Dollar,** it cost me a
dollar
kostspielig, expensive, costly
die **Kraft, -, ⁼e,** strength, power
krank, sick, ill
die **Krankheit, -, -en,** sickness, illness
das **Kraut, -(e)s, ⁼er,** plant, vegetable,
herb, weed; (*dialect*) cabbage
die **Krawatte, -, -n,** necktie, cravat

die **Kreide, -,** chalk
der **Kreis, -es, -e,** circle
die **Kreisbahn, -, -en,** orbit
kriechen, kroch, ist gekrochen, to
creep
der **Krieg, -(e)s, -e,** war
krumm, crooked
die **Küche, -, -n,** kitchen
die **Kugel, -, -n,** bullet, ball, sphere
die **Kuh, -, ⁼e,** cow
kühl, cool
der **Kummer, -s,** (*no pl.*), sorrow, grief,
worry, trouble
sich **kümmern um,** to worry (care) about
die **Kunst, -, ⁼e,** art
der **Künstler, -s, -,** (*male*) artist
die **Künstlerin, -, -nen** (*female*) artist
künstlerisch, artistic
künstlich, artificial, synthetic
kurz, short

L

lächeln, to smile
lachen, to laugh; **— über** (*w. acc.*), to
laugh at
der **Laden, -s, ⁼,** store
lahm, lame
das **Lamm, (-e)s, ⁼er,** lamb
die **Lampe, —, -n,** lamp
das **Land, -(e)s, ⁼er,** land, country; **aufs
—,** to the country; **auf dem —e,** in
the country
lang, long; **einen Fuß —,** a foot
long
lange, (for) a long time
langsam, slow(ly)
langweilig, tedious, boring
der **Lärm, -(e)s,** noise
lassen, ließ, gelassen, läßt, to let,
leave; have done; **sich** (*dat.*) **das
Haar schneiden —,** to have one's
hair cut
laufen, lief, ist gelaufen, läuft, to
run; **Schlittschuh —,** to skate
laufend, current (of time); **auf dem
laufenden,** up-to-date; running;
mit laufendem Motor, with engine
running
die **Laune, -, -n,** mood, humor; **guter
—** (*gen.*) **sein,** to be a in good mood
lauschen, to listen
laut, loud(ly), aloud
der **Laut, -(e)s, -e,** sound
das **Leben, -s, -,** life

leben, to live
das **Leder, -s, -,** leather
leer, empty
legen, to lay, place, put
sich **lehnen an** (*w. acc.*), to lean on
lehren, to teach; **sie lehrte ihn das Lied,** she taught him the song
der **Lehrer, -s, -,** (*male*) teacher
die **Lehrerin, -, -nen,** (*female*) teacher
der **Lehrling, -s, -e,** apprentice
leicht, easy; light; **—en Herzens,** with a light heart
leiden, litt, gelitten, to suffer
leider (*adv.*), unfortunately; (*interj.*), alas
leid tun (*impers.*), to be sorry; **es tut mir leid,** I am sorry
leisten, to perform, accomplish; **sich** (*dat.*) **—,** to afford
leiten, to lead, guide
die **Lerche, -, -n,** lark
lernen, to learn, study
lesen, las, gelesen, liest, to read
letzt-, last
Leute, - (*pl.*), people
das **Licht, -(e)s, -er,** light
lieb, dear
die **Liebe, -, -n,** love
lieben, to love
lieber (*comp. of* **lieb**), dearer; (*comp. of* **gern**), rather
lieblich, lovely, sweet
der **Liebling, -s, -e,** favorite; darling
das **Lied, -(e)s, -er,** song
liefern, to supply, furnish, deliver, render, yield
liegen, lag, gelegen, to lie; be situated
die **Limonade, -, -n,** soda, lemonade
die **Linde, -, -n,** linden
der **Lindenbaum, -(e)s, -e,** linden tree
link-, left
links, on the left; **nach —,** to the left
die **Lippe, -, -n,** lip
die **Literatur, -, -en,** literature
loben, to praise
das **Loch, -(e)s, -er,** hole
der **Löffel, -s, -,** spoon
los, rid of; **ich bin es —,** I am rid of it; **was ist —?** what is the matter?
das **Löschblatt, -(e)s, -er,** (sheet of) blotting paper
löschen, to blot; quench
lösen, to loosen; solve (*a puzzle*); buy (*a ticket*); **sich —** (*refl.*), to loosen, become detached, be released
loslassen, ließ los, losgelassen, läßt los, to release, let go

der **Löwe, -n, -n,** lion
die **Luft, -, -e,** air
die **Luftdichte, -,** air density
das **Luftschiff, -(e)s, -e,** airship
der **Luftverkehr, -s,** air traffic
die **Lüge, -, -n,** lie, falsehood
lügen, log, gelogen, to (tell a) lie
lustig, merry, gay

M

machen, to make, do; **eine Reise (einen Spaziergang, eine Prüfung) —,** to take a trip (walk, examination); **sich** (*dat.*) **Sorgen — um,** to worry about; **man machte ihn zum Präsidenten,** he was made president
die **Macht, -, -e,** might, power
mächtig, mighty; (*w. gen.*) master (*or* in control) of
das **Mädchen, -s, -,** girl
die **Mahlzeit, -, -en,** meal
der **Mai, -(e)s** (*or* -), **-e,** May
das **Mal, -(e)s, -e,** time; **das erste —** (*or* **erstemal**), the first time
malen, to paint
der **Maler, -s, -,** painter; artist
malerisch, artsitic, picturesque
man (*indef. pron.*), one, they, people
mancher, manche, manches, many a; (*pl.*) some
manchmal, sometimes, many a time
der **Mann, -(e)s, -er,** man
der **Mantel, -s, -,** cloak; overcoat
die **Mark, -,** mark (*monetary*)
der **Markt, -(e)s, -e,** market
das **Maß, -es, -e,** measure
das **Material, -s, -ien,** material, substance, matter
der **Mathematiker, -s, —,** mathematician
die **Mauer, -, -n,** (*outside*) wall
die **Maus, -, Mäuse,** mouse
das **Meer, -(e)s, -e,** sea, ocean
mehr (*comp. of* **viel**), more
mehrere (*pl.*), several, a number of
die **Meile, -, -n,** mile
mein, meine, mein (*poss. adj.*), my
meinen, to mean (*only of people*), think, believe
die **Meinung, -, -en,** opinion
meist- (*superl. of* **viel**), most
der **Meister, -s, -,** master; expert; master tradesman
die **Meldung, -, -en,** message, report
der **Mensch, -en, -en,** man, human being

das **Merkmal, -s, -e,** characteristic, feature, symptom
die **Messe, -, -n,** fair, market
messen, maß, gemessen, mißt, to measure
das **Messer, -s, -,** knife
das **Metall, -s, -e,** metal
das **Meter, -s, -,** meter (39.37 inches)
die **Milch, -,** milk
die **Miliarde, -, -n,** milliard (*one thousand millions*)
die **Million, -, -en,** million
die **Minute, -, -n,** minute
mischen, to mix
mißverstehen, mißverstand, mißverstanden, to misunderstand
mit (*prep. w. dat.*), with
mitbringen, brachte mit, mitgebracht, to bring along
das **Mitglied, -(e)s, -er,** member
mithelfen, half mit, mitgeholfen, hilft mit, to help along
der **Mittag, -(e)s, -e,** noon; **am —,** at noon
die **Mitte, -,** middle
mitten in, in the middle of
der **Mittwoch, -(e)s, -e,** Wednesday
mögen, mochte, gemocht, mag, to like to, care for; **er möchte (gern) mitgehen,** he would like to go along; **er mochte wohl dreißig Jahre alt sein,** he was probably thirty years old; **das mag sein,** that may be
möglich, possible
der **Monat, -(e)s, -e,** month
monatelang, for months
der **Mond, -(e)s, -e,** moon
der **Montag, -(e)s, -e,** Monday
morgen (*adv.*), tomorrow
der **Morgen, -s, -,** morning; **am —** (des **—s** *or* **morgens**), in the morning; **eines —s,** one morning; **heute morgen,** this morning
müde (*adj. w. gen. or acc.*), tired; **ich bin des Lebens —,** I am tired of life; **ich bin es —,** I am tired of it
die **Mühe, -, -n,** trouble; **der —** (*gen.*) **wert sein,** to be worth the trouble
die **Mühle, -, -n,** mill
der **Müller, -s, -,** miller
der **Mund, -(e)s, -er,** mouth
das **Museum, -s, Museen,** museum
die **Musik, -,** music
müssen, mußte, gemußt, muß, to be obliged, have to, must
das **Muster, -s, -,** model, sample, pattern

der **Mut, -(e)s,** courage
mutig, courageous
die **Mutter, -, -,** mother

N

nach (*prep. w. dat.*), after; toward; according to; **— Hause,** home, homeward
der **Nachbar, -s**(*or* **-n**), **-n,** (*male*) neighbor
die **Nachbarin, -, -nen,** (*female*) neighbor
nachdem (*conj.*), after
nachher (*adv.*), afterwards
nachlaufen, lief nach, ist nachgelaufen, läuft nach, to run after
der **Nachmittag, -(e)s, -e,** afternoon; **am —** (des **—s** *or* **nachmittages**), in the afternoon; **eines —s** (*indef. time*), one afternoon; **heute nachmittag,** this afternoon
die **Nachricht, -, -en,** news, information
nächst- (*superl. of* **nah**), next, nearest; **—es Jahr,** next year
die **Nacht, -, -e,** night; **in der —,** at night
nackt, naked, bare
die **Nadel, -, -n,** needle
der **Nagel, -s, -,** nail
nah(e) (**näher, nächst-**) (*w. dat.*), near
die **Nähe, -, -n,** vicinity, neighborhood; **in seiner —,** near him
sich **nähern** (*w. dat.*), to approach
nähren, to nourish
der **Name, -ns, -n,** name; **beim Namen nennen,** to call by name
namens, named, by the name of; **ein Mann — Schmidt,** a man named Smith
nämlich, namely
der **Narr, -en, -en,** fool
die **Nase, -, -n,** nose
naß, wet
die **Natur, -, -en,** nature
natürlich, natural(ly)
der **Nebel, -s, -,** fog
neben (*prep. w. dat. or acc.*), beside, by the side of, next to
das **Nebenzimmer, -s, -,** adjoining room
necken, to tease
der **Neffe, -n, -n,** nephew
nehmen, nahm, genommen, nimmt, to take
nein, no

nennen, nannte, genannt, to name, call; **er nannte ihn beim Namen,** he called him by name

das Nest, -es, -er, nest

nett, pleasant; pretty; tidy; nice; **ein —es Mädchen,** a nice girl

das Netz, -es, -e, net

neu, new

neulich, recently

neutral, neutral

nicht, not; **gar —,** not at all; **noch —,** not yet; **— einmal,** not even; **— nur ... sondern auch,** not only ... but also; **— wahr?** right? not so?

nichts, nothing; **gar —,** nothing at all; **das geht ihn — an,** that does not concern him

die Niederlande, - (*pl.*), Netherlands

sich niederlegen, legte nieder, niedergelegt, to lie down

niedrig, low

nie(mals), never

niemand, -(e)s, nobody

nirgend (*neg. of* irgend; *used in various compounds*), no-

nirgends, nowhere

noch, still, yet; **— einmal,** again; **— ein,** another; **— immer** (*or* immer **—**), still; **— nicht,** not yet; **weder ... —,** neither ... nor; **was —?** what else?

der Norden, -s, north

die Not, -, ⁻e, need, necessity; trouble

nötig, necessary; **ich habe es —,** I need it

die Nummer, -, -n, number

nun (*adv.*), now; (*part.*) now, well

nur, only

die Nuß, -, Nüsse, nut

nützlich, useful

O

ob (*conj.*), whether, if; **als —,** as if

oben (*adv.*), above, at the top of, up; upstairs

oberhalb (*prep. w. gen.*), above

die Oberfläche, -, -n, surface

obgleich (*conj.*), although

das Obst, -es, fruit

der Obstbaum, -(e)s, ⁻e, fruit tree

obwohl (*conj.*), although

der Ochse, -n, -n, ox

oder (*conj.*), or

der Ofen, -s, ⁻, stove

offen (*adj.*), open

öffnen, to open

oft, often

ohne (*prep. w. acc.*), without

das Ohr. -(e)s, -en, ear

der Oktober, -(s), -, October

das Öl, -(e)s, -e, oil

der Onkel, -s, -, uncle

die Oper, -, -n, opera

das Opfer, -s, -, victim, sacrifice

opfern, to sacrifice

organisch, organic

die Orgel, -, -n, organ

der Ort, -(e)s, -e, place

der Osten, -s, east

Ostern (*pl., w. sing. vb.*), Easter

der Ozean, -s, -e, ocean

P

das Paar, -(e)s, -e, pair; **ein paar,** several, a few

packen, to pack; to seize

das Papier, -s, -e, paper

der Park, -(e)s, -e, park

passen (*w. dat.*), to fit; be convenient, suit

die Perle, -, -n, pearl

die Person, -, -en, person

die Pfalz, the Palatinate

die Pfeife, -, -n, pipe; whistle

pfeifen, pfiff, gepfiffen, to whistle

der Pfennig, -s, -e, pfennig (1/100 *mark*)

das Pferd, -(e)s, -e, horse

die Pflanze, -, -n, plant

pflanzen, to plant

pflegen, to take care of; be accustomed; **wie er zu sagen pflegt,** as he usually says

das Pfund, -(e)s, -e, pound

der Physiker, -s, -, physicist

physiologisch, physiological

der Plan, -(e)s, ⁻e, plan

planen, to plan

der Planet, -en, -en, planet

das Platin, -s, platinum

der Platz, -es, ⁻e, place; seat; square; **nehmen Sie —!** be seated

plötzlich, sudden(ly)

der Polizist, -en, -en, policeman

die Post, -, -en, mail; post office; **auf die — bringen,** to mail

die Postkarte, -, -en, postal card

der Präsident, -en, -en, president

der **Preis, -es, -e,** price; prize
Preußen, -s, (*neut.*), Prussia
der **Prinz, -en, -en,** prince
der **Professor, -s, -en,** professor
die **Prüfung, -, -en,** examination
das **Pult, -(e)s, -e,** desk
der **Punkt, -(e)s, -e,** point, dot, period;
— **zwei Uhr,** at two o'clock sharp,
on the dot of two
pünktlich, punctual(ly)
putzen, to clean, shine; (*refl.*), to dress
up

Q

der **Quarz, -es, -e,** quartz, crystal
die **Quelle, -, -n,** spring; source
die **Quittung, -, -en,** receipt

R

die **Rache, -,** revenge
sich **rächen an** (*w. dat.*), to take revenge on
das **Rad, -(e)s, ⁼er,** wheel; bicycle
der **Radarstrahl, -(e)s, -en,** radar beam
das **Radarteleskop, -s, -e,** radar telescope
der **Rand, -(e)s, ⁼er,** edge
rasch, quick(ly)
rasieren, to shave (*often refl.*)
der **Rat, -(e)s, -schläge,** (piece of) advice
der **Rat, -(e)s, ⁼e,** councilor, adviser
raten, riet, geraten, rät (*w. dat.*), to
advise; (*w. acc.*), to guess
das **Rathaus, -es, /häuser,** city hall
das **Rätsel, -s, -,** riddle, puzzle
die **Ratte, -, -n,** rat
der **Räuber, -s, -,** robber
rauchen, to smoke
der **Raum, -(e)s, ⁼e,** room, space
das **Raumfahrzeug, -s, -e,** space ship
der **Raumflug, -(e)s, ⁼e,** space flight
die **Raumkapsel, -, -n,** space capsule
rauschen, to rustle
die **Rechnung, -, -en,** bill
recht, right; **er hat —,** he is right; **es
geschieht ihm —,** it serves him
right
rechts, on the right; **nach —,** to the
right
die **Rede, -, -n,** speech, discourse
reden, to speak, talk
der **Redner, -s, -,** speaker, orator
die **Regel, -, -n,** rule; **in der —,** as a
rule
regelmäßig, regular(ly)

der **Regen, -s, -fälle** (*or* **Niederschläge**),
rain
der **Regenschirm, -(e)s, -e,** umbrella
regieren, to rule
die **Regierung, -, -en,** government
regnen, to rain; **stark —,** to rain hard
regulieren, to regulate, govern, control
reiben, rieb, gerieben, to rub
reich, rich; **— an** (*w. dat.*), rich in
das **Reich, -(e)s, -e,** empire, realm, state;
system of government
reif, ripe; mature
die **Reihe, -, -n,** row; **ich bin an der —**
(*or* **die — ist an mir**), it is my turn
rein, pure, clean, clear
reinigen, to clean
die **Reise, -, -n,** trip, journey; **eine —
machen,** to take a trip
reisen, reiste, ist gereist, to travel
das **Reiseziel, -(e)s, -e,** destination of a
trip
reißen, riß, gerissen, to tear
reiten, ritt, ist geritten, to ride (horseback)
der **Reiter, -s, -,** rider, horseman
reizen, to excite, irritate
reizend (*pres. p. used as adj.*), charming
rennen, rannte, ist gerannt, to run
die **Republik, -, -en,** republic
retten, to save, rescue
der **Rhein, -(e)s,** Rhine
der **Richter, -s, -,** judge
richtig, correct
riechen, roch, gerochen, to smell;
— nach, to smell of
der **Riese, -n, -n,** giant
riesig, gigantic
der **Ring, -(e)s, -e,** ring
der **Ritter, -s, -,** knight
der **Rock, -(e)s, ⁼e,** coat
roh, raw
rollen, rollte, ist gerollt, to roll
die **Rose, -, -n,** rose
rot, red
der **Rücken, -s, -,** back
rücken, to move
die **Rücksicht, -, -en,** consideration
rufen, rief, gerufen, to call
die **Ruhe, -,** peace, quiet, rest
ruhig, quiet(ly)
der **Ruhm, -(e)s,** fame
sich **rühmen** (*w. gen.*), to boast of
rühren, to stir, move; (*often refl.*) —
Sie sich nicht von der Stelle! don't
move from the spot
rund, round

S

der **Saal, -(e)s, Säle,** hall

die **Sache, -, -n,** thing; matter; **er ist seiner — gewiß,** he knows what he is about

der **Sack, -(e)s, ⁓e,** sack

die **Sage, -, -n,** legend, tradition; **der — nach,** according to legend

sagen, to say, tell; **— wollen,** to mean

das **Salz, -es, -e,** salt

sammeln, to collect

der **Samstag, -(e)s, -e,** Saturday

sanft, mild(ly), gentle, gently

der **Sänger, -s, -,** (*male*) singer

die **Sängerin, -, -nen,** (*female*) singer

der **Satellit, -en, -en,** satellite

der **Satz, -es, ⁓e,** sentence

sauber, clean

sauer, sour

schade (*interj.*), too bad, (what) a pity

schaden (*w. dat.*), to hurt, injure

das **Schaf, -(e)s, -e,** sheep

sich **schämen,** (*w. gen. or* **über** *& acc.*), to be ashamed of

scharf, sharp

der **Schatten, -s, -,** shade, shadow

der **Schatz, -es, ⁓e,** treasure; sweetheart

schätzen, to appreciate

schauen, to look

scheiden, schied, geschieden (*tr.*), to separate; (*intr. w.* **sein**) to take leave

der **Schein, -(e)s, -e,** light, brilliancy

scheinen, schien, geschienen, to shine; appear, seem

schelten, schalt, gescholten, schilt, to scold; call names

schenken, to give, present (*as a gift*)

die **Schicht, -, -en,** layer, stratum

schicken, to send

das **Schicksal, -(e)s, -e,** fate, destiny

schieben, schob, geschoben, to shove

schief, uneven, crooked, wry

schießen, schoß, geschossen, to shoot

das **Schiff, -(e)s, -e,** ship

der **Schild, -(e)s, -e,** shield

das **Schild, -(e)s, -er,** sign(board); door plate

der **Schimpanse, -n, -n,** chimpanzee

der **Schirm, -(e)s, -e,** shelter; shade, screen

die **Schlacht, -, -en,** battle

der **Schlaf, -(e)s,** sleep

schlafen, schlief, geschlafen, schläft, to sleep

schläfern (*impers.*), to be sleepy; **mich schläfert,** I am sleepy

schläfrig, sleepy

der **Schlag, -(e)s, ⁓e,** blow; stroke

schlagen, schlug, geschlagen, schlägt, to strike, hit

schlank, slender, slim

schlau, sly, cunning

schlecht, bad

schließen, schloß, geschlossen, to close, lock

schlimm, bad(ly)

der **Schlittschuh, -(e)s, -e,** skate; — **laufen,** to skate

das **Schloß, Schlosses, Schlösser,** castle

der **Schluß, Schlusses, Schlüsse,** end

der **Schlüssel, -s, -,** key

schmal, narrow; thin, slender

schmecken, to taste

schmeicheln (*w. dat.*), to flatter; (*refl.*), to flatter oneself; **du schmeichelst dir,** you flatter yourself

schmelzen, schmolz, ist geschmolzen, schmilzt, to melt

der **Schmerz, -es, -en,** pain; **toll vor —,** frantic with pain

schmerzlich, painful(ly); **er empfindet es —,** it pains him

schmücken, to adorn

schmutzig, dirty

der **Schnee, -s,** snow

schneiden, schnitt, geschnitten, to cut

der **Schneider, -s, -,** tailor

schneien, to snow

schnell, quick(ly)

der **Schnellzug, -(e)s, ⁓e,** express train

schon, already

schön, beautiful(ly)

die **Schönheit, -, -en,** beauty

der **Schrank, -(e)s, ⁓e,** cupboard, cabinet

schreiben, schrieb, geschrieben, to write; **ich schreibe meinem Freund einen Brief** (*or* **ich schreibe einen Brief an meinen Freund**), I write my friend a letter

schreien, schrie, geschrien, to scream

die **Schrift, -, -en,** writing

schriftlich, in writing, written

der **Schuh, -(e)s, -e,** shoe

die **Schuld, -, -en,** guilt; debt

schuldig, guilty; indebted; **ich bin ihm nichts —,** I owe him nothing

die **Schule, -, -n,** school; **in der —,** in school; **nach der —,** after school; **in die** (*or* **zur**) **— gehen,** to go to school

der **Schüler, -s, -,** (*male*) pupil

die **Schülerin, -, -nen,** (*female*) pupil

die **Schulter, -, -n,** shoulder

der **Schupo, -s, -s** (*abbr. for* der **Schutzpolizist**), policeman

die **Schüssel, -, -n,** dish; platter; bowl

schütteln, to shake

schützen, to protect

schwach, weak

der **Schwager, -s, ",** brother-in-law

schwarz, black

der **Schwarzwald, -(e)s,** Black Forest

schweben, to hover, float, hang, be suspended

schweigen, schwieg, geschwiegen, to be silent

die **Schweiz, -,** Switzerland

schwer, heavy; difficult; **— arbeiten,** to work hard

die **Schwester, -, -n,** sister

schwierig, hard, difficult

schwimmen, schwamm, ist geschwommen, to swim

der **See, -s, -n,** lake

die **See, -, -n,** ocean, sea

die **Seele, -, -n,** soul

segeln, to sail

sehen, sah, gesehen, sieht, to see; **haben Sie ihn kommen —?** did you see him coming?

sich **sehnen nach,** to long for

sehr, very (much)

die **Seide, -, -n,** silk

sein, war, ist gewesen, ist, to be; **mir ist,** it seems to me; **mir ist schlecht zumute,** I am in a bad humor

sein, seine, sein (*poss. adj.*), his, its

seiner, seine, seines (*poss. pron.*), his, its

seit (*prep. w. dat.*), since, for; **— wann?** since when?

seitdem (*adv. & conj.*), since

die **Seite, -, -n,** side; page

seither (*adv.*), since then

die **Sekunde, -, -n,** second

selbst (*indecl. adj. and pron.*), self; (*adv.*) even

selig, blessed; blissful(ly)

selten, seldom, rare(ly)

seltsam, peculiar

senden, sandte, gesandt, to send

setzen, to set, place; (*refl.*), to sit down; **er setzt sich an den Tisch,** he sits down at the table

sicher (*adj. w. gen.*) sure; (*adv.*), surely, safe(ly)

der **Sieg, -(e)s, -e,** victory

siegen, to conquer

das **Signal, -s, -e,** signal, sign

das **Silber, -s,** silver

silbern (*adj.*), (of) silver

singen, sang, gesungen, to sing

sinken, sank, ist gesunken (*intr.*), to sink

der **Sinn, -(e)s, -e,** mind; sense

sitzen, saß, gesessen (*intr.*), to sit; **er sitzt am Tisch,** he sits at the table

so, so, thus, as

sobald, as soon as

sofort, at once

sogar, even

sogleich, at once, immediately

der **Sohn, -(e)s, "e,** son

solcher, solche, solches, such

der **Soldat, -en, -en,** soldier

sollen, sollte, gesollt, soll, to be (required) to; be said; **er hätte arbeiten —,** he should have worked; **er soll reich sein,** he is said to be rich; **er sollte** (*imperf. subj.*) **arbeiten,** he should (*or* ought) to work

der **Sommer, -s, -,** summer

der **Sommermonat, -(e)s, -e,** summer month

sonderbar, unusual, peculiar

sondern, but; **nicht nur . . . — auch,** not only . . . but also

der **Sonnabend, -s, -e,** Saturday

die **Sonne, -, -n,** sun

die **Sonnenfinsternis, -, -se,** solar eclipse

der **Sonnenschein, -(e)s,** sunshine

das **Sonnensystem, -s, -e,** solar system

sonnig, sunny

der **Sonntag, -(e)s, -e,** Sunday

sonst, otherwise

die **Sorge, -, -n,** care, worry; **sich** (*dat.*) **—n machen um,** to worry about

sorgen für, to care for, take care of

sorgfältig, careful(ly)

die **Spalte, -, -n,** crack, cleft, fissure, split, gap

sparen, to save, economize

der **Spaß, -es, "e,** joke

spät, late

spazierengehen (*conjugated like* **gehen**), to go walking; **ich bin spazierengegangen,** I went for a walk

der **Spaziergang, -(s), "e,** walk; **einen — machen,** to take a walk

die **Speise, -, -n,** food, dish

der **Spiegel, -s, -,** mirror

das **Spiel, -(e)s, -e,** play, game

spielen, to play

die **Spitze, -, -n,** tip, head, point; lace
spitzen, to sharpen

die **Sprache, -, -n,** language
sprechen, sprach, gesprochen, spricht, to speak; — **über** (*w. acc.*) *or* **von** (*w. dat.*) to talk about

das **Sprichwort, -(e)s, ̈er,** proverb
springen, sprang, ist gesprungen, to jump
spüren, to feel, notice

der **Staat, -(e)s, -en,** state

der **Stab, -(e)s, ̈e,** staff, stick

die **Stadt, -, ̈e,** city

der **Stall, -(e)s, ̈e,** stable

der **Stand, -(e)s, ̈e,** standing; class
stark, strong; — **regnen,** to rain hard
starr, fixed; stiff
statt (= **anstatt**)(*prep. w. gen.*), instead of
stattfinden, fand statt, stattgefunden, to take place
stattlich, stately

der **Staub, -(e)s, -e,** dust
stechen, stach, gestochen, sticht, to prick, sting
stecken, to stick; put; — **Sie das in die Tasche!** put that in your pocket
stehen, stand, gestanden, to stand
stehlen, stahl, gestohlen, stiehlt, to steal; **er hat mir die Uhr gestohlen,** he stole my watch
steigen, stieg, ist gestiegen, to climb, mount, rise, ascend
steil, steep

der **Stein, -(e)s, -e,** stone

die **Stelle, -, -n,** spot, place; position
stellen, to place, put; **eine Frage an eine Person** (*acc.*) —, to ask a person a question

die **Stellung, -, -en,** position; rank
sterben, starb, ist gestorben, stirbt, to die

der **Stern, -(e)s, -e,** star

die **Sternwarte, -, -n,** observatory
stets, always
still, quiet, still

die **Stimme, -, -n,** voice

der **Stock, -(e)s, ̈e,** cane, stick

der **Stoff, -(e)s, -e,** material; matter
stolz, proud; — **sein auf** (*w. acc.*), to be proud of
stören, to disturb
stoßen, stieß, gestoßen, stößt, to push
strafen, to punish
strahlen, to shine, be radiant

der **Strand, -(e)s, -e,** shore

die **Straße, -, -n,** street

die **Straßenbahn, -, -en,** streetcar

die **Stratosphäre, -,** stratosphere

der **Streit, -(e)s, -e,** (*or* —**igkeiten**), quarrel, fight, strife
streng, strict, severe

der **Strom -(e)s, ̈e,** river, stream

die **Stube, -, -n,** room

das **Stück -(e)s, -e,** piece

der **Student, -en, -en,** student
studieren, to study

die **Stufe, —, -n,** step

der **Stuhl, -(e)s, ̈e,** chair
stumm, dumb, mute, silent
stumpf, blunt, without a point

die **Stunde, -, -n,** hour; **ich nehme —n,** I take lessons

der **Sturm, -(e)s, ̈e,** storm
stürmisch, stormy
stützen, to support; (*refl. w.* **auf** & *acc.*), to lean on
suchen, to look for, seek

der **Süden, -s,** south

die **Summe, -, -n,** amount, sum

die **Suppe, -, -n,** soup
süß, sweet

die **Szene, -, -n,** scene

T

tadeln, to criticize, rebuke

die **Tafel, -, -n,** blackboard

der **Tag, -(e)s, -e,** day; — **für** —, day after day; **einen — um den anderen,** every other day; **am —e,** in the daytime; **eines —es** (*indef. time*), one day; **heute über acht —e,** a week from today; **vor acht —en,** a week ago
täglich, daily

das **Tal, -(e)s, ̈er,** valley

die **Tanne, -, -n,** fir (tree)

die **Tante, -, -n,** aunt

der **Tanz, -es, ̈e,** dance
tanzen, to dance
tapfer, brave(ly)

die **Tapferkeit, -,** bravery

die **Tasche, -, -n,** pocket

das **Taschentuch, -(e)s, ̈er,** handkerchief

die **Taschenuhr, -, -en,** (pocket) watch

die **Tasse, -, -n,** cup

die **Tat, -, -en,** deed; **in der —,** indeed, in fact
tätig, active

die **Tätigkeit, -, -en,** activity, action
tauchen, tauchte, ist getaucht, to dive
taugen, to be fit (good, useful)

tauschen, to exchange
täuschen, to deceive
tausend (*num. adj.*), thousand
das Tausend, -(e)s, -e, thousand
tausendmal, a thousand times
der Techniker, -s, -, technician
technisch, technical
der Tee, -s, -s, tea
der Teil, -(e)s, -e, part
die Teilung, -, -en, division
das Telefon -s, -e, telephone
telefonieren to telephone
telefonisch, by phone; — erreichen,
to reach by phone
telegrafieren, to telegraph
das Teleskop, -s, -e, telescope
der Teller, -s, —, plate
das Temperament, -s, -e, temperament
die Temperatur, -, -en, temperature
der Tenor, -s, ⁼e (*or* -e) tenor
teuer, dear; expensive
der Teufel, -s, -, devil
das Theater, -s, -, theater; ins — gehen,
to go to the theater
tief, deep
die Tiefe, -, -n, depth
das Tier, -(e)s, -e, animal
die Tinte, -, -n, ink
der Tisch, -es, -e, table; den — decken,
to set the table; nach —, after dinner
das Tischtuch, -(e)s, ⁼er, tablecloth
die Tochter, -, ⁼, daughter
der Tod, -es, -esfälle, death
toll, mad, crazy; — vor Schmerz,
frantic with pain
der Ton, -(e)s, ⁼e, tone, sound
das Tonbandgerät, -s, -e, tape recorder
tot, dead
töten, to kill
tragen, trug, getragen, trägt, to carry;
wear
die Träne, -, -n, tear
der Trank, -(e)s, ⁼e, drink, beverage
der Traum, -(e)s, ⁼e, dream
träumen, to dream
traurig, sad
treffen, traf, getroffen, trifft, to meet;
hit
treiben, trieb, getrieben, to drive; be
engaged in
trennen, to separate
die Treppe, -, -n, stairs
treten, trat, ist getreten, tritt, to step
treu, faithful(ly), true
trinken, trank, getrunken, to drink
das Trinkgeld, -(e)s, -er, tip
trocken (*adj.*), dry
trocknen, to dry

trösten, to comfort, console
trotz (*prep. w. gen.*), in spite of
trotzdem, nevertheless, in spite of it
die (*or* das) Trübsal, - (*or* -s), -e, affliction, trouble
der Trunk, -(e)s, ⁼e, drink, draught
die Tschechoslowakei, Czechoslovakia
das Tuch, -(e)s, ⁼er, cloth
tüchtig, capable; strong; — studieren, to study hard
tun, tat, getan, tut, to do; act, pre-
tend; er tut als ob, he acts as if
die Tür, -, -en, door
die Türkei, -, Turkey
der Turm, -(e)s, ⁼e, tower

U

üben, to practice
über (*prep.w. dat. or acc.*), over, above
überall, everywhere
überhaupt, on the whole, altogether;
— nicht, not at all
übermorgen, day after tomorrow
überráschen, to surprise
der Überrock, -(e)s, ⁼e, overcoat
überschwémmen, to flood
übersétzen, to translate
überwinden, überwand, überwunden, to overcome
die Übung, -, -en, exercise
das Ufer, -s, -, shore, river bank
die Uhr, -, -en, watch; clock; o'clock;
um zwei —, at two o'clock; wieviel
— ist es? what time is it?
um (*prep. w. acc.*) around, about; —
drei Uhr, at three o'clock; — ...
willen, for ... sake; — ... zu (*w.
pres. inf.*) in order to
umsonst, in vain
unbemannt, unmanned, pilotless
und, and
unehrlich, dishonest
ungefähr, about, approximately
das Unglück, -(e)s, -sfälle, misfortune
unglücklich, unhappy, unlucky
die Universität, -, -en, university;
(*student*) auf der —, (*professor*) an
der —, at the university
unmöglich, impossible
unser, uns(e)re, unser (*poss. adj.*), our
uns(e)rer, uns(e)re, uns(e)res (*poss.
pron.*) our
unten (*adv.*), below; downstairs
unter (*prep. w. dat. or acc.*), under, below, beneath; among

die **Untergrundbahn, -, -en,** subway
unterhalb (*prep. w. gen.*), below
unterhálten, unterhielt, unterhalten, to entertain; (*refl.*) to converse
der **Unterschied, -(e)s, -e,** difference
unterscheíden, unterschied, unterschieden, to distinguish
untersúchen, untersuchte, untersucht, to examine, test, investigate
die **Untersuchung, -, -en,** investigation, test
unzufrieden, dissatisfied
der **Urgroßvater, -s, ⁔,** great-grandfather
der **Urlaub, -(e)s, -e,** vacation, leave
die **Ursache, -, -n,** cause
urteilen, urteilte, geurteilt, to judge

V

der **Vater, -s, ⁔,** father
das **Vaterland, -(e)s, ⁔er,** fatherland, native land
die **Vaterstadt, -, ⁔e,** native city
verándern, to change, alter, transform
verbergen, verbarg, verborgen, verbirgt, to hide, conceal
verbessern, to correct
sich **verbeugen vor** (*w. dat.*), to bow to (*or* before)
verbieten, verbot, verboten (*w. dat. of the pers.*), to forbid
verbinden, verband, verbunden, to unite
verbrennen, verbrannte, verbrannt (*tr.*) to burn up; (*intr. w.* **sein**) to burn up
verbringen, verbrachte, verbracht, to pass, spend time
verdanken (*w. dat. of the pers.*), to owe
verdienen, to earn; deserve
der **Verein, -(e)s, -e,** club
die **Vereinigten Staaten, -** (*pl.*), United States
die **Verfassung, -, -en,** constitution
verfolgen (*w. acc.*), to pursue
die **Vergangenheit, -, -en,** past, time gone by
vergeben, vergab, vergeben, vergibt (*w. dat. of the pers.*), to forgive
vergebens, in vain
vergehen, verging, ist vergangen, to pass; elapse; disappear
vergessen, vergaß, vergessen, vergißt, to forget
vergleichen, verglich, verglichen, to compare
das **Vergnügen, -s, -,** pleasure

das **Verhältnis, -ses, -se,** relation
verkaufen, to sell
verlangen, to demand
verlassen, verließ, verlassen, verläßt, to leave, forsake; leave behind; sich **— auf** (*w. acc.*), to depend (*or* rely) on
verlegen, to misplace
sich **verlieben in** (*w. acc.*), to fall in love with
verlieren, verlor, verloren, to lose
sich **verloben mit,** to become engaged to
vermissen, to miss
das **Vermögen, -s, -,** fortune
verpassen, to miss (*as a train*)
der **Verrat, -(e)s,** treason
sich **versammeln,** to gather, assemble
versäumen, to miss (*as a train*)
verschieden (*adj.*), different; (*pl.*) several, various
verschlingen, verschlang, verschlungen, to devour
verschwenden, to squander
verschwinden, verschwand, ist verschwunden, to disappear
die **Versicherungsgesellschaft, -, -en,** insurance company
versprechen, versprach, versprochen, verspricht, to promise
verstehen, verstand, verstanden, to understand; **das versteht sich,** that is self-understood
versuchen, to try, experiment
verteidigen, to defend
vertreten, vertrat, vertreten, vertritt, to represent
verwandt (*adj.*), related
der **Verwandte, -n, -n** (*w. adj. decl.*), relative; **ein —r,** a relative; **meine —n,** my relatives
verwenden, verwandte, verwandt to utilize, apply
die **Verwendung, -, -en,** use, application
verwöhnen, to spoil, pamper
verzeihen, verzieh, verziehen (*w. dat.*), to pardon
der **Vetter, -s, -n,** (*male*) cousin
das **Vieh, -(e)s,** cattle
viel (mehr, meist-), much, a great deal; (*pl.*) many; **—es,** many things
vielleicht, perhaps
vielmehr, rather
vier, four; **auf allen —en,** on all fours
viert-, fourth
das **Viertel, -s, -,** quarter, one-fourth
die **Viertelstunde, -, -n,** quarter of an hour

der **Vogel, -s, ⸚,** bird
das **Volk, -(e)s, ⸚er,** people, nation
das **Volkslied, -(e)s, -er,** folksong
    voll, full
    vollständig, complete(ly)
    von (*prep. w. dat.*), of, from
    vor (*prep. w. dat. or acc.*), before, in front of; (*w. dat. only*), ago; — **einem Monat,** a month ago; **ich bin außer mir — Freude,** I am beside myself with joy; **er brennt — Ungeduld,** he burns with impatience
    vorbei, past, over
    vorbeifliegen, flog vorbei, ist vorbeigeflogen, to fly past (*w. an & dat.*)
    vorbereiten, to prepare; (*refl. w. auf & acc.*), to prepare for
    vorgehen, ging vor, ist vorgegangen, to precede; **die Uhr geht vor,** the clock is fast
    vorgestern, day before yesterday
    vorig, last, previous; —**e Nacht,** last night
    vorkommen, kam vor, ist vorgekommen, to happen; occur; appear
    vorlesen, las vor, vorgelesen, liest vor, to read aloud to
    vorletzt-, before (the) last; —**es Jahr,** year before last
der **Vormittag, -(e)s, -e,** forenoon
    vorn (*adv.*), in front
die **Vorstadt, -, ⸚e,** suburb
die **Vorstellung, -, -en,** performance
    vorwärts, forward

W

    wach, awake; — **sein,** to be awake
    wachsen, wuchs, ist gewachsen, wächst, to grow
die **Waffe, -, -n,** weapon
der **Wagen, -s, -,** wagon, carriage; car (*of a train*); auto
    wagen, to dare
die **Wahl, -, -en,** choice, selection; election
    wählen, to choose; elect
    wahr, true; **nicht —?** right? not so?
    während (*prep. w. gen.*), during; (*conj.*), while
die **Wahrheit, -, -en,** truth
    wahrscheinlich, probable, probably
der **Wald, -(e)s, ⸚er,** forest
die **Wand, -, ⸚e,** wall
    wandern (*w. sein*), to walk, travel (*on foot*), go; wander

die **Wandkarte, -, -n,** wall map
die **Wange, -, -n,** cheek
    wann (*inter. adv.*), when; **seit —?** since when?
die **Ware, -, -n,** ware; (*pl.*) merchandise
    warnen, to warn
    warten, to wait; — **auf** (*w. acc.*), to wait for
    warum, why
    was (*inter. pron.*), what; (*rel. pron.*), what, that which; **alles, was ich habe,** all (that) I have; — **für ein,** what kind of
    waschen, wusch, gewaschen, wäscht, to wash; **ich wasche mir die Hände,** I wash my hands; (*dir. refl.*), **ich wasche mich,** I wash (myself)
das **Wasser, -s, -,** water
der **Wasserfall, -(e)s, ⸚e,** waterfall
    weder . . . noch, neither . . . nor
der **Weg. -(e)s, -e,** way; **gehe deines —es!** go your way
    wegen (*prep. w. gen.*), on account of; **meinet—,** on my account
    weggehen, ging weg, ist weggegangen, to go away
    weh tun, to hurt; **es tut mir weh,** it hurts me
das **Weib, -(e)s, -er,** woman (*usually contemptuous*)
    weich, soft
die **Weihnachten, -** (*pl. w. sing. vb.*), Christmas
    weil, because
der **Wein, -(e)s, -e,** wine
    weinen, to weep
die **Weise, -, -n,** way, manner; **auf diese —,** in this manner
    weise, wise
die **Weisheit, -, -en,** wisdom
    weiß, white
    weit, wide; far
    welcher, welche, welches (*rel. & inter. adj. & pron.*), which (one), what (one), who; (*in excls.*) what; **welch eine Stadt!** what a city!
die **Welle, -, -n,** wave
die **Welt, -, -en,** world
    weltbekannt, known worldwide
der **Weltmeister, -s, -,** world champion
der **Weltraum, -(e)s,** (outer) space
der **Weltraumfahrer, -s, -,** space traveler
der **Weltraumflug, -(e)s, ⸚e,** space flight
das **Weltraumschiff, -(e)s, -e,** space ship
die **Weltraumstrahlung, -,** cosmic radiation
    wenden, wandte, gewandt, to turn

wenig, little, not much
wenige (*pl.*), few
wenigstens, at least
wenn, if, whenever
wer (*inter. pron.*), who; (*indef. rel. pron.*) he who, whoever
werden, wurde, ist geworden, wird, to become; — aus, to become of
werfen, warf, geworfen, wirft, to throw
das Werk, -(e)s, -e, work, deed, opus
die Werkstatt, -, ᵘe, workshop
wert, worth; einen Dollar —, worth a dollar; der Mühe (*gen.*) —, worth the trouble; der Rede —, worth mentioning
der Wert, -(e)s, -e, worth
wesentlich, essential, intrinsic
weshalb, why
wessen (*gen. of wer*), whose
der Westen, -s, west
wetten, to bet, wager
das Wetter, -s, -, weather
wichtig, important
wider (*prep. w. acc.*), against
widerspréchen, widersprach, widersprochen, widerspricht (*w. dat.*), to contradict
wie, how; as
wieder, again
wiederhólen, wiederholte, wiederholt, to repeat
das Wiedersehen, -s, auf —! goodbye, au revoir
die Wiege, -, -n, cradle
die Wiese, -, -n, meadow
wieviel, how much; der wievielte ist heute? what is today's date?
willkommen (*adj.*), welcome
der Wind, -(e)s, -e, wind
windig, windy
winken, to wink, beckon; einem mit den Augen —, to wink at a person; mit der Hand —, to beckon, wave
der Winter, -s, -, winter
der Wipfel, -s, -, tree top
wirken, to be effective, make an impression
wirklich, real(ly)
die Wirklichkeit, -, -en, reality
der Wirt, -(e)s, -e, host, innkeeper
wissen, wußte, gewußt, weiß, to know (*a fact*)
das Wissen, -s, knowledge, learning; meines —s, as far as I know
die Wissenschaft, -, -en, science; knowledge
der Wissenschaftler, -s, -, scientist

wissenschaftlich, scientific
der Witz, -es, -e, joke
wo, where
die Woche, -, -n, week
wöchentlich, weekly
wofür, for what (*or* which)
woher, from where, whence; — wissen Sie das? how do you know that?
wohin, whither, to what place
wohl, well; indeed; probably
wohnen, to live, dwell
die Wohnung, -, -en, residence
der Wolf, -(e)s, ᵘe, wolf
die Wolke, -, -n, cloud
wolkenerfüllt, cloud-filled
wollen, wollte, gewollt, will, to want, wish; er will morgen abfahren, he intends to leave tomorrow; er will eine reiche Tante haben, he professes to have a rich aunt; er will es getan haben, he claims to have done it; er wollte eben ausgehen, he was (just) on the point of going out
womit, with what (*or* which)
das Wort, -(e)s, -e (*in connected discourse*), ᵘer (*disconnected words*), word; er hält —, he keeps his word
das Wörterbuch, -(e)s, ᵘer, dictionary
wörtlich, literally
das Wunder, -s, -, wonder, miracle
sich wundern über (*w. acc.*), to be surprised at
wunderschön, exceedingly beautiful
der Wunsch, -es, ᵘe, wish, desire
wünschen, to wish
die Würde, -, -n, dignity
würdig, worthy; (*w. gen.*) worthy of
die Wurst, -, ᵘe, sausage
die Wut, -, rage
wüten, to rage
wütend, raging, very angry

Z

die Zahl, -, -en, number
zahlen, to pay
zählen, to count
zahllos, countless, innumerable
zahlreich, numerous
zahm, tame
der Zahn, -(e)s, ᵘe, tooth
der Zahnarzt, -es, ᵘe, dentist
das Zahnweh, -(e)s, toothache
zart, tender, delicate

der **Zauber, -s, -,** charm, magic
der **Zaun, -(e)s,** Zäune, fence
z.B. (= **zum Beispiel**), for example
zehn, ten
das **Zeichen, -s, -,** sign, signal
zeichnen, to draw
zeigen, to show
die **Zeile, -, -n,** line
die **Zeit, -, -en,** time; **zur —, als (da** or **wo),** at the time when
das **Zeitalter, -s, -,** age; era; **das atomische —,** atomic age
die **Zeitschrift, -, -en,** magazine
die **Zeitung, -, -en,** newspaper
zerbrechen, zerbrach, zerbrochen, zerbricht, to break (to pieces)
zerfleischen, to mangle
zerreißen, zerriß, zerrissen, to tear (to pieces)
der **Zeuge, -n, -n,** witness
die **Ziege, -, -n,** goat
ziehen, zog, gezogen, to pull; (*intr. w.* sein), to go, move
das **Ziel, -(e)s, -e,** aim, goal
ziemlich, rather
das **Zimmer, -s, -,** room
der **Zimmermann, -(e)s,** Zimmerleute, carpenter
zittern, to tremble
zornig, angry
zu (*prep. w. dat.*), to; at; for; (*adv.*) too; **— Hause,** at home; **— Weihnachten,** for (or at) Christmas
der **Zucker, -s,** sugar
zuerst, at first
zufällig, accidental(ly); **er war — zu Hause,** he happened to be at home
zufälligerweise (*adv.*), by chance; **— war ich auch da,** I happened to be there too
zufrieden, satisfied

zufriedenstellend, satisfactory
der **Zug, -(e)s,** ̈e, train; draught; feature
zugleich, at the same time
zuhören, hörte zu, zugehört (*w. dat.*), to listen to
die **Zukunft, -,** future
zuletzt, finally, at the end
zum (= **zu dem**), to (at or for) the; **— Geburtstag,** for one's birthday
zumachen, machte zu, zugemacht, to close
zunächst, first of all
die **Zunge, -, -n,** tongue
zur (= **zu der**), to (at or for) the; **— Zeit als (da** or **wo),** at the time when
zurückkehren, kehrte zurück, ist zurückgekehrt, to turn (or come) back, return
zusammen, together
zusammenbringen, brachte zusammen, zusammengebracht, to bring together; gather
der **Zustand, -(e)s,** ̈e, condition
zuverlässig, reliable, dependable
zuvor, before
zuweilen, occasionally
zuwenden, wandte zu, zugewandt, to turn to(ward); **er wandte mir den Rücken zu,** he turned his back on me
zwanzig, twenty
zwar, to be sure, I admit
der **Zweck, -(e)s, -e,** purpose
zweierlei, of two kinds
der **Zweifel, -s, -,** doubt
der **Zweig, -(e)s, -e,** twig
zweimal, twice
der **Zwerg, -(e)s, -e,** dwarf
zwingen, zwang, gezwungen, to force
zwischen (*prep. w. dat. or acc.*), between

English-German
Vocabulary

A

a, an, ein; **not —,** kein

able: to be —, können, konnte, gekonnt, kann

about (= *approximately*), ungefähr; **to talk —,** sprechen von (*w. dat.*) *or* über (*w. acc.*) **what was it (all) — ?** um was handelte es sich?; **do you know what you are — ?,** sind Sie Ihrer Sache gewiß? **he was — to leave,** er wollte eben abfahren (*or* er war im Begriff abzufahren)

above, über (*w. dat. or acc.*); oberhalb (*w. gen.*)

absent, abwesend; **to be —,** fehlen; **he is —,** er fehlt

accompany, begleiten

accomplishment, die Leistung, -, -en

according to, nach (*w. dat.*)

account: on — of, wegen (*w. gen.*); **on — of the weather,** wegen des Wetters (*or* des Wetters wegen); **on my —,** meinetwegen; **on your —,** Ihretwegen

accuse of, ánklagen *or* beschuldigen (*w. acc. of the pers. & gen. of the th.*)

accustomed: become — to, sich gewöhnen an (*w. acc.*); **I am — to it,** ich bin daran gewöhnt; *or* ich bin es gewohnt

acquaintance, der Bekannte, -n, -n (*w. adj. decl*); ein Bekannter; **I made his —,** ich lernte ihn kennen, *or* ich machte seine Bekanntschaft

acquainted: to be — with, kennen, kannte, gekannt

acquire (*knowledge or information*), Kenntnisse erlangen

across, durch (*w. acc.*)

act (= *pretened*), tun, tat, getan, tut; **he acts as if,** er tut, als ob

actually (= *really*), wirklich; (= *indeed*) in der Tat

add, hinzufügen, fügte hinzu, hinzugefügt

address, die Adresse, -, -n

admire, bewundern

advance, der Fortschritt, -(e)s, -e

advice, der Rat, -(e)s, -schläge

advise, raten, riet, geraten, rät (*w. dat.*)

afford, sich (*dat.*) leisten

afraid: to be — of, sich fürchten vor (*w. dat.*); **to be — that,** fürchten, daß

Africa, (das) Afrika, -s

after, nach (*w. dat.*); **— dinner,** nach Tisch; **— school,** nach der Schule; (*conj.*), nachdem

afternoon, der Nachmittag, -(e)s, -e; **this —,** heute nachmittag; **tomorrow —,** morgen nachmittag; **yesterday —,** gestern nachmittag; **the whole —,** den ganzen Nachmittag (*duration of time*); **one —,** eines Nachmittags (*indef. time*); **in the —,** am Nachmittag (des Nachmittags *or* nachmittags)

afterwards, nachher, darauf, danach

again, wieder, noch einmal

against, gegen (*w. acc.*); wider (*w. acc.*)

age, das Alter, -s, -; (= *period of time*) das Zeitalter; **atomic —,** das atomische Zeitalter; **Middle Ages,** das Mittelalter

ago, vor (*w. dat.*), her; **two years —,** vor zwei Jahren; **a week —,** vor acht Tagen; **that was long —,** das ist schon lange her

agreeable, angenehm

air, die Luft, -, ⸚e

air density, die Luftdichte, -

air layer, die Luftschicht, -, -en

airplane, das Flugzeug, -(e)s, -e

airship, das Luftschiff, -(e)s, -e

air traffic, der Luftverkehr, -s

all, alle; ganz; — **Europe,** ganz Europa; **for — I care,** meinetwegen; **it was — the same to me,** es war mir ganz gleich; **almost — week,** fast die ganze Woche; — **I have,** alles, was ich habe; — **good things,** alles Gute; — **else,** alles andere; **not at —,** gar nicht; **nothing at —,** gar nichts

allow, erlauben (*w. dat.*)

allowed: to be —, dürfen, durfte, gedurft, darf

almost, fast, beinah(e)

alone, allein

along (*prep.*), entlang (*usually w. acc.*); **he is going — the river,** er geht den Fluß entlang; (*adv.*), mit; **come —,** kommen Sie mit!

aloud, laut; **to read —,** vorlesen

alphabet, das Alphabet, -(e)s, -e

alphabetically, nach dem Alphabet

Alps, die Alpen (*pl.*)

already, schon

als, auch

although, obgleich

altitude, die Höhe, -, -n

always, immer, stets

America, (das) Amerika, -s

American, amerikanisch (*adj.*)

among unter (*w. dat. or acc.*); — **other things,** unter ander(e)m

and, und; **colder — colder,** immer kälter

anger, der Zorn, -(e)s

angry, zornig, böse; — **with,** böse auf (*w. acc.*); **he is — with me,** er ist mir böse; *or* er ist böse auf mich

animal, das Tier, -(e)s, -e; **domestic —,** das Haustier

another, noch ein; (= *a different one*) ein anderer; **one after —,** einer nach dem anderen

answer die Antwort, -, -en; **an — to,** eine Antwort auf (*w. acc.*)

answer, antworten (*w. dat. of the pers.*); — **a question,** auf eine Frage (*acc.*) antworten, *or* eine Frage (*dir. obj.*) beantworten; **I — him,** ich antworte ihm

any, etwas (*indecl. w. sing. noun or alone as pron.*); irgend- (*in various combinations*); (irgend) welche (*w. a pl. noun*); **not —,** kein; **I haven't — money,** ich habe kein Geld; **not — longer,** nicht mehr

anybody, (irgend) jemand

anyhow (= *somehow*), irgendwie, auf irgendeine Weise; (= *in any case*), jedenfalls

anyone, (irgend) jemand; — **else,** jemand anders, sonst jemand

anything, (irgend) etwas

appear, erscheinen, erschien, ist erschienen

appetite, der Appetit, -(e)s, -e

apple, der Apfel, -s, ⸚

apply for, sich bewerben um (*w. acc.*)

approach, sich nähern (*w. dat.*)

April, der April -(e)s, -e

arm, der Arm, -(e)s, -e

army, das Heer, -(e)s, -e

around, um (*w. acc.*)

arrest, verhaften

arrive, ankommen, kam an, ist angekommen

art, die Kunst, -, ⸚e

article, der Artikel, -s, -

artificial, künstlich

artist, der Künstler, -s, -

artistic, künstlerisch, artistisch

as wie; (*causal*) da; (*temp.*) indem; **white — snow,** weiß wie Schnee; **he was famous — an orator,** als Redner war er berühmt; — **if** als ob; — **far —,** bis; — **soon —,** sobald; — **long —,** solange; — **often —,** sooft; — **well —,** so gut wie; **just —,** ebenso

ascend, steigen, stieg, ist gestiegen; aufsteigen

ashamed: to be — (of), sich schämen (*w. gen. or* über *& acc.*)

Asia, (das) Asien, -s

ask, fragen; — **a person a question,** eine Frage an eine Person (*acc.*) stellen; — **for something,** um etwas (*acc.*) bitten; — **about,** fragen nach (*w. dat.*)

asleep: fall —, einschlafen, schlief ein, ist eingeschlafen, schläft ein

assert, behaupten

associated with, verbunden mit

assume, annehmen, nahm an, angenommen, nimmt an

astonished, erstaunt; — **at,** erstaunt über (*w. acc.*)

astronaut, der Astronaut, -en, -en

astronomer, der Astronom, -en, -en

at, an, auf, in, bei, zu (*w. dat.*); — **eight o'clock,** um acht Uhr; — **the top of,** oben auf; — **his house,** bei ihm; — **home,** zu Hause; — **once,** gleich, sogleich, sofort; — **the time when,** zur Zeit, als (da *or* wo); (*student*) — **the university,** auf der Universität; (*professor*) — **the university,** an der Universität; — **night,** in der Nacht

atmosphere, die Atmosphäre, -, -en

atomic, atomisch; — **Age,** das atomische Zeitalter

attain, erreichen

attempt, versuchen

attend (*a school*), besuchen; (*a performance*), beiwohnen (*w. dat.*); (*a lecture*), einem Vortrag beiwohnen; eine Vorlesung hören (*or* besuchen)

attention, die Aufmerksamkeit, -, -en; **to pay —,** aufpassen, paßte auf, aufgepaßt; **I paid no — to it** (*didn't care*), ich kümmerte mich nicht darum

attentive, aufmerksam

August, der August, -, -e

aunt, die Tante, -, -n; **at my —'s,** bei meiner Tante

auto, das Auto, -s, -s

autumn, der Herbst, -es, -e

avail oneself of, sich bedienen (*w. gen.*); von etwas (*dat.*) Gebrauch machen

aviator, der Flieger, -s, -

awake, wach; **to be —,** wach sein

awaken (*tr.*), aufwecken; (*intr.*) aufwachen, wachte auf, ist aufgewacht

aware of, bewußt (*adj. w. gen.*); **not that I am aware,** nicht daß ich wüßte

away, fort, weg

B

back (*adv.*), zurück

back, der Rücken, -s, -

bad, schlecht, böse, übel; schlimm; **— times,** schlechte Zeiten; **that is not a — idea,** das ist kein übler Einfall; **that is too —,** schade!

bake, backen, buk, gebacken, bäckt

bakery, die Bäckerei, -, -en

ball, der Ball, -(e)s, ̈e

balloon, der Ballon, -s, -e *or* -s

bank (*of a river*), das Ufer, -s, -; (*for money*) die Bank, -, -en

barber, der Barbier, -s, -e

bark, bellen

bathe, baden

bathroom, das Badezimmer, -s, -

Bavaria, (das) Bayern, -s

be (= *exist*), sein, war, ist gewesen, ist; (= *be situated*) liegen, lag, hat gelegen; Köln liegt am Rhein; **— it early or late,** sei es früh, sei es spät; **how are you?** wie geht es Ihnen?; **that is** (= *i.e.*) das heißt (*abbr.* d.h.); **there is (are),** es gibt (*w. acc.*); **he is right,** er hat recht

beach, der Strand, -(e)s, -e; **to go to the —,** an den Strand gehen

beard, der Bart, -(e)s, ̈e

beautiful, schön; **most — of all,** allerschönst-

because (*conj.*), weil, denn; **— of** (*prep.*), wegen (*w. gen.*)

become, werden, wurde, ist geworden, wird; **what will — of him?** was wird aus ihm werden?

bed, das Bett, -(e)s, -en; **to go to —,** zu Bett gehen; **in —,** im Bett

bedroom, das Schlafzimmer, -s, -

beer, das Bier, -(e)s, -e; **dark (light) —,** dunkles (helles) Bier

before, vor (*w. dat. or acc.*); **day — yesterday,** vorgestern; **year — last,** vorletztes Jahr; (*conj.*), ehe, bevor; (*adv.*), vorher, früher; **the day —,** den Tag vorher

begin, beginnen, begann, begonnen, beginnt; anfangen, fing an, angefangen, fängt an; **— at the beginning,** fangen Sie von vorn an!

beginning, der Anfang, -(e)s, ̈e

behave, sich betragen (*or* benehmen) (*str.*)

behind (*prep.*), hinter (*w. dat. or acc.*); (*adv.*), hinten

believe, glauben (*w. dat. of the pers. & acc. of the th.*); **— in,** glauben an (*w. acc.*); **he believes me (it),** er glaubt mir (es); **he believes in me (in it),** er glaubt an mich (daran); meinen (*to have an opinion*)

bell, die Glocke, -, -n; die Klingel, -, -n; **the — rings,** es klingelt

belong to, gehören (*w. dat. = ownership*); gehören zu (= *to be part or member of*)

below, unter (*w. dat. or acc.*), unterhalb (*w. gen.*)

bench, die Bank, -, ̈e

beside, bei (*w. dat.*), neben (*w. dat. or acc.*); **I am — myself with joy,** ich bin außer mir vor Freude

best, best-; **— of all,** allerbest-; **I like it —,** es gefällt mir am besten; *or* ich habe es am liebsten; **the — I have,** das Beste, was ich habe

betray, verraten, verriet, verraten, verrät

better, besser (*comp. of* gut)

between, zwischen (*w. dat. or acc.*)

Bible, die Bibel, -, -n

bicycle, das Fahrrad, -(e)s, ̈er; das Rad, -(e)s, ̈er

big, groß

biological, biologisch

biology, die Biologie, -; die Lebenslehre, -

bird, der Vogel, -s, ̈

birthday, der Geburtstag, -(e)s, -e; **for one's —,** zum Geburtstag

bite, beißen, biß, gebissen

black, schwarz

(black)board, die Tafel, -, -n
blame, die Schuld, -, -en; he is to — for that, er ist schuld daran
blind, blind; — in, blind auf (w. dat.)
blond, blond
blue, blau
board, das Brett, -(e)s, -er; (of a ship), der Bord, -(e)s,
boast of, prahlen mit (w. dat.); sich rühmen (w. gen.)
body, der Körper, -s, -; celestial —, der Himmelskörper
bold, kühn; frech (impudent)
book, das Buch, -(e)s, ᵘer
bored: to be —, sich langweilen, langweilte, gelangweilt
born, geboren (p.p of gebären); was — (of the dead), wurde geboren; (of the living), ist geboren; when were you —? wann sind Sie geboren?
both, beide; — brothers, beide (or die beiden) Brüder
bother about, sich kümmern um (w. acc.)
bottle, die Flasche, -, -n
box, der Kasten , -s, -; die Kiste, -, -n
boy, der Junge, -n, -n; der Knabe, -n, -n
brave, tapfer
bread, das Brot, -(e)s, -e
break, brechen, brach, gebrochen, bricht; — one's arm, sich (dat.) den Arm brechen; — to pieces, zerbrechen
breakfast, das Frühstück, -(e)s, -e; for —, zum Frühstück; after —, nach dem Frühstück; to eat —, frühstücken, frühstückte, gefrühstückt
breath, der Atem, -s, -züge; to take —, Atem holen
breathe, atmen
breathless, atemlos
bridge, die Brücke, -, -n
bright, hell
bring, bringen, brachte, gebracht; — along, mitbringen
broad, breit
brook, der Bach, -(e)s, ᵘe
brother, der Bruder, -s, ᵘ
brown, braun
brush, (sich) bürsten; — one's teeth, sich (dat.) die Zähne putzen
build, bauen
building, das Gebäude, -s, -
bundle, das (or der) Bündel, -s, -
burn, brennen, brannte, gebrannt; — with (fig.), brennen vor
business, das Geschäft, -(e)s, -e to go into —, ein Geschäft eröffnen (or gründen)
busy, beschäftigt
but, aber; sondern

butcher, der Fleischer, -s, -; der Metzger, -s, -
butter, die Butter, -
buy, kaufen
by, von (pers. agent), mit, bei (all w. dat.); durch (means or instrument; w. acc.); an, neben (both w. dat. or acc.); — heart, auswendig; — steamer, mit dem Dampfer; — rail, mit der Eisenbahn

C

cake, der Kuchen, -s, -
call, rufen, rief, gerufen; (= to name), nennen, nannte, genannt; (= to be called), heißen, hieß, geheißen; (= to call names) schimpfen (wk.); schelten, schalt, gescholten, schilt; — on (= to visit), besuchen; (to recite), aúfrufen; — up (on the phone), ánrufen; — for (= to pick up), ábholen
Canada, (das) Kanada, -s
canal, der Kanal, -s, ᵘle
candle, die Kerze, -, -n
cane, der Stock, -(e)s, ᵘe
cap, die Mütze, -, -n
capable (of), fähig (w. gen.)
capital, die Hauptstadt, -, ᵘe
capitalize, großschreiben
car, das Auto, -s, -s; der Wagen, -s, -; streetcar, die Straßenbahn, -, -en
care, die Sorge, -, -n; for all I —, meinetwegen; to take —, sich in acht nehmen; to take — of, sorgen für (w. acc.)
care (for) (= to like), mögen, gern haben
careful, sorgfältig; (= cautious) vorsichtig; to be —, sich in acht nehmen
carpenter, der Zimmermann, -(e)s, Zimmerleute
carry, tragen, trug, getragen, trägt; to — away, fórttragen
carry out, ausführen, führte aus, ausgeführt; durchführen, führte durch, durchgefürt
case (= circumstance or grammatical), der Fall, -(e)s, ᵘe; in — (sub. conj.), falls; in any —, jedenfalls
cash, das Bargeld, -(e)s
cask, das Faß, Fasses, Fässer
castle, das Schloß, Schlosses, Schlösser; die Burg, -, -en;
cat, die Katze, -, -n
catch, fangen, fing, gefangen, fängt; — (a) cold, sich erkälten; — sight of, erblicken
cathedral, der Dom, -(e)s, -e

cause, die Ursache, -, -n; der Grund, -(e)s, ²e

celebrate, feiern

cellar, der Keller, -s, -

cent, der Cent, -(s), -(s); **twenty —s' worth of stamps,** für zwanzig Cent Briefmarken

century, das Jahrhundert, -(e)s, -e

certain(ly), gewiß

chain, die Kette, -, -n

chair, der Stuhl, -(e)s, ²e

chalk, die Kreide, -

chancellor, der Kanzler, -s, -

change, die Ábwechs(e)lung, -, -en; **for a —,** zur Abwechs(e)lung

change (= *to alter*), ändern; (*for better or worse*) (sich) verändern; (= *to exchange*) wechseln; **— money,** Geld wechseln; **— cars,** úmsteigen (*w.* sein); **— clothes,** sich umziehen (*or* úmkleiden); **— one's mind,** sich anders besinnen; **you have changed very much,** Sie haben sich sehr verändert; **I have changed my place of residence,** ich habe meine Wohnung gewechselt (*or* ich bin umgezogen)

Charlemagne, Karl der Große

charm, bezaubern

charming, reizend

cheap, billig

cheek, die Wange, -, -n

cheese, der Käse, -s, -

chess, das Schach, -(e)s; **a game of —,** eine Partie Schach

child, das Kind, -(e)s, -er

chimpanzee, der Schimpanse, -n, -n

choose, wählen

Christmas, (die) Weihnachten, - (*pl. form w. sing. vb.*); **for** (*or* **at**) **—,** zu Weihnachten

church, die Kirche, -, -n

cigar, die Zigarre, -, -n

cigarette, die Zigarette, -, -n

circle, der Kreis, -es, -e

circumstance, der Umstand, -(e)s, ²e

circus, der Zirkus, -, -se

citizen, der Bürger, -s, -

city, die Stadt, -, -e; **the — of Hamburg,** die Stadt Hamburg

city hall, das Rathaus, -es, / häuser

claim (= *assert*), behaupten; wollen, wollte, gewollt, will; **he claims to have done it,** er will es getan haben

clap, klatschen; **— one's hands,** in die Hände klatschen

class, die Klasse, -, -n; **to travel second —,** zweiter Klasse (*gen.*) fahren

classroom, das Klassenzimmer, -s, -

clean (*adj.*), rein

clean, reinigen; **— up,** aúfräumen

clear(ly) (= *bright*), hell; klar; (= *distinct*) deutlich

cleft, die Spalte, -, -n

clever, klug

cliff, der Felsen, -s, -

climb (up), klettern (*w.* sein) auf (*w. acc.*)

clock, die (Wand)uhr, -, -en

close, zumachen, machte zu, zugemacht; schließen, scholß, geschlossen

cloth, das Tuch, -(e)s, ²er

clothes, Kleider (*pl. of* das Kleid)

club (*social*), der Verein, -s, -e

coal, die Kohle, -, -n; **rich in —,** reich an Kohlen

coast, die Küste, -, -n

coat, der Rock, -(e)s, ²e

coat of ice, die Eisdecke, -, -n

coffee, der Kaffee, -s

coffee cup, die Kaffeetasse, -, -n

cold (*adj.*), kalt; **I am —,** mir ist kalt

cold (*weather*), die Kälte, -; (*respiratory*) die Erkältung, -, -en; **to catch (a) —,** sich erkälten; **I caught a bad —,** ich habe mich stark erkältet

collar, der Kragen, -s, -

collect, sammeln

Cologne, (das) Köln, -s

color, die Farbe, -, -n

comb, der Kamm, -(e)s, ²e

comb, kämmen

come, kommen, kam, ist gekommen; **— back,** zurückkommen; **— up,** heraúfkommen; **— in** (= *enter*), hereínkommen; **— in** (*of money*), eínkommen; **— late,** zu spät kommen; **he came running,** er kam gelaufen; **come along,** Kommen Sie mit!

comfortable, bequem

command, befehlen, befahl, befohlen, befiehlt (*w. dat.*)

company (= *society*), die Gesellschaft, -; -en; (= *visitors*) der Besuch, -(e)s, -e, **we had —,** wir hatten Besuch (*or* Gäste)

comparatively, verhältnismäßig

compare, vergleichen

compel, zwingen, zwang, gezwungen

complain about, klagen über (*w. acc.*)

complete (*adj.*), ganz, vollständig, fertig, vollendet

complete, vollenden

composition (= *essay*), der Aufsatz, -es, ²e

confirm, bestätigen

congratulate, gratulieren (*w. dat.*); **I — you on your great success,** ich gratuliere Ihnen zu Ihrem großen Erfolg

conquer (*intr.*), siegen; (*tr.*) besiegen

consequence, die Folge, -, -n; **as a —,** zur Folge

consequently, infolgedessen

consist of, bestehen aus (*w. dat.*)

construct, konstruieren, bauen

contain, enthalten, enthielt, enthalten, enthält

continually, fortwährend

continue, fortfahren, fuhr fort, hat fortgefahren, fährt fort; — **reading,** lesen Sie weiter!; **he continued reading,** er hat fortgefahren zu lesen

contradict, widerspréchen (*w. dat.*)

contrary to, gegen (*w. acc.*)

control: in — of, mächtig (*w. gen.*)

conversation, das Gespräch, -(e)s, -e

converse, sich unterhálten

convince, überzeúgen

cook, kochen

cool, kühl

copy, abschreiben, schrieb ab, abgeschrieben

corner, die Ecke, -, -n

correct (*adj.*), richtig

correct, verbessern, korrigieren

cosmic, kosmisch

cosmic radiation, die kosmische Strahlung, -; die Weltraumstrahlung, -

cosmic rays, kosmische Strahlen (*or* Ultrastrahlen), *m. pl.*; Höhenstrahlen, *m. pl.*

cost, kosten; **it — me a dollar,** es kostete mich (*or* mir) einen Dollar

could (= was able), konnte (*refers to a fact*); (= would be able) könnte (*contrary to fact*); **he — have done it,** er hätte es tun können

countless, zahllos

country, das Land, -(e)s, ⁻er; **in the —,** auf dem Lande; **to the —,** aufs Land

couple, das Paar, -(e)s, -e

course (*of a meal*), der Gang, -(e)s, ⁻e; (*of time*) der Lauf, -(e)s, ⁻e; **in the — of time,** im Laufe der Zeit

court, der Hof, -(e)s, ⁻e; (*of justice*) das Gericht, -(e)s, -e; **at —,** am Hofe

cousin (*male*), der Vetter, -s, -n; (*female*), die Cousine, -, -n

cover, bedecken

covered, bedeckt

cow, die Kuh, -, ⁻e

cowardly, feige

crazy, verrückt

crooked, krumm

crowd, die Menge, -, -n

cruel, grausam; — **to,** grausam gegen (*w. acc.*)

cup, die Tasse, -, -n

curious, neugierig

custom, die Sitte, -, -n

cut, schneiden, schnitt, geschnitten; **to — class,** schwänzen

Czechoslovakia, die Tschechoslowakei

D

dance, der Tanz, -es, ⁻e

dance, tanzen

dangerous, gefährlich

Danube, die Donau, ⁻

dare, wagen

dark, dunkel

darkness, die Finsternis, -, -se

date, das Datum, -s, Daten; **what is today's —?** der wievielte ist (*or* den wievielten haben wir) heute?

daughter, die Tochter, -, ⁻

day, der Tag, -(e)s, -e; — **before yesterday,** vorgestern; — **after tomorrow,** übermorgen; **one —** (*indef. time*), eines Tages; **all —** (*duration of time*), den ganzen Tag; — **after —,** Tag für Tag; **every other —,** einen Tag um den anderen; **the — before,** den Tag vorher

daytime: in the —, am Tage

dead, tot

deaf, taub

deal: a great — (*of*), viel

dear (*beloved*), lieb, teuer; (*expensive*) teuer

death, der Tod, -(e)s, -esfälle

debt, die Schuld, -, -en

December, der Dezember, -(s), -

decide, sich entschließen; **I have decided upon a trip,** ich habe mich zur Reise entschlossen; **I have decided to work hard,** ich habe mich entschlossen, schwer zu arbeiten

decorate, schmücken

deed, die Tat, -, -en

deep, tief; **a foot —,** einen Fuß tief

defend, verteidigen

deliver (*a speech*), halten, hielt, gehalten, hält; **he delivered a long speech,** er hat eine lange Rede gehalten

dentist, der Zahnarzt, -es, ⁻e

deny, leugnen; (= *refuse*) verweigern

depend, darauf ánkommen; **that depends,** es kommt darauf an; **it all depends on the weather,** alles hängt vom Wetter ab

dependent, abhängig

describe, beschreiben, beschrieb, beschrieben

desk, das Pult, -(e)s, -e

dessert, der Nachtisch, -es, -e; **for —,** zum Nachtisch

destroy, zerstören
devil, der Teufel, -s, -
dictionary, das Wörterbuch, -(e)s, ⁔er
die, sterben, starb, ist gestorben, stirbt; —
of, sterben an (w. dat.)
difference, der Unterschied, -(e)s, -e; that
makes no —, das macht nichts aus
different, ander-; verschieden
difficult, schwer
difficulty, die Schwierigkeit, -, -en; (obstacle), das Hindernis, -ses, -se
diligent(ly), fleißig
dining room, das Eßzimmer, -s, -
dinner, das Mittagessen, -s, -; is — ready?
ist das Mittagessen fertig? after —, nach
dem Mittagessen (or nach Tisch)
direct (vb.), richten; — toward (aim at),
richten auf (w. acc.)
direction, die Richtung, -, -en; in all —s,
nach allen Richtungen
dirty, schmutzig
disappear, verschwinden, verschwand, ist
verschwunden
disappointed, enttäuscht
discharge, entlassen, entließ, entlassen,
entläßt
discover, entdecken
discoverer, der Entdecker, -s, -; der Erfin-
der, -s, - (inventor)
discovery, die Entdeckung, -, -en; die Erfindung, -, -en (invention)
discuss, besprechen (str.)
dish, die Schüssel, -, -n; to wash dishes,
Geschirr (neut. sing.) ábwaschen
dishonest, unehrlich
dissatisfied, unzufrieden
distance, die Ferne, -, -n; die Entfernung,
-, -en; from a —, aus der Ferne; at a —,
in der Ferne
disturb, stören
divide, teilen
dizzy, schwind(e)lig; she is —, ihr ist
schwind(e)lig (or ihr schwindelt)
do, tun, tat, getan, tut; machen; what are
we to —? was sollen wir tun? he does
me a favor, er tut mir einen Gefallen;
he does his lessons, er macht seine
Aufgaben
doctor, der Arzt, -es, ⁔e; der Doktor, -s,
-en
dog, der Hund, -(e)s, -e
doll, die Puppe, -, -n
dollar, der Dollar, -s, -(s); a thousand —s,
tausend Dollar; a —'s worth of sugar,
für einen Dollar Zucker
domesticated, zahm
door, die Tür, -, -en; front —, Haustür

doubt, der Zweifel, -s, -
doubt, bezweifeln (tr.)
doubtless, wohl (often w. fut.); ohne Zweifel
down, nieder; hinab, hinunter; to lie —,
sich niéderlegen; to settle —, sich niéder-
lassen; to go —, hinúntergehen, hináb-
steigen (substitute prefix her- if denoting
motion toward the observer)
downstairs, (nach) unten; to go —, nach
unten gehen (or die Treppe hinúntergeh-
en)
dozen, das Dutzend, -s, -e; half a —, ein
halbes Dutzend
dragon, der Drache, -n, -n
drama, das Drama, -s, Dramen
draught, der Zug, -(e)s, ⁔e
draw (pull), ziehen, zog, gezogen; (sketch)
zeichnen
dream, der Traum, -(e)s, ⁔e
dream, träumen
dress, das Kleid, -(e)s, -er
dress (oneself), sich ánziehen (or ánkleiden)
drink, trinken, trank, getrunken (of people);
saufen, soff, gesoffen, säuft (of animals)
drive, treiben, trieb, getrieben (to go driving), fahren, fuhr, ist gefahren, fährt; to
— a car, (ein) Auto fahren (tr.)
drop, der Tropfen, -s, -
drop, fallen lassen; she dropped her handkerchief, sie hat das Taschentuch fallen
lassen
drown (tr.), ertränken (wk.)
drowned: to be —, ertrinken, ertrank, ist
ertrunken
drugstore, die Apotheke, -, -n
dry (adj.), trocken
dry, trocknen; — dishes, Geschirr (neut.
sing.) ábtrocknen
duke, der Herzog, -(e)s, -e (or ⁔e)
during, während (w. gen.)
dusty, staubig
duty, die Pflicht, -, -en
dwarf, der Zwerg, -(e)s, -e

E

each, jeder, — other, einander (or sich)
ear, das Ohr, -(e)s, -en
early, früh; — in the morning, frühmorgens
earn, verdienen
earth, die Erde, -
easily, leicht
east, der Osten, -s; — of, östlich von (w.
dat.)

Easter, Ostern (*pl. form w. sing. vb.*)

easy, leicht

eat, essen, aß, gegessen, ißt (*of people*); fressen, fraß, gefressen, frißt (*of animals*); **what does he — for breakfat?** was ißt er zum Frühstück?

eclipse (*lunar*), die Mondfinsternis, -, -se; (*solar*), die Sonnenfinsternis, -, -se

educated, gebildet

egg, das Ei, -(e)s, -er

eight, acht; die Acht

eighteen, achtzehn

eighty, achtzig

either, (= *both*) beide; (= *each*) jeder, **on — side,** auf jeder Seite (*or* bedien Seiten); **I did not see — of them,** ich habe keinen von ihnen gesehen

either . . . or (*conj.*), entweder . . . oder; (*adv.*) **nor I —,** ich auch nicht

elderly, älter-,

eldest, ältest-

elect, wählen

election, die Wahl, -, -en

electric, elektrisch

elevated railroad, die Hochbahn, -, -en

eleven, elf

else (= *otherwise*), sonst; ander-; **no one —,** niemand anders (*or* sonst niemand); **someone** (*or* **anyone**) **—,** jemand anders (*or* sonst jemand)

embarrassed, verlegen

emperor, der Kaiser, -s, -

empire, das Reich, -(e)s, -e

empty, leer

end, das Ende, -s, -n; **at the —,** am Ende

end, enden

enemy, der Feind, -(e)s, -e

engaged, verlobt; **to become — to,** sich verloben mit

England, (das) England, -s

English, englisch; **he is learning —,** er lernt Englisch; **in —,** auf englisch

English-German (*adj.*), englisch-deutsch; **an — dictionary,** ein englisch-deutsches Wörterbuch

enjoy, genießen, genoß, genossen; froh werden (*w. gen.*)

enough, genug

enter, eíntreten (gehen *or* kommen) in (*w. acc.*) (*often w. the separable prefixes* herein *and* hinein

entire, ganz

entrance, der Eingang, -(e)s, ⸗e

especially, besonders

Europe, (das) Europa, -s

even (*adj.*), eben, gerade; (*adv.*), sogar, selbst; **— a physician,** selbst ein Arzt; **— if he were here,** wenn er auch hier wäre

evening, der Abend, -s, -e; **this —,** heute abend; **tomorrow —,** morgen abend; **yesterday —,** gestern abend; **one —** (*indef. time*), eines Abends; **all —** (*duration of time*), den ganzen Abend; **in the —,** am Abend (abends *or* des Abends); **good —,** guten Abend!

ever (= *always*), immer; (= *at any time*), je(mals)

every, jeder, jede, jedes

everybody, jedermann, -s

everything, alles, **— he had,** alles, was er hatte; **— possible,** alles mögliche; **— else,** alles andere; **— good,** alles Gute

everywhere, überall

evil, übel

exact(ly), genau

examination, die Prüfung, -, -en; das Examen, -s, Examina; **to take an —,** eine Prüfung machen; **to pass an —,** eine Prüfung bestehen; **to fail an —,** bei einer Prüfung durchfallen (*w. sein*)

example, das Beispiel, -(e)s, -e; **for —,** zum Beispiel (*abbr.* z.B.)

excited, aufgeregt

exercise, die Aufgabe, -, -n; die Übung, -, -en

exercise, üben (*often refl.*)

expect, erwarten

expensive, teuer, kostspielig

experience, das Erlebnis, -ses, -se; die Erfahrung, -, -en

experience, erleben; erfahren

experiment, der Versuch, -s, -e

explain, erklären

expose, aussetzen, setzte aus, ausgestzt

express, aúsdrücken

expression, der Ausdruck, -(e)s, ⸗e

express train, der Schnellzug, -(e)s, ⸗e

extremely, höchst; äußerst

eye, das Auge, -s, -n

F

face, das Gesicht, -(e)s, -er

fact, die Tatsache, -, -n; **in —,** in der Tat

fail (*an examination*), (bei einer Prüfung) durchfallen, fiel durch, ist durchgefallen, fällt durch

fair, die Messe, -, -n

fairy tale, das Märchen, -s, -

faithful, treu (*w. dat.*)

fall (*season*), der Herbst, -es, -e

fall, fallen, fiel, ist gefallen, fällt; **to — asleep,** einschlafen, schlief ein, ist eingeschlafen, schläft ein; **to — in love with,** sich verlieben in (*w. acc.*)

family, die Familie, -, -n
famous, berühmt; — for, derühmt durch
(*w. acc.*) *or* wegen (*w. gen.*)
far, weit; — and wide, weit und breit; as
— as I know, soviel ich weiß (*or* meines
Wissens); as — as (*prep.*), bis
fare, der Fahrpreis, -es, -e
farewell, leben Sie wohl!
farmer, der Bauer, -s (*or* -n), -n
fast, schnell; my watch is —, meine Uhr
geht vor
father, der Vater, -s, ⁔
fault, die Schuld, -, -en; it is not his —,
er kann nichts dafür
favor, der Gefallen, -s, -; he does me a —,
er tut mir einen Gefallen
favorable, günstig
fear, die Furcht, -
fear, fürchten; sich fürchten vor (*w. dat.*);
fürchten, daß
February, (der) Februar, -(s), -e
Federal Republic of Germany, die
Bundesrepublik Deutschland
feed, füttern
feel, fühlen; sich fühlen (*or* befinden); how
do you — (= *how are you*)? wie geht es
Ihnen?
fell (= *cut down*), fällen
fellow, der Kerl, -(e)s, -e
fence, der Zaun, -(e)s, ⁔e
few, wenige; a —, ein paar (*indecl.*)
field, das Feld, -(e)s, -er; in the —, auf dem
Feld
fifteen, fünfzehn
fifty, fünfzig
fight, der Kampf, -(e)s, ⁔e
fight, kämpfen; (= *come to blows*) sich
prügeln
fill, füllen
finally, endlich, schließlich, zuletzt
find, finden, fand, gefunden
fine, fein; very — (*sarcastic*), sehr schön
finger, der Finger, -s, -
finish, vollenden
fire, das Feuer, -s, -
firm (*adj.*), fest
firm, die Firma, -, Firmen
first, erst-; in the — place, erstens; at —,
zuerst
fish, der Fisch, -es, -e
fishing : to go —, fischen gehen; I went —,
ich bin fischen gegangen
fist, die Faust, -, ⁔e
five, fünf
flag, die Fahne, -, -n
flame, die Flamme, -, -n
flat, flach
flatter, schmeicheln (*w. dat.*); you — yourself, du schmeichelst dir

flee, fliehen, floh, ist geflohen
floor, der Boden, -s, ⁔ (*or* -); ground —,
das Erdgeschoß; first —, der erste Stock;
top —, der oberste Stock
flour, das Mehl, -(e)s, -e (*or* -arten)
flow, fließen, floß, ist geflossen
flower, die Blume, -, -n
fluent(ly), fließend
fly, fliegen, flog, ist geflogen; (*of time*) vergehen, verging, ist vergangen; how time
flies! wie schnell die Zeit vergeht!
flyer, der Flieger, -s, -
folksong, das Volkslied, -(e)s, -er
follow, folgen, folgte, ist gefolgt (*w. dat.*)
fool, der Narr, -en, -en
foolish, närrisch
foot, der Fuß, -es, ⁔e; on —, zu Fuß
for, für (*w. acc.*); — what reason? aus
welchem Grunde?; — example, zum
Beispiel; — heaven's sake! um Himmels willen! — all I care, meinetwegen;
— two years, zwei Jahre lang; he is going to the country — a month, er geht
auf einen Monat aufs Land; I have been
here — a month, ich bin seit einem
Monat hier; to ask —, bitten um (*w. acc.*);
to long —, sich sehnen nach
for (*causal conj.*), denn
force, die Gewalt, -, -en
foreign, fremd; — language, die Fremdsprache, -, -n
forenoon, der Vormittag, -(e)s, -e (*see*
afternoon *phrases*)
forest, der Wald, -(e)s, ⁔er,
forget, vergessen, vergaß, vergessen, vergißt
fork, die Gabel, -, -n
form, die Form, -, -en; — of government, die Regierungsform
former, jener (*in contrast with* dieser);
vorher erwähnt (previously mentioned)
formerly, früher
fortunately, glücklicherweise
fortune (*good luck*), das Glück, -(e)s;
(*wealth*), das Vermögen, -s, -
fountain, der Brunnen, -s, -
fountain pen, die Füllfeder, -, -n
four, vier
fourfold, vierfach
fourteenth, vierzehnt-
fourth (*num. adj.*), viert-; (*noun*), das Viertel,
-s, -
fox, der Fuchs, -es, Füchse
France, (das) Frankreich, -s
frantic, toll; — with pain, toll vor Schmerz
free, frei
freedom, die Freiheit, -, en
freeze, frieren, fror, gefroren; it froze
hard, es hat stark gefroren

French, französisch; **do you speak —?** sprechen Sie Französisch?

Frenchman, der Franzose, -n, -n

fresh, frisch

Friday, der Freitag, -(e)s, -e

friend (*male*), der Freund, -(e)s, -e; (*female*) die Freundin, -, -nen; **a — of mine,** ein Freund von mir

friendly, freundlich; **he is — to me,** er ist mir freundlich (*or* er ist freundlich gegen mich)

friendship, die Freundschaft, -, -en

frighten (*tr.*), erschrecken (*wk.*)

frightened: to be — (*intr.*), erschrecken erschrak, ist erschrocken, erschrickt

from, von, aus (*both w. dat.*)

front: in — of, vor (*w. dat. or acc.*)

fruit, die Frucht, -, ⁀e; das Obst, -es

full, voll

fun, der Spaß, -es, ⁀e

funny, komisch

furious, wütend

further, weiter

future (*adj.*), (zu)künftig

future, die Zukunft, -; **— plan,** der Zukunftsplan, -(e)s, ⁀e

G

game, das Spiel, -(e)s, -e; **football —,** das Fußballspiel; **to play a — of chess,** eine Partie Schach spielen

garden, der Garten, -s, ⁀

gas, das Gas, -es -e

gay, fröhlich, lustig, heiter

generally, gewöhnlich, in der Regel

gentleman, der Herr, -n, -en

German, deutsch; **in —,** auf deutsch; **are you studying —?** lernen Sie Deutsch? (*native of Germany*), der Deutsche, -n, -n (*w. adj. decl.*); ein Deutscher

Germany, (das) Deutschland, -s

get (= *to receive*), erhalten, erhielt, erhalten, erhält; bekommen, bekam, bekommen; **— in,** einsteigen, stieg ein, ist eingestiegen; **— to be** (= *become*), werden, wurde, ist geworden, wird; **— up,** aufstehen, stand auf, ist aufgestanden; **— used to,** sich gewöhnen an (*w. acc.*)

giant, der Riese, -n, -n

giant, gigantic, riesig

gift, das Geschenk, -(e)s, -e

girl, das Mädchen, -s, -

give, geben, gab, gegeben, gibt; **it gives me pleasure,** es macht mir Freude

glad, froh; **I am — of it;** ich freue mich darüber (*or* es freut mich)

glass, das Glas, -es, ⁀er; **a — of beer,** ein Glas Bier

glasses (= *spectacles*), die Brille, -, -n

glee club, der Gesangverein, -(e)s, -e

glove, der Handschuh, -(e)s, -e; **a pair of —s,** ein Paar Handschuhe

go, gehen, ging, ist gegangen; (= *to travel*) fahren, fuhr, ist gefahren, fährt; reisen, reiste, ist gereist; **— home,** nach Hause gehen; **— to bed,** zu Bett gehen; **— walking,** spazierengehen (*or* einen Spaziergang machen); **— to school,** in die (*or* zur) Schule gehen; **— to the theater (to the opera),** ins Theater (in die Oper) gehen; **— away,** fortgehen; **— along** mitgehen; **— out** (hin)ausgehen; **— down,** hinúntergehen; **— to sleep,** einschlafen, schlief ein, ist eingeschlafen, schläft ein; **— out of the door,** zur Tür hináusgehen; **he goes second class,** er fährt zweiter Klasse; **the fire is going out,** das Feuer geht aus

God, der Gott; -es, ⁀er

gold, das Gold, -(e)s

golden, golden

good, gut; **to have a — time,** sich amüsieren

goodbye, auf Wiederseh(e)n!

goods, die Waren (*pl. of* die Ware)

gorgeous, prächtig

govern, regieren

grade (*school mark*), die Zensur, -, -en; die Note, -, -n

gradually, allmählich, nach und nach

grammar, die Grammatik, -, -en

grandfather, der Großvater, -s, ⁀

grandmother, die Großmutter, -, ⁀

grandparents, die Großeltern, -, (*pl.*)

grandson, der Enkel, -s, -

grape, die Traube, -, -n

grass, das Gras, -es, ⁀er

grateful, dankbar (*w. dat.*)

grave, das Grab, -(e)s, ⁀er

gray, grau

great, groß

green, grün

greet, grüßen

groan, stöhnen

ground, der Boden, -s, ⁀ (*or* -); der Grund, -(e)s, ⁀e

group, die Gruppe, -, -n

grow, wachsen, wuchs, ist gewachsen, wächst

guard, bewachen

guess (= *guess right, solve*), erraten, erriet, erraten, errät; **to — at,** raten, riet, geraten, rät

guest, der Gast, -es, ⁀e

guilty, schuldig

gymnasium, (*physical education*) die Turn-halle, -, -n; (*German high school*) das Gymnasium, -s, Gymnasien
gymnastic, gymnastisch

H

hail, hageln
hair, das Haar, -(e)s, -e; **I had my — cut,** ich habe mir das Haar schneiden lassen; **my — stood on end,** mir standen die Haare zu Berge
half (*adj.*), halb; **one and a —,** anderthalb; **at — past nine,** um halb zehn; **— a pound,** ein halbes Pfund
half, die Hälfte, -, -n
hall, der Saal, -(e)s, Säle
halt, halten, hielt, gehalten, hält; anhalten
hammer, der Hammer, -s, ̈
hand, die Hand, -, ̈e; **on the other —,** dagegen
handful, die Handvoll, -, -
handkerchief, das Taschentuch, -(e)s, ̈er
happen, geschehen, geschah, ist geschehen, geschieht; vorkommen, kam vor, ist vorgekommen; passieren (*w.* sein); **he happened to be at home,** er war zufällig (*or* zufälligerweise war er) zu Hause
happiness, das Glück, -(e)s
happy, glücklich, fröhlich; **I am — about it,** ich freue mich darüber (*or* es freut mich)
harbor, der Hafen, -s, ̈
hard, hart; schwer; **to study (work) —,** fleißig (tüchtig *or* schwer) studieren (arbeiten); **to rain —,** stark regnen
hardly, kaum
harm, schaden (*w. dat.*)
harmful, schädlich (*w. dat.*)
hat, der Hut, -(e)s, ̈e
hate, hassen
hatred, der Haß, Hasses
have, haben, hatte, gehabt, hat; **to — a good time,** sich amüsieren; **to — something done,** etwas tun lassen; **to — to,** müssen, mußte, gemußt, muß; **I have to go,** ich muß gehen; **you don't have (= need) to do that,** das brauchen Sie nicht zu tun; **I had a new suit made,** ich habe mir einen neuen Anzug machen lassen
he, er
head, der Kopf, -(e)s, ̈e; das Haupt, -(e)s, ̈er
headache, das Kopfweh, -(e)s; **I have a —,** ich habe Kopfweh
health, die Gesundheit, -, -en

healthy, gesund
heap, der Haufe(n), -ns, -n
hear, hören; **I heard him sing,** ich habe ihn singen hören
heart, das Herz, -ens, -en; **by —,** auswendig
hearty, herzlich
heat, die Hitze, -
heaven, der Himmel, -s, -; **for —'s sake,** um Himmels (*or* Gottes) willen!
heavy, schwer
height, die Höhe, ̈, -n
help, helfen, half, geholfen, hilft (*w. dat.*); **I couldn't — it,** ich konnte nichts dafür; **I couldn't — telling him the truth,** ich konnte nicht umhin, ihm die Wahrheit zu sagen; **to — out,** aushelfen
help, die Hilfe, -, -n
her (*pers. pron.*), ihr (*dat.*); sie (*acc.*); (*poss. adj.*), ihr, ihre, ihr
here, hier; **spring is —,** der Frühling ist gekommen; **come —!** kommen Sie her!
hero, der Held, -en, -en
hers (*poss. pron.*), ihrer, ihre, ihres; der (die *or* das) ihre (*or* ihrige)
herself (*refl. pron.*), sich; (*intens.*) selbst; **she —,** sie selbst (*or* selber)
hesitate, zögern
high, hoch; **a foot —,** einen Fuß hoch
hill, der Hügel, -s, -
him (*pers. pron.*), ihm (*dat.*); ihn (*acc.*)
himself (*refl. pron.*), sich; (*intens.*) selbst; **he —,** er selbst (*or* selber)
his (*poss. adj.*), sein, seine, sein; (*poss. pron.*), seiner, seine, seines; der (die *or* das) seine (*or* seinige)
historic, historisch
history, die Geschichte, -, -n
hit, treffen, traf, getroffen, trifft; schlagen, schlug, geschlagen, schlägt
hold, halten, hielt, gehalten, hält; fassen; **— together,** zusámmenhalten
holidays, die Ferien, -, (*pl.*)
holy, heilig
home, das Heim, -(e)s, -e; (= *dwelling*), das Haus, -es, Häuser; (= *native place*) die Heimat, -, -en; **at —,** zu Hause (*or* daheim); **make yourself at —,** machen Sie es sich (*dat.*) bequem!
homeland, die Heimat, -, -en
homeward, heim(wärts), nach Hause
honest, ehrlich
honesty, die Ehrlichkeit, -
honor, die Ehre, -, -n
hope, hoffen; **— for,** hoffen auf (*w. acc.*)
hope, die Hoffnung, -, -en
horn, das Horn, -(e)s, ̈er
horse, das Pferd, -(e)s, -e
horseback: **on —,** zu Pferde
hostile, feindlich (gesinnt) (*w. dat.*)

hot, heiß

hotel, das Gasthaus, -es, / häuser; das Hotel, -s, -s

hotelkeeper, der Wirt, -(e)s, -e

hour, die Stunde, -, -n; **half an —,** eine halbe Stunde; **an — and a half,** anderthalb Stunden; **zero —,** die Angriffszeit, -, die Nullzeit, -

house, das Haus, -es, Häuser; **at his —,** bei ihm; **at whose —?** bei wem?

how, wie; **— much?** wieviel?; **— many?** wie viele? **— long?** wie lange?; **— are you?** wie geht es Ihnen?; **— do you know that?** woher wissen Sie das?; **— much does it cost?** was kostet es?

however, aber; doch

huge, ungeheuer; riesig (*gigantic*)

humor (= *mood*), die Laune, -, -n; **he is in a good —,** er ist guter Laune (*gen.*)

hundred (*num. adj.*)*:* **a —,** hundert (*no art.*)

hundred, das Hundert, -(e)s, -e

hungry, hungrig; **I am —,** ich bin hungrig (*or* ich habe Hunger)

hunt (*noun*), die Jagd, -, -en

hunt, jagen, auf die Jagd gehen

hunter, der Jäger, -s, -

hurry, eilen (*w.* sein); sich beeilen

hurt, schaden (*w. dat.*); **— oneself,** sich (*dat.*) weh tun [*or* sich (*acc.*) verletzen]; **that will — your health,** das wird Ihrer Gesundheit schaden; **it hurts me,** es tut mir weh

husband, der Gatte, -n, -n; der Mann, -(e)s, ꞈer

hydrogen, der Wasserstoff, -(e)s

I

I, ich; **nor —,** ich auch nicht

idea, der Einfall, -(e)s, ꞈe; die Idee, -, -n; **that is not a bad —,** das ist kein übler Einfall

idiomatic, idiomatisch

if, wenn, falls; ob (*in indir. ques.*)*;* **as —,** als ob

ill, krank

imagine, sich (*dat.*) denken (éinbilden *or* vórstellen)

immediately, sogleich, gleich, sofort

impatience, die Ungeduld, -; **he is burning with —,** er brennt vor Ungeduld

impatient, ungeduldig

implore, bitten, bat, gebeten, bittet

importance, die Wichtigkeit, -; die Bedeutung, - (*significance*)

important, wichtig; bedeutend (*significant*)

impossible, unmöglich

impression, der Eindruck, -(e)s, ꞈe

in (*prep.*)*,* in, an, auf (*w. dat. or acc.*)*;* **— 1974,** im Jahre 1974; **— German,** auf deutsch

inch, der Zoll, -(e)s, -

incombustible, unverbrennbar

income, das Einkommen, -s, -

indeed, wirklich, in der Tat; **they would be stupid —,** sie wären schön dumm!

independent, unabhängig

Indian, der Indianer, -s, -

individual, (*adj.*), einzeln

individual, das Individuum, -s, Individuen

industrious, fleißig

industry (= *diligence*), der Fleiß, -es

inevitable, unvermeidlich

information, die Nachricht, -, -en; die Auskunft, -, ꞈe

inhabit, bewohnen

inhabitant, der Einwohner, -s, -

injustice, das Unrecht, -(e)s

ink, die Tinte, -, -n

inn, das Gasthaus, -es, /häuser

in order to (*conj.*), damit; (*prep.*), um . . . zu; **— learn,** um zu lernen

inquire about, sich erkundigen nach

insist (up)on, bestehen auf (*usually w. dat.*)

in spite of, trotz (*w. gen.*)

instance, das Beispiel, -(e)s, -e; **for —,** zum Beispiel (*abbr.* z.B.)

instead of, (an)statt (*w. gen.*)*;* **— working,** anstatt zu arbeiten

intend, beabsichtigen; vórhaben; wollen, wollte, gewollt, will; **he intends to leave tomorrow,** er will morgen abfahren

intentionally, absichtlich

interest, das Interesse, -s, -n; **to bear —** (on money), Zinsen tragen; **to take an — in,** sich interessieren für (*w. acc.*)

interested: to be — in, sich interessieren für (*w. acc.*)

interesting, interessant

interrupt, unterbréchen

into, in (*w. acc.*)

introduce, vórstellen; **he introduced him to me,** er hat ihn mir vorgestellt

in vain, vergebens, umsonst

invention, die Erfindung, -, -en

investigate, untersúchen

investigation, die Forschung, -, -en; die Untersuchung, -, -en; die Prüfung, -, -en

investigator, der Forscher, -s, -; der Untersucher, -s, -

invite, einladen, lud ein, eingeladen, ladet (*or* lädt) ein; **he invited me for supper,** er hat mich zum Abendessen eingeladen

iron, das Eisen, -s
island, die Insel, -, -n
it, es (*nom. & acc.*); ihm (*dat.*); is — he ? ist
er es ?; — is he, er ist es; *da-forms:* damit,
darauf, *etc.*
Italian, italienisch
Italy, (das) Italien, -s
its, sein (*refers to masc. & neut. nouns*); ihr
(*refers to fem. nouns*)

J

January, der Januar, -(s), -e
jet (aircraft), das Strahlflugzeug, -(e)s, -e
joke, der Scherz, -es, -e; der Spaß, es, ᵘe
joke, scherzen
joy, die Freude, -, -n
judge, der Richter, -s, -
July, der Juli, -(s), -s
jump, springen, sprang, ist gesprungen
June, der Juni, -(s), -s
just (*adj.*), gerecht; (*adv.*), gerade; eben; —
try it, versuchen Sie es nur!; she is —
as industrious as he, sie ist ebenso
fleißig wie er
justice, die Gerechtigkeit, -, -en

K

keep, behalten behielt, behalten, behält; he
keeps his word, er hält Wort
key, der Schlüssel, -s, -
kill, töten; ermorden (*to murder*)
kilometer, das Kilometer, -s, -
kind (*adj.*), gütig
kind, die Art -, -en; what — of, was für;
four kinds of, viererlei
king, der König, -(e)s, -e
kitchen, die Küche, -, -n
knee, das Knie, -s, -
knife, das Messer, -s, -
knight, der Ritter, -s, -
knighthood, das Rittertum, -s
knock at, klopfen an (*w. acc.*)
know (= *to know a fact*), wissen, wußte,
gewußt, weiß; (= *to be acquainted with*)
kennen, kannte, gekannt; (= *to have
learned by study*) können, konnte, gekonnt,
kann; how do you — that ? ·woher
wissen Sie das ? do you — what you are
about ? sind Sie Ihrer Sache gewiß ? he
knows German, er kann Deutsch; as far
as I —, soviel ich weiß

knowledge, die Kenntnis, -, -se; (= *science*)
die Wissenschaft, -, -en
known (= *well-known*), bekannt

L

labor, die Arbeit, -, -en
lady, die Dame, -, -n
lamp, die Lampe, -, -n
land, das Land, -(e)s, ᵘer; native —, das
Vaterland
land, landen, landete, ist gelandet; — on,
landen auf (*w. dat.*)
landscape, die Landschaft, -, -en
language, die Sprache, -, -n; foreign —,
die Fremdsprache
lap, der Schoß, -es, ᵘe
large, groß
last (*adj.*), letzt-; next to —, vorletzt-
last, dauern
late, spät; to come —, zu spät kommen
later on, späterhin
latter, der (die, das) letztere; dieser (*in
contrast with* jener)
laugh, lachen; to — at, aúslachen (*tr.*),
lachen über (*w. acc.*)
laughter, das Lachen, -s; there was much
—, es wurde viel gelacht
law, das Gesetz, -es, -e
lawyer, der Advokat, -en, -en
lay, legen
layer of air, die Luftschicht, -, -en
laziness, die Faulheit, -
lazy, faul
lead (*noun*), das Blei, -(e)s, -e
lead, führen, leiten
leader, der Führer, -s, -
leaf, das Blatt, -(e)s, ᵘer
leap, spring, sprang, ist gesprungen
leap, der Sprung, -(e)s, ᵘe
learn, lernen; erfahren (über) w. acc.
least: at —, wenigstens; — of all, am
allerwenigsten
leather, das Leder, -s, -
leave, lassen, ließ, gelassen, läßt; (= *to
bequeath*) hinterlassen; (= *to depart*)
abfahren, fuhr ab, ist abgefahren, fährt
ab; to — behind (= *to forsake*), verlassen, verließ, verlassen, verläßt; to
take —, sich empfehlen, empfahl, empfohlen, empfiehlt
lecture, die Vorlesung, -, -en; der Vortrag,
-(e)s, ᵘe
left (*adj.*), link-; (*adv.*), links; on the —,
links; to the —, nach links

left (over), übrig; **I have only three bottles —,** ich habe nur drei Flaschen übrig
leg, das Bein, -(e)s, -e
legend, die Sage, -, -n; **according to —,** der Sage nach
lend, leihen, lieh, geliehen
less, weniger
lesson, die Lektion, -, -en; die Aufgabe, -, -n; **to take —s,** Stunden nehmen
let, lassen, ließ, gelassen, läßt
let know, wissen lassen; **let me know,** lassen Sie mich wissen
letter, der Brief, -(e)s, -e
library, die Bibilothek, -, -en; **to take books out of the —,** Bücher aus der Bibliothek entnehmen
lie (*falsehood*), die Lüge, -, -n
lie (*tell a lie*) lügen, log, gelogen; (*be situated*), liegen, lag, gelegen; **to — down,** sich (hin)legen
life, das Leben, -s, -; **to lead a simple —,** ein einfaches Leben führen
lift, heben, hob, gehoben; aúf heben
light (= *bright*), hell; (= *of small weight*) leicht
light, das Licht, -(e)s, -er
light, anzünden
like (*adj.*), gleich (*w. dat.*); ähnlich (*w. dat.*)
like, gern haben; gefallen (*w. dat.*); mögen; **to be —** (= *to resemble*), gleichen (*w. dat.*), ähnlich sein (*w. dat.*); **I — it,** ich habe es gern (es gefällt mir *or* ich mag es); **I — to read,** ich lese gern; **I — best to read,** ich lese am liebsten; **he would — to go along,** er möchte mitgehen
line (*of print*), die Zeile, -, -n; (*geometric*) die Linie, -, -n; **a straight —,** eine gerade Linie
lion, der Löwe, -n, -n
lip, die Lippe, -, -n
listen to, zuhören (*w. dat.*); (*tr.*) anhören
little (*as to size*), klein; (*as to quantity*) wenig; **a —,** ein wenig (*or* bißchen)
live, leben; (= *dwell*) wohnen, bewohnen
long (*adj.*), lang; **a foot —,** einen Fuß lang; (*adv.*) (= *for a long time*), lange; **how — (a time)?** wie lange?
longer, länger; **no —,** nicht mehr
long for, sich sehnen nach
look, aussehen, sah aus, ausgesehen, sieht aus; **to — at,** ánsehen; **— for,** suchen; **— forward with pleasure to,** sich freuen auf (*w. acc.*); **— out of the window,** zum Fenster hinaussehen; **he looks as if he were ill,** er sieht aus, als ob er krank wäre; **I am looking for it,** ich suche es; **she is looking out of the window,** sie sieht zum Fenster hinaus

Lord, der Herr, -n
lose, verlieren, verlor, verloren; **— one's way,** sich verirren
loss, der Verlust, -es -e
loud, laut
love, lieben; **to fall in — with,** sich verlieben in (*w. acc.*)
love, die Liebe, -, -n
luck: good —, das Glück, -(e)s
lunch, der Imbiß, Imbisses, Imbisse

M

magazine, die Zeitschrift, -, -en
maiden, die Jungfrau, -, -en
mail (*noun*), die Post, -, -en
mail, auf die Post bringen; **he mailed the letter,** er hat den Brief auf die Post gebracht
maintain (= *to assert*), behaupten
make, machen; **— up** (*work, lessons, etc.*), nachholen; **— up one's mind,** sich entschließen; **— money,** Geld verdienen; **— a speech,** eine Rede halten; **that makes no dißerence,** das macht nichts aus; **he was made king,** man machte ihn zum König; **I made his acquaintance,** ich lernte ihn kennen
man, der Mann, -(e)s, ̈er; (= *human being*) der Mensch, -en, -en
manner, die Weise, -, -n; **in this —,** auf diese Weise
many, viele; **— a,** mancher; **— things,** vieles; **— beautiful things,** viel Schönes; **how —?** wie viele?
March, der März, -(es), -e
mark (*money*), die Mark, -; (*school grade*), die Zensur, -, -en; die Note, -, -n
market, der Markt, -(e)s, ̈e
married, verheiratet
marry, heiraten; sich verheiraten
master, der Herr, -n, -en
mathematics, die Mathematik, -
matter, die Sache, -, -n; die Angelegenheit, -, -en; **what is the —?** was ist los?; **what is the — with him?** was fehlt ihm?
May, der Mai, -(e)s, -e
may (= *to be permitted*), dürfen, durfte, gedurft, darf; mögen, mochte, gemocht, mag; **that — be,** das mag (*or* kann) sein; **whoever she — be,** wer sie auch sein mag; **however that — be,** wie das auch sein mag (*or* wie dem auch sei)
mayor, der Bürgermeister, -s, -

me, mir (*dat.*); mich (*acc.*)

meadow, die Wiese, -, -n

meal, das Essen, -s, -; die Mahlzeit, -, -en

mean, meinen (*of people*); bedeuten (*of things*); what (in the world) do you — ? was fällt Ihnen denn ein?

means: by no —, keineswegs, durchaus nicht

means (= *expedient, contrivance*), das Mittel, -s, -, (*pl. often = resources*)

meantime: in the —, inzwischen, währenddessen

meanwhile, *see* meantime

meat, das Fleisch, -es

medicine, die Medizin, -, -en

medieval, mittelalterlich

meet, begegnen, begegnete, ist begegnet (*w. dat.*); treffen, traf, getroffen, trifft (*w. acc.*)

melt, schmelzen, schmolz, ist geschmolzen, schmilzt

member, das Mitglied, -(e)s, -er

mention, erwähnen

merchant, der Kaufmann, -(e)s, Kaufleute

merry, fröhlich, lustig, munter

meter, das Meter, -s, - (39.37 U.S. inches)

middle, die Mitte, -; in the — of the forest, mitten (*adv.*) im Walde

midnight, die Mitternacht, -

might, (= *power*), die Macht, -, ⁼e; die Gewalt, -, -en

might, dürfte, könnte; — I ask you for the book? dürfte ich Sie um das Buch bitten?; that — be, das könnte (*or* dürfte) sein

mighty, mächtig, gewaltig

mile, die Meile, -, -n

milk, die Milch, -

miller, der Müller, -s, -

million, die Million, -, -en

millionairre, der Millionär, -s, -e ⁻

mind (= *memory*), das Gedächtnis, -ses, -se; der Sinn, -(e)s, -e; to make up one's —, sich entschließen

mine (*poss. pron.*), meiner, meine, meines; der (die *or* das) meine (*or* meinige); a friend of —, ein Freund von mir

minute, die Minute, -, -n

mirror, der Spiegel, -s, -

misfortune, das Unglück, -(e)s, -sfälle

misplace, verlegen

miss (*a person*), vermissen; (*a train*) versäumen, verpassen

mistake, der Fehler, -s, -

mistaken: to be —, sich irren

misunderstand, mißverstehen, mißverstand, mißverstanden

model, das Muster, -s, - (*pattern, sample*)

model airplane, das Musterflugzeug, -s, -e; das Flugzeugmodell, -s, -e

modern, modern

modest, bescheiden

moment, der Augenblick, -(e)s, -e; wait a —, warten Sie einen Augenblick!

monarchy, die Monarchie, -, -n

money, das Geld, -(e)s, -er; to make —, Geld verdienen; to save (spend, squander) —, Geld sparen (ausgeben, verschwenden)

month, der Monat, -(e)s, -e; for months, monatelang

monthly, monatlich

moon, der Mond, -(e)s, -e

more, mehr; — and —, immer mehr; — beautiful, schöner; the — ..., the —, je mehr ... desto mehr

morning, der Morgen, -s, -; good —, guten Morgen! tomorrow —, morgen früh; early in the —, frühmorgens; all —, den ganzen Morgen; this —, heute morgen

mortal, sterblich

most (*adj.*), meist-; — people, die meisten Leute (*def. art. required*)

most (*adv.*), am meisten; — interesting, höchst interessant

mostly, meistens, meistenteils

mother, die Mutter, -, ⁼

mother-in-law, die Schwiegermutter, -, ⁼

mountain, der Berg, -(e)s, -e; we are going to the —s, wir gehen in die Berge (*or* ins Gebirge)

mouse, die Maus, -, Mäuse

mouth (*of a pers.*), der Mund, -(e)s, Münder (*rarely* Munde *and* Münde); (*of an animal*) das Maul, -(e)s, ⁼er; (*of a river*) die Mündung, -, -en

move (*tr.*), bewegen; (*intr.*) ziehen, zog, ist gezogen; (*refl.*) sich bewegen (*or* rühren); (= *to change residence*) sich úmziehen; I have moved, ich bin umgezogen; don't — from the spot! rühren Sie sich nicht von der Stelle!

movie, der Film, -s, -e; is there a good movie playing tonight? gibt's heute abend einen guten Film?

movies, das Kino, -s, -s; we rarely go to the —, wir gehen selten ins Kino

Mr., Herr; — Wagner's overcoat, Herrn Wagners Mantel

Mrs., Frau; — Wagner's gloves, Frau Wagners Handschuhe

much (*quantity*), viel; (*degree*) sehr; how —? wieviel?; how — does it cost? was kostet es?; twice as —, zweimal soviel; he suffers —, er leidet sehr

Munich, (das) München, -s; **of —** (*adj.*), Münch(e)ner (*indecl.*)
museum, das Museum, -s, Museen
music, die Musik, -
must, müssen; **you — not do that,** das dürfen Sie nicht tun
my (*poss. adj.*), mein, meine, mein; **for — sake,** um meinetwillen
myself (*refl. pron.*), mich (*acc.*); mir (*dat.*); (*intens.*), ich selbst (*or* selber); **I seat —** (*or* sit down), ich setze mich; **I hurt —,** ich habe mir weh getan

N

nail, der Nagel, -s, ⸚
naked, nackt; **with the — eye,** mit bloßem Auge
name (*noun*), der Name, -ns, -n; **his — is,** er heißt
name, nennen, nannte, genannt; **to be named** (*or* called), heißen, hieß, geheißen
narrow, eng
nation, das Volk, -(e)s, ⸚er; die Nation, -, -en
native land, das Vaterland, -(e)s, ⸚er
natural(ly), natürlich
nature, die Natur, -, -en
near, nah(e) (*w. dat.*); **— them,** in ihrer Nähe (*or* ihnen nahe)
necessary, nötig
neck, der Hals, -es, Hälse
need, brauchen, nötig haben, bedürfen *w. gen.*)
need, die Not, -, ⸚e; **in — of repair** (*adj.*), ausbesserungsbedürftig
neighbor, (*male*) der Nachbar, -s (*or* -n), -n; (*female*) die Nachbarin, -, -nen
neither (*conj.*), weder; **— ... nor,** weder ... noch; **— the father nor the mother,** weder der Vater noch die Mutter
nest, das Nest, -es, -er
Netherlands, die Niederlande, -, (*pl.*)
network, das Netz, -es, -e; das Netzwerk -(e)s, -e; **— communication,** der Netzverkehr, -s
never, nie(mals)
nevertheless, trotzdem, dessenungeachtet
new, neu; **the — year,** das neue Jahr; **what's —?** was gibt's Neues?
news, die Nachricht, -, -en; die Neuigkeit, -, -en
newspaper, die Zeitung, -, -en
New Year('s Day), das Neujahr, -(e)s, -e
next, nächst-; **the —** (= *adjoining*) **room,** das Nebenzimmer

night, die Nacht, -, ⸚e; **at —,** in der Nacht; **last —,** gestern nacht (*or* abend), vorige Nacht; **one —** (*indef. time*), eines Nachts
nine, neun
ninth, neunt-
no (*adj.*), kein, keine, kein; **— one,** keiner; niemand, -(e)s; **— one else,** niemand anders, sonst niemand; **— such,** kein solch
no (*adv.*), nein; **— more,** nicht mehr
nobility, der Adel, -s
noble, edel; vornehm
nobody, niemand, -(e)s
none (*pron.*), keiner, keine, keines
nonsense, der Unsinn, -(e)s
nor, noch; **neither ... —,** weder ... noch; **— I,** ich auch nicht
north, der Norden, -s; **— of,** nördlich von (*w. dat.*)
northeast (*adj.*), nordöstlich; (*noun*), der Nordosten, -s
northwest (*adj.*), nordwestlich; (*noun*), der Nordwesten, -s
nose, die Nase, -, -n
not, nicht; **— a, any,** kein; **— at all,** gar nicht; **— yet,** noch nicht; **— even,** nicht einmal; **— only ... but also,** nicht nur ... sondern auch; **— until seven o'clock,** erst um sieben Uhr
notebook, das Heft, -(e)s, -e
nothing, nichts; **— at all,** gar nichts; **— (that) he has,** nichts, was er hat; **— new,** nichts Neues; **— will come of it,** nichts wird daraus werden
notice, bemerken
November, der November, -(s), -
now, jetzt
nowadays, heutzutage
nowhere, nirgendwo, nirgends
number, die Nummer, -, -n (*cipher; size; issue*); die Zahl, -, -en; **the even —s,** die geraden Zahlen; **a — of,** mehrere
numberless, zahllos
numerous, zahlreich
nurse, die Krankenschwester, -, -n
nurse, pflegen

O

obey, gehorchen (*w. dat.*)
objection: I have no — to that, ich habe nichts dagegen
observe (*to look at*), betrachten; bemerken; (*take note of*), beobachten

obstacle, das Hindernis, -ses, -se
occasionally, dann und wann, gelegentlich
occupy (*live in*), bewohnen (*w. dir. obj.*), wohnen in (*w. dat.*); (*busy oneself*), sich beschäftigen; (*take possession of*), besetzen
occur to, einfallen, fiel ein, ist eingefallen, fällt ein (*w. dat.*); **that never occurred to me,** das ist mir nie eingefallen
ocean, der Ozean, -s, -e;
o'clock: at two —, um zwei Uhr
of, von (*w. dat.*); **— course,** natürlich, selbstverständlich; **I think — him,** ich denke an ihn; **full —,** voll(er); **the square is full — people,** der Platz ist voll(er) Menschen; (*Often omitted:* **the city — Munich,** die Stadt München; **a pound — butter,** ein Pfund Butter
offer, bieten, bot, geboten; anbieten
office, das Amt, -(e)s, ⸗er; (*place of business*) das Büro, -s, -s
official, der Beamte, -n, -n (*w. adj. decl.*); ein Beamter
official (*adj.*), offiziell, amtlich
official record, der offizielle Rekord, -s
often, oft
old, alt; **— age,** das Alter, -s
on, auf, an (*w. dat. or acc.*); **— Monday,** am Montag (*or* Montags); **— my account,** meinetwegen; **— condition that,** unter der Bedingung, daß
once, einmal; **at —,** sogleich, gleich, sofort; **— upon a time there was,** es war einmal; **— more,** noch einmal
one (*num. adj.*), ein; (= *single*) einzig; **— and a half,** anderthalb
one (*indef. art.*), ein, eine, ein
one (*pron.*), einer, eine, ein(e)s; man (*indef., used only in nominative*); **which —?** welcher?; **— of the pupils,** einer von den Schülern
onion, die Zwiebel, -, -n
only (*adj.*), einzig; (*adv.*), nur, bloß; erst; **not — ... but also,** nicht nur ... sondern auch; **it is — two o'clock,** es ist erst zwei Uhr
open (*adj.*), offen
open, öffnen, aufmachen
opinion, die Meinung, -, -en
opportunity, die Gelegenheit, -, -en
opposite, gegenüber (*w. dat.*); **we live — the park,** wir wohnen dem Park gegenüber
or, oder; **either ... —,** entweder ... oder
oral, mündlich
orange, die Orange, -, -n, die Apfelsine, -, -n
orator, der Redner, -s, -

order (*command*), der Befehl, -(e)s, -e; (*arrangement*), die Ordnung, -, -en; **to give an — for,** bestellen; **to put something in —,** etwas in Ordnung bringen; **it might perhaps be in —,** es wäre wohl an der Zeit; **in — to** (*conj.*), damit; (*prep.*) um ... zu (*w. inf.*)
order, befehlen, behahl, befohlen, befiehlt (*w. dat.*); (*to give an order for*), bestellen; **to — a taxi,** ein Taxi bestellen
originally, ursprünglich
originate, entstehen, entspringen (*both str. & w. sein*)
other (*adj.*), ander-
other (*pron.*), der (die *or* das) andere, (*pl.*) die anderen; **they love each —,** sie lieben einander (*or* sich)
otherwise, sonst; anders, auf andere Weise
ought (= *should*), sollte (*imperf. subj. of* sollen*); **I — to work,** ich sollte arbeiten
our (*poss. adj.*), unser, unsere, unser
ours (*poss. pron.*), uns(e)rer, uns(e)re, uns(e)res; der (die *or* das) unsrige *or* uns(e)re
ourselves (*refl.*), uns (*dat. & acc.*); (*intens.*) **we —,** wir selbst (*or* selber)
out (*w. vbs. of motion*), hinaus, heraus; (= *outside*) draußen; (= *not at home*) nicht zu Hause, ausgegangen
out of, aus (*w. dat.*); **— what?** woraus? **— it,** daraus
outside, draußen; **— of,** außerhalb (*w. gen.*)
over (*prep.*), über (*w. dat. or acc.*)
over (*adv.*), vorüber; (*to this side*) herüber; (*to that side*) hinüber; (*on the other side*) drüben; (= *in excess; remaining*) übrig; (= *past*) vorüber; **I have only ten marks left —,** ich habe nur zehn Mark übrig; **winter is —,** der Winter ist vorüber
overcoat, der Überrock, -(e)s, ⸗e; der Mantel, -s, ⸗
overcome, überwinden, überwand, überwunden
own (*adj.*), eigen
own, besitzen, besaß, besessen

P

page, die Seite, -, -n
pain, der Schmerz, -es, -en; **frantic with —,** toll vor Schmerz
paint (*art*), malen; (*as a house*), anstreichen, strich an, angestrichen

painter, der Maler, -s, -
painting, das Gemälde, -s, -
pair, das Paar, -(e)s, -e; **a — of gloves,** ein Parr Handschuhe
palace, der Palast, -(e)s, ⁼e
pale, blaß
paper, das Papier, -s, -e; (*newspaper*), die Zeitung, -, -en
pardon, die Verzeihung, -; **I beg your —,** (ich bitte um) Verzeihung!
pardon, entschuldigen (*wk. w. acc.*); verzeihen, verzieh, verziehen (*w. dat.*)
parents, die Eltern, -, (*pl.*)
park, der Park, -(e)s, -e
part, der Teil, -(e)s, -e; **for the most —,** meistens, meistenteils
part (*take leave*), Abschied nehmen, sich verabschieden
party (*social gathering*), die Gesellschaft, -, -en; (*picnic*), die Landpartie, -, -n; (*political party*), die Partei, -, -en
pass (*elapse*), vergehen, verging, ist vergangen; (*spend time*) verbringen, verbrachte, verbracht; **— by,** vorübergehen, ging vorüber, ist vorübergegangen (*w. an & dat.*); vorbeigehen (*w. sein, an & dat.*); **— an examination,** eine Prüfung (*or* ein Examen) bestehen (*str.*); **how do you — your leisure time?** wie verbringen Sie Ihre Mußestunden?; **time passes,** die Zeit vergeht
passenger, der Passagier, -s, -e
past (*adv.*), vorüber; **half — twelve,** halb eins
past, die Vergangenheit, -
path, der Pfad, -(e)s, -e
patience, die Geduld, -
patient, geduldig
pay, bezahlen; **— attention,** aufpassen, paßte auf, aufgepaßt
pea, die Erbse, -, -n
peace, der Friede(n), -ns
peasant, der Bauer, -s (*or* -n), -n
peculiar, sonderbar
pen, die Feder, -, -n; **fountain —,** die Füllfeder, -, -n
pencil, der Bleistift, -(e)s, -e
people, die Leute, -, (*pl.*); die Menschen (*pl.*); (= *nation*) das Volk, -(e)s, ⁼er; man (*indef. pron. w. sing. vb.*)
pepper, der Pfeffer, -s, -
perceive, gewahr werden (*w. gen.*)
perhaps, vielleicht; **that might — be in order,** das wäre wohl an der Zeit
permission, die Erlaubnis, -, -se
permit, erlauben (*w. dat.*)

permitted, erlaubt; **to be —,** dürfen, durfte, gedurft, darf
personified, selbst; **kindness —,** die Güte selbst
persuade, überreden, überredete, überredet (*w. acc. of the pers.*)
physician, der Arzt, -es, ⁼e
physicist, der Physiker, -s, -
physics, die Physik, -
piano, das Klavier, -s, -e; **to play —,** Klavier (*no art.*) spielen
pick, pflücken; **to — up,** aúfheben; (*receive, record*), aufnehmen, nahm auf, aufgenommen, nimmt auf
picture, das Bild, -(e)s, -er; **to take —s of,** Aufnahmen machen von (*w. dat.*)
picturesque, malerisch
piece, das Stück, -(e)s, -e; **to tear to —s,** zerreißen, zerriß, zerrissen
pipe, die Pfeife, -, -n
pity, das Mitleid, -(e)s; **that would be a —,** das wäre schade! **what a —,** schade! **for —'s sake,** um Gottes (*or* Himmels) willen!
pity, sich erbarmen (*w. gen. or* über & *acc.*); Mitleid haben mit (*w. dat.*)
place, der Platz, -es, ⁼e; die Stelle, -, -n; (= *locality*) der Ort, -(e)s, -e; **I would do it if I were in your —,** ich täte es an Ihrer Stelle
place (*in a horizontal position*), legen; (*in an upright position*), stellen; (= *to set*) setzen
plan, der Plan, -(e)s, ⁼e; **to carry out a —,** einen Plan aúsführen
plan, planen
planet, der Planet, -en, -en
plant, die Pflanze, -, -n
plant, pflanzen
plate, der Teller, -s, -
play, spielen; **to — the piano,** Klavier (*no art.*) spielen; **to — ball,** Ball spielen
pleasant, angenehm
please, gefallen, gefiel, gefallen, gefällt (*w. dat.*); (**if you**) **—,** bitte; **it pleases me** (= *I like it*), es gefällt mir
pleasure, die Freude, -, -n; das Vergnügen, -s, -; **to look forward to with —,** sich freuen auf (*w. acc.*); **I look forward with — to the vacation,** ich freue mich auf die Ferien; **I take — in it,** ich finde meine Freude daran; **it gives me —,** es macht mir Freude
plum, die Pflaume, -, -n
pocket, die Tasche, -, -n
poem, das Gedicht, -(e)s, -e; **a — by Goethe,** ein Gedicht von Goethe

poet, der Dichter, -s, -
poetic, poetisch
point, der Punkt, -(e)s, -e; he was on the — of going out, er wollte eben ausgehen (or er war im Begriff auszugehen)
point, zeigen
police, die Polizei, -
policeman, der Polizist, -en, -en; der Schutzmann, -(e)s, ⸗er (or Schutzleute); der Schupo, -s, -s (abbr. for der Schutzpolizist)
polite, höflich; — to, höflich gegen
poor (adj.), arm; — in, arm an (w. dat.)
poor person, der (or die) Arme, (pl.) die Armen
popular, beliebt
population, die Bevölkerung, -, -en
porter, der Gepäckträger, -s, -
position, die Stellung, -, -en; die Stelle, -, -n (more menial position; place)
possess, besitzen, besaß, besessen
possession, der Besitz, -es; to take — of, etwas (acc.) in Besitz nehmen
possessor, der Besitzer, -s, -
possible, möglich; (Possibility is often expressed by the subjunctive)
post office, das Postamt, -(e)s, ⸗er; die Post, -, -en
postpone, aufschieben, schob auf, aufgeschoben; — to, verschieben auf (w. acc.)
potato, die Kartoffel, -, -n
pound, das Pfund, -(e)s, -e; half a —, ein halbes Pfund; a — and a half, anderthalb Pfund; two marks a —, zwei Mark das Pfund
pour, gießen, goß, gegossen
powder (for the face), der Puder, -s, -
power, die Macht, -, ⸗e; die Gewalt, -, -en
powerful, mächtig, gewaltig
practice, üben (often refl.); he practices fencing (swimming), er übt sich im Fechten (Schwimmen)
praise, das Lob, -(e)s
praise, loben
pray, beten
prayer, das Gebet, -(e)s, -e
prefer, vorziehen, zog vor, vorgezogen; lieber haben; I — it, ich habe es lieber; I — to do it, ich tue es lieber
prepare, bereiten; vórbereiten; (often refl.) to — for, sich vórbereiten auf (w. acc.); I was preparing for the examination, ich bereitete mich auf die Prüfung vor
prepared, bereit; vorbereitet; he is — for the worst, er ist auf das Schlimmste gefaßt

present (in attendance), anwesend; (= at present) gegenwärtig
present (= gift), das Geschenk, -(e)s, -e; (time) die Gegenwart; for the —, vorläufig (adv.)
presént (as a gift), schenken
preserve, erhalten, erhielt, erhalten, erhält
president, der Präsident, -en, -en
press (clothes), bügeln
pretty, hübsch, schön
pride, der Stolz, -es
prince, der Fürst, -en, -en; der Prinz, -en, -en
princess, die Prinzessin, -, -nen
print, drucken
prison, das Gefängnis, -ses, -se
prisoner, der Gefangene (w. adj. decl.); ein Gefangener
prize, der Preis, -es, -e
probability, die Wahrscheinlichkeit, -, -en
probably, wahrscheinlich; wohl (often w. fut. tenses); he was — twenty years old, er mochte wohl zwanzig Jahre alt sein
procession, der Zug, -(e)s, ⸗e
profess, wollen, wollte, gewollt, will; he professes to have a rich uncle, er will einen reichen Onkel haben
professor, der Professor, -s, -en; he is a — at the university, er ist Professor an der Universität
prominent, hervorragend
promise, das Versprechen, -s, -
promise, versprechen, versprach, versprochen, verspricht
pronounce, aússprechen; he always pronounces the word wrong, er spricht das Wort immer falsch aus
proof, der Beweis, -es, -e
property, das Eigentum, -(e)s, ⸗er
protect, (be)schützen
proud, stolz; — of, stolz auf (w. acc.)
prove, beweisen, bewies, bewiesen
proverb, das Sprichwort, -(e)s, ⸗er
provoked: to be — at, sich ärgern über (w. acc.)
Prussia, (das) Preußen, -s
public(ly), öffentlich; — library, die Volksbibliothek, -, -en
punctual(ly), pünktlich
punish, strafen, bestrafen
pupil, (male) der Schüler, -s, -; (female) die Schülerin, -, -nen
pure, rein
pursue, verfolgen (w. acc.)

put (*in a horizontal position*), legen; (*in an upright position*) stellen; (= *to set*) setzen; híntun; **to — a question,** eine Frage stellen; **— it there,** tun Sie es hin!
put on (*clothes, shoes*) [sich (*dat.*) *w. dir. obj.*] anziehen, zog an, angezogen; (*hat, glasses*) aufsetzen, setzte auf, aufgesetzt

Q

quarrel, der (Wort)streit, -(e)s, -e (*or* Streitigkeiten)
quarrel, streiten, stritt, gestritten
quarter, das Viertel, -s, -; **a — to nine,** ein Viertel vor neun; **a — after three,** ein Viertel nach drei; **a — of an hour,** eine Viertelstunde; **a — of a dollar,** ein Vierteldollar (*masc.*)
queen, die Königin, -, -nen
quench, löschen
question, die Frage, -, -n; **to ask a —,** eine Frage stellen; **to answer a —,** eine Frage beantworten (*or* auf eine Frage antworten)
quick(ly), schnell
quiet(ly), ruhig
quiet, die Ruhe,
quite, ganz

R

rabbit, das Kaninchen, -s, -
radiation, die Strahlung, -; **cosmic —,** die kosmische Strahlung, die Weltraumstrahlung
radio, das Radio, -s, -s; der Rundfunk, -s; **to listen to (turn on, turn off) the —,** das Radio ánhören (ánstellen, ábstellen); **— set,** der Radioapparat, -(e)s, -e
rage, die Wut, -
railway, die Eisenbahn, -, -en; **by —,** mit der Eisenbahn; **— station,** der Bahnhof, -(e)s, ᵘe; **elevated —,** die Hochbahn, -, -en
rain (*noun*), der Regen, -s, -fälle (*or* Niederschläge)
rain, regnen; **to — hard,** stark regnen
raincoat, der Regenmantel, -s, ᵘ
raise, heben, hob, gehoben, hebt; aúfheben
rapid(ly), schnell
rare, selten
rat, die Ratte, -, -n
rather, ziemlich

reach, reichen; erreichen (*attain*); **he cannot be reached by phone,** er ist telefonisch nicht zu erreichen
read, lesen, las, gelesen, liest; **to — aloud to,** vórlesen (*w. dat. of the pers.*); **to — through,** zu Ende lesen
reading, das Lesen, -s
ready (= *finished*), fertig; (= *prepared*) bereit; **he is — for everything,** er ist zu allem bereit
real(ly), wirklich
realize, einsehen, sah ein, eingesehen, sieht ein; sich (*dat.*) etwas vórstellen
rear (= *to bring up*), erziehen, erzog, erzogen
reason, der Grund, -(e)s, ᵘe; **for what —?** aus welchem Grunde?
receive, erhalten, erhielt, erhalten, erhält; bekommen, bekam, bekommen; (= *to welcome*), freundlich empfangen, empfing, empfangen, empfängt; (*messages, etc.*), aufnehmen, nahm auf, aufgenommen, nimmt auf
recently, neulich, kürzlich, vor kurzem
recognize, erkennen, erkannte, erkannt
recommend, empfehlen, empfahl, empfohlen, empfiehlt
recover (= *recuperate*) **from,** sich erholen von (*w. dat.*)
red, rot
reference: with — to, in bezug (*or* Bezug) auf (*w. acc.*)
refuse, verweigern (*w. dat. of the pers. & acc. of the th.*)
regard: with — to, hinsichtlich (*w. gen.*); in bezug auf (*w. acc.*)
regards, der Gruß, -es, ᵘe; **best — to your father,** besten Gruß an Ihren Vater
region, die Gegend, -, -en
regret, bedauern
regulate, regulieren
rejoice at, sich freuen über (*w. acc.*)
relate, erzählen
relatively, relativ; **in a — short time,** in relativ kurzer Zeit
reliable, zuverlässig
religion, die Religion, -, -en
rely on, sich verlassen auf (*w. acc.*)
remain, bleiben, blieb, ist geblieben; verbleiben
remark, die Bemerkung, -, -en
remark, bemerken
remarkable, merkwürdig
remember, sich erinnern [*w. gen. or an & acc. (more modern)*]; gedenken (*w. gen.*)
remind, erinnern; **— me of that,** erinnern Sie mich daran!

remove (*as hat, glasses*), abnehmen, nahm ab, abgenommen, nimmt ab; (*as clothes, shoes*) ausziehen, zog aus, ausgezogen

rent, die Miete, -, -n

rent (*from a pers*), mieten; (*to a pers.*) vermieten

repair, ausbessern, besserte aus, ausgebessert; reparieren

repeat, widerhólen, wiederholte, wiederholt

reply, antworten (*w. dat. of the pers.*); erwidern

reply, die Antwort, -, -en

report, der Bericht, -(e)s, -e

report, berichten

represent, vertreten, vertrat, vertreten, vertritt

representative, der Vertreter, -s, -

republic, die Republik, -, -en

request, die Bitte, -, -n

require, verlangen, fordern

research, die Forschung, -, -en

researcher, der Forscher, -s, -

resemble, gleichen (*w. dat.*), ähnlich sein (*w. dat.*)

reside, wohnen

respect, die Hinsicht, -, -en; in this —, in dieser Hinsicht

responsible, verantwortlich; — for, verantwortlich für

rest, die Ruhe, -

rest, sich aúsruhen

restaurant, das Restaurant, -s, -s

result, die Folge, -, -n; as a —, zur Folge; as a — of that, infolgedessen

return (= *to go back*), zurückkehren, kehrte zurück, ist zurückgekehrt; (= *to give back*) zurückgeben, gab zurück, zurückgegeben

revolution, die Revolution, -, -en

Rhine, der Rhein, -(e)s

ribbon, das Band, -(e)s, ᵘer

rich, reich; — in, reich an (*w. dat.*)

riches, der Reichtum, -(e)s, ᵘer

rid of, los; he is — it, er ist es los

riddle, das Rätsel, -s, -

ride (= *journey*), die Fahrt, -, -en

ride (*on horseback*), reiten, ritt, ist geritten; (*travel*) fahren, fuhr, ist gefahren, fährt

rider, der Reiter, -s, -

right, recht; he is —, er hat recht; it serves him —, es geschieht ihm recht; to the —, nach rechts; on the —, rechts; I shall be there — away, ich bin gleich da

ring, der Ring, -(e)s, -e

ring, läuten; klingeln; the bell is ringing, es klingelt

ripe, reif

rise (*of persons*), aufstehen, stand auf, ist aufgestanden; (*of the sun and moon*) aufgehen, ging auf, ist aufgegangen; (*of a river*) entspringen, entsprang, ist entsprungen; steigen, stieg, ist gestiegen *or* aufsteigen (*esp. of a rocket*)

river, der Fluß, Flusses, Flüsse

road, der Weg, -(e)s, -e

roar (*as a lion*), brüllen

roast, braten, briet, gebraten, brät

rob, rauben (*w. dat. of the pers. & acc. of the th.*), berauben (*w. acc. of the pers. & gen. of the th.*); they robbed him of everything, man hat ihm alles geraubt; they robbed him of all his money, man hat ihn seines ganzen Geldes beraubt

robber, der Räuber, -s, -

rock, der Felsen, -s, -

rocket, die Rakete, -, -n

roof, das Dach, -(e)s, ᵘer

room, das Zimmer, -s, -; die Stube, -, -n; (= *hall*) der Saal, -(e)s, Säle; (= *space*) der Raum, -(e)s, ᵘe

rope, der Strick, -(e)s, -e

rose, die Rose, -, -n

rouge, die Schminke, -, -n

round, rund

row, die Reihe, -, -n

row, rudern

royal, königlich

ruin, die Ruine, -, -n; castle —s, Schloßruinen

rule, die Regel, -, -n; (= *rulership*) die Herrschaft, -, -en; as a —, in der Regel

run, laufen, lief, ist gelaufen, läuft; rennen, rannte, ist gerannt

S

sad, traurig

safe, sicher

said, gesagt; to be —, sollen; he is — to be rich, er soll reich sein

sake: for the — of . . . um . . . willen; for my —, um meinetwillen; for heaven's —, um Himmels willen!

same: the —, derselbe, dieselbe, dasselbe; it is all the — to me, es ist mir ganz gleich (*or* einerlei)

satellite, der Satellit, -en, -en

satisfied, zufrieden

Saturday, der Samstag, -(e)s, -e; der Sonnabend, -s, -e; on —(s), am Samstag (*or* Samstags) save (*by economizing*), sparen; (= *to rescue*), retten; — me the trouble, ersparen Sie mir die Mühe!

say, sagen

saying, der Spruch, -(e)s, ⁼e

scarcely, kaum

school, die Schule, -, -n; in —, in der Schule; to —, in die (*or* zur) Schule; after —, nach der Schule

schoolmate, der Schulkamerad, -en, -en

science, die Wissenschaft, -, -en

scientific, wissenschaftlich

scientist, der Wissenschaftler, -s, -; der Forscher, -s, -

scold, schelten, schalt, gescholten, schilt

scratch, kratzen

sea, die See, -, -n; das Meer, -(e)s, -e

seasick, seekrank

seasickness, die Seekrankheit, -, -en

season, die Jahreszeit, -, -en

seat, der Sitz, -es, -e; der Platz, -es, ⁼e

seated: be —, setzen Sie sich (*or* nehmen Sie Platz)!

second (*adj.*), zweit-; in the — place, zweitens

second, die Sekunde, -, -n

secret, das Geheimnis, -ses, -se

secretly, heimlich

see, sehen, sah, gesehen, sieht; — to it, sorgen Sie dafür; have you seen him working ?, haben Sie ihn arbeiten sehen?

seek, suchen

seem, scheinen, schien, geschienen

seize (= *to grasp*), fassen; (= *to take possession of*) sich bemächtigen (*w. gen.*)

seldom, selten

self, selbst, selber

sell, verkaufen

semester, das Semester, -s, -

send, senden, sandte, gesandt; schicken; to — by mail, mit der Post schicken; to — for, holen (*or* kommen) lassen; did you — for the doctor, haben Sie den Arzt holen (*or* kommen) lassen?

sense, der Sinn, -(e)s, -e; there is no — in doing such a thing, es hat keinen Sinn, so etwas zu tun; he is not in his —s, er ist nicht bei Sinnen

sentence, der Satz, -es, ⁼e

separate, trennen

September, der September, -(s), -

serious, ernst(haft)

servant, der Diener, -s, -; — girl, das Dienstmädchen, -s, -

serve, dienen (*w. dat.*); that serves him right, das geschieht ihm recht

set (= *to place, put*), setzen; (*of the sun and moon*) untergehen, ging unter, ist untergegangen; — the table, den Tisch decken

seven, sieben

seventeen, siebzehn

seventeenth, siebzehnt-

seventh, sieb(en)t-

several, mehrere, ein paar (*indecl.*)

severe (*as sickness*), schwer; (= *strict*) streng

shade, der Schatten, -s, -

shadow, *see* shade

shady, schattig

shall (*aux. of fut. tenses*), werden; (*to denote moral obligation*) sollen

shape, die Gestalt, -, -en; die Form, -, -en

sharp, scharf; we left at ten o'clock —, Punkt zehn Uhr sind wir abgefahren

sharpen (*as a pencil*), spitzen

shave (oneself), sich rasieren; to get shaved, sich rasieren lassen

she, sie

shine, scheinen, schien, geschienen

ship, das Schiff, -(e)s, -e

shirt, das Hemd, -(e)s, -en

shoe, der Schuh, -(e)s, -e

shoot, schießen, schoß, geschossen

shore, das Ufer, -s, -

short, kurz

shot, der Schuß, Schusses, Schüsse

should (= *ought*), sollte (*imperf. subj. of* sollen); he — go, er sollte gehen; he — have gone, er hätte gehen sollen; I — like to travel, ich möchte (*imperf. subj. of* mögen) (gern) reisen

shout, schreien, schrie, geschrien

show, zeigen; — honor to, Ehre erweisen (*w. dat.*)

shudder, grauen (*impers.*); I —, mir graut

sick, krank

side, die Seite, -, -n; on this — of, diesseits (*w. gen.*); on that — of, jenseits (*w. gen.*)

sight (= *something worth seeing*) die Sehenswürdigkeit, -, -en; (= *aspect*) der Anblick, -(e)s, -e

sign, das Zeichen, -s, -

sign, unterschreíben, unterschrieb, unterschrieben; unterzeichnen

signature, die Unterschrift, -, -en

significance, die Bedeutung, -; die Wichtigkeit,

silent (*adj.*), still, schweigsam; to be —, schweigen, schwieg, geschwiegen

silk, die Seide, -, -n; (*adj.*), seiden

silver, das Silber, -s; (*adj.*), silbern

similar, ähnlich (*w. dat.*)

simple, simply, einfach

since (*prep.*), seit (*w. dat.*); — **when ?,** seit wann ?

since (*conj.*), seitdem (*temp.*); da (*causal*)

since (*adv.*), seitdem; — **then,** seitdem

sincere(ly), aufrichtig; **—ly yours,** Ihr (ganz) ergebener

sing, singen, sang, gesungen

singer (*male*), der Sänger, -s, -; (*female*) die Sängerin, -, -nen

single (= *only, sole*), einzig; (= *individual*), einzeln; (= *unmarried*), ledig

sink (*intr.*), sinken, sank, ist gesunken; versinken (*w.* sein); (*tr.*) versenken (*wk.*)

sister, die Schwester, -, -n

sit, sitzen, saß, gesessen; — **down,** sich setzen

situated : to be — on, liegen (*str.*) an (*w. dat.*)

six, sechs

sixteen, sechzehn

sixteenth, sechzehnt-

sixth, sechst-

sixty, sechzig

size, die Größe, -, -n

skate (*noun*), der Schlittschuh, -(e)s, -e

skate, Schlittschuh laufen; **I went skating,** ich bin Schlittschuh gelaufen

skip, überspríngen, übersprang, übersprungen; **he skipped a grade,** er hat eine Klasse übersprungen

slave, der Sklave, -n, -n

sleep, schlafen, schlief, geschlafen, schläft; **go to — ** (= *to fall asleep*), einschlafen (*w.* sein)

sleepy, schläfrig

sleeve, der Ärmel, -s, -

slide (= *slip*), gleiten, glitt, ist geglitten

slow(ly), langsam

small, klein

smell, riechen, roch, gerochen; — **of,** riechen nach (*w. dat.*)

smoke, der Rauch, -(e)s

smoke, rauchen

smoking, das Rauchen, -s; — **is forbidden,** das Rauchen ist verboten

snore, schnarchen

snow, der Schnee, -s

snow, schneien

so (*adv.*), so; **and — forth,** und so weiter (*abbr.* usw.)

sob, schluchzen

so-called, sogenannt

sofa, das Sofa, -s, -s

soft(ly) (= *not hard*), weich; (= *not loud*) leise

soldier, der Soldat, -en, -en

solve, lösen; — **a puzzle,** ein Rätsel lösen

some, etwas (*indecl.; w. sing. noun*); einige (*w. pl. noun*); — **... or other,** irgendein (*adj.*)

somebody, someone, jemand, -(e)s; irgend jemand; — **else,** jemand anders (*or* sonst jemand)

something, etwas (*indecl.*); — **he likes,** etwas, was er gern hat; — **good,** etwas Gutes; — **else,** etwas anderes

sometimes, dann und wann, zuweilen, gelegentlich, manchmal

somewhat, etwas; — **sour,** etwas sauer

somewhere, irgendwo(hin)

son, der Sohn, -(e)s, ⁼e

song, das Lied, -(e)s, -er

soon, bald; **as — as,** sobald

sooner (= *earlier*), früher; (= *rather*) lieber

sorrow, der Kummer, -s,

sorry : to be —, leid tun; **I am — for him,** er tut mir leid (*or* es tut mir leid um ihn)

sort, die Art, -, -en; **what — of (a),** was für ein; **what — of** (*pl.*), was für; **all —s of,** allerlei (*indecl.*)

so that, damit; um ... zu (*w. pres. inf.*)

soul, die Seele, -, -n

sound (*adj.*) (= *well*), gesund; (= *stout or strong*), stark; (= *firm*) fest

sound, der Laut, -(e)s, -e

soup, die Suppe, -, -n

sour, sauer

source, die Quelle, -, -n

south, der Süden, -s; — **of,** südlich von (*w. dat.*)

southeast (*adj.*), südöstlich; (*noun*), der Südosten, -s

southwest (*adj.*), südwestlich; (*noun*), der Südwesten, -s

space, der Raum, -(e)s, ⁼e; der Weltraum (*outer space*)

space flight, der Raumflug, -(e)s, ⁼e

space ship, das Raumschiff, -(e)s, -e

space traveler, der Raumfahrer, -s, -

Spain, (das) Spanien, -s

Spanish, spanisch

spare (= *unoccupied*), frei; — **time,** die Mußestunden (*leisure*)

speak, sprechen, sprach, gesprochen, spricht; — **about,** sprechen über (*w. acc.*) *or* von (*w. dat.*)

speech, die Rede, -, -n; **to make a —,** eine Rede halten

spend (*time*), verbringen, verbrachte, verbracht; (*money*) ausgeben, gab aus, ausgegeben, gibt aus

spit, speien, spie, gespie(e)n

spite: **in — of** (*prep.*), trotz (*w. gen.*)*;* **in — of that,** trotzdem, dessenungeachtet

spoil (= *pamper*), verwöhnen

spring (*of water*), die Quelle, -, -n; (*the season*) der Frühling, -s, -e; **in —,** im Frühling; **— is here,** der Frühling ist gekommen

squander, verschwenden, vergeuden

stamp, die Briefmarke, -, -n

stand, stehen, stand, gestanden

star, der Stern, -(e)s, -e

start, ánfangen (*str.*), beginnen (*str.*)*;* (*on a journey*) ábreisen (*wk. intr. w.* sein), sich auf den Weg machen; starten (*to take off*)

starve, verhungern, verhungerte, ist verhungert

state, der Staat, -(e)s, -en

station (= *rank*), der Stand, -es, -e; (= *situation*) die Stelle, -, -n; (= *position*) die Stellung, -, -en (= *railroad depot*) der Bahnhof, -(e)s, ᵘe; (= *stopping place*) die Station, -, -en; die Haltestelle, -, -n; **at the —,** auf dem Bahnhof; **to call for someone at the —,** jemand vom Bahnhof abholen; **radio,** die Funkenstation, die Sendestation, der Sender

stay, bleiben, blieb, ist geblieben; **— at home,** zu Hause bleiben

steamer, der Dampfer, -s, -; **by —,** mit dem Dampfer

steel, der Stahl, -(e)s, ᵘe

stem, der Stamm, -(e)s, ᵘe; der Stengel, -s, -

step, der Schritt, -(e)s, -e; **to keep —,** Schritt halten

step, treten, trat, ist getreten, tritt

stick, stecken

stiff, steif

still (*adj.*), still, ruhig

still (= *yet*), noch, immer noch; (= *nevertheless*), doch

stingy, geizig

stocking, der Strumpf, -(e)s, ᵘe

stomach, der Magen, -s, -

stone, der Stein, -(e)s, -e

stop, halten, hielt, gehalten, hält; ánhalten; **it has stopped snowing,** es hat aufgehört zu schneien; **suddenly he stopped,** plötzlich blieb er stehen; **my watch has stopped,** meine Uhr ist stehengeblieben

store, der Laden, -s, ᵘ

stork, der Storch, -(e)s, ᵘe

storm, das Gewitter, -s, -

story, die Geschichte, -, -n; (*of a house*) das Stockwerk, -(e)s, -e

stove, der Ofen, -s, ᵘ

straight: **a — line,** eine gerade Linie; **— ahead,** geradeaus (*adv.*)

straighten (**oneself**) **up,** sich aúfrichten

strange, fremd (*w. dat.*)

stranger, der Fremde, -n, -n (*w. adj. decl.*)*;* ein Fremder; **he is a — to me,** er ist mir fremd

stratosphere, die Stratosphäre, -

stream, der Strom, -(e)s, ᵘe

street, die Straße, -, -n; **in** (*or* **on**) **the —** auf der Straße

streetcar, die Straßenbahn, -, -en; **by —,** mit der Straßenbahn

strict, streng

strike, schlagen, schlug, geschlagen, schlägt

strive for, streben nach (*w. dat.*)

strong, stark

student, der Student, -en, -en; **to be a — at a university,** auf einer Universität Student sein

study, das Studium, -s, Studien; (*subject in school*) das Fach, -(e)s, ᵘer

study (*of students*), studieren; (*of pupils*) lernen; **to — hard,** fleißig (schwer, tüchtig) studieren (*or* lernen)

stumble, stolpern

stupid, dumm; **that would be — indeed,** das wäre schön dumm!

stupidity, die Dummheit, -, -en

style, die Mode, -, -n; **it is in —,** es ist (in der) Mode

subject (*in school*), das Fach, -(e)s, ᵘer

suburb, die Vorstadt, -, ᵘe

subway, die Untergrundbahn, -, -en

succeed, gelingen, gelang, ist gelungen (*impers. w. dat.*)*;* **I have not succeeded in deciphering your handwriting,** es ist mir nicht gelungen, Ihre Handschrift zu entziffern

success, der Erfolg, -(e)s, -e

successful, erfolgreich

such, solcher, solche, solches; **— a storm,** solch ein (*or* ein solches) Gewitter; **he is no — fool,** er ist kein solcher Narr

suddenly, plötzlich, auf einmal

suffer, leiden, litt, gelitten

suger, der Zucker, -s

suit (*of clothes*), der Anzug, -(e)s, ᵘe

suit, passen (*w. dat.*)

suitcase, der Handkoffer, -s, -

summer, der Sommer, -s, -; **in —,** im Sommer

sun, die Sonne, -, -n; the — rises (sets), die Sonne geht auf (unter)

sunburnt, sonnverbrannt

Sunday, der Sonntag, -(e)s, -e

sunny, sonnig

sunrise, der Sonnenaufgang, -(e)s, -e

sunset, der Sonnenuntergang, -(e)s, -e

sunshine, der Sonnenchein, -(e)s

supper, das Abendessen, -s, -; after —, nach dem Abendessen; for —, zum Abendessen

sure, sicher; — of, sicher (w. gen.)

surface, die Oberfläche, -, -n

surprise, die Überraschung, -, -en

surprise, überraschen, überraschte, überrascht

sweetheart, der Schatz, -es, ᵘe

swim, schwimmen, schwamm, ist geschwommen

Switzerland, die Schweiz

sword, das Schwert, -(e)s, -er

sympathetic(ally), mitleidsvoll

sympathy, das Mitleid, -(e)s

system, das System, -s, -e

T

table, der Tisch, -es, -e; to sit at (the) —, am Tisch(e) sitzen; to sit down at (the) —, sich an den Tisch setzen

tachometer, der Geschwindigkeitsmesser, -s, -

tail, der Schwanz, -es, ᵘe

tailor, der Schneider, -s, -

take, nehmen, nahm, genommen, nimmt; — a walk (a trip, an examination), einen Spaziergang (eine Reise, eine Prüfung) machen; — off (as clothes, shoes), [sich (dat.) w. dir. obj] ausziehen; (as hat, glasses), abnehmen; — part in, teilnehmen an (w. dat.); — leave, sich empfehlen, empfahl, empfohlen, empfiehlt; will you — tea or coffee?, wollen Sie Tee oder Kaffee?

talk, sprechen, sprach, gesprochen, spricht; — about, sprechen über (w. acc.) or von (w. dat.); — to oneself, vor sich (acc.) hinsprechen; he talks to himself, er spricht vor sich hin

tall, hoch; von hoher Gestalt; groß; lang

tape recorder, das Tonbangerät, -s, -e

taste, der Geschmack, -(e)s, ᵘe

taste, schmecken; — of, schmecken nach (w. dat.); it tastes of sour milk, es schmeckt nach saurer Milch

tax, die Steuer, -, -n

tea, der Tee, -s, -s

teach, lehren (w. two accs.); she taught him the song, sie lehrte ihn das Lied

teacher (male), der Lehrer, -s, -; (female) die Lehrerin, -, -nen

team (in a game), die Mannschaft, -, -en

tear, reißen, riß, gerissen; — to pieces, zerreißen

technical, technisch; — dictionary, das Fachwörterbuch, -(e)s, ᵘer; — term, der Fachausdruck, -(e)s, ᵘe

technician, der Techniker, -s, -; der Facharbeiter, -s, -

telegraph, telegrafieren

telephone, telefonieren; he cannot be reached by —, er ist telefonisch (adv.) nicht zu erreichen

telescope, das Teleskop, -s, -e; das Fernrohr, -s, -e

television, das Fernsehen; — set, der Fernsehapparat

tell, erzählen, sagen

temperature, die Temperatur, -, -en

temptation, die Versuchung, -, -en

ten, zehn; — times, zehnmal

tennis, das Tennis, -

tenor, der Tenor, -s, ᵘe

tent, das Zelt, -(e)s, -e

tenth, zehnt-

terrible, schrecklich

test, die Prüfung, -, -en; der Versuch, -(e)s, -e

test, prüfen

than, als

thank, danken; — for, danken (w. dat. of the pers) für (w. acc.); — a person for something, sich bei einer Person für etwas bedanken

thankful, dankbar (w. dat.)

that (conj.), daß; so —, damit; um ... zu (w. pres. inf.)

that (one) (dem. adj. & pron.), jener, jene, jenes; der, die, das; that is (i.e), das heißt (d.h.)

that (rel pron. = which), der, die, das; welcher, welche, welches

thaw, tauen

theater, das Theater, -s, -; to go to the —, ins Theater gehen

theft, der Diebstahl, -s, ᵘe

their (poss. adj), ihr, ihre, ihr

theirs (poss. pron.), ihrer, ihre, ihres

them, ihnen (dat.); sie (acc.)

themselves (refl. pron.), sich (dat. & acc.); (intens.) selbst (or selber); they —, sie selbst (or selber) then (*adv.*), damals; dann; da; denn; **now and —,** dann und wann; **not till —,** erst dann; **what — ?** was dann? **well —,** nun gut denn

there, da, dort; **— is (are),** es gibt (*w. acc.*), es ist (sind) (*w. nom.*)

thereafter, danach, nachher

therefore, darum, deshalb, deswegen, daher, also

thereupon, darauf

they, sie

thick, dick; **a foot —,** einen Fuß dick

thief, der Dieb, -(e)s, -e

thin, dünn

thing, die Sache, -, -n; das Ding, -(e)s, -e; **main —,** die Hauptsache; **most beautiful —,** das Schönste (*adj. used as a noun*); **such a —,** so etwas (*indecl.*); **such —s,** dergleichen (*indecl.*); **all good —s,** alles Gute; **among other —s,** unter ander(e)m; **many —s,** vieles

think, denken, dachte, gedacht; **— of,** denken an (*w. acc.*); **he has thought out a good plan,** er hat sich einen guten Plan ausgedacht

third, dritt-; das Drittel, -s, -

thirst, der Durst, -es

thirsty, durstig

thirteenth, dreizehnt-

thirtieth, dreißigst-

thirty, dreißig

this, dieser, diese, dieses; **on — side of** (*prep. w. gen.*) diesseits

thorough(ly), gründlich

thought, der Gedanke, -ns, -n

thousand (*adj.*), tausend

thousand, das Tausend, -(e)s, -e; **two —,** zweitausend; **many —s,** viele Tausende

threaten, drohen (*w. dat.*)

three, drei; **— times,** dreimal; **of — kinds,** dreierlei (*invar.*)

threefold, dreifach

three-legged, dreibeinig

three-stage, dreistufig; **— rocket,** die dreistufige Rakete

through (*prep.*), durch (*w. acc.*); **the whole year —,** das ganze Jahr hindurch; (*adj. = finished*), fertig

throw, werfen, warf, geworfen, wirft

thumb, der Daumen, -s, -

thunder, der Donner, -s, -

thunder, donnern

Thursday, der Donnerstag, -(e)s, -e

thus, so; auf diese Weise

ticket, die Fahrkarte, -, -n; **— of admission,** die Eintrittskarte, -, -n

tie, die Krawatte, -, -n; der Schlips, -es, -e; die Halsbinde, -, -n

tie, binden, band, gebunden

tiger, der Tiger, -s, -

time, die Zeit, -, -en; (= *occasion*) das Mal, -(e)s, -e; **at what — ?** um wieviel Uhr? **what — is it?** wieviel Uhr ist es? **to have a good —,** sich amüsieren; **at the — when,** zur Zeit, als (da *or* wo); **for the first —,** zum ersten Male (*or* zum erstenmal); **(for) a long —,** lange; **how long a — ?** wie lange? **ten —s,** zehnmal; **old(en) —s,** die alten Zeiten

tip, das Trinkgeld, -(e)s, -er

tired, müde; **he is — of life,** er ist des Lebens müde; **he is — of it,** er ist es müde

title, der Titel, -s, -

to (*prep.*), zu, nach (*both w. dat.*); auf, in, bis (*all w. acc.*); **— my brother's (house),** zu meinem Bruder; **(up) — the window,** bis an das Fenster; **to go — the theater,** ins Theater gehen; **to go — the country,** aufs Land gehen; **to go — school,** in die (*or* zur) Schule gehen; **(in order) —,** um ... zu (*w. pres. inf.*) [*or* damit (*sub. conj.*)]

tobacco, der Tabak, -(e)s

today, heute; **a week from —,** heute über acht Tage; **what is —'s date?,** der wievielte ist (*or* den wievielten haben wir) heute?

together, zusammen

tomato, die Tomate, -, -n

tomorrow (*adv.*), morgen; **— morning,** morgen früh; **— afternoon,** morgen nachmittag; **day after —,** übermorgen

tongue, die Zunge, -, -n

tonight, heute abend (*or* nacht)

too, zu; (= *in addition, also*) auch

tooth, der Zahn, -(e)s, ⸗e

toothache, das Zahnweh, -(e)s; **I have a —,** ich habe Zahnweh (*no art.*)

top, die Spitze, -, -n; (*of a mountain*) der Gipfel, -s, -; **at the — of,** oben auf; **on the — floor,** im obersten Stock(werk)

toward (*prep.*), gegen (*w. acc.*); entgegen (*w. dat.*)

tower, der Turm, -(e)s, ⸗e

town, die Stadt, -, ⸗e; **in —,** in der Stadt; **to —,** in die Stadt

toys, die Spielsachen (*pl.*)

train, der Zug, -(é)s, ⸗e

translate, übersétzen, übersetzte, übersetzt; **— into English,** ins Englische übersetzen

translation, die Übersetzung, -, -en

transmit, übertrágen, übertrug, übertragen

transparent, durchsichtig

travel, reisen, reiste, ist gereist; fahren, fuhr, ist gefahren, fährt; **he travels second class,** er fährt zweiter Klasse

traveler, der Reisende, -n, -n; (*w. adj. decl.*) ein Reisender

treason, der Verrat, -(e)s

treasure, der Schatz, -es, ⸗e

treat, behandeln

tree, der Baum, -(e)s, ⸗e

tremble, zittern

trick (= *prank*), der Streich, -(e)s, -e

trip, die Reise, -, -n; **to take a —,** eine Reise machen

trouble, die Mühe, -, -n; **it is not worth the —,** es ist nicht der Mühe wert

trouble oneself about, sich kümmern um (*w. acc.*)

true, wahr; (= *faithful*) treu

trunk, der Koffer, -s, -

truth, die Wahrheit, -, -en

try, versuchen

Tuesday, der Dienstag, -(e)s, -e

tune, die Melodie, -, -n (*pl. w. four syllables*)

tunnel, der Tunnel, -s, -s (or -)

turkey (*cock*), der Truthahn, -(e)s, ⸗e; der Puter, -s, -

Turkey, die Türkei, -

turn, die Reihe, -, -n; **it is my —,** ich bin an der Reihe (*or* die Reihe ist an mir); **his — has come,** er ist an die Reihe gekommen

turn, kehren; wenden, wandte, gewandt; (= *to become*) werden; **— on** (*light, gas, water*), ándrehen, (*radio*) ánstellen; **to — off,** ábdrehen, ábstellen; **— one's back on someone,** jemand (*dat.*) den Rücken zúwenden; **he turned pale with fright,** vor Schreck ist er blaß geworden

twelve, zwölf

twenty, zwanzig

twice, zweimal; **— as much,** zweimal soviel

two, zwei; beide (*or* die beiden); **his — sons,** seine beiden Söhne

undertake, unternéhmen, unternahm, unternommen, unternimmt

undress (oneself), sich áusziehen (*str.*)

unemployed (*adj.*), arbeitslos

unemployed, der Arbeitslose, -n, -n

unexpected, unerwartet

unfinished, unvollendet

unfortunately, leider

unhappy, unglücklich

unite, vereinigen

United States, die Vereinigten Staaten

university, die Universität, -, -en; **to be a student at the —,** auf der Universität Student sein; **to be a professor at the —,** an der Universität Professor sein

unjust, ungerecht

unknown, unbekannt

unless, wenn . . . nicht; (*after a neg. statement*) es sei denn, daß . . .

until (*prep.*), bis (*w. acc.*) **not —,** erts; **not — seven,** erst um sieben Uhr

unusual, ungewöhnlich

up, auf; **— and down,** auf und ab

upset, úmstürzen (*wk. tr. w.* haben; *intr. w.* sein)

upstairs, oben; **he goes —,** er geht nach oben (*or* die Treppe hinauf)

urge, treiben, trieb, getrieben

us, uns (*dat. and acc.*)

use (*noun*), der Gebrauch, -(e)s, ⸗e; **to make — of,** sich bedienen (*w. gen.*)*;* Gebrauch von etwas (*dat.*) machen; **of what — is that to you?** was nützt Ihnen das?

use, gebrauchen; verwenden, verwandte (*or* verwendete) verwandt (*or* verwendet)

used to (= *accustomed*), gewohnt (*w. acc. & no prep.*)*;* **he is — it,** er ist es gewohnt (*or* daran gewöhnt); **to become —,** sich gewöhnen an (*w. acc.*)*;* **he used to smoke,** er pflegte zu rauchen; früher rauchte er

useful, nützlich (*w. dat.*)

usual(ly), gewöhnlich

U

umbrella, der Regenschirm, -(e)s, -e

unable: to be —, nicht können; **he is — to go,** er kann nicht gehen

uncle, der Onkel, -s, -

under (*prep.*), unter (*w. dat. or acc.*)

understand, verstehen, verstand, verstanden; **that is understood,** das versteht sich (von selbst) (*or* das ist selbstverständlich)

V

vacation, die Ferien (*pl.*)*;* der Urlaub, -(e)s, -e

vain: in —, vergebens, umsonst

valuable, wertvoll

value, der Wert, -(e)s, -e

various, verschieden

vast, riesig; unermesslich (*immeasurable*)

velocity, die Geschwindigkeit, -

velvet, der Samt, -(e)s, -e

verb, das Zeitwort, -(e)s, ⸗er; das Verb(um), -s, Verben

verse, der Vers, -es, -e
very, sehr
vest, die Weste, -, -n
vicinity, die Nähe, -, -n
victim, das Opfer, -s, -
Vienna, (das) Wien, -s
view, die Aussicht, -, -en
view, betrachten
village, das Dorf, -(e)s, ⸚er
vinegar, der Essig, -s, -e
violent, heftig
virtue, die Tugend, -, -en
visit, der Besuch, -(e)s, -e
visit, besuchen
voice, die Stimme, -, -n
volume, der Band, -(e)s, ⸚e
vote, die Stimme, -, -n
vote for, stimmen für (*w. acc.*)

W

wait, warten; — **for,** warten auf (*w. acc.*)
waiter, der Kellner, -s, -
wake, aufwecken (*tr.*); aúfwachen (*intr. w.* sein)
walk, der Spaziergang, -(e)s, ⸚e; **to take a** —, einen Spaziergang machen
walk, gehen, ging, ist gegangen; zu Fuß gehen
walking: to go —, spazierengehen; **he went** —, er ist spazierengegangen
wall, die Wand, -, ⸚e; (*outside*) die Mauer, -, -n
wander, wandern (*w.* sein)
want (*noun*) (= *need*), die Not, -, ⸚
want, (= *desire*), wollen, wollte, gewollt
war, der Krieg, -(e)s, -e
ware, die Ware, -, -n
warm, warm
warn, warnen
wash, waschen, wusch, gewaschen, wäscht; **to** — **dishes,** Geschirr (*neut. sing.*) ábwaschen; **I** — **my hands,** ich wasche mir die Hände; **I** — **(myself),** ich wasche mich
waste (= *squander*), verschwenden
wastepaper basket, der Papierkorb, -(e)s, ⸚e
watch, die (Taschen)uhr, -, -en
watch, bewachen
water, das Wasser -s, -
wave, die Welle, -, -n
way, der Weg, -(e)s, -e; **go your** —, gehe (*or* ziehe) deines Weges!
we, wir
weak, schwach

wear, tragen, trug, getragen, trägt
wear out, abnutzen, nutzte ab, abgenutzt
wearability, die Abnutzbarkeit, -
weather, das Wetter, -s, -; — **forecast,** die Wettervoraussage, -, -n; — **information,** die Wetternachrichten (*pl.*)
wedding, die Hochzeit, -, -en
Wednesday, der Mittwoch, -(e)s, -e
week, die Woche, -, -n; **once a** —, einmal die Woche; **a** — **ago,** vor acht Tagen; **a** — **from today,** heute über acht Tage; **for a** —, auf eine Woche
weekly, wöchentlich
weep, weinen
welcome, begrüßen, freundlich empfangen (*str.*)
welfare (= *prosperity*), der Wohlstand, -(e)s
well, gut; wohl (*occurs only in a few set phrases as adv. of* well); **I am very** —, es geht mir sehr gut; **did you sleep** —? haben Sie gut geschlafen? **fare you** —, leben Sie wohl! **sleep** —, schlafen Sie wohl!
well-known, bekannt
well-meant, wohlgemeint
well off, wohlhabend
west, der Westen, -s; — **of,** westlich (*adj.*) von (*w. dat.*)
wet, naß
what (*inter.*), was; — **is today's date?** der wievielte is heute (*or* den wievielten haben wir heute)?; **out of** —? woraus?; **with** —? womit?; (*inter. adj.*) welcher, welche, welches; (*adj. in excl.*) welch; — **a man!** welch ein Mann! — **time is it?** wieviel Uhr ist es? — **kind of,** was für ein, (*pl.*) was für
whatever, was; was . . . auch; — **he says,** was er auch sagt
wheel, das Rad, -(e)s, ⸚er; (= *bicycle*) das (Fahr)rad
when, wann (*inter.*); (= *whenever*) wenn; (*relating to one def. past action*) als; **since** —? seit wann?
whenever, wenn
where, wo (*w. vb. of rest*); wohin (*w. vb. of motion*)
whether, ob
which, der, die, das; welcher, welche, welches; — **one?** welcher? welche? welches?
while (*conj.*), während; indem
while (*noun*), die Weile, —; **for a** —, eine Zeitlang; **a little** — **ago,** vor kurzer Zeit (*or* vor kurzem)
whisper, flüstern
whistle, pfeifen, pfiff, gepfiffen

white, weiß
who (*inter.*), wer
whoever, wer; wer ... auch; — she may be, wer sie auch sein mag
whole, ganz
whom (*inter.*), wem (*dat.*), wen (*acc.*); (*rel.*) dem, der, dem, (*pl.*) denen (*dat.*); den, die, das, (*pl.*) die (*acc.*); (*or proper forms of* welcher)
whose (*inter.*), wessen; at — house? bei wem?
whose (*rel.*), dessen, deren, dessen, (*pl.*) deren
why, warum
wide, weit; breit; a foot —, einen Fuß breit
wife, die Frau, -, -en; die Gattin, -, -nen
wild, wild
will (*in fut. tenses*), werden
will, der Wille, -ns, -n
win, siegen
wind, der Wind, -(e)s, -e
wind (*a watch*), aúfziehen (*str.*)
window, das Fenster, -s, -; to the —, ans Fenster; at the —, am Fester; to look out of the —, zum Fenster hinaússehen
windy, windig
wine, der Wein, -(e)s, -e
wing, der Flügel, -s, -
winter, der Winter, -s, -; in —, im Winter
wise, weise, klug
wish, der Wunsch, -es, ⁐e
wish, wollen, wollte, gewollt, will; wünschen (*w. zu & dep. inf.*); (= *to long for*) sich sehnen nach
with (*prep.*), mit, bei (*both w. dat.*); to fall in love —, sich verlieben in (*w. acc.*); have you any money — you? haben Sie etwas Geld bei sich?; — what? womit?; — it, damit
within (*prep.*), innerhalb (*w. gen.*); — a short time, in kurzer Zeit
without (*prep.*), ohne (*w. acc.*)
witness, der Zeuge, -n, -n
wolf, der Wolf, -(e)s, ⁐e
woman, die Frau, -, -en
wonderful, wunderbar
wood, das Holz, -es, ⁐er
wooden, hölzern
word, das Wort, -(e)s -er (*disconnected*), -e (*in connected discourse*); he keeps his —, er hält Wort
work, die Arbeit, -, -en; das Werk, -(e)s, -e; Schiller's —s, Schillers Werke
work, arbeiten; to — hard, schwer (fleißig or tüchtig) arbeiten; to go to —, an die Arbeit gehen

world, die Welt, -, -en
worry about (= *be anxious*), sich (*dat.*) Sorgen machen um; (= *bother about*) sich (*acc.*) kümmern um
worth (*adj.*), wert; it is — a dollar, es ist einen Dollar (*acc.*) wert; it is not — the trouble, es ist nicht der Mühe (*gen.*) wert; five marks' — of sugar, für fünf Mark Zucker
worth, der Wert, -(e)s, -e
worthy of, würdig (*w. gen.*)
would: — like, möchte (gern) (*w. inf.*); he — like to go to the theater, er möchte (gern) ins Theater gehen
wrap up, eínwickeln; wrap it up in clean paper, wickeln Sie es in saubres Papier ein!
write, schreiben, schrieb, geschrieben; — on the (black)board, an die Tafel schreiben; I wrote my friend a letter, ich habe meinem Freund einen Brief geschrieben (*or* ich habe einen Brief an meinen Freund geschrieben)
writing (*noun*), das Schreiben, -s; — is difficult for him, das Schreiben ist (*or* fällt) ihm schwer
written (*adj.*), schriftlich
wrong: he is —, er hat unrecht

Y

yard (*courtyard*), der Hof, -(e)s, ⁐e; (*measure*) das (*or* der) Meter, -s -
year, das Jahr, -(e)s, -e; leap —, das Schaltjahr; she is five —s, old, sie ist fünf Jahre alt
yell, schreien, schrie, geschrien
yellow, gelb
yes, ja; — indeed, jawohl
yesterday, gestern; day before —, vorgestern
yet, noch; not —, noch nicht; (= *nevertheless*) doch
you, du, ihr, Sie (*nom.*); dir, euch, Ihnen (*dat.*); dich, euch, Sie (*acc.*)
young, jung
your (*poss. adj.*), dein, deine, dein (*sing. fam.*); euer, eu(e)re, euer (*pl. fam.*); Ihr, Ihre, Ihr (*formal*)
yours (*poss. pron.*), deiner, deine, deines; eurer, eure, eures; Ihrer, Ihre, Ihres
yourself (*refl. pron.*), dich, euch, sich (*all acc.*); dir, euch, sich (*all dat.*); (*intens.*) du ihr, Sie selbst (*or* selber)
youth, die Jugend, -

Z

zeal, der Eifer, -s
zealous, eifrig

zero, die Null, -, -en
zero hour, die Angriffszeit, -; die Nullzeit, -
zoölogical, zoologisch; — garden, der
Tiergarten, -s, -; der zoologische Garten
zoölogy, die Zoologie, -; die Tierkunde, -

Index